IDIOMS: Processing, Structure, and Interpretation

IDIOMS: Processing, Structure, and Interpretation

Edited by

Cristina Cacciari

University of Bologna, Italy

Patrizia Tabossi

University of Ferrara, Italy

LEA LAWRENCE ERLBAUM ASSOCIATES, PUBLISHERS
1993   **Hillsdale, New Jersey**   **Hove and London**

Lawrence Erlbaum Associates, Inc., Publishers
365 Broadway
Hillsdale, New Jersey 07642

Library of Congress Cataloging-in-Publication Data

Idioms: processing, structure, and interpretation / edited by Cristina
   Cacciari and Patrizia Tabossi.
      p. cm.
   Includes bibliographical references and index.
   ISBN 0-8058-1038-2
   1. Idioms. 2. Psycholinguistics. 3. Language acquisition.
  4. Semantics. I. Cacciari, C. (Cristina) II. Tabossi, Patrizia.
P301.5.I34I3   1993
401'.9—dc20

92–28580
CIP

Books published by Lawrence Erlbaum Associates are printed on acid-free paper, and their
bindings are chosen for strength and durability.

Printed in the United States of America

10 9 8 7 6 5 4 3 2 1

CONTENTS

Foreword

If natural language had been designed by a logician, idioms would not exist. They are a feature of discourse that frustrates any simple logical account of how the meanings of utterances depend on the meanings of their parts and on the syntactic relation among those parts. Idioms are transparent to native speakers, but a course of perplexity to those who are acquiring a second language. If someone tells me that Mrs. Thatcher has become the Queen of Scotland, I am likely to say: "That's a tall story. Pull the other one!" As anyone struggling to learn English will aver, stories cannot be tall—they have no height, and so the expression violates a restriction on the normal sense of the word. Similarly, to pull something is a physical event, and "one" is a pronoun that normally harks back to something that has occurred in the discourse. But I am certainly not inviting you to make any physical action. "Tall" has an idiomatic sense of improbable or farfetched. "Pull the other one" has an idiomatic sense that relates to another idiom: "to pull someone's leg," which means to joke or to tease someone. "To pull the other one" stands in for "to pull my other leg," and is accordingly an ironic invitation to tell me another joke.

A simple litmus, though not an infallible one, for whether a sense is idiomatic is to consider its expression in another language. An Italian speaker, for example, does not say, "Mi stai tirando la gamba" [literally, you are pulling my leg] to express the idea of a joke, but rather: "Mi prendi in giro." This expression is purely idiomatic. It does not have a literal meaning, though it clearly relates to: "Fammi fare un giro," which means you are taking me on a tour. Hence, some expressions have both a literal and an idiomatic meaning, such as "It's better than a poke in the eye with a burnt stick," and others have only an idiomatic interpretation, such as "You're giving me the run around." All this linguistic filigree is interesting no doubt, but does it really call for psycholinguistic studies, and for the book of scholarly essays that you presently hold in your hand? The answer is: yes. And to justify this claim, I will briefly explain why idioms are important, why their study is so central to current psychological investigations of language, and why indeed all students of language as a mental phenomenon are likely to benefit from reading the chapters in this book. Then I will pass you on to the editors of the volume to introduce its contents to you.

The logical approach to language relegates idioms to the sidelines. Speakers use idiomatic expressions, on this account, as though they were words or phrases that have become frozen into a single form with a special meaning. Somewhere in the mind these expressions are stored as exceptions, much as they might be listed at the end of a dictionary. Listeners first try to make a literal interpretation of an utterance. The literal meaning can be constructed compositionally, that is, it can be composed from the meanings of its parts according to the syntactic relations amongst them. Words have meanings; each syntactic rule in the grammar has a corresponding semantic principle. As the mental parser makes its way through a sentence, it uses syntactic rules to analyze the sentence, and whenever it uses a syntactic rule, it also uses the corresponding semantic principle to build up an interpretation of the sentence. The literal meaning of "You are pulling my leg" can be constructed compositionally, and so different arguments for the verb are intersubstitutable, i.e., "You are pulling the part of my leg that hurts." Different superficial re-arrangements of the constituents are also acceptable, i.e., "My leg is being pulled by you." The idiomatic sense, however, is not fully compositional. "My leg" does not refer to my leg, but to me, and, unlike the compositional case, listeners cannot make this interpretation of the noun phrase in isolation from the rest of the sentence. They need the expression as a whole to recognize that it has an idiomatic interpretation. Idioms are accordingly relatively fixed in syntactic and lexical form. Speakers who say, " You are pulling my legs," or "You are pushing my legs," or "You're pulling my foot," have not quite mastered the idiom. Yet a fluent speaker might invent such expressions to convey idiomatically some subtle aspect of the situation: "You are pulling my legs" because you have told me *two* improbable stories. If a compositional interpretation is nonsensical in the context of the utterance, then the listener is supposed to check whether an idiomatic sense is listed and whether it makes better sense. In short, idioms are exceptions to the general rule of compositionality, and where the general rule fails, the list of exceptions (e.g., frozen idioms) is examined to see whether it provides a more appropriate interpretation. This sort of proposal has been advanced from many quarters, particularly by philosophers, logicians, and those housebound cartographers who rely solely on intuition to draw maps of the mind.

The facts tell a different story. Why, for example, do idioms exist? Their origin is singularly mysterious in the logical account of language. It is not at all obvious why speakers should use expressions that cannot be understood in the normal way. Idioms should be rare exceptions comparable to slips of the tongue. Yet it is difficult to speak spontaneously without lapsing into idiomatic usage. Try it with a foreigner, and you will see that you are often aware of using an idiom only after the event. Even in explaining an idiom, you can find to your expense that you are using another. Hence, the first reason for the importance of idioms is that they are pervasive.

One reaction to this pervasiveness is to argue that all usage is idiomatic. (Connectionists have a natural inclination to make such claims.) And this hypothesis has the advantage that it removes at a stroke the mystery of the origin of idioms: They arise in the natural use of natural language. Yet fish are unaware of the water—that is to say, if all is idiom, why do we ever draw the distinction between the literal and the idiomatic? Clearly, utterances with a literal interpretation are just as pervasive as idioms. There may be a continuum from clear cases of literal usage to clear cases of idiomatic usage, but the two ends of the continuum are plain enough. The creative use of language—at any level from phonology to pragmatics—is a natural part of discourse. Speakers—some more than others—invent words and phrases to force us to pay attention, to amuse us, to astonish us, and to challenge us. And they create new ways to convey old meanings for the sheer joy of invention. But the creation of idioms also reflects new conceptions of the world, new ways in which individuals construct mental models of the world, and new ways in which to convey their contents vividly. It is through idioms—and I include those special cases that rhetoricians dignify as tropes, such as metaphor, irony, metonymy, and synecdoche—that the truly creative nature of human expression reveals itself. Idioms are the poetry of daily discourse. That is the second reason for their importance.

Alas, we are not all capable of idiomatic invention, but most of us do pick up, borrow, or steal the idioms of others. Our linguistic usage is full of second-hand idioms, dead metaphors, and stale similes. We use these clichés without thinking; and we understand them equally automatically. However, if we are supposed to try to make a literal interpretation before we seek an idiomatic one, then we should understand literal meanings faster than idioms. In fact, as a number of experiments have shown, we can understand idioms just as fast as literal usages. For twenty years or more, psycholinguists have pursued an intensive examination of how the mental parser works. Compositional interpretation is, in principle, straightforward. But how are idioms interpreted? Speakers certainly acquire a knowledge of familiar idioms, and this knowledge somehow enables them to cope as readily with idiomatic usage as with literal meaning. Idioms are easy, and this surprising fact is the third reason for their importance.

We have the ability to speak in riddles. These riddles are neither constructed nor interpreted in the normal way. Yet we use them so readily that we are usually unaware of their special character—unless we have the misfortune *not* to be a native speaker. We call these special riddles idioms. They are one of the many ways in which natural languages differ from those artificial languages that experts have designed on logical principles—mathematical calculi, computer programming languages, and systems of formal logic. Idioms are mysterious. They are pervasive, poetic, and easy. How they are understood is a mystery that the contents of this book go some way to dispelling.

P. N. Johnson-Laird

Preface

According to the Oxford Dictionary (5th ed.), an idiom can be the "language of a people or country," or a "form of expression peculiar to a language." It is in the second of the two senses, obviously related to each other, that idioms[1], along with metaphors, proverbs, indirect speech acts, etc., are part of the vast family of figurative expressions. The interest in these expressions has a longstanding tradition. Within European structuralism, for instance, linguists have studied figurative expressions primarily in the attempt to shed light on the synchronic regularities and the diachronic changes of languages (for a recent approach to language changes, cf. Sweetser, 1991). In a similar vein, anthropologists have devoted much of their attention to studying how a figurative expression is formed or why it becomes an appropriate description of an event in one speech community, but not in another (Basso, 1976; Fernandez, 1991; Holland & Quinn, 1987; Ruwet, 1983). These lines of research, aiming at elucidating the linguistic and social sources of figurative language, have successfully shown that any facts, beliefs, cultural models, natural events, etc. shared by the members of a speech community at a given time can give rise to figurative expressions (Ammer, 1989; Makkai, 1987). The introduction of railways, electricity, and other technological innovations, for instance, has enriched the figurative basis of many languages providing a whole new set of ways of describing reality, which was not available, say, in seventeenth century France, where many figurative expressions were related to religion (Ullmann, 1962).

More recently, the interest in the origins of figurative language has received further impulse thanks to a new approach that sees the *substratum* of figurative

---

[1]We will use "idiom" and "idiomatic expression" as synonyms.

expressions in people's cognitive structure (e.g., Holland & Quinn, 1987; Nayak & Gibbs, 1990; Sweetser, 1991). In this perspective, the historical origins of figurative expressions, whether or not they are still transparent to the speakers of a community, provide useful information on how people organize their conceptual and lexical knowledge, and establish connections across domains. A well-known example of this sort is the relation between the temporal and spatial domain, where many concepts of the former are borrowed from the latter, as illustrated by the numerous spatial terms used—at least in English—for referring to time.

In this long and uninterrupted tradition, figurative language has typically been viewed as a relatively homogeneous topic. No doubt, there are differences among, for instance, a metaphor and a proverb, but both are likely to have similar origins and serve similar purposes within a linguistic community. Moreover, a widely shared assumption is that, theoretically, the most prominent form is metaphor, whereas the other expressions are mostly derivative topics. Idioms, in particular, have often been considered "dead metaphors"—i.e., expressions that were once innovative, but are now conventionalized and frozen—and hence scarcely relevant in comparison with metaphor.

Only recently has this belief come to be challenged, and idiomatic expressions come to be considered for their own sake. This book takes up this perspective, and although several chapters discuss the relation between idioms and other forms of figurative language—notable, metaphor—its main focus is on aspects that are peculiar to idioms. Thus, the book deals primarily with questions such as how idioms are mentally represented, understood, and acquired by children, what are the neurological structures involved in their comprehension, how can their syntactic behavior be explained, and what is their place in our languages.

This approach is grounded in the conviction that problems of representation, parsing and interpretation are different for metaphors and idioms, each of which has specific properties and characteristics, and requires, therefore, different explanations. This is not to deny the unquestionable relation between the two forms. To the contrary, one fascinating aspect of idioms—extensively explored in the book—is precisely the fact that idioms appear to be at a crossroad, sharing aspects of different linguistic objects. Thus, although lacking the semantic richness and flexibility of metaphors, idioms share some of the features of that "most luminous" and vital trope. For instance, individual words in idiomatic expressions, as in metaphors, do not generally have the same meaning they have in literal strings. As Levinson (1983) has noted for metaphors, in order to make sense of both types of expressions one must take into account the "connotative penumbra" of their words. However, unlike metaphors, whose interpretation is built compositionally, the meaning of many idiomatic expressions seems to become available, as the meaning of lexical items, through processes of retrieval from memory. Yet again, unlike actual words, idioms have a syntactic structure that at times is frozen, but on occasions is very flexible and can be modified in various ways, depending also upon the extent to which the figurative meaning of the string is related to its literal meaning (Cutler, 1982; Gibbs & Nayak, 1989; Gibbs, Nayak, Bolton, & Keppel, 1988; Nunberg, 1978; Wasow, Sag, & Nunberg, 1983).

Indeed, as pointed out by almost all of the authors in this book, idioms are very elusive, and the difficulty of exactly characterizing them is perhaps one of the reasons why relatively little attention has traditionally been accorded to these expressions, in spite of their unquestionable relevance, which resides in at least two considerations: Idioms are a clear challenge to current compositional models of language comprehension, and their use in the language is so widespread to justify Searle's (1975) informal rule of conversation: "Speak idiomatically unless there is some good reason not to do so."

The multifaceted nature of idioms has, among its consequences, the fact that it is virtually impossible for any single approach or methodology to fully capture it. Moreover, our current knowledge of these expressions is such that the picture that emerges from their study is still rather fragmentary. Both these aspects are reflected in the book, and although linguistic, computational, psychological, and neuropsychological approaches are all present, providing an interdisciplinary, cognitive science perspective on the study of idioms, no attempt has been made to force the different trends of research into a coherent framework. Instead, the chapters offers an updated account of many of the problems that are currently discussed, along with the explanatory attempts produced so far.

The book is divided into three parts. Part I is dedicated to the interpretation of idioms and to the relations between their literal and the figurative meanings. Glucksberg's claim is that idioms are not unanalyzable wholes, but can be decomposed into linguistic and conceptual elements, even though the literal meanings of the linguistic elements alone are insufficient, and other sources of meaning—in particular, stipulated and allusional—must also be considered in order for the complete interpretation of these expressions to be obtained.

The notions of literal and metaphorical meanings are also discussed in the chapter by Cacciari. She argues that for many idioms the meanings of their individual words and the rhetorical structure of the expressions—whether metaphorical, analogical, or other—are both available to people. This information is not always used, but is employed when required either by a specific task, or by the need to interpret unfamiliar idiomatic expression.

Gibbs' chapter is aimed at demonstratiang the fallacy of the "dead metaphor view of idiomaticity." The author argues that many idioms are "very much alive metaphorically", and that people are able to make sense of the figurative meaning of many unfamiliar idioms precisely because they can rely on the metaphorical interpretation of these expressions. Finally, Flores d'Arcais examines the processes of comprehension of an idiomatic phrase with respect to its familiarity, its uniqueness point—i.e., the point at which the idiom becomes uniquely identifiable—and its syntactic flexibility. He also presents data suggesting that people interpret unfamiliar idioms much like metaphors, relying whenever possible on similarities with more familiar expressions.

Part II of the book deals with how children learn to use idiomatic expressions and how these are represented and processed by adults. In her chapter on acquisition, Levorato argues that learning to use an idiom is not the same as learning to associate the string with its meaning, as it would be if idioms were acquired like words. Rather, it is a process that requires the development of figurative competence, and is achieved in different stages during which the ability to comprehend and produce idioms grows in parallel with the child's increasing mastery of linguistic and communicative abilities.

Botelho and Cutler's chapter presents data on memory for Portuguese idioms with and without a literal counterpart. The authors argue that their results support the lexical representation hypothesis (originally proposed by Cutler and Swinney in 1979), one of the most influential psycholinguistic models of idiom processing and representation. In contrast to this view, Tabossi and Zardon claim that idioms are mentally represented not as lexical items, but as configurations of words, much like poems. Accordingly, the meaning of these expressions is retrieved not as the meaning of individual words, but triggered only after sufficient information is available to the listeners to recognize the idiomatic "configuration."

Colombo's paper deals with an old issue in psycholinguistic research—namely, the ambiguity of idioms and the effects that context has on the biasing of their literal and figurative interpretation. The results of her study appear to indicate that the idiomatic meaning of an ambiguous string is activated in a context that biases that meaning. No such activation is found, however, in a neutral context or in a context that biases the literal meaning of the string.

In the last chapter of the section, Peterson and Burgess argue for the relevance of neurolinguistic as well as psycholinguistic evidence in the study of idioms. In fact, both types of data presented in their chapter appear to converge, indicating a dissociation between the syntactic and semantic processing of idiomatic expressions. In particular, the syntactic analysis of an idiom is computed even when such an analysis is no longer used to contruct the literal interpretation of the string.

In Part III, the chapter by Stock, Slack, and Ortony and that by Pulman both tackle one of the best known and least understood problems involving idioms: their flexibility. As Pulman correctly points out, the major difficulty with idioms is not "that their meaning cannot by derived compositionality, . . . because this could by overcome by treating them as multi-word lexical items . . . The problem is that unlike (most) lexical items, (most) idioms have considerable internal structure which seems to interact with the usual productive syntactic and semantic mechanisms of a language."

Stock et al. address this thorny problem in a computational model where the flexibility of an idiom, or the lack thereof, is determined by whether or not the thematic structure of its linguistic form (e.g., "kick the bucket") is equivalent to the thematic structure of its associated semantic representation (e.g., "die").

In a similar vein, Pulman argues that the flexibililty of idioms is not and should not be explained by a theory of syntax, but depends on the semantics of the idioms and on the contextual interpretation of the utterances in which they occur. Given a sentence, the processing system parses it and, applying compositional semantic rules, gives the logical forms of the sentence which in turn can serve as input to an inferential mechanism that has access to meaning postulates and idiom rules. These can add figurative interpretations to the string. The sets of literal and figurative interpretations are then evaluated contextually.

Fellbaum's chapter is more specific in scope. After an analysis of the distribution and role of determiners in idiomatic strings such as "spill the beans" or "have an axe to grind," Fellbaum discusses the results of the investigation in the light of a theory of compositionality.

In the final chapter, Makkai explores universal constraints on the formation of idioms, and discusses the role that this process fullfils in a language. Makkai claims that language develops through phases, the last of which is characterized by the arbitrary attribution of sound strings to concepts. However, when concepts develop even further, a "point of saturation" is reached in the process of designating new concepts and objects arbitrarily. The speech community starts then to borrow images and similes for what is to be expressed, and recombines existing signs in new ways, in this way creating idioms.

This brief presentation should suffice to give the reader a flavor of the variety of topics that are currently under debate, and of the different approaches that co-exist in the field. In fact, as already pointed out, many aspects concerning idioms remain controversial, and perhaps many questions are still waiting to be asked in the appropriate way. However, along with the differences, the chapters in this book also suggest that, at least on some issues, convergent attitudes are starting to emerge. For instance, the traditional, noncompositional approach to idiomatic meaning, once unchallenged, has recently been criticized on several grounds, and the view that the meanings of the constituent words of an idiom do play a role in its comprehension is now winning a growing consensus among cognitive scientists. We hope that this book will contribute to the further development of interdisciplinary research, offering a useful tool to all those interested in the study of idioms and in the better comprehension of language, whether figurative or not.

Cristina Cacciari
Patrizia Tabossi

REFERENCES

Ammer, C. (1989). *It's raining cats and dogs . . . and other beastly expressions*. New York: Laurel Books.
Basso, K. H. (1976). "Wise Words" of the Western Apache: Metaphor and semantic theory. In K.

H. Basso (Ed.), *Meaning in anthropology* (pp. 93–121). Albuquerque: University of New Mexico Press.

Cutler, A. (1982). Idioms: the older the colder. *Linguistic Inquiry, 13,* 2, 317–320.

Fernandez, J. W. (1991). (Ed.). *Beyond metaphor. The theory of tropes in anthropology.* Stanford, CA: Stanford University Press.

Gibbs, W. R., Nayak, N. P., Bolton, J. L., & Keppel, M. (1988). Speakers assumptions about the lexical flexibility of idioms. *Memory & Cognition, 17,* 1, 58–68.

Gibbs, W. R., & Nayak, N. P. (1989). Psycholinguistic studies on the syntactic behavior of idioms. *Cognitive Psychology, 21,* 100–138.

Holland, D., & Quinn, N. (1987). (Eds.). *Cultural models in language and thought.* New York: Cambridge University Press.

Levinson, S. C. (1983). *Pragmatics.* London: Cambridge University Press.

Makkai, A. (1987). Idiomaticity and phraseology in post-chomskian linguistics. The coming-of-age of semantics beyond the sentence. *Semiotica, 64,* 1-2, 171–187.

Nayak, P. N., & Gibbs, W. R. (1990). Conceptual knowledge in the interpretation of idioms. *Journal of Experimental Psychology: General, 119,* 115–130.

Nunberg, G. (1978). *The pragmatics of reference.* Bloomington, Indiana: Indiana Linguistic Club.

Ruwet, N. (1983). Du bon usage des expressions idiomatiques. *Recherches Linguistiques, 11,* 5–84.

Searle, J. (1975). Indirect speech acts. In P. Cole & J. L. Morgan (Eds.), *Syntax and semantics speech acts* (pp. 59–82). New York: Academic Press.

Sweetser, E. (1991). *From etymology to pragmatics. Metaphorical and cultural aspects of semantic structure.* Cambridge: Cambridge University Press.

Swinney, D. A., & Cutler, A. (1979). The access and processing of idiomatic expressions. *Journal of Verbal Learning and Verbal Behavior, 18,* 523–534.

The Concise Oxford Dictionary, Fifth Edition, Oxford: The Clerendon Press.

Ullmann, S. (1962). *Semantics: An introduction to the study of meaning.* Oxford: Basil Blackwell & Mott.

Wasow, T., Sag, I., & Nunberg, G. (1983). Idioms: An interim report. In S. Hattori & K. Inoue (Eds.), *Proceedings of the XIIIth International Congress of Linguistics* (pp. 102–105). Tokyo.

List of Contributors

Teresa Botelho da Silva   Department of Linguistics, University of Cambridge, Sidewick Avenue, Cambridge CB3 9DL United Kingdom.

Curt Burgess   Department of Psychology, 1419 Life Science Building, University of California, Riverside, CA 92521–0426.

Cristina Cacciari   Dipartimento di Psicologia, Viale Berti-Pichat 5, 40127 Bologna, Italy.

Lucia Colombo   Dipartimento di Psicologia Generale, Piazza Capitaniato 3, 35139 Padova, Italy.

Anne Cutler   MRC Applied Psychology Unit, 15 Chaucer Rd., Cambridge CB2 2EF United Kingdom.

Christiane Fellbaum   Cognitive Science Laboratory, Princeton University, 221, Nassau Street, Princeton, NJ 08542.

Giovanni Battista Flores d'Arcais   Dipartimento di Psicologia dello Sviluppo e della Socializzazione, Via Beato Pellegrino 26, 35137 Padova, Italy.

Ray W. Gibbs   Program in Experimental Psychology, Clark Kerr Hall, University of California, Santa Cruz, Santa Cruz, CA 95064.

Sam Glucksberg   Department of Psychology, Green Hall, Princeton University, Princeton NJ 08544–1010.

Maria Chiara Levorato   Dipartimento di Psicologia dello Sviluppo e della Socializzazione, Via Beato Pellegrino 26, 35137 Padova, Italy.

Adam Makkai   M/c 237, University of Illinois at Chicago, POB # 4348, Chicago IL 60680.

Andrew Ortony   Institute for the Learning Sciences, 1980 Maple Avenue, Evanston, IL 60201.

Robert Peterson   Department of Psychology, Indiana University, Bloomington, IN 47405.

Steve G. Pulman   SRI International, Cambridge Computer Science Research, Millers Yard, Mill Lane, Cambridge CB2 1RQ United Kingdom.

Jon Slack   IRST, 38050 Povo (Trento), Italy.

Oliviero Stock   IRST, 38050 Povo (Trento), Italy.

Patrizia Tabossi   Facoltà di Letteu e Filosofia, Via Savonarola 38, 44100 Ferrara, Italy.

Francesco Zardon   Dipartimento di Psicologia, Viale Berti-Pichat 5, 40127 Bologna, Italy.

IDIOM INTERPRETATION AND THE LITERAL FIGURATIVE DISTINCTION

1 Idiom Meanings and Allusional Content

Sam Glucksberg
Princeton University

> *People who live in glass houses should not throw stones.*

For most readers, this proverb should elicit the experience of apprehending several kinds of meanings simultaneously. The meaning of the sentence itself— the literal meaning—would be apprehended by anyone who reads English fluently. In addition, readers familiar with the proverb will apprehend immediately a second kind of meaning, the meaning of the proverb. The expression is not just about glass houses and stones, but also about the vulnerability of people criticizing others for faults that they themselves have. The idiomatic meaning itself derives from the allusion to the glass house as a metaphor for vulnerability. Despite being able to determine both the literal and idiomatic meanings of the proverb, however, few readers experience the most important meaning of all: What did I, the writer, intend by my use of this proverb? In the absence of any relevant contextual information, the proverb can be understood only as an example or illustration of some point, which of course it is.

The proverb is one example of the class of expressions that mean something other than their constituent words and phrases. At one end of the continuum are phrases such as *by and large,* which seem to be nothing more than long words. Furthermore, not only does this expression mean something other than its constituents, its meaning seems to bear no relation to those constituents. At the other extreme are familiar proverbs and idioms that allude to apocryphal events, such as residents of glass houses throwing stones, people carrying coals to Newcastle, and farmers locking barn doors after horses have been stolen. In these cases, the meanings of the constituents are relevant, but the meaning of each expression is not just something other than the meanings of the constituent parts. The ex-

3

pression's meaning is also something more than the meanings of the parts. The expression itself alludes to an archetypical case of the class of events that it typifies. It does not matter one whit whether anyone actually threw any stones while living in a glass house, or carried coal to the English city of Newcastle, or ever locked a barn door after having horses stolen. These expressions are, in essence, metaphors for the general situations or events that they typify.

In between the wordlike by-and-large idioms and the metaphorlike coals-to-Newcastle idioms are those that can have quite variable relations between their constituent and idiom meanings. Like *by and large,* phrasal idioms such as *kick the bucket* have meanings that bear no discernible relation to their idiomatic meanings, in this case "to die." Like *coals to Newcastle,* other phrasal idioms such as *spill the beans* bear a somewhat metaphorical relation to their idiomatic meanings, in this case *divulge secrets.* Given the diversity among the idioms people use in everyday discourse, it should not be surprising that theories of idiom comprehension are diverse as well.

Idiomatic Meaning: Direct Access Versus Compositional

Two classes of models have been proposed for idiom comprehension. Reflecting the characteristics of such idioms as *by and large* and *kick the bucket,* one class treats idioms as expressions that have meanings that are stipulated arbitrarily. According to this class of models, idioms are understood simply by retrieving the meaning of an idiom as a whole. I refer to this type of model as a *direct look-up model.* The second class of models reflects the characteristics of such idioms as *carrying coals to Newcastle.* The meanings of these kinds of idioms are not arbitrary. The relation of coals to Newcastle is a matter of historical fact, and the literal act of carrying coals to the coal-mining center of Newcastle is a stereotypical instance of uselessly bringing something to some place. According to this second class of models, idioms are understood by ordinary linguistic processing combined with a pragmatic interpretation of the use of the expression in discourse contexts. I refer to this class of models as *compositional.*

Direct Look-Up. Three versions of direct look-up models have been proposed: (a) the idiom list hypothesis (Bobrow & Bell, 1973), (b) the lexicalization hypothesis (Swinney & Cutler, 1979), and (c) the direct access hypothesis (Gibbs, 1984). All share the assumption that idiom meanings are apprehended by direct memory retrieval, not by linguistic processing. The three differ in relatively unimportant ways. Bobrow and Bell proposed that idioms are represented in a mental idiom list, that is, an idiom lexicon that parallels the mental word lexicon. Idiomatic meanings are sought when a linguistic analysis fails to yield an interpretable result. When linguistic analysis fails, people turn to a search of the idiom list, and if the linguistically recalcitrant expression is found, then the idiom meaning is taken as the intended meaning. This model is rejected easily by the robust finding that idioms are understood at least as quickly as comparable literal expressions (Gibbs, 1980; Ortony, Schallert, Reynolds, and Antos, 1978). If expressions must always be analyzed literally before any idiomatic meanings are sought, then literal meanings should always be understood more quickly than idiomatic ones. Contrary to Bobrow and Bell, the literal meanings of conventional idiomatic expressions are never understood more quickly than their idiomatic ones.

Swinney and Cutler's (1979) lexicalization hypothesis accounts quite nicely for the relative ease of understanding familiar idioms. Idioms are represented simply as long words, together with all the ordinary words in the mental lexicon. When a familiar idiomatic expression is encountered, linguistic processing proceeds normally. Lexical access, of course, proceeds as part of linguistic processing, and lexicalized phrases such as *by and large* or *kick the bucket* are routinely found in the mental lexicon along with their constituent words, *by, and, large,* and so on. Which of the two meanings—literal or idiomatic—is apprehended first depends on the relative speed with which full linguistic processing and lexical/idiom access can be completed. Normally, idiom access will be completed more quickly because it does not require the lexical, syntactic, and semantic processing required for full linguistic analysis. Thus, familiar idioms will be understood more quickly than comparable literal expressions.

Gibbs' (1984) direct access proposal is an extreme version of the Swinney and Cutler (1979) model. Rather than posit a race between idiom-meaning access and linguistic processing, Gibbs argued that linguistic processing may be bypassed entirely if an expression is recognized immediately as an idiom. In essence, idiom-meaning access may be so rapid as to obviate any linguistic analysis at all. Gibbs himself soon adopted a more compositional view of idiom comprehension, based in part on some of his own observations of lexical and syntactic phenomena involved in idiom use.

Compositional.   As we have already seen, idioms can vary from apparently unitary phrases (e.g., *by and large*) to expressions whose idiomatic meanings derive jointly from their literal meanings and allusional content (e.g., *carry coals to Newcastle*). Nunberg (1978) tried to capture this variability by proposing that idioms can be ordered along a continuum of compositionality. Ordinary language is, by definition, compositional. The meaning of any given linguistic expression is determinable from the meanings of its constituent parts and the syntactic and semantic relations among those parts. The meaning of any idiom, in the standard view, is determinable entirely from its stipulated meaning, whether that meaning is represented in a special idiom list or simply as part of the mental lexicon.

As usual, a simple dichotomy fails to capture natural complexity. In an extension of Nunberg's (1978) original proposal, Gibbs and his colleagues have shown that people can reliably judge degrees of compositionality of idioms (Gibbs,

Nayak, Bolton, & Keppel, 1989; Gibbs, Nayak, & Cutting, 1989). Idioms such as *spill the beans,* for example, are considered relatively compositional (in Gibbs' terms, analyzable), in contrast to idioms such as *kick the bucket,* which are considered noncompositional. In either case, linguistic processing proceeds in parallel with direct idiom-meaning look-up, with direct look-up usually being faster than full linguistic analysis.

A somewhat similar proposal was offered by Cacciari and Tabossi (1988). Linguistic processing and idiom look-up can occur in parallel, but idiom look-up cannot begin until the idiom itself is recognized as a configuration, that is, as a unitary expression with a meaning beyond that of its constituents. This model along with the race models mentioned earlier seem to fit most closely with what we know about idiom processing. In the next section, important idiom phe- nomena are considered in the context of the issue of look-up versus composi- tionality.

HOW IDIOMS ARE UNDERSTOOD

Idioms as Long Words

The primary evidence for direct look-up of idiom meaning is the relative speed of idiom comprehension. Idioms are understood more quickly in their idiomatic senses than in their literal senses. The to-die meaning of *kick the bucket,* for example, is understood more quickly than the literal meaning of striking a pail with one's foot (Gibbs, 1980). Similarly, it takes less time to understand the expression *spill the beans* than to understand the literal paraphrase, *tell the secrets* (McGlone, Glucksberg, & Cacciari, in press; see also, Ortony et al., 1978). These data suggest that an idiom's meaning may be retrieved from memo- ry without full linguistic processing, on the assumption that direct memory retrieval takes less time than would standard linguistic processing.

Idioms as Linguistic Expressions

Whatever else they may be, idioms are composed of words that in turn form phrases and sentences. In general, people cannot inhibit their language-process- ing system. If someone attends to a word, for example, then they cannot ignore that word's meaning. Even if people are asked explicitly to ignore a word's meaning, as in Stroop's classic color-naming experiment, the meaning still comes through. People who try to name the color of the ink that a color name is printed in are delayed momentarily when the color name and ink color differ (e.g., when the word *red* is printed in green ink; Stroop, 1935). Given the automaticity of the language-processing system, it should not be surprising to find evidence for the ubiquity of lexical and syntactic operations during idiom comprehension.

Phrases Versus Words.   Perhaps the most compelling case for idioms as long words can be made with such idioms as *by and large*. Like a long word, such idioms can be negated, as in:

> Tom: By and large, the economy seems to be doing well.
> Ned: Not so by and large: Have you seen the latest unemployment figures?

Unlike a word, however, such idioms can be negated internally, as in:

> Ned: By but not so large! Have you considered. . . .

If the string *by and large* were indeed nothing more than a long word, then substituting *but* for *and*, together with inserting two additional words, *not* and *so*, should produce an unacceptable string. Not only is the string acceptable, it is perfectly interpretable. Phrases such as *by and large*, however much they might behave like long words, are still phrases and treated as such.

Do Words Matter? Semantic Compatibility Effects.   Some phrasal idioms seem odd when synonyms are substituted for the original words, and indeed may not even be recognized as idioms; for example, people rarely realize that *boot the pail* is a paraphrase of *kick the bucket* (Gibbs, Nayak, & Cutting, 1989). Other phrasal idioms, especially those that are judged to be compositional, can survive lexical substitutions, but the substitutions are constrained jointly by the idiom's meaning and the semantics of the words themselves. The idiom *break the ice,* for example, refers to a more or less discrete event that results in a relaxation of a stiff, awkward, chilly social situation. Substituting the word *crack* for *break* in this idiom is relatively acceptable. In contrast, the words *crush, grind,* or *shave* would not be acceptable in this idiom, even though these actions are perfectly appropriate to the actual object, *ice.* Can the proverbial ice be melted? Perhaps, but only if a gradual change in the social atmosphere were involved. These examples illustrate the potential role of literal word meanings in idiomatic use and comprehension. Lexical substitutions are not only possible but also are semantically constrained precisely because idioms must be processed lin-guistically, even when such processing is not necessary for determining the idiom's meaning.

Semantic Constraints on Idiom Use.   Idioms such as *kick the bucket* tend to resist lexical substitutions. Nevertheless, the semantic properties of their constit-uents may still play important roles in use and in comprehension. Even though there is no apparent relation between the meanings of the words kick and bucket and the concept "to die," word meanings and idiomatic meaning may still interact to guide and constrain this idiom's use. On the one hand, our understand-ing of what it means to die guides and constrains how the idiom kick the bucket may be used. People can die silently, and so it makes sense to say, "He silently kicked the bucket." People cannot die "sharply," so even though one can kick sharply, one cannot say "He sharply kicked the bucket." On the other hand, the meanings of the words kick and bucket can also play important roles. Kicking is a discrete act, and so, even though one can say, "He lay dying all week," one cannot say, "He lay kicking the bucket all week" (Wasow, Sag, & Nunberg, 1983). This is because the only way one can kick a bucket all week is to kick it over and over again, but one cannot die over and over again.

How real is the bucket? Once used in discourse, the proverbial bucket behaves just as would any other discourse referent, as shown by its availability as an anaphoric referent. Consider the following conversational fragment:

> George: Did the old man kick the bucket last night?
> Edward: Nah, he barely nudged it.

In this context, the relation of *nudge* to *kick* and the use of the pronoun *it* to refer to *bucket* are clearly interpretable. Barely nudging as compared to kicking the bucket denotes not even coming close to kicking it, and so this variant is taken to mean not even close to dying. In this example, the concept of death and the semantics of the idiom's constituents jointly constrain idiom use and comprehension, reflecting again the joint operation of idiom meaning and the language itself.

Idiom Variants: Semantic Productivity.   When familiar idioms are used as variants of their canonical forms, the discrepancy between original and new wordings may form the basis of newly created idiom meanings. If, for example, someone were to say *crack the ice* instead of *break the ice* to refer to a change in a social situation, no particular communicative intent would be inferred. *Crack* and *break* would be seen as mere stylistic variants of one another. If, on the other hand, someone were to say *shatter the ice,* then this would not be interpreted as a mere stylistic variant. Instead, the difference between the meaning of break and the meaning of shatter creates a new idiomatic meaning, something like "break down an uncomfortable and stiff social situation flamboyantly in one fell swoop." Thus, this is not simply an example of lexical flexibility, it is an example of semantic productivity.

Such semantically productive idiom variants appear in everyday conversation and in the media. One striking example appeared in a *New York Times* article on the rise and fall of the Wall Street firm Drexel Burnham Lambert (Drexel). Drexel had made a fortune on junk bonds and then found themselves seriously short of cash. Before declaring bankruptcy, the firm's assets were distributed among the senior executives in the form of very substantial cash bonuses. As a direct result of this bonus distribution, Drexel's cash reserve was depleted, forcing the firm into bankruptcy. In this context, the meaning of this twist on a familiar idiom is clear: "Drexel's senior executives, not content with collecting one golden egg after another, seem to have insisted then on eating the goose." Similarly, Donald Barthelme's title for an essay on contemporary literature— "Convicted Minimalist Spills Bean"—makes perfect sense to those who know of his reputation as a minimalist writer. Even young children spontaneously use idioms productively in discourse, once the original idioms have been learned. One 5-year-old girl learned the expression *spill the beans* as meaning "tell a secret." Later that same day, she told her father, "Don't throw the beans to Rebecca! She's not supposed to know!" (Greenberg-Concool, 1990).

Direct Access and Linguistic Processing Reconsidered

The evidence for direct access is straightforward yet inconclusive: (a) Familiar idioms in their original, canonical form are understood more quickly than comparable literal expressions; and (b) Familiar idioms in canonical form also are understood more quickly than their variants (McGlone, Glucksberg, & Cacciari, in press). The expression *didn't spill the beans,* for example, is understood more quickly than the relatively novel expression *didn't spill a single bean.* Taken together, these data suggest but do not force the conclusion that familiar idioms need not be processed linguistically because their meanings can be retrieved directly from memory. In contrast, nonidiomatic expressions, as well as variants of familiar idioms, presumably must be processed linguistically because their meanings are not stipulated and stored in memory.

At the same time, familiar idioms must be processed linguistically even though initial meaning access may be quite independent of linguistic analysis. Evidence that even familiar idioms are fully analyzed includes the reciprocal constraints of idiom meaning and literal meaning on idiom use, and the ability of people to understand idiom variants quite readily. The question remains, however, how do people determine the meaning of idiom variants? An adequate answer to this question might provide the answer to the question of how people understand idioms more generally.

UNDERSTANDING IDIOMS AND THEIR
VARIANTS: A PARADIGM CASE

How do people manage to understand an expression such as "He didn't spill a single bean"? Clearly, the meaning of this expression cannot be stored in memory because the expression is novel, albeit based on the familiar idiom *spill the beans.* If a variant idiom's meaning is not available to be retrieved from memory, then the meanings of the constituent words must be used in some fashion to determine the variant's meaning. There are at least two ways that word meanings could be used. One way would involve comparing the meanings of the original and variant idiom constituents, determining the relation between those meanings, and inferring, by analogy, the meaning of the variant with respect to the meaning of the original. Such a strategy would involve at least the following six discrete operations:

1. Recognize novel idiom as a variant of a conventional idiom.
2. Retrieve meaning of original idiom.
3. Identify word meanings of both variant and original idioms.
4. Compare the word meanings of the two idiom forms.
5. Identify the relation(s) between those word meanings.
6. Take this relation(s) between the word meanings to infer, by analogy, the relation(s) between the meanings of the original and variant idioms.

If, for example, the substituted words were antonyms, then the variant idiom's meaning would be taken to be the opposite of the original, as in *got up on the right side of the bed* versus *got up on the wrong side of the bed.* If the relation between the substituted words is one of quantity, then this would be taken as the relation between the variant idiom and the original, as in *spill a single bean* versus *spill the beans.* More complex relations are also possible, as in the Drexel Burnham example, where the proverbial golden goose can be said to be eaten instead of killed to imply unseemly greed and gorging oneself in addition to simply destroying a source of wealth. Similarly, to say that "we'll jump off that bridge when we come to it" instead of "we'll cross that bridge when we come to it" suggests self-destructive or suicidal behavior in addition to lack of foresight or planning.

This kind of sequential, multistep model is perfectly compatible with the traditional view of idioms as long words (or as phrases) whose meanings are simply retrieved from a mental idiom lexicon. Individual word meanings, of course, must be used when conventional idioms are varied in some way, but word meanings still would play no role in understanding familiar idioms in their canonical form. One implication of this view is that variant idioms should take considerably longer to understand than idioms in their original forms. Original idioms require only one operation, retrieval of a meaning from a stored list of meanings (Operation 2 from previous six-item list). Variant idioms, on this model, would require at least the five additional operations listed earlier. Even if some of these operations could be done in parallel (e.g., retrieving the meaning of the original idiom and activating word meanings), variant idioms still should take more time to process than original idioms, and certainly more time to process than literal expressions of comparable length and complexity.

A much simpler alternative model uses the meanings of the words of the variant idiom to arrive at the variant's meaning. The core assumption of this model is that the words of familiar idioms have become polysemous through frequent use in idiom contexts. The verb and noun in the idiom *spill the beans*, for example, have at least two meanings: their default context-free literal meanings, and the meanings that are induced by the idiom context. In nonidiomatic contexts, the verb *spill* will have the meaning "to be lost from a container" and the word *beans* the meaning "edible legumes." In the idiom context, these words have a dual meaning, retaining their literal meanings but also acquiring the idiomatic meanings of "reveal" and "information-that-should-have-been-kept-confidential." With repeated usage, such idioms become able to induce polysemy, adding the idiomatic meanings to each word's set of possible meanings.

Once this property has developed for any particular idiom and its constituent words, variants of the idiom could be processed just as one would process any other phrase or sentence: by accessing the contextually appropriate word meanings and performing ordinary linguistic analyses on the words and their relations with one another. In the case of familiar idioms, this will result in at least two products: the literal meaning and the idiomatic meaning (including the idiomatic senses of the words of the idiom). Because this model depends on the assumption of phrase-induced dual meanings, we refer to it as the *phrase-induced polysemy* (PIP) model of idiom comprehension.[1]

The PIP model has at least two interesting advantages over the standard idiom look-up model. First, it allows for rapid and easy comprehension and production of variant idioms. Second, it is parsimonious in that the same model would account for both conventional and variant idiom processing. The PIP model can be tested by assessing the relative comprehension time for variant idioms and comparable literal expressions. According to the PIP model, variants such as *didn't spill a single bean* should take more time than original idioms such as *spill the beans* precisely because the variants must be analyzed as if they were literal strings. If this is so, then a variant idiom such as *didn't spill a single bean* should take no longer to process than its literal paraphrase *didn't say a single word*. In contrast, the standard model assumes that variant idioms require several more processing operations than comparable literal expressions. Therefore, the standard model predicts that variant idioms should take longer to process than their literal paraphrases.

Following this logic, McGlone et al. (in press) compared comprehension times for original and variant idioms and their literal paraphrases. Original idioms were faster than both their literal paraphrases and their variants. More interesting, variant idioms were understood just as quickly as their literal paraphrases: For example, *didn't spill a single bean* was understood as quickly as *didn't say a single word*. How can this pattern of results be explained? The relative speed of understanding original idioms can be accounted for by assuming that once an idiom is recognized, then its meaning can be accessed directly from

---

[1]As Wasow et al. (1983) pointed out, "a full account of idioms must await a theory of meaning transfers" (p. 114). The PIP model is a step toward explicating such a theory.

memory, often before linguistic processing is completed. This is essentially a restatement of the lexical representation and direct access hypotheses (Gibbs, 1980; Swinney & Cutler, 1979). Additional assumptions are needed, however, to account for the finding that variant idioms can be understood as rapidly as their literal paraphrases. The most parsimonious processing assumption that accounts for the entire pattern of results is that variant idioms, like literal expressions, require linguistic processing, whereas original idioms do not (at least for initial interpretation).

STRING MEANINGS AND CONSTITUENT WORD MEANINGS

Consider how idiom meanings are acquired in the first place. As the standard view suggests, idiom meanings are acquired by stipulation. The meaning of an idiom is learned simply as an arbitrary relation between a phrase and its meaning, just as the meaning of a word is learned as an arbitrary relation between a linguistic unit and its referent. The meaning of *spill the beans,* for example, is memorized, roughly, as "reveal the secrets." This paraphrase is not precise, nor is it limited to the particular words *reveal* or *secrets.* Other literal paraphrases would suit as well, such as "divulge/tell/inform about" [the] "information/plans/confidential stuff, and so forth. Although the wording may vary, the basic conceptual referents and the relations among them are, of course, invariant. With repeated use, it would not be surprising if the pairing of a word such as *spill* and the concept of "divulge" would come to be represented in lexical memory. In the context of a phrase containing the word *beans,* the idiomatic meaning of *spill* would be activated automatically, just as the context-appropriate meaning of any polysemous word is activated automatically (Tabossi, 1988). More specifically, the two words, *spill* and *beans,* come to function as minimal contexts for one another, making available the dual meanings of *spill* and *beans* during comprehension.

After such idiomatic word meanings have been acquired, then the meanings of familiar idioms could be either retrieved or generated. Retrieval would be accomplished by direct access of the stipulated idiomatic meaning. Generation would be accomplished by ordinary linguistic processing, using the contextually appropriate idiomatic meanings of the idiom's constituent words.[2] Because direct access can be accomplished more quickly than linguistic processing, familiar idioms can be understood more rapidly than comparable literal expressions, because such idioms do not require linguistic processing whereas ordinary literal

---

[2]The polysemy of idiom constituents, in fact, is recognized by lexicographers. For example, the Random House Dictionary of the American Language lists, as one entry for the word *spill,* "to divulge, disclose or tell" (p. 1266).

expressions do. However, if direct access fails, as when memory retrieval might fail, then an idiom might still be understood via linguistic processing. Because variant idioms use words that do not match the canonical form of the original idiom, direct access would fail. However, if the constituent words of the original idiom have acquired phrase-specific idiomatic meanings, then the meaning of a variant idiom could be generated relatively quickly via ordinary linguistic processing.

The phrase-induced polysemy hypothesis can be summarized quite briefly. The constituent words of familiar idioms acquire, through repeated use in idiom contexts, the meanings that are appropriate for the idioms in which they appear. After these phrase-specific meanings have been acquired, then idiom variants that preserve the relationships among the constituent idiomatic concepts can be understood via ordinary linguistic processing. In this way, idiom variants can be understood exactly as literal expressions are understood—by accessing context-appropriate constituent word meanings and identifying the syntactic and semantic relations among those constituents.

Implications for Idiom Productivity

Compositionality and Communicative Intentions.   Not all idioms, of course, involve phrase-induced idiomatic word meanings. Consider, first, phrasal idioms such as *spill the beans* and *pop the question*. Such idioms can vary in the extent to which they are compositional (Cacciari & Glucksberg, 1991; Gibbs & Nayak, 1989; Nunberg, 1978). In fully compositional idioms, the constituent words can be mapped directly onto their idiomatic referents. In the idiom *pop the question,* for example, the verb *pop* and the noun phrase *the question* can be mapped directly onto their respective idiomatic referents "suddenly ask" and "marriage proposal." In general, idioms that permit word-to-referent mapping will express n-argument predicates, where $n > 1$, as in *spill the beans.* In contrast, the constituent words in less compositional idioms such as *kick the bucket* cannot be mapped individually in a one-to-one fashion to the idiom's meaning of "die"; only the phrase as a whole can be mapped. Because it is impossible to have a one-to-one mapping from multiple constituents to a single-argument predicate, such idiom constituents would not develop phrase-induced idiomatic meanings. Accordingly, such idiom types generally will not be used in variant forms. Gibbs, Nayak, and Cutting (1989) reported data consistent with this argument. Less compositional idioms are less flexible both lexically and syntactically than are more compositional ones (see also Gibbs & Nayak, 1989).

Compositionality, however, is neither a necessary nor a sufficient condition for an idiom to be varied productively because idioms can be productive even when their constituent words do not acquire phrase-specific idiomatic meanings. Consider idioms that express single-argument predicates, such as *two left feet* to express clumsiness. The noun phrase *two left feet* contains three constituent words, and these three words, perforce, cannot be mapped individually onto the idiomatic referent "clumsy." These words therefore will not acquire phrase-specific idiomatic meanings. Nevertheless, idioms of this type still can be productive because the semantics of the phrase itself can have direct functional relations with the idiom's stipulated meaning. Variations of an idiom will be productive if the variation plausibly exploits such relations. The phrase *two left feet,* for example, alludes to the grace (or lack of same) with which someone might dance if he or she did in fact have two left feet, hence the general idiomatic meaning of clumsiness. Changing the quantifier from *two* to *three* simply modifies the degree of clumsiness. If *two left feet* implies clumsy, then *three left feet,* by ordinary discourse processes, implies more than usual clumsiness.

When an idiom's constituents bear functional relations to the idiom's meaning, then operations such as quantification, antonymy, and negation will be productive provided that a plausible communicative intent can be inferred (Cacciari & Glucksberg, 1991). The change from plural to singular in Donald Barthelme's essay "convicted minimalist spills bean," for example, is productive because of the relation between the singular form of the noun *bean* and the concept of minimalism. Similarly, the phrase *popped the question* would normally be difficult to interpret because one usually proposes marriage to only one person at a time. If, however, the question popper were a notorious bigamist, then pluralization of the word *question* might make sense. The constraints of general world knowledge, together with rules of discourse and conversation, seem as important for idiom flexibility and productivity as are more formal linguistic factors such as compositionality.

Why Spilling the Peas Is Like Kicking the Pail.   We are now in a position to speculate about why certain lexical substitutions seem to be productive, whereas others are not. Consider, first, the circumstances under which a speaker might use a variant form of a familiar idiom. Least interesting are those occasions when a speaker simply misspeaks, as when a colleague recently complained that "research grants were becoming scarce as pig's teeth!" The speaker obviously intended the meaning of the original idiom (scarce as hen's teeth) and did not notice his error. More interesting, the listeners in the room at the time understood the intended meaning, and some did not even notice the error, even though the substitution of *pig* for *hen* was contradictory. After all, pigs have teeth, so saying that something is as scarce as pig's teeth is to say that it is not scarce at all. Nevertheless, because the phrase was immediately recognizable as a misspoken form of the original (perhaps because of the close semantic relation between pigs and hens as barnyard animals), the intended and contextually appropriate idiomatic meaning of scarcity came through. Normally, unintentional lexical substitutions are semantically related to the correct or intended word (Fromkin, 1971), as when, for example, a speaker substitutes *swallow the bullet* for *bite the bullet.*

In each of these examples, a lexical substitution was made unintentionally, but because the original idiom was called to mind, the utterances were understood appropriately in context. More interesting are those cases where a speaker fully intends the variant form. What kinds of variations do speakers (or writers) use? Perhaps this question might be better if posed in the negative: What kinds of variations rarely, if ever, are seen? It is difficult to imagine a context in which someone would choose to say "kick the pail" instead of "kick the bucket" to refer to someone's death. It is also difficult to imagine a context in which someone would say "spill the peas" instead of "spill the beans" to refer to secrets being divulged. In the pail-bucket example, the original idiom is noncompositional and opaque, whereas in the peas-beans example, the original idiom is compositional and transparent. Nevertheless, both variants seem distinctly odd, most likely because no motivation for the lexical substitutions is apparent. What communicative intent might lead a speaker to choose *pail* over *bucket* or *peas* over *beans?*

In cases where no communicative intent can be inferred, listeners either may be totally confused, or might be reminded of the original idiom and simply accept the variant utterance as a mistake on the speaker's part (especially if the situation and context were appropriate to the original idiom). If listeners do accept the variant as a synonym of the original, then the idiom is said to be lexically flexible. In lexically flexible idioms, near-synonyms may be used in place of the original words, often inadvertently, without making the idiom unrecognizable. In contrast to accidental variations, speakers intentionally will create novel idiom forms by using words that bear an interpretable relation to the original, as in *pour the beans* to communicate that someone were divulging secrets quite lavishly. If a listener decides that a speaker's choice of *pour* over *spill* is intentional, then the listener might interpret the varied idiom as denoting a more vigorous and egregious disclosure of information than usual. If, however, the choice of *pour* were to be perceived as a mistake, then no such communicative intent would be inferred.

Speakers, then, seem to produce idiom variants in two ways: inadvertently, with no communicative intent, and deliberately, to communicate an intended modification of an original idiom's conventional meaning. The former case involves lexical flexibility, and this seems to be governed primarily by the relative recognizability of an utterance as a variant of the original idiom. Thus, in phrasal idioms that contain both a verb and a noun phrase, changing either the verb or the noun has less of an adverse effect than changing both. Few people would recognize *boot the pail* as a variant of *kick the bucket,* for example. The more interesting case, when speakers intend the variant, involves semantic productivity. Semantic productivity requires an interpretable relation between original constituents and their substitutes such that a communicative intent can be inferred. Semantic productivity, as we noted earlier, is the ability of people to create new idiomatic meanings by changing relevant aspects of an idiom's individual elements. In contrast to simple and unmotivated synonym substitutions, semantically productive operations serve communicative functions: They are motivated by communicative intentions and so they should be informative. Some relatively simple productive operations have been subsumed under the rubric of syntactic or lexical flexibility. Among these are:

1. Adjectival modification, as in "When drugs are involved, it's time to speak your *parental* mind."
2. Adverbial modification, as in "Did he *finally* speak his mind?"
3. Quantification, as in "As a diverse but purposeful group, you should speak your *minds.*"
4. Tense marking, as in "He *spoke* his mind."
5. All of the above, as in, "The tenants' association finally spoke their collective minds."

What is noteworthy about this example is not only that an idiom can be semantically productive, but that this particular idiom is one of a group of noncompositional (nonanalyzable) idioms used by Gibbs, Nayak, and Cutting (1989). Recall that noncompositional idioms should tend to be both lexically and syntactically frozen, yet this idiom seems to be quite productive.

This example suggests that semantic productivity can be independent of both syntactic and lexical flexibility, and it may be independent of compositionality as well. Instead, semantic productivity seems to be governed by the same principles that govern such discourse phenomena as adjectival and adverbial modification, quantification, and negation. For example, one can sing sweetly if one actually were singing a song, but one cannot sing sweetly if one is singing to the police. In this latter context, singing refers not to a musical activity but to an act of divulging incriminating information about others. Thus, even though one cannot sing sweetly to the police, one still can sing like a canary, that is, sing volubly and with unseemly verve and enthusiasm. Notably, there is nothing in the lexical or syntactic form of the idiomatic verb *to sing* that constrains adjectival modification, only the notion of what it means to "sing" to the authorities. Similarly, there is nothing in the lexical or syntactic form of *speak your mind* that constrains any of its variants, other than the communicative intentions that can motivate a speaker to use a variant.

TOWARD A FUNCTIONAL TYPOLOGY OF IDIOMS

Compositionality and Transparency

We begin with the assumption that all idioms, regardless of their degree of compositionality, are automatically processed linguistically, that is, lexically, syntactically, and semantically. For compositional idioms, the results of linguistic analysis will be consistent with the stipulated idiomatic meaning, especially when phrase-induced polysemy has developed. In such cases, stipulated and linguistic meanings coincide, and so comprehension should be facilitated. For noncompositional idioms, stipulated and linguistic meanings will conflict, and so comprehension should be more difficult. The evidence favors this initial classification: Compositional idioms are understood more quickly than are noncompositional idioms (Gibbs, Nayak, & Cutting, 1989).

For compositional idioms, some relationship between an idiom's component words and its stipulated meaning can be discerned. In such idioms, the particular relationship, together with pragmatic considerations, will determine how an idiom may be understood and used. There are at least three ways that word meanings can map onto the stipulated meaning of an idiom (Cacciari & Glucksberg, 1991). The first type of mapping involves compositional idioms that are opaque. In this idiom type, the relations between an idioms' elements and the idiom meaning are not apparent, but the meanings of individual words nevertheless can constrain both interpretation and use. For the idiom *kick the bucket,* for example, the semantics of the verb *to kick* constrain both interpretation and discourse productivity (see aforementioned examples). Such idioms were dubbed *compositional-opaque* (Type CO) by Cacciari and Glucksberg (1991).[3]

A second idiom type consists of idioms that are compositional and transparent, Type CT. In these idioms, there are one-to-one semantic relations between the idiom's words and components of the idiom's meaning, usually because of metaphorical correspondences between an idiom's words and components of the idiom's meaning. In the idiom *break the ice,* for example, the word *break* corresponds to the idiomatic sense of changing a mood or feeling, and the word *ice* corresponds to the idiomatic sense of social tension. Similarly, the elements of the idiom *spill the beans* map onto the components of the idiom's meaning. *Spill* corresponds to the act of revealing or letting out, and *beans* corresponds to the material that heretofore had been concealed or otherwise unknown. Furthermore, in such idioms the words themselves have acquired individual idiomatic meanings, so that one sense of *spill* in the context of the idiom is "to reveal," and one sense of *beans* in this context is "information." Included in this class of idioms are both the normally and abnormally decomposable idioms of Nunberg's (1978) and Gibbs, Nayak, and Cutting's (1989) classification. According to Gibbs, Nayak, and Cutting, normally decomposable idioms have quasi-literal relations between elements and meanings, as in *pop the question,* whereas in abnormally decomposable idioms these relations are more

---

[3]Cacciari and Glucksberg (1991) and others have used the term *analyzable* instead of *compositional* in their discussions of idiom types. I prefer the term compositional because it connotes comprehension and use. In contrast, the term analyzable suggests a judgmental operation, not interactive language use.

or less metaphorical, as in *spill the beans* or *break the ice*. We see no compelling reason to distinguish between these two subtypes, because phrase-induced poly-semy should develop regardless of the initial kind of relations between an idiom's component words and that idiom's component idiomatic meanings.

The third type of idiom distinguished by Cacciari and Glucksberg (1991) is Type M, quasi-metaphorical. In these idioms the literal referent of the idiom is itself an instance of the idiomatic meaning; for example, *giving up the ship* is simultaneously an ideal or prototypical exemplar of the act of surrendering and a phrase that can refer to any instance of complete surrender. Other examples of this idiom type are *carry coals to Newcastle* to refer to any instance of bringing something to a place that already has a surfeit of that something, *count your chickens before they are hatched* to refer to any instance of premature confidence in an outcome, and so forth. Included in this class of idioms are such metonymic phrases as *bury the hatchet,* where the action of burying a hatchet was once an actual part of the ritual of making peace, but is now used to refer to any instance of peace making in its entirety.

Quasi-metaphorical idioms convey meaning via their allusional content—they call to mind a prototypical or stereotypical instance of an entire category of people, events, situations, or actions. These idioms use the same communicative strategy as do metaphor vehicles in expressions such as "my lawyer was a *shark*" or "my job is a *jail.*" In these metaphors, vehicles such as *shark* or *jail* allude to ideal exemplars of their metaphoric categories—cutthroat people and confining, unpleasant situations, respectively—and simultaneously as names for those categories (Brown, 1958; Glucksberg, in press; Glucksberg & Keysar, 1990). These metaphors are used to characterize their referents by assigning them to categories that are diagnostic and often evaluative, as in "Margaret Thatcher *was a bulldozer*" (Glucksberg & Keysar, 1990; Keysar & Glucksberg, in press). Quasi-metaphorical idioms function precisely as do such nominative metaphors. They simultaneously refer to an idea exemplar of a concept (e.g., total surrender) while characterizing some event, person, or object as an instance of that concept, as in:

> Nick: "I don't know what to do about Henry, he continues to do so poorly in school."
> Alice: "Don't give up the ship. I'm sure he'll do better once he im-proves his study habits."

In this interchange, Alice identifies despair about Henry as an instance of sur-render by using the idiom, *don't give up the ship*. This is accomplished by implicitly grouping the two actions into the same category: Despairing of Henry and giving up a ship are analogues of one another, and both are instances of the category of actions that constitute total surrender. Total surrender, in turn, is referred to by the allusion to an ideal exemplar of surrender, giving up a ship.

This rough classification of idioms into three general types suggests some determinants of idiom comprehension and use. Comprehension and use should be governed by the functional relations between an idiom's elements and the idiom meaning. Lexical substitutions, syntactic operations, and discourse productivity should be possible whenever those functional relations are preserved. In addition, there must be some discernible communicative or discourse purpose that is served by using an idiom in some form other than the original. As argued earlier, a listener or reader must be able to infer a reason for any change. It thus follows that no typology, whether structural or functional, will be fully sufficient. Both the internal semantics of the idiom and the pragmatics of the discourse context will always jointly determine idiom comprehension and use, including idiom variation. To illustrate this approach, I consider how each idiom type may be used both in their original and in variant forms.

Idiom Flexibility and Productivity

Idioms vary considerably in the extent to which they may sustain lexical substitutions, syntactic operations, and semantic productivity. In general, the more compositional an idiom, the more likely will it be available for variation of one type or another, but as we already have seen, compositionality alone is insufficient to constrain idiom use. Consider a noncompositional idiom such as *by and large.* Such idioms are considered noncompositional because a semantic and syntactic analysis of the idiom and its elements fails to produce anything that is relevant to the idiom's stipulated meaning. Hence, word substitutions should not be acceptable. If someone were to say, for example, "by plus large," most hearers would not recognize the utterance as a misspoken form of *by and large.* Similarly, saying "by and small" to communicate the opposite of *by and large* also would fail because it, too, would not be recognized as a variant of the original. The primary reason for such failures is that the component words of noncompositional idioms do not map onto the idiom's meaning except in the most general of ways.

To the extent that there is any semantic relation between an idiom's elements and the idiom meaning, some semantic productivity should be possible. The word *large* bears some relation to the idiom meaning of "generally," and so relevant modifications should be possible, as in *by and not-so-large* in a context that would support this qualification. The productive use of negation in this idiom points up another problem for the view of idioms as purely noncompositional strings. If an idiom is truly an unanalyzable whole, then the scope of negation—or more generally, scope of modification—must be limited to the entire string. A negation or an adjective cannot be used to modify a semantically empty element or constituent within a string (Cruse, 1986). In some cases, modification of idiom constituents, as in *break the proverbial ice* can be treated as a metalinguistic comment on the expression as a whole. Nevertheless, there is a clear and important theoretical difference between such metalinguistic comments and true semantic modification, as in the aforementioned by-and-large example, or in such cases as "he broke the really frigid ice," where the concept of social lack of warmth is intensified, not merely commented on. These examples suggest that the idiom *by and large* is not purely or completely noncompositional because the semantics of *large* do bear some functional relation to the idiom's meaning. Thus, this idiom is partially, if minimally, compositional. Indeed, purely noncompositional idioms may not exist at all. To the extent that a constituent of an idiom may be modified independently of the idiom as a whole, it is compositional and so could be used productively in discourse.

More compositional idioms, whether opaque or transparent, are more flexible, but here too pragmatic considerations will be central. For opaque idioms such as *kick the bucket,* where the idiom's component words have nothing to do with the idiom's meaning, lexical substitutions will be comprehensible only if the original idiom is called to mind. Even then, no communicative intent could be inferred because there are no interpretable relations between a substituted word and the original. As discussed previously, variants such as *boot the bucket* and *kick the pail* might be recognized as meaning "to die" (Gibbs, Nayak, & Cutting, 1989), but people would be at a loss to understand why someone would use these variants. Neither the substitution of *boot* for *kick* nor *pail* for *bucket* seems motivated by any communicative purpose, and so would not be considered acceptable, unless used by a nonnative speaker. In this latter case, the usage would be understood but recognized as a mistake. When near-synonyms are substituted for both the verb and the noun, as in *boot the pail,* then the idiomatic meaning of "to die" is not recognized (Gibbs, Nayak, & Cutting, 1989). For opaque idioms, then, lexical substitution by near-synonyms are either not understood, or viewed as mistakes.

Syntactic operations for idioms also are constrained primarily by the semantics and pragmatics of an idiom's components and idiomatic meaning. Consider how *kick the bucket* might be varied syntactically. Kicking is a discrete action, and so even though one can lie dying for a week, one cannot say "he lay kicking the bucket for a week." One can say, for the same kinds of reasons, "almost, will, can, might, may, should, or didn't kick the bucket . . . " The operation of semantic constraints can be seen in two examples of adjectival modification, one acceptable, the other not. It would be acceptable to say "he silently kicked the bucket" because both kicking and dying can be accomplished silently. It would not be acceptable to say "he sharply kicked the bucket" because there is no way clear way to understand how anyone could die "sharply" (cf. Wasow et al., 1983).

The operation of pragmatic constraints is illustrated by the nonacceptability of the passive voice for this idiom. People tend to reject "the bucket was kicked by John" as a paraphrase of "John kicked the bucket." The communicative role of the passive form provides a good reason for not using it for such idioms. Passives are used to put focus on the object of a clause or sentence, usually when there is some prior topicalization, as in: (a) The woman had just turned the corner when *she was hit by a car;* or (b) What happened to John? *He was hit by a truck.* No such communicative purpose can be served by topicalizing *bucket,* and so the passive form is uninterpretable; that is, the use of the passive would not be motivated. The general principle we propose is: A syntactic operation on an idiom will be acceptable if and only if it produces a comprehensible difference in interpretation; that is, a reasonable communicative intention can be inferred. For opaque idioms, the passive form rarely if ever will be acceptable because there rarely would be any reason to topicalize or focus on a grammatical or logical object. Tense markings for opaque idiom, in contrast, would be acceptable and interpretable provided that those tense markings would make sense for the idiomatic meaning itself; for example, one can die in the future and so one can also kick the bucket in the future.

Comprehension and use of transparent idioms, such as *break the ice* and *spill the beans* are governed by the same principles that govern opaque idiom use. A central difference, however, is that the elements of transparent idioms can be mapped onto the components of the idiom's meaning. Any operations that (a) respect the semantics of each element, (b) preserve the relationship between an idiom's elements and meaning components, and (c) respect the idiom meaning itself should be acceptable and interpretable provided that a reasonable communicative intent can be inferred. Lexical substitutions should be acceptable if they satisfy these conditions, and so, as we have seen previously, variants of *break the ice* such as *crack the ice, break the frost,* and *break the chill* could be acceptable. In each of these cases, the concept of abrupt breaking is preserved and the metaphorical relation between physical temperature and interpersonal warmth/coolness is also preserved.

Lexical variants that violate the conditions just specified should be considered unacceptable. To say *crush the ice* would be unacceptable, primarily because the kind of metaphorical ice involved in this idiom is not the kind that can be crushed: It is, metaphorically speaking of course, thin and brittle, capable of being cracked or, perhaps, even shattered. This example illustrates again how the semantics of an idiom's elements can govern idiom use and productivity at the lexical level.

At the syntactic level, the same principles apply: Any syntactic operations that satisfy both the semantics and pragmatics of the idiom's elements and the idiom's meaning would be appropriate—again with the proviso that a communicative purpose can be inferred by listeners. Accordingly, passive transforms would be acceptable if it would be appropriate to focus on a grammatical object, as in "the ice was finally broken" or "despite days of intensive questioning not a bean was spilled." Note that in this latter expression *bean* was used in the singular. Pluralization operations also will be acceptable if they would be appropriate for the idiom's meaning. *Beans* in this context can be either singular or plural because *secrets* can be singular or plural: The pragmatics of the idiom's referent are the governing factor. The *ice* in *break the ice* cannot be varied in quantity because the social tension referred to by the term *ice* is a singular, momentary state. In other contexts, of course, both ice and social tensions can be quantified.

Allusional Content: Quasi-Metaphorical Idioms.   The insufficiency of compositionality as a determiner of idiom use and productivity is illustrated clearly by quasi-metaphorical idioms. These idioms are fully compositional in that a linguistic analysis yields a completely adequate interpretation. The literal meaning of *carrying coals to Newcastle,* for example, is relevant and intended, even though this literal meaning is insufficient. Speakers using such idioms intend the literal meaning and simultaneously allude to the action of carrying coals to Newcastle as an ideal exemplar of the situation that is the momentary topic of conversation. Even though the idiom itself is fully compositional, lexical substitution is highly constrained. For example, "carrying wood to Birmingham" communicates nothing even close to the original meaning. When, however, a communicative intent can be inferred, then well-chosen paraphrases can be effective. A newspaper article once reported on the dismal failures of a nuclear generating plant at Shoreham, Long Island, that was being converted to conventional fuels. The headline read, "Carrying Coals to Shoreham." This headline served to remind readers of the original idiom, and familiarity with the Shoreham nuclear dilemma made the innovative idiom's meaning clear.

Within the constraints imposed by the metaphorical nature of the coals-to-Newcastle idiom, lexical substitutions and variants are freely available. The verb *to carry* can be replaced by another verb so long as the action involved is consistent with the intended meaning and context. Thus, bringing to or from, sending, selling, offering, can be used when appropriate. Like any metaphor, quasi-metaphorical idioms can be tailored to suit discourse purposes.

The principles that govern syntactic operations in general also apply to quasi-metaphorical idioms. Syntactic operations must be communicatively motivated, and so any changes they make in an idiom's meaning must be interpretable in context. Consider the passive form. For most quasi-metaphorical idioms, no purpose would be served by focusing on the grammatical object. For this reason, it would make no sense to say "Newcastle was where the coals were carried to." This constraint, however, is not a general one. There can be metaphorical idioms that would make sense in the passive form, as in "after intensive discussions among the warring parties, the hatchet was finally buried once and for all." In this case, the grammatical object, *hatchet,* can be the focus of the expression. The applicability of any syntactic operation will be governed by such communicative considerations.

Discourse productivity, as before, also will be governed primarily by pragmatic considerations. For example, one can easily imagine a context for the following interchange:

Ken: Don't worry, I'll cross that bridge when I come to it.
Ann: By that time they will have burnt it down!

Here, as in earlier examples, the semantics of an idiom element (in this example, *bridge*) can be used to generate appropriate conversational responses to the original idiom. While retaining its role as symbol, *bridge* still can be treated as a real bridge so long as its symbolic function is preserved.

IDIOM MEANINGS: LINGUISTIC, STIPULATED, AND ALLUSIONAL

Integrating Linguistic and Other Meanings

All idioms, by definition, have at least two meanings: the linguistic meaning of the words and phrases themselves, and the stipulated, idiomatic meaning. We began this essay with an analysis of the direct access hypothesis, which effectively denied the role of linguistic meanings in idiom use and comprehension. We have argued that even for seemingly unanalyzable idioms such as *by and large,* linguistic meanings play important roles. For such idioms, as well as for other, more compositional idiom types, linguistic meanings are generated automatically and are available for use in the context of discourse. Sometimes, as for relatively noncompositional idioms such as *kick the bucket,* the linguistic meanings play no initial roles and do not contribute to initial interpretation (Gibbs, 1984). For relatively compositional idioms such as *spill the beans,* the component words have acquired idiom-specific meanings, and so a linguistic analysis produces an interpretation that is consistent with the stipulated, idiomatic meaning. In all cases, the linguistic and stipulated meanings of idioms always are generated and must be integrated within the discourse context to provide an interpretation of the speaker's intended meaning.

Allusional Content.   In addition to linguistic and stipulated meanings, many idiomatic expressions also have what I call *allusional content.* Whenever an expression calls to mind a specific action, event, situation, or person, then use of that expression can be said to be an allusion to that action, event, situation, or person. When speakers make an allusion to something, listeners must infer the speaker's communicative intent. Citing a proverb, a line of poetry, or a song title are examples of explicit allusions. The literal meaning of an allusive expression is always intended, but is never enough to convey the full speaker's intention. Consider, for example, someone reciting these words of a familiar song, "I want a gal, just like the gal that married dear old Dad." If uttered in the context of a wedding ceremony, it might be taken as a comment on the similarity of the bride to the groom's mother. If uttered in the context of a performance of *Oedipus Rex,* it would be taken as a satiric and perhaps tasteless comment on the Oedipus legend itself.

Here, as with ordinary phrasal idioms, the literal meaning of an expression is not irrelevant, but instead is an important element of the speaker's intended meaning. Listeners, in constructing interpretations of speakers' intentions, must integrate the linguistic, stipulated, and allusional content with the discourse context. Because the relevance of any one of these three sources of meaning cannot be determined in advance, one comprehension strategy would be to automatically compute all the meaning types that are available in any given utterance: (a) literal, (b) stipulated-idiomatic, and (c) allusional. More often than not, all three sources of meaning are relevant, and this strategy seems efficient as well. Just as people do not—indeed cannot—isolate or ignore the meanings of words and phrases when engaging in discourse, people cannot ignore those familiar, memorized "chunks" of speech whose meanings derive not from the language itself but from their role in everyday experience. Included in this category of language are all those word strings that people learn, such as movie and book titles, song titles and lyrics, poetry, proverbs, cliches, morals, and so forth. These expressions have explicit allusional content. We turn now to a class of idioms that have implicit allusional content: those idioms that reflect underlying conceptualizations of complex concepts.

Implicit Allusional Content: Accessing Conceptual Knowledge

Many idioms in common use seem to reflect underlying conceptual metaphors (Nayak & Gibbs, 1990). Anger, for example, can be expressed with such idioms as *blow up, blow one's top, let off steam, cool down,* all reflecting the conceptual metaphor of anger as heat in a pressurized container (Lakoff, 1987; Lakoff & Johnson, 1980). Such idioms are not used interchangeably, but are chosen so as to reflect the particular conceptualization that is appropriate in a given discourse. For example, people preferred to say "flip one's lid" rather than "get hot under the collar" when a provoking incident was serious, but the reverse when a provoking incident was fairly mild (Nayak & Gibbs, 1990). Nayak and Gibbs studied idioms that expressed emotions, and found that idiom choice and interpretation were consistent with people's underlying conceptualizations of those emotions. These findings provide evidence that people exploit the implicit allusions to emotional states that are available in such idioms as *play with fire* (for danger), *touch bottom* (for despair), and *shake in one's shoes* (for fear).

In essence, idioms such as these are no different from the quasi-metaphorical idioms discussed earlier. *Shaking in one's shoes* can be understood as a metonymic allusion to a stereotypically fearful behavior, just as *burying the hatchet* can be understood as a metonymic allusion to a stereotypical part of a peace-making ceremony. Both of these idioms rely on all three forms of meaning—literal, stipulated, and allusional—for their communicative effectiveness. Speakers apparently recognize, albeit implicitly, that some choices of idioms are more appropriate in context than others, as when *flip one's lid* is chosen over *did a slow burn* to express a particular kind of anger in a specific situation.

Do speakers use word meanings more generally in their choice of idioms? When, for example, might someone choose to say *kick the bucket* rather than *give up the ghost* to refer to someone's death? One possibility is that the *kick* idiom might be chosen when the death was perhaps unanticipated and abrupt, and *give up* when the death had been expected and the dying more or less gradual. Word and idiom choice as a function of specific idiomatic meanings may well be governed in general by the relations among an idiom's component elements, the stipulated (idiomatic) meaning, and the context of use. Far from being unanalyzable wholes, these idioms seem fully operational as linguistic and conceptual entities, even though their linguistic meanings are insufficient for complete interpretation.

The precise ways in which the three sources of meaning involved in idiom use—literal, stipulated, and allusional—are used by speakers have yet to be examined in detail. The precise ways in which these three kinds of meaning are integrated in comprehension is as yet not understood. What is clear, however, is that a focus on only one or two of these kinds of meaning to the exclusion of the others will fail to yield an adequate account of idiom use and comprehension. More specific criticisms of much of the current psychological, linguistic, and philosophical work in the area of figurative language could be appropriate here, but then, people in glass houses should not throw stones.

ACKNOWLEDGMENTS

I am grateful for the financial support provided by the National Science Foundation, Grants BNS 8519462 and BNS 8819657, and by the Public Health Service, Grant HD25826-01 to Princeton University, and to the Council for International Exchange of Scholars for a Fullbright travel grant to C. Cacciari, who contributed in important ways to much of my thinking on figurative language. I also thank Mary Brown, Kay Deaux, Boaz Keysar, and Matthew McGlone for their valuable discussions, comments, and suggestions. Correspondence can be sent to Sam Glucksberg, Department of Psychology, Princeton University, Princeton, New Jersey 08544-1010.

REFERENCES

Bobrow, S., & Bell, S. (1973). On catching on to idiomatic expression. *Memory & Cognition, 1*, 343–346.

Brown, R. (1958). *Words and things*. New York: Free Press.

Cacciari, C., & Glucksberg, S. (1991). Understanding idiomatic expressions: The contribution of word meanings. In G. B. Simpson (Ed.), *Understanding word and sentence* (pp. 217–240). Amsterdam, Netherlands: Elsevier Science Publishers (North Holland).

Cacciari, C., & Tabossi, P. (1988). The comprehension of idioms. *Journal of Memory and Language, 27,* 668–683.

Cruse, D. A. (1986). *Lexical semantics*. New York: Cambridge University Press.

Fromkin, V. A. (1971). The non-anomalous nature of anomalous utterances. *Language, 47,* 27–52.

Gibbs, R. W. (1980). Spilling the beans on understanding and memory for idioms in context. *Memory & Cognition, 8,* 149–156.

Gibbs, R. W. (1984). Literal meaning and psychological theory. *Cognitive Science, 8,* 275–304.

Gibbs, R. W., & Nayak, N. (1989). Psycholinguistic studies on the syntactic behavior of idioms. *Cognitive Psychology, 21,* 100–138.

Gibbs, R. W., Nayak, N. P., Bolton, J. L., & Keppel, M. E. (1989). Speakers' assumptions about the lexical flexibility of idioms. *Memory & Cognition, 17,* 58–68.

Gibbs, R. W., Nayak, N., & Cutting, C. (1989). How to kick the bucket and not decompose: Analyzability and idiom processing. *Journal of Memory and Language, 28,* 576–593.

Glucksberg, S. (in press). How metaphors work. In A. Ortony (Ed.), *Metaphor and thought* (2nd ed.). Cambridge, England: Cambridge University Press.

Glucksberg, S., & Keysar, B. (1990). Understanding metaphoric comparisons: Beyond similarity. *Psychological Review, 97,* 3–18.

Greenberg-Concool, N. (1990). *Don't throw the beans: A study of a young child's comprehension of idioms* (unpublished research report). Princeton, NJ: Princeton University.

Keysar, B., & Glucksberg, S. (in press). Metaphor and communication. *Poetics Today.*

Lakoff, G. (1987). *Women, fire and dangerous things*. Chicago: University of Chicago Press.

Lakoff, G., & Johnson, M. (1980). *Metaphors we live by*. Chicago: Chicago University Press.

McGlone, M. S., Glucksberg, S., & Cacciari, C. (in press). Semantic productivity and idiom comprehension. *Discourse Processing.*

Nayak, N. P., & Gibbs, R. W. (1990). Conceptual knowledge in the interpretation of idioms. *Journal of Experimental Psychology: General, 119,* 315–330.

Nunberg, G. (1978). *The pragmatics of reference*. Bloomington: Indiana University Linguistics Club.

Ortony, A., Schallert, D. L., Reynolds, R. E., & Antos, S. J. (1978). Interpreting metaphors and idioms: Some effects of context on comprehension. *Journal of Verbal Learning and Verbal Behavior, 17,* 465–477.

Stroop, J. R. (1935). Studies of interference in serial verbal reactions. *Journal of Experimental Psychology, 18,* 643–662.

Swinney, D. A., & Cutler, A. (1979). The access and processing of idiomatic expressions. *Journal of Verbal Learning and Verbal Behavior, 18,* 523–534.

Tabossi, P. (1988). Accessing lexical ambiguity in different types of sentential contexts. *Journal of Memory and Language, 27,* 324–340.

Wasow, T., Sag, I., & Nunberg, G. (1983). Idioms: An interim report. In S. Hattori & K. Inoue (Eds.), *Proceedings of the XIIIth International Congress of Linguistics,* Tokyo.

2 The Place of Idioms in a Literal and Metaphorical World

Cristina Cacciari
University of Bologna, Italy

Idiomatic expressions belong to the vast family of fixed phrases, cliches, proverbs, indirect speech acts, speech formulas, and so forth, that shares some degree of conventionalization of meaning yet at the same time differs in semantic as well as syntactic properties. As many authors have noted (Coulmas, 1981; Hoffman & Honeck, 1980; Honeck & Hoffman, 1980; Pollio & Burns, 1977), a large part of our everyday linguistic repertoire is formed by these "conventionalized ways of saying things" (Fillmore, 1978, p. 170), so that the usage of idiomatic expressions seems to be governed by the following informal rule: "Speak idiomatically unless there is some good reason not to do it" (Searle, 1975). Not only is their meaning stipulated, but so also is their correct intonation (cf. Hockett, 1958, on politeness formulas), the context, and the linguistic as well as interpersonal functions.

Nonetheless, the task of defining what an idiomatic expression is, and how it is acquired and understood, is still a rather difficult and controversial one. To the same extent, the border between literal and idiomatic expressions, on the one hand, and metaphorical and idiomatic expressions, on the other, is also controversial. The difficulty in defining idioms is due to several factors that are examined in several chapters of this book. Among the possible sources of such difficulty one might include the fact that, as Michiels (1977) noted, idiomatization is a process. A given structure is not idiomatic once and for all, but gradually acquires its idiomaticity. Furthermore, idioms are at the same time holistic and analyzable (Coulmas, 1981): They are composed of freely occurring units whose global meaning cannot be reduced simply to the meanings of these units. But at the same time, for most idioms, people have strong intuitions as to the relationship between the meaning of the constituent words and the idiomatic referent

(Nayak & Gibbs, 1990). Last, idioms are not all created equal. As we see, idiomaticity, as a general notion, has come to include very different linguistic phenomena: from partially frozen constructions where the individual words retain roughly the same meaning they have in isolation to constructions whose meaning is totally different from that of the constituents (Lehrer, 1974); from phrasal verbs to compounds; from indirect speech acts to formulaic expressions.

THE NOTION OF LITERAL MEANING

Idiomatic language always has been defined by differentiating it from literal language, which also has functioned as an anchor point for defining metaphorical language. Therefore, an interesting and crucial question is what kind of notion of literal language do researchers implicitly or explicitly assume while defining idioms. We briefly sketch the main approaches to literal meaning before going on to consider the place of idioms in a literal and metaphorical world.

Dascal (1987) argued that the notion of literal meaning so far has been considered so central and unproblematic to become an axiomlike notion in theories of language. In successive waves, philosophers, linguists, and then psychologists have criticized the priority accorded to this notion, up to the point of questioning its psychological reality (cf. Gibbs, 1984).

The more common notion of literal language still used in linguistics as well as in psychological literature is the one proposed by Katz and Fodor in 1963 that is based on "the anonymous letter criterion": A person receives an anonymous letter containing only a single sentence. No specification whatsoever about motives, circumstances, or any contextual information is given. What the addressee will understand is the *sentence meaning* (its literal meaning), its semantic interpretation rather than the *utterance meaning*. The latter in fact requires contextual information that is totally absent in the anonymous letter case aforementioned. One can consider properly only the sentence meaning of the string as its literal meaning.

Evidence coming from different linguistic phenomena (deictics, indirect speech acts, conversational implicatures, irony, etc.) has been used to question the plausibility of such a notion of literal language as well as of the assumption of "zero context" implicit in Katz and Fodor's (1963) proposal. It has been argued that their proposal is deficient in many respects because it did not take into account linguistic presuppositions, background knowledge, and more broadly the role of world knowledge in comprehension processes (Clark & Carlson, 1981).

Gibbs (1984, 1988) and Dascal (1987) recently challenged the plausibility of the general notion of literal language adopted in psychological research, but the issue has been raised previously by other scholars as well (cf. Clark, 1978, 1979, 1983; Clark & Clark, 1977; Glucksberg, 1991; Nunberg, 1978, 1979).

Gibbs (1984) claimed that the "literal language hypothesis," according to which sentences possess well-defined literal meanings whose computation is the first and necessary step of comprehension processes, is based on a rather unplausible model of humans' linguistic behavior. According to Gibbs, evidence coming from psycholinguistic studies on literal and figurative language comprehension showed that the same processes are at work in the comprehension of both types of language. He therefore posited that the meaning of highly conventionalized string of words, such as idioms or indirect speech acts, is accessed directly without any need to compute their literal meanings.

Although Dascal (1987) also maintained the need for questioning the priority accorded to the notion of literal meaning, he did not push things as far as Gibbs did. In fact, Dascal claimed that parts of the literal meaning of a figurative expression could play a role in the construction of its meaning, even without being present in the final interpretation (e.g., in irony). He therefore proposed the "moderate literalism hypothesis" according to which the notion of literal meaning must be broadened in order to include conventional meaning attached to certain expressions. So, for instance, the figurative meaning of frozen metaphors (such as JOHN IS A LION) must be considered as "literal" because of its conventionality. The figurative meaning of idioms, indirect speech acts, and so on, are accessed directly precisely because their literal meaning has come to include also all conventionalized aspects of meaning that were once metaphorical or indirect.

One might argue that the notion of conventionality is at the same time too general and vague to be a good candidate as a substitute for the notion of literal meaning. Furthermore, if all language is by nature conventional, how should one distinguish between different types of conventionality? In any case, the notion of conventionality seems to be open to the same criticisms addressed to the notion of literal meaning.

According to Lakoff (1986; but see also Fillmore, 1979), the notion of literal language has been defined in terms of an idealized and oversimplified model of language and thought with at least four different and rather unspecified senses attributed to the word *literal:*

Literal 1. *Conventional literality,* that is, ordinary conventional language contrasting with poetic language.

Literal 2. *Subject matter literality,* that is, the language normally used to talk about some domain.

Literal 3. *Nonmetaphorical literality,* that is, directly meaningful language whose understanding does not require any borrowing from other domains of thought and experience, nor any indirect intervention of metaphor or metonymy.

Literal 4. *Truth-conditional literality,* that is, language capable of "fitting the world."

According to Lakoff, it is necessary to acknowledge that the notion of literality is theory-dependent and that differences of stress on one or another of the four levels aforementioned are often to be attributed to a need for internal coherence of a given theory. Lakoff's notion of literal meaning rests on the prior notion of semantic autonomy (more or less Level 3) (cf. Lakoff & Turner, 1989). An expression in a language is semantically autonomous if it is meaningful completely on its own terms; namely, it does not derive any of its meanings from conceptual metaphors. One can see easily that such a definition leaves almost no theoretical room for the notion that it claims to define.

Defining literal meaning seems to be risky in that one easily can end up taking for granted the plausibility of the notion of literal meaning in order to define literality, nonetheless one might want to take this risk of such a *cercle vicieux* precisely in order to correspond to a basic intuition of native speakers of a language. As Rumelhart noted (1979), the classification of an utterance as to whether it involves literal or metaphorical meanings is analogous to our judgment as to whether a bit of language is formal or not. Both judgments can reliably be made while being fully aware that a particular utterance may be more or less figurative or more or less literal. Purely figurative and purely literal utterances are at best "rare," but still we are aware of the existence of, and able to use, such a distinction. This does not imply, according to Rumelhart, any claim or need to postulate different processing mechanisms or strategies.

IDIOMS AND METAPHORS

Idiomatic expressions are taken as one of the most challenging phenomena for traditional theories of literal language. In fact, idioms behave at the same time as words and as larger-than-word units (Nagy, 1978). Even in the most frozen of idioms, the semantics of the single constituent words seem to be still available (cf. the semantic constraints of the verb *kick* in *kick the bucket,* Nunberg, 1978; see also Glucksberg, chapter 2 of this book) even though these idioms behave much as words, with their meaning acquired and stored in memory, as for other memorized string of words (lines of poetry, snatches of songs, etc.). Idiomatic expressions are thus a good test for alternative notions of literality and conversely of figurativeness.

But idiomatic expressions highlight also the need for moving from a one-dimensional level such as the one represented by the dichotomy of literality versus nonliterality, toward more complex issues, such as, for instance, the one implicit in defining what aspects of the meaning of the constituent words of a given idiomatic expression enter into the comprehension and the interpretative process, if any. Several relationships can exist between a sentence and its referent aside from its being literal or figurative: A sentence in fact can be literal, metaphorical, vague, indeterminate, anomalous, polysemous, indirect, ambiguous, and so forth. The literal-metaphorical dimension is only but one of many, and also a rather controversial one.

Several authors (Fernando, 1978; Fernando & Flavell, 1981; Lehrer, 1974; Makkai, 1972) have taken the view that idiomaticity is more a matter of degrees than an "all-or-nothing" property of a string in a given language. This is considered to be generally true for all figurative language (Clark, 1978, 1979; Gibbs, 1984; Rumelhart, 1979). It has been suggested, therefore, that literal and figurative might be the endpoints of a continuum along which one can situate different types of expressions, according to their level of literality, idiomaticity, or metaphoricity. But is the decision as to whether to locate a given sentence depending on some well-established criterion or is it purely subjective? We thus are faced again with the problem of determining the border between literal, idiomatic, and metaphorical language.

It the last 20 years, several linguistic tests have been proposed, quite unsuccessfully, to assess such a border and identify idioms (Hockett, 1958; Makkai, 1972). Among the more important are the following two: (a) test by substitution or replacement whereby any morpheme replaceable by another of the same class identifies it as nonidiomatic; and (b) once an expression already has been tested by means of (a) (and has also a noncompositional meaning), expose it to as many transformational changes as its internal structure will permit. But as Fernando and Flavell (1981) noted, this attempt to classify idioms in terms of their surface form, and to distinguish them from metaphors on this basis, got stranded in a sea of counterexamples and exceptions. Fernando and Flavell argued that the only possible distinctive criterion is a pragmatic one, namely the one established by the concrete usage of idiomatic expressions by native speakers that is grounded in their intuitions on language.

Cruse (1986) proposed to distinguish between literal, idiomatic, and metaphorical expressions on the basis of their relative degree of semantic transparency (i.e., the degree to which an expression is divisible into semantic constituents) or of opaqueness. The degree of opaqueness is definable in terms of two components:

1. The extent to which the constituents of an opaque expression are "full semantic indicators" (i.e., their meaning contributes to the global sense of the word): *Blackbird* is therefore less opaque than *ladybird* because it has two full indicators whereas the latter has only one (*bird*). They are in turns less opaque than *red herring* or *in a brown study,* which contain no indicators at all.

2. The discrepancy between the combined semantics of the indicators and the overall meaning of the idiom.

Bound collocations (i.e., sequences of lexical items that habitually co-occur) such as "torrential rain" or "heavy drinker" fell outside this typology because, according to Cruse, each of the lexical items composing them at the same time preserves its semantics. Accordingly, dead metaphors are not to be considered as idioms because the hearer can still trace the metaphorical origin, even though the metaphorical meaning is possibly encoded by the hearer as one of the standard senses of the expression (cf. Lakoff & Turner, 1989).

It might be worth noting that Ruwet (1983) argued that one of the possible ways of escaping from the theoretical swamp of the discussion on idioms is to study them *in statu nascenti,* namely to study the figurative origin of idioms (be it metaphorical or metonymical).

The life cycle that goes from a metaphor to an idiom has been traced by Hobbs (1979) in the following way. In the first phase a metaphor is creative and alive: A term belonging to a conceptual domain is extended to another domain and inferential paths allow it to be interpreted. In the second phase the metaphor is already familiar and the interpretive path starts to be established and therefore less complex. In the third phase the metaphor is already "tired"; a direct link is formed between the two domains. In the fourth and final phase the metaphor is a dead one. One no longer can trace the metaphorical origin of the expression. The expression is conceived of as a way of denoting the object, action, or event that once was connotated only metaphorically as such (e.g., the case of "set a variable to a value" or the use of space for designing time expressions).

The relevance of the figurative genesis of idiomatic expressions for a theory of idioms has been stressed by many linguists and psychologists. A still disputed issue however is the scope of such an interest: (a) Are we simply interested in knowing how it came to be that "die" has been conceptualized in terms of kicking and buckets?; (b) do we want to understand the movement of the meaning from the concreteness of literal language to the abstractness of idiomaticity (Fernando, 1978; Fernando & Flavell, 1981)?; or (c) do we believe that for most idioms the meanings of the constituent words and their internal structure (metaphorical, metonymical, based on analogies, and the like) are available and still play a role in understanding and interpreting idioms?

A new wave of studies on idioms shares the idea that the latter is the case: There is already evidence enough to refute the traditional idea that idioms that once had metaphorical origins have lost their metaphoricity over time and are now fixed expressions directly stipulated in the lexicon with no possible use of the semantics of the words composing them. Several studies (Gibbs, Nayak, Bolton, & Keppel, 1988; Gibbs, Nayak, & Cutting, 1989; Nayak & Gibbs, 1990) were aimed at demonstrating that speakers have reliable intuitions about the analyzability of idioms, and that these intuitions do play an important role in determining certain syntactic behavior of idioms, their ease of comprehension, and the extent to which idioms can be semantically productive. One therefore can consider some classes of idioms as motivated string of words and such motivation, far from being a simple etymological fancy, is available and usable in comprehension and interpretation. Before trying to offer more arguments and evidence in favor of this view, the "canon" that has based the standard definition of idioms (i.e., their being noncompositional lexical units) has to be considered, partly to see if anything of the standard view still holds true or can be integrated in a revised form into a theory of idiom representation and comprehension. After all, we certainly do not want to throw away the baby with the bath water.

IDIOMS AS NONCOMPOSITIONAL UNITS

The issue of compositionality of idioms has figured prominently in linguistic and psychological discussions of idiomaticity. Defining an idiom as an expression whose meaning is not formed by the composition of the meanings of the constituent words, according to the morpho-syntactic rules of the language (Katz, 1973), has seemed for years the more straightforward way of defining it. The points supporting this claim were of three sorts and we briefly review them.

First, although the semantic interpretation of expressions such as "he broke the cup" only requires the knowledge of the meanings of the constituent words and of morpho-syntactic rules, it seems not to be so for the figurative meaning of *break the ice*. Such figurative meaning must, according to the noncompositionality hypothesis, be retrieved from lexical memory.

Second, the lack of compositionality represents for some authors (e.g., Cruse, 1986) one of the few criteria for distinguishing between idioms and metaphors. In fact, according to this proposal, whereas the metaphor exploits the meanings of the words in order to induce the hearer to see a thing, a state of affairs, or even in terms of something else, the constituent words of an idiom are semantically empty.

This claim mirrors the opposition between metaphors that are creative (and exploit the "connotative penumbra," Levinson, 1983, p. 150, of the words) and idioms that have fixed and frozen meanings. This opposition between creativity and fixedness is due to the fact that in "figurative formulas" (such as proverbs, idioms, cliches) the metaphorical structure or more generally the "history" that once motivated them is now unperceivable. At best, idioms might be conceived of as frozen or dead metaphors. But as Tannen (1989) recently argued, most of our speech is prepatterned, which does not amount to saying that language is fixed and "tired." She argued that in the prepatterning of language (including what is usually called idiomaticity or formulaicity), there is a pragmatically motivated interplay between fixity and novelty, between "echos" of already spoken words (as Bachtin and Barthes stated many years ago) and simple repetition. This interplay has a major role in everyday conversation and is a resource of creativity.

The third argument used to sustain the noncompositionality of idiomatic expressions is their high degree of internal cohesiveness (or frozenness), a consequence of their being *multiword lexical units* (Fraser, 1970; Swinney & Cutler, 1979). So, just as one cannot modify internally a word without changing its meaning (aside from morphological modifications, of course), the same holds true for idioms (Chafe, 1970; Cruse, 1986). For instance, any adjectival modification of an idiomatic expression will produce either a switch toward the literal meaning of the string (if any) or a metalinguistic comment on the idiom as a unit (e.g., *she or he kicked the proverbial bucket*), where the scope of the modification ranges over the entire string and not, as in literal language, only over the constituent to the right of the adjective.

Before briefly considering the arguments raised against the idea of a strict noncompositionality of idioms, it might be worth noting that idioms are so internally heterogeneous that the generalization of one characteristic (e.g., noncompositionality or syntactic frozenness) to the entire class of expressions can be highly problematic. As Davies (1982/1983) noted, a definition based only on semantic noncompositionality does not uniquely identify idioms with respect, for instance, to compound words: There are, in fact, other expressions that can be defined as "syntactically complex expressions whose meanings are not determined by the semantic properties of the constituents and modes of combination" (p. 71), for instance, combinations such as "carpet sweeper" and "vacuum cleaner." In both cases, in fact, one cannot work out the meaning from the constituents and their modes of combination alone: A carpet sweeper sweeps carpets but a vacuum cleaner does not clean vacuums; instead, it cleans by means of a vacuum (cf. Lehnert, 1986, for a detailed analysis of nominal compounds). A more complex definition of idioms, taking into account at the same time both cases of noncompositionality and of semantic transparency, seems necessary in order to uniquely define idiomatic expressions.

SOME CRACKS ON AN "AXIOMATIC IDEA"

First linguists (Gaatone, 1981; Nunberg, 1979; Ruwet, 1983; Wasow, Sag, & Nunberg, 1983) then psychologists (Cacciari & Glucksberg, 1990; Gibbs, Nayak, Bolton, & Keppel, 1988; Glucksberg, 1991) insisted that the "axiomatic idea" (Wasow et al., 1983, p. 107) that the meaning of an idiom is not a function of the meanings of its parts is deficient in several respects (I am concerned mainly with semantic compositionality). Essentially this axiom is not able to account for (a) the fact that parts of idioms can be modified by means of adjectives (e.g., *leave no* legal *stone unturned* where the scope of the adjective does not range over the entire idiom but only locally); (b) quantification (e.g., *pull a string or two*) and focusing effects (e.g., *those strings he wouldn't pull for you*) seem to work to the same extent as for literal language; and (c) parts of idioms can be omitted in elliptical constructions (e.g., *my goose is cooked, but yours isn't*).

Wasow et al. (1983) qualified their break with the previous linguistic literature by claiming that parts of an idiom have typically identifiable meanings that combine to produce the figurative meaning as a whole. The idiomatic meaning is derived from the literal meaning of the constituent words in conventionalized and not totally arbitrary ways through meaning transfer mechanisms that they do not specify fully.

Nunberg (1979) stated that the failure to explain idioms purely on the basis of the syntactic form or of the content demonstrated that their behavior must be accounted for on the basis of the relation between these two levels (cf. also Ruwet, 1983). Nunberg's claim is that these relations are unperceivable if one still believes that phrasal idioms possess a single semantic representation generally unrelated to the meanings of their parts. The first step is therefore to recognize that idioms can be partially analyzable, namely to acknowledge that there are idioms for which we can perceive a still vivid synchronic relation to the literal meaning.

As work by Gibbs and collaborators demonstrated, speakers do have assumptions about the rationale whereby *pull strings* or *kick the bucket* mean what they mean, that is, a rationale that one can define as the *motivation* for an idiom. Not only can this rationale affect the way in which an idiom is used, but also it can affect its syntactic behavior (Gibbs & Gonzales, 1985). Of course not all idioms behave the same, therefore Nunberg (1979) distinguished among (a) normally decomposable idioms that are analyzable and imply conventions whereby each of the idiom's constituents can be used to refer to the idiomatic referent (e.g., *pop the question, keep the pot boiling, break the ice,* etc.); (b) abnormally decomposable idioms where we are able to identify this relation only by virtue of conventional metaphors that govern the mapping from constituents to idiomatic meanings (e.g., *hit the ceiling, hit the panic button, throw in the sponge,* etc.); and (c) nondecomposable, that is, opaque, idioms (cf. Gibbs, Nayak, & Cutting, 1989).

THE NOTION OF MOTIVATION IN IDIOMS

The notion of motivation partly overlaps with similar notions that have been used by linguists and psychologists who adhere to this new view of idioms. It may prove helpful to try to specify them. An idiom can be *semantically compositional* in the sense that its meaning is entirely derivable given the knowledge of the meanings of the constituent words and an ability to detect and use as an inferential tool the rhetorical structure underlying an idiom (e.g., analogical relations, metonymical relations, etc.; we return to this issue later). The *analyzability* of an idiom is the extent to which a speaker of the language can trace the relations between the two levels of meaning (literal-local and figurative-global). A fairly different notion is that of *predictability*. According to Nunberg (1978), a regular word use is predictable for a given speaker if she or he believes that it is rational, namely, is following the normal conventions governing its use and beliefs. A purely conventionalized use of a word has no regularity and therefore it is not predictable, although there can be different levels of motivation. In this sense, one hardly can predict the rationale whereby, for instance, a certain noun phrase (NP) was selected to be an idiomatic vehicle. One can speculate on its general semantic features that can make it a good candidate for a certain figurative referent, as in, for example, the case of *spill the beans*. Beans are countable, numerable, discrete, and so on; therefore they can be taken to represent secrets much more efficiently than *mud*, which is a mass noun. But the reasons why *beans* were selected instead of *pebbles* is rather opaque, although it has been argued that symbolization processes are not totally arbitrary and are culturally bound (cf. for instance Holland & Quinn, 1987).

The notion of motivation has a long history : Ullmann (1962), for instance, claimed that any language has both conventional and motivated terms. It is as difficult to imagine a language with no onomatopoeic terms or transparent metaphors as it is to imagine a language with only motivated terms. There are at least three possible levels of motivation: the phonetic motivation (e.g., "boom"), the morphological motivation (e.g., "retell" or "thinker," where the knowledge of morphological rules will guide the interpretation), and the semantic motivation, as in figurative expressions (e.g., "the turning point of the question"). Both morphological and semantic motivations contain a level of arbitrariness: In fact, whereas affixes are motivated, the components are as arbitrary as the relationship between the words and the objects designated by the metaphor of the turning point.

Recently, Lakoff (1987) and Gibbs and collaborators (Gibbs & Nayak, 1991; Nayak & Gibbs, 1990) argued that idioms are not dead metaphors with arbitrarily determined meanings. The figurative meanings of idioms are motivated by speakers' tacit knowledge of the conceptual metaphors underlying them (e.g., THE MIND IS A CONTAINER or LIFE IS A JOURNEY). These conceptual metaphors form part of the link between an idiom and its figurative meaning and constrain the way people understand them, or how people form mental images (Gibbs & O'Brien, 1990). These mappings of source and target domains exist independently in the conceptual system and function, according to the proponents of cognitive linguistics, to structure and organize many aspects of our thought and reasoning. According to this view, metaphorical motivation of idioms is rooted at the level of these conceptual structures, and not in a correlation between word meanings: The motivation is thus at the conceptual, not at the lexical level.

Although interesting, the idea of conceptual templates shaping all aspects of language production and interpretation seems not to take fully into account certain important aspects of language use. First, words do have meanings that are computed automatically and cannot be simply bypassed. Second, words are grouped together in idiomatic expressions most often not arbitrarily but according to principles that are per se meaningful (use of pars-pro-toto principles, analogies, extensions of prototypical cases, etc.). Third, people can interpret language sensibly at that level, and do so in a creative way (see later). So it is not simply a matter of componential meaning (as it was according to standard theories of idioms), but of the interaction between all the meanings (be they central or peripheral ones) that are carried by the words composing the idiom and the structure underlying the idioms. Although idioms possess established meanings that are easy to conceive of in terms of stored semantic concepts, they simultaneously exploit the senses of the words, the structure underlying their grouping in an idiom, and possibly also conceptual templates such as the ones postulated by Lakoff and Gibbs (cf. Gibbs & Nayak, 1991; Kreutz & Graesser, 1991).

THE ROLE OF THE CONSTITUENT WORDS
IN IDIOMS' INTERPRETATION

One might argue that we now are faced with another *cercle vicieux:* How can we distinguish different degrees of transparency of an idiom when we already know its meaning? Reagan (1987) argued that when faced with the problem of semantic decomposability of idioms, one has to distinguish between *breaking down* meaning into parts and *building up* meaning from parts. These two mechanisms should allow different predictions as to the level of semantic transparency of idioms. As Ruwet (1983) noted, the confusion between acquisition and interpretation has favored the idea of semantic opaqueness of idioms' constituents.

Coulmas (1981) considered the case of non-native speakers faced with the problem of making sense of idioms as a heuristic model. A possible and sensible assumption a non-native speaker might make is that any incomprehensible expression she or he might run across could be an idiom. He or she can use three possible sources of knowledge in order to reduce the range of possible meanings: the logic of everyday activity, because most communicative acts take place in stereotypical social situations; the structure of the lexical phrase; and the awareness of the fact that most languages have "idiom-prone lexemes," as *take, put,* and so forth. By using together all these sources, a non-native speaker might arrive at the idiomatic meaning "by inference" rather than "by instruction." This knowledge, coupled with an attention toward context, can help him or her to arrive at the meaning, or at least at the semantic domain to which the idiom belongs, although it will not be sufficient to tell when and how to use it appropriately.

There are several ways that one can investigate the role of the meanings of the words that form an idiomatic expression. Cacciari and Glucksberg (1990) (see also Glucksberg, McGlone, and Cacciari, in press, and Glucksberg, chapter 2 of this volume), for instance, studied the semantic productivity of idioms, namely the ability of people to understand and produce new idiomatic meanings by changing, in a pragmatically sensible way, various aspects of an idiom's individual elements (e.g., *burn the candle at three ends* instead of *burn the candle at both ends*). They showed that, according to the principles that govern discourse processing, idioms are analyzed both semantically and syntactically. The "literal meanings" of the constituent words are available and used when necessary, that is, especially when idioms are analyzable and direct, one-to-one mappings from idiomatic constituents to idiomatic referents are possible. The words composing such idioms can acquire new senses, that is, the ones they get from being part of an idiom. So *spill* can come to acquire a "divulge" sense, even though not as a dominant one, precisely because of the repeated usage of the idiom *spill the beans* together with some level of conventionalization of a figurative and partly motivated origin. Therefore its meanings will be available and activated according to different processing needs, types of contexts, tasks, and so on.

Additional sources of evidence for this role of the meanings of the constituents are represented by production phenomena such as slips of the tongue, where a semantically related word is substituted (e.g., *swallow the bullet* instead of *bite the bullet;* cf. Cacciari & Glucksberg, 1990; Fromkin, 1971); advertising in media, and intentional switches between literal and figurative senses of words as the ones exemplified in the following passages taken from Broderick (1975): (a) "Baldwin occasionally stumbles over the truth, but he always hastily picks himself up and hurries on as if nothing had happened" (Winston Churchill; p. 8); and (b) "Kennedy won by an eyelash and some thought it was a false eyelash" (Howard K. Smith; p. 9). Broderick interpreted these two examples as cases where the literalization of some words (e.g., *stumble over*) resurrects the metaphor. The two passages illustrate the possibility of multiple semantic processing, namely the simultaneous processing of the semantics of an idiom and of its literalization, at the same time accounting for metaphorical processes at work in the literalization.

But it seems also possible to interpret the two passages in a different way. The two passages play exactly on the overlapping of the literal semantics of the words, that is, the ones they possess if taken outside the idiom, as well as the aspect of meaning they acquire when embedded in figurative expressions. It is precisely because the meanings are still available that one can produce such an effect: It is a movement that backgrounds and foregrounds the literal and the figurative meanings of the words, that is, pushes them on stage and back to the backstage, according to the communicative needs of the moment. A movement not dissimilar from the one that we experience when faced with perceptually ambiguous stimuli: Once we see a vase, but a moment later we see two profiles. The two images can even co-occur for a while; in any case we are aware of their coexistence as we are aware of the existence and interplay of the two meanings: the literal and the figurative.

As we mentioned earlier, the idea that idioms still have an internal semantics that can be used per se in order to allow people to interpret them (the so-called transparency of the figurative meaning) might lead to a chicken-or-egg critique:

Do we arrive at the figurative meaning and then have intuitions about the idiom's analyzability because we already know its conventionalized meaning (the "break down hypothesis" made by Reagan, 1987) or do we arrive directly at such a figurative meaning building it up from its "building blocks" (as for metaphors that do not have a stipulated meaning)?

The idea of a continuum from opacity to transparency leads us to hypothesize the existence of four possible types of idioms: (1) totally opaque idioms; (b) retrospectively transparent idioms: namely, transparent once you either know the meaning (and this allows one to trace the correspondence between literal constituents and figurative referents) or are reminded of the episode or setting that originated the idiom; (c) directly transparent idioms: the senses of the words leading one to the idiomatic meaning of the string, perhaps by means of the re-creation of an analogical or metaphorical mapping; (d) figuratively transparent idioms: idioms composed of other idioms, or parts that appear in other idioms or as metaphorical vehicles.

What remains nonetheless unclear is whether the idea of such a continuum bears any correspondence to the interpretative strategies used in idiomatic language interpretation or whether it merely represents an exercise in the stylistic properties of language. As it might prove useful for most chicken-or-egg problems, it is worth trying to look at it from different perspectives and gather evidence to try to transform it into a more manageable issue. The preliminary results of some experiments on adults and children might shed some light on the issue of idiom transparency and interpretation.

COPING WITH UNKNOWN IDIOMS: STRATEGIES FOR INTERPRETATIONS

The first experiment was conducted on 32 adults.[1] They were given a written questionnaire containing a list of unfamiliar idioms (each embedded in a short sentence containing a personal pronoun + idiom, e.g., "He made the feathers fly") taken from a study on idiom familiarity (Schweigert, 1986). The experimental materials consisted of 48 idioms divided into four lists (see Appendix A), and subjects were assigned randomly to one of them. The subjects' task was twofold: They first were requested to give a paraphrase and rate their confidence on it (on a 7-point scale going from 1:very unsure to 7:very sure) for each of the idioms whose meaning they thought they knew. For those that they were uncer-

---

[1]This pilot study was conducted in collaboration with Dr. Boaz Keisar (currently at the University of Chicago) and Sachi Kumon (Princeton University) while I was a Fullbright visiting scholar at the Department of Psychology of the University of Princeton. Eleven subjects were students at the Princeton University and 21 were American students at the Johns Hopkins University in Bologna, Italy. All served as unpaid volunteers.

tain of or did not know the meaning, they were requested to make a guess and write down a paraphrase on a separate side of the questionnaire. Once finished with this first task, they were asked to go back through all the guessed idioms and briefly write under the guessed paraphrase how they arrived at the meanings of those idioms, namely "what made you choose the specific interpretation, did you use something as a cue, were you reminded of something?" The aim of this pilot study was to investigate people's ability to make sense of unfamiliar idioms, namely their ability to use different sources of knowledge and strategies in order to assign a meaning to a string of words.

The responses were discussed and evaluated both separately and collectively by the researchers with over 86% agreement. The written self-reports were used in order to outline the strategies that students used during the guessing phase. Five such strategies were identified. Sometimes students made mistakes: They were sure that they knew the meaning of the idiom, and that was not always the case. Sometimes subjects confused two similar idioms and the like (47.6% of the total answers were correct, with an average confidence rate of 6.4; 11.7% were incorrect, with a confidence rate of 2.1; and 35.2% were guessing; 5.5% were incomprehensible or missed).

We were not particularly interested in the average error rate, that is, in the performance per se, nor in which of the strategies was more effective in guessing the correct meaning. Rather, we were mainly interested in students' self-report of the principles they thought governed their interpretation, and in this respect they were quite cooperative and accurate. I therefore report here only on the five strategies we identified. These types of interpretative paths are interesting even when they led to wrong solutions. In fact, as we see, sometimes students ended up with wrong meanings, although the inferential path was sensible.

Type 1. Look for another idiom that is similar to some extent. This general principle can be instantiated in different ways:

1. See whether one part or construction (e.g., one or more constituents) is interpretable according to other idioms. Examples are the *by the board* in *go by the board* interpreted as "by the book" in "go by the book"; *feathers* of *make the feathers fly* interpreted as in "smooth someone's feathers."

2. Search for another idiom having a related word (e.g., an antonymous word) or the same verb in the same position and interpret it accordingly or change a constituent and interpret the idiom accordingly. Examples are *drop* instead of *explode* in *explode a bombshell;* or *dry behind the ears* interpreted as "wet," so "innocent"; *take the bit in one's mouth* interpreted by inverting the active and passive poles, therefore as a passive action.

3. See if there is another idiom that uses a semantic associate of one of the words of the idiom and interpret it accordingly. An example is *get out of the hole,* which was interpreted according to "put yourself in a hole."

Type 2.   Interpret one constituent literally and use also the other words composing its semantic field to infer the meaning of the idiom. Some examples are: for *hose somebody down:* Hose = clean, so clean somebody up = defeat somebody in a game, therefore hose down = defeat; for *polish the apple:* polish = clean, improve, and apple = perfection, so polish the apple = reach perfection.

Type 3.   Look for a cause–effect relationship between the action described by the idiom and select either the cause or the effect as the meaning of the idiom. Take for example *grease the wheels:* "greasing the wheels allows the machinery to start moving" so the idiom means "go faster."

Type 4.   Consider the semantics of the words composing the idioms and try to derive a possible meaning for the idiom. This can imply:

1. Consider the literal semantic of one word. Some examples are *back* interpreted as "beginning" or "source" as in *back to the salt mines;* or *hammer* in *under the hammer*—what is a hammer used for? Breaking things that are hard (e.g., nuts), so the idiom could mean examine very careful and intensely a problem. *Asleep at the switch* "has its sense because of interpretation of the word meaning. Switch: railroad switching station."
2. Consider the literal meaning of the entire string, and possible outcomes (reconstruction of the analogy). For example, *asleep at the switch* implies being not careful, not alert. For *take the bit in one's mouth,* "if you relate the idiom to riding horses, its meaning becomes clear." For *darken one's door,* "the person's shadow appears on the door when he or she comes to visit."
3. Interpret the words metaphorically. For example, for *a straw in the wind, straw* is a symbol of weakness, of no direction, "a straw blowing helplessly in the wind." For *the bottom dropped out,* "the bottom symbolizes the depression." For *darken one's door,* "cast a shadow implies darkness, a negative meaning; the door stands for one's self, home."

Type 5.   Try to visualize an image of the action/state described. For example, for *bow and scrape:* "I had a sort of visual interpretation. I pictured someone acting sort of like a puppy when it begs"; for *make the feathers fly:* "causing fluster or upset, the visual image of feathers flying."

What the results of this pilot study seem to show is that the ability to make sense of idioms is not restricted to the simple mechanism of retrieving an idiom's meaning from lexical memory.[2] In case of familiar idioms, people certainly

[2]Fillmore, Kay, and O'Connor (1988) noted that there are idioms (as *let alone,* or *the most . . . the most*) that are partly open and must be filled in according to semantic as well as pragmatic constraints. In these cases, the mental lexicon must incorporate different levels of informa-

retrieve the meaning stored in memory, often together with information much more complex than a simple paraphrase. In fact, it has been argued that many idioms have rich semantic descriptions associated with them that might not be fully captured by a single word paraphrase (Gibbs & Nayak, 1991; Michiels, 1977; Mueller & Gibbs, 1987; Nunberg, 1978). In fact to use an idiom such as *kick the bucket* does not simply mean "die," but also dying in a certain way. For example, one would not use it to refer to a relative, or in any respectful circumstance or the like. Some idioms also can take slightly but relevant different nuances of sense depending on the context, showing that their general meaning must be instantiated according to the available information. In fact, one might think of the function of idioms in terms of specification of existing concepts in a way that is not already specified in semantic memory by existing lexical items.

There are thus semantic as well pragmatic constraints on idioms' use that go beyond the scope of a simple paraphrase. These constraints show that people possess much more knowledge of idioms than simple paraphrases. Of course, they actualize and make use of such knowledge and interpretative paths (based on similarity, analogical transfer, inferences, etc.) only when necessary and that is obviously the case for unfamiliar idioms (that might be reasonably seen as metaphors).

It is precisely such complexity that renders idioms so difficult to manage for a non-native speaker. As Coulmas (1981) noted, she or he has to learn that in many cases linguistic meaning is vastly more complicated than the simple computation of the meaning components of identifiable parts, and includes also the range of appropriate circumstances and applications.

But is there anything special about the strategies people use when trying to make sense of unfamiliar idioms; namely, is there anything new or different from what we routinely do during a conversation or while reading a newspaper article? More generally, is there anything special in making sense of figurative language with respect to literal language, lexical or sentential innovations, and so on? There is not enough evidence to sustain the idea of a principled difference between types of knowledge, strategies, and meaning construal rules used for understanding and interpreting one or another type of language (if such a sharp distinction still holds, which is highly disputable). In fact, first we make use of the same types of knowledge (although different priority in accessing one or another source of knowledge might occur). Second, we spend most of our activity of listening or reading in filling gaps, drawing inferences not always triggered by conversational implicatures *à la* Grice, looking for prototypical cases or similar situations that might function as anchor points, and the like. As evidence on lexical innovations, eponymes, indirect speech acts, "nonce"

---

tion, from grammatical patterns, to an entailment relation in the background of a presupposed semantic scale for idioms such as *let alone;* in fact the interpretation of any *let alone* sentence requires seeing the two parts of the construction as "points on a scale."

senses, and complex concepts showed (Clark, 1983; Clark & Gerrig, 1983; Gerrig, 1989; Gerrig & Murphy, 1991; Medin & Shoben, 1988; Murphy, 1988), we have developed a fairly efficient ability to decode and assign meaning and coherence even to contradictory or incomplete verbal materials. The general mechanisms for meaning extractions are so powerful and efficient that it is difficult to accept the idea of something special used only for figurative language, as most stage models posited (e.g., Searle, 1979). The general idea underlying stage models is that figurative meaning understanding depends on the recognition of some sort of contextual deficiency of the sentence, if taken literally. But this has led to predictions that generally have been disconfirmed by the existing evidence (cf. Gibbs, 1984; Glucksberg, Gildea, & Bookin, 1982).

HOW CHILDREN ASSIGN A MEANING
TO IDIOMS

For many years, the predominant view was that children up to the teenage years were unable to understand idiomatic expressions. Recent work on the development of figurative competence (Ackerman, 1982; Cacciari & Levorato, 1989; Levorato & Cacciari, 1992; Winner, 1988) has cast doubt on this assumption. A growing body of evidence now suggests that even 7-year-old children are able to understand idiomatic expression, especially when embedded in highly informative contexts. It therefore can be of some interest to see the strategies adopted by fifth-grade children (10-year-olds) when asked to assign meanings to idiomatic expressions. This could shed light on both their metalinguistic awareness and their figurative competence.

As part of a larger set of studies on the developmental trend of the acquisition and production of idiomatic expression,[3] Levorato and I gave a questionnaire to 45 Italian fifth graders and a group of 30 university students (I will not report on their results here). Three lists of 10 frequent idioms each, being either semantically transparent idioms (e.g., *cry over spilled milk*), quasi-metaphorical idioms (based on a figurative comparison as in *to be as two drops of water,* which means to be very similar), and opaque idioms (e.g., *break the ice*) were prepared (see Appendix B). Each list was assigned to a group of 15 fifth graders. For each idiom, the child was requested to write down (a) a paraphrase of the idiom meaning, (b) the reasons motivating the meaning of the idiom, (c) whether a first grader (a 6-year-old) might understand it, and (d) what the 6-year-old can do in order to understand it. The questionnaire was the same for children and adults because the latter acted as baseline. Adults therefore were advised that this was

---

[3]For more details, see Cacciari and Levorato (1989), Levorato and Cacciari (1992), Cacciari & Levorato (1991), and chapter 6 by Levorato in this book.

part of a study on children's acquisition of figurative language. Let us see some of the results concerning children's answers.

First of all, as was predicted on the basis of previous studies, 10-year-old children already have a good competence on idiom meaning, especially for the quasi-metaphorical ones (henceforth, QM) (69.9% of correct paraphrases, 51.9% for opaque idioms [O] and 47.9% for transparent idioms [T]). Not many children wrote that they had no ideas as an answer to the question: "Why do we say so," namely the reasons motivating the idiom (13.3% of the total answers). The explanations of the correct meaning of the idioms (43.3 for QM, 26.6% for T, and 15.9% for O) were classified according to the following categories:

1. *Usage conditions:* "we use it for saying it," "it's a way of speaking," "it's a proverb."

2. *Causal explanations:* e.g., in the case of *fall from the clouds* (that means "be astounded"): "clouds are far away, so if someone is on the clouds is far away from reality that's why she or he doesn't realize what is really happening."

3. *Explanations based on the literal state or action expressed by the idiom,* its impossibility, outcomes, or agents: e.g., in the case of *make a hole in the water* ("be unsuccessful"): "it is impossible to make a hole in the water, so you lose time and realize nothing"; or, for *drown oneself in a glass of water* ("get lost for nothing"): "it is impossible because a glass is too small, so it means that you are worried for nothing"; or for *be as dumb as a fish* (that means to be silent and keep secrets): "fishes do not speak."

4. *Explanation based on the literal and figurative outcomes of the idiomatic action:* e.g., for *touch the sky with a finger* ("be extremely happy"): "in order to touch the sky one has to make huge jumps that are possible only if one is very happy"; for *break the ice:* "we say like that because the ice is tough and the more the time is passing and the more the silence gets iced," or "because words glide as the ice, and breaking it is like getting to the point."

5. *Explanation based on analogies:* e.g., for *close shop:* "closing the shop is like to stop working, which means that you keep silent and do not speak to other people"; or for *look for a needle in a haystack* ("do something that is impossible"): "because looking for a needle in a haystack is as much difficult as looking for answers to impossible questions"; or for *be among the clouds* ("be very absent-minded"): "because if one is among the clouds she or he is not on the earth; that is there is metaphor: earth stands for reality, clouds stand for fantasy."

6. *Explanations based on perceived symbols:* e.g., for *be at the seventh sky* ("be in seventh heaven"): "we all know that sky is wonderful, so if there was a seventh one, can you imagine?"; "in the heaven everything is happy and nice."

7. *Explanations based on other idioms:* e.g., for *touch the sky with a finger:* "because we can also say to be on the stars, because when one is very happy she or he seems to fly."

Children were requested also to answer a question concerning younger children's ability to understand idioms and a possible way for them to get to the right meaning. The rationale of the question was to elicit as much information as possible on the tacit knowledge children possess on idioms, namely to gather other evidence on both the perception of a semantic motivation and the strategies for interpretation. As a side effect, it revealed the level of metalinguistic awareness of 10-year-old children, and that children indeed possess a naive theory on younger children's knowledge and reasoning abilities.

First, many children think that first graders can understand idioms (QM: 38.6%; T: 43.9%; O: 40.6%). Their answers to the question "What can she or he do in order to understand it?" were classified according to the following types:

1. *Exemplification* (5.7% on the total of the answers).
2. *Perform the idiomatic action* (20.1%).
3. *Perform the literal action* (12.2%).
4. *Ask adults* (15.5%).
5. *By reasoning* on the constituent words and on the action described by the idiom (9.2%).
6. *By a correct similitude* (the child either depicts a similitude or relates the action to her or himself) (11.7%).[4]

Let us see some examples associated with the three different types of idioms.

Quasi-Metaphorical Idioms. The more preferred answers are: by a similitude (22.6%) (for *be as dumb as a fish:* "You must say to her or him that fishes don't speak, but also that you can say the same thing also for human beings"; "make him think how can she or he possibly speak under the water"); for *feel as a fish outside the water:* "It is enough to try to imagine to be a fish and then to try to figure out how can feel a fish without its water" by reasoning on the words and on the action (18.6%) ("In order to understand, she or he can reason about it, pay attention, or observe the others"; "examine carefully the meaning of the words"); perform the literal action (16.6%) (for *be afraid also by one's own shadow:* "Stand in front of a light bulb and watch at his shadow"; "it is enough that it enters his consciousness the idea that phantoms and living shadows do not exist"; for *be as dumb as a fish:* "She or he goes to the zoo, and touches the aquarium, if she or he doesn't hear any noise, she or he will understand that fishes are dumb"; for *go backwards as crayfishes:* "She or he goes to the seaside, looks for a crayfish, and then makes it walk"); to ask adults (15.9%)

---

[4]There were two other groups of answers: a group formed by answers such as "I don't know," incorrect analogy or incorrect idiom (7.3%), and another one formed by answers such as "she or he cannot understand because she or he is too young" (4.6%).

("you don't have to be a genius for understanding it, but first graders are small so an older person must explain the meaning"); perform the idiomatic action (7.9%) (for *be as dog and cat;* i.e., "enemies": "She or he can try to argue with its best friend"); exemplification (5.9%) (for *be as two drops of water:* "One must explain to him that they are as similar as two white sheets used for drawing").

Transparent Idioms.   The answers were classified as follows: Perform the idiomatic action (34.6%) (for *look for a needle in a haystack:* "They too can understand, because they too have lost several things that ended up being somewhere," or "if she or he looks for a small thing in a huge room, it's impossible to find it"; for *cry over spilled milk:* "I'll show them a movie with a man that has repented for having done so many bad things"); perform the literal action (18.6%) (for *cost an eye of the head,* i.e., "an arm and a leg": "thinking to buy something and paying for it with an eye"; for *make a hole in the water,* i.e., "be unsuccessful": "Let him try to make a hole in the water, he'll see it's impossible"; for *cry over spilled milk:* "One can spill some milk and then become desperate"; for *be among the clouds,* i.e., "be absent-minded": "One can draw the picture of a child on a cloud that is not thinking of anything"); by similitude (8.6%) (for *cry over spilled milk:* "I'll tell her or him that as when someone spills milk and cannot then pick it up, when one performs badly she or he cannot remedy it"; for *cost an eye of the head:* "She or he has to think how unhappy must be a person without an eye"); ask adults (7.9%); exemplification (5.9%) (for *be among the clouds:* "I'll make her or him an example: While the teacher is explaining the lesson you're thinking of something else"; for *be on the thorns,* i.e., "be very anxious about something happening": "I'll use the example of cartoons: When the cartoon is split and you don't know the end"; for *make chickens laugh,* i.e., "be socially unsuccessful," namely to tell something that is neither amusing nor believable: "She or he can try to make chickens laugh; it's impossible"). Few children, many less than with QM idioms, quoted the self-reasoning strategy (1.9%), which can imply that children thought T idioms were more semantically complex than QM idioms.

Opaque Idioms.   Although children provided answers for most of the QM and T idioms, there were fewer answers for O idioms (21.2% of the total are missing, vs. 17.2% for T idioms and 1.3% for QM idioms). The answers were distributed according to the following categories: Ask adults (22.6%); perform the idiomatic action (17.9%) (for *cut the rope,* i.e., "escape": "She or he should try to be feared and escape very quickly"); by reasoning on the words (7.2%) (for *break the ice:* "she or he can dwell in the word *break*); by exemplification (3%) (for *give oneself some air,* i.e., "beast": "She or he can arrive at understanding by reasoning on the fact that the words do not mean take a fan, but something else"; for *touch the sky with a finger:* "if he or she thinks that in order to touch the sky with a finger one has to make extremely high jumps that are possible only when one is very happy"; "think to the fact that the sky is the happiest place so how can one be unhappy there?"). Almost absent is the perform-the-literal-action answer (1.3%) (for *fall from the clouds,* i.e., "be astounded": "make her or him fall from the bed, and see the reaction"). Table 2.1 summarizes the preferences accorded to the different answers.

There was also a group of answers that one can define as "reflections on younger children's ability" where 10-year-old children declared why younger ones cannot understand a particular idiom of the list (3.9% on the total of QM idioms, 0.7% of T idioms, 9.3% for O idioms). Here are some examples for the idioms where such an answer is more frequent, opaque idioms: for *cut the rope,* i.e., "escape": "because he or she really believes that it really means to cut a rope"; for *break the ice:* "She or he won't understand because listening to someone who is breaking the ice she or he will not think to make friends"; for *touch the sky with a finger:* "She or he won't understand because touching the sky with a finger doesn't seem to be such a happy thing."

The three types of idioms seem to elicit different responses and interpretative strategies. One might attribute this to experimental artifacts such as our choice of the materials and of the categories as well as the decisions concerning the best fit between answers and categories. However, we believe that our data reflect a genuine effect that can be explained on more motivated grounds, namely that idioms do differ according to their semantic structure and that children are sensitive to such differences. As a consequence, the interpretative strategies children thought of as more appropriate reflect the perception of the semantic characteristics and cognitive complexities of idioms. Of course, children's answers also reflect a difference in the availability of sources of information and experiential bases.

Let us compare two types of answers: the perform-the-idiomatic-action answer and the perform-the-literal-action one. The first prevails in both T idioms (34.6%) and O idioms (17.9), although is much more present in T idioms. This

TABLE 2.1
Percentages of Answers to the Question
"What Can She or He Do in Order to Understand It?"

Types of Answer	QM	T	O
Exemplification	5.9%	5.9%	5.3%
Perform the Literal Action	16.6%	18.6%	1.3%
Perform the Idiomatic Action	7.9%	34.6%	17.9%
Ask Adults	15.9%	7.9%	22.6%
By Reasoning	18.6%	1.9%	7.2%
By a Correct Similitude	22.6%	8.6%	3.9%
No Answer	1.3%	17.2%	21.2%
Other Answers	6.9%	4.1%	10.9%

result seems coherent with evidence on adults reported by Popiel and McRae (1988) and Cronk (1990), namely that many idioms that possess a possible literal interpretation are interpreted mostly figuratively because the likeliness of their literal usage is very low. So the children who chose this answer may have relied on the action referred to by the idiomatic meaning as the more salient and plausible, although possibly not for the same reason for the two types of idioms. The perform-the-literal-action answer is used more frequently in T idioms (18.6%) and QM idioms (16.6%) than in O idioms (1.3%). In the first case this might be because the literal meaning of T idioms, by definition, bears a certain similarity to its figurative meaning and the constituent words map onto their idiomatic referent in a quite direct way. Therefore children might have thought that performing the literal action is a good strategy for getting to the figurative meaning. In fact, such a strategy is virtually absent for O idioms (1.3%). The preference for this answer in QM idioms (16.6%) can be largely due to these idioms being built upon a comparison that specifies a certain state, property, or action with respect to a metaphorical vehicle that seems to represent it in a more appropriate or prototypical way. Thus the literal information is actively part of the idiom's meaning. The fact that "by reasoning" and "by a correct similitude" are used almost only with QM idioms (18.6% and 22.6%, respectively) can be due to the structural characteristics aforementioned. In fact, the comparative structure is set already and much more information already is given with respect to T and O idioms. The child had only to fill in an empty slot in the comparison or to figure out the relevant property that is to be transferred to the object or person compared and that is typified by the metaphorical vehicle; for example, *be as dumb as a fish* makes use of a property of fishes, that is, not speaking, for referring to someone who is able to be silent and keep secrets; in *be as two drops of water* one has to guess what two things by definition identical could share, that is, the relevant property at issue and so on.

CONCLUSION

In this chapter, I examined some of the core notions that constitute the theoretical field of idiom representation and comprehension: (a) the notion of literal meaning and its relationship with compositionality and figurative language, (b) the concept of motivation in idioms, and (c) the role of speakers' intuitions about idiom meaning and structure. I presented a new set of linguistic and psychological studies on idioms that progressively abandon an "axiomatic idea," the non-compositionality of idioms. In order to clarify the possible roles of both the structure of the idiom and the meanings of the words composing it on the strategies people follow in interpretation, I presented some evidence coming from two studies: one concerned with the interpretative strategies adopted by adults when faced with unfamiliar idioms and the other with the interpretative paths followed by children when asked to perform some metalinguistic tasks on idioms.

What is the picture that emerges from the literature and evidence I have been examining? At the very beginning, I mentioned that researchers in the field perceive a need to reform the traditional idea that idioms are no more than lexical units stored in the lexicon with no semantic as well syntactic structure. The motivation for this change arises from experimental evidence as well as from the progresses made in the area of meaning representation and processing. First, there is a need to differentiate between types of idioms according to their semantic as well syntactic characteristics. One relevant dimension certainly can be the degree of semantic transparency of idioms, as reflected by both speakers' intuitions and on-line processing measures. Second, we need to recognize that the meanings of the words forming an idiom and its underlying structure (being more or less deeply rooted in the cognitive structure) are both available and play a role when necessary for communicative purposes, that is, when one has, for instance, to understand unfamiliar idioms, or to produce a pragmatically motivated variation on a classical idiom, and so forth. As a sort of processing default, it seems still plausible to speak in terms of activation of the meanings of the words and of the semantic description associated with an idiom. Still, the senses of the words are available, at least up to and even some time after an idiom's recognition occurs (cf. Cacciari & Tabossi, 1988; Tabossi & Cacciari, 1988), and these word senses are usable in cases such as the previous ones.

Just as an example, let us take an Italian idiom *to make a hole in the water* that means to perform an activity in a rather unsuccessful way. Suppose one hears the following sentence: "Doing X is like making holes in the water." In order to infer the semantic domain to which the idiom's meaning makes reference (if not the meaning in itself) and that serves as a basis for the intended judgment on the action, one has to retrieve the meanings of the words composing it (lexical-local level), form a candidate interpretation of the figurative action (there is no plausible literal meaning in this case), then reason that making holes in the water is quite an unsuccessful activity, in that it serves as a prototypical instance of uselessness and infer, by analogy, the intended values of "doing X" (conceptual-analogical level). This example briefly illustrates some of the abilities and informative sources that are at work when an unknown idiom is met. In everyday conversation, of course, we do not need to use such an amount of processing and inferential energies; nonetheless this is what understanding idioms is all about.

ACKNOWLEDGMENTS

I am grateful to The Council for International Exchange of Scholars for a Fullbright travel grant in 1987 that allowed me to think more deeply about idiom, to enjoy the hospitality of the Department of Psychology of Princeton University, and to start a wonderful collaboration with Sam Glucksberg, whom I again thank. Part of the results of the studies contained in this chapter was presented first at the Syilvia Beach Conference on Language Comprehension in 1991. I want to thank Morton Ann Gernsbacher for her hospitality and useful comments.

REFERENCES

Ackerman, B. P. (1982). On comprehending idioms: Do children get the picture? *Journal of Experimental Child Psychology, 33,* 439–454.

Broderick, J. P. (1975). Metaphors in idioms: A problem for linguistic theory. *The USF Language Quarterly, XIII,* 3–4, 7–12.

Cacciari, C., & Glucksberg, S. (1990). Understanding idiomatic expressions: The contribution of word meanings. In G. B. Simpson (Ed.), *Understanding word and sentence* (pp. 217–240). Amsterdam, Netherlands: Elsevier.

Cacciari, C., & Levorato, M. C. (1989). How children understand idioms in discourse. *Journal of Child Language, 16,* 387–405.

Cacciari, C., & Levorato, M. C. (1991, November). Spilling the beans on children's comprehension and production of idioms. Paper presented at the 32nd Annual Meeting of The Psychonomic Society, San Francisco.

Cacciari, C., & Tabossi, P. (1988). The comprehension of idioms. *Journal of Memory and Language, 27,* 668–683.

Chafe, W. (1970). *Meaning and the structure of language.* Chicago: University of Chicago Press.

Clark, H. H. (1978). Inferring what is meant. In J. M. Levelt & G. B. Flores d'Arcais (Eds.), *Studies in the perception of language* (pp. 295–322). Chichester, England & New York: Wiley.

Clark, H. H. (1979). Responding to indirect speech acts. *Cognitive Psychology, 11,* 430–477.

Clark, H. H. (1983). Making sense of nonce sense. In G. B. Flores d'Arcais & R. J. Jarvella (Eds.), *The process of language understanding* (pp. 297–331). Chichester, England: Wiley.

Clark, H. H., & Carlson, T. B. (1981). Context for comprehension. In J. Long & A. Baddeley (Eds.), *Attention and performance* (Vol. 9, pp. 313–330). Hillsdale, NJ: Lawrence Erlbaum Associates.

Clark, H. H., & Clark. E. (1977). *Psychology and language.* New York: Harcourt Brace Janovich.

Clark, H. H., & Gerrig, R. J. (1983). Understanding old words with new meanings. *Journal of Verbal Learning and Verbal Behavior, 22,* 591–608.

Coulmas, F. (1981). Idiomaticity as a problem of pragmatics. In H. Parret & M. Sbisa' (Eds.), *Possibilities and limitations of pragmatics* (pp. 139–151). Amsterdam, Netherlands: John Benjamins.

Cronk, B. (1990, June). *Familiarity and likeliness for figurative and literal meanings of idioms.* Poster presented at the 2nd Annual Convention of the American Psychological Association, Dallas.

Cruse, D. A. (1986). *Lexical semantics.* New York: Cambridge University Press.

Dascal, M. (1987). Defending literal meaning. *Cognitive Science, 11,* 259–281.

Davies, M. (1982/1983). Idiom and metaphor. *Proceedings of the Aristotelian Society, 83,* 67–85.

Fernando, C. (1978). Towards a definition of idiom, its nature and function. *Studies in Language,* 2(3), 313–343.

Fernando, C., & Flavell, R. H. (1981). On idiom. Critical views and perspectives. *Exter Linguistics Studies, 5,* pp. 1–S4.

Fillmore, C. J. (1978). On the organization of the semantic information in the lexicon. In D. Farkas, W. M. Jacobsen, & K. W. Todrys (Eds.), *Papers from the parasession on the lexicon* (pp. 148–173). Chicago: Chicago Linguistic Society.

Fillmore, C. J. (1979). Innocence: A second idealization for linguistics. *Proceedings of the annual meeting of the Berkeley Linguistic Society,* (pp. 63–76).

Fillmore, C. J., Kay, P., & O'Connor, M. C. (1988). Regularity and idiomaticity in grammatical constructions: The case of "let alone." *Language, 64,* 501–538.

Fraser, B. (1970). Idioms within a transformational grammar. *Foundations of Language, 6*(1), 22–42.

Fromkin, V. A. (1971). The non anomalous nature of anomalous utterances. *Language, 47,* 27–52.

Gaatone, D. (1981). Les locutions verbales: Pourquoi faire? *Revue Romane, 16,* 49–73.

Gerrig, R. J. (1989). The time course of sense creation. *Memory & Cognition, 17,* 194–207.

Gerrig, R. J., & Murphy, G. L. (1991, November). *Contextual influences on the comprehension of complex concepts.* Poster presented at the 32nd Annual Meeting of The Psychonomic Society, San Francisco.

Gibbs, R. W. (1984). Literal meaning and psychological theory. *Cognitive Psychology, 8,* 191–219.

Gibbs, R. W., & Gonzales, G. P. (1985). Syntactic frozenness in processing and remembering idioms. *Cognition, 20,* 243–259.

Gibbs, R. W., & Nayak, N. P. (1991). Why idioms mean what they do. *Journal of Experimental Psychology: General, 120,* 93–95.

Gibbs, R. W., Nayak, N. P., Bolton, J. L., & Keppel, M. (1988). Speakers' assumptions about the lexical flexibility of idioms. *Memory & Cognition, 17*(1), 58–68.

Gibbs, R. W., Nayak, N. P., & Cutting, N. (1989). Psycholinguistic studies on the syntactic behavior of idioms. *Cognitive Psychology, 21,* 100–138.

Gibbs, R. W., & O'Brien, J. E. (1990). Idioms and mental imagery: The metaphorical motivation for idiomatic meaning. *Cognition, 36,* 35–68.

Glucksberg, S. (1991). Beyond literal meanings. The psychology of allusion. *Psychological Science, 2,* 146–152.

Glucksberg, S., Gildea, P., & Bookin, M. B. (1982). On understanding non-literal speech: Can people ignore metaphors? *Journal of Verbal Learning and Verbal Behavior, 21,* 85–98.

Glucksberg, S., McGlone, M., & Cacciari, C. (in press). *Semantic productivity and idioms: Discourse processes.*

Hobbs, J. (1979). Metaphor, metaphor schemata and selective inferencing. *Technical Note No. 204 SRI International,* Menlo Park, CA.

Hockett, C. F. (1958). Idiom formation. In M. Halle et al. (Eds.), *For Roman Jakobson* (pp. 222–229). The Hague, Netherlands: Mouton.

Hoffman, R. R., & Honeck, R. P. (1980). A peacock looks at its legs: Cognitive science and figurative language. In R. P. Honeck & R. R. Hoffman (Eds.), *Cognition and figurative language* (pp. 3–24). Hillsdale, NJ: Lawrence Erlbaum Associates.

Holland, D., & Quinn, N. (Eds.). (1987). *Cultural models in language and thought.* New York: Cambridge University Press.

Honeck, R. P., & Hoffman, R. R. (1980). (Eds.). *Cognition and figurative language.* Hillsdale, NJ: Lawrence Erlbaum Associates.

Katz, J. J. (1973). Compositionality, idiomaticity and lexical substitution. In S. R. Anderson & P. Kiparsky (Eds.), *A festschrift for Morris Halle* (pp. 357–376). New York: Holt, Reinhart & Winston.

Katz, J. J., & Fodor, J. (1963). The structure of a semantic theory. *Language, 39,* 170–210.

Kreutz, R. J., & Graesser, A. C. (1991). Aspects of idiom interpretation: Comment on Nayak and Gibbs. *Journal of Experimental Psychology: General, 120*(1), 90–92.

Lakoff, G. (1986). The meanings of literal. *Metaphor and Symbolic Activity, 1*(4), 291–296.

Lakoff, G. (1987). *Women, fire and dangerous things.* Chicago: University of Chicago Press.

Lakoff, G., & Turner, M. (1989). *More than cool reason. A field guide to poetic metaphor.* Chicago: University of Chicago Press.

Lehnert, W. G. (1986). The analysis of nominal compounds. *VS, 44/45,* 155–180.

Lehrer, A. (1974). *Semantic fields and lexical structure.* Amsterdam, Netherlands: North Holland.

Levinson, S. C. (1983). *Pragmatics.* London: Cambridge University Press.

Levorato, M. C., & Cacciari, C. (1992). Children's comprehension and production of idioms: The role of context and familiarity. *Journal of Child Language, 13,* 415–433.

Makkai, A. (1972). *Idiom structure in English.* The Hague, Netherlands & Paris: Mouton.

Medin, D., & Shoben, E. (1988). Context and structure in conceptual combination. *Cognitive Psychology, 20,* 158–190.

Michiels, A. (1977). Idiomaticity in English. *Revue des Langues Vivantes, 43,* 184–199.

Mueller, R. A. G., & Gibbs, R. W. (1987). Processing idioms with multiple meanings. *Journal of Psycholinguistic Research, 16*(1), 63–81.

Murphy, G. L. (1988). Comprehending complex concepts. *Cognitive Science, 12,* 529–562.

Nagy, W. (1978). Some non-idiom larger-than-word units in the lexicon. In D. Farkas, W. M. Jacobsen, & K. W. Todrys (Eds.), *Papers from the parasession on the lexicon* (pp. 289–311). Chicago: Chicago Linguistic Society.

Nayak, N. P., & Gibbs, W. R. (1990). Conceptual knowledge in the interpretation of idioms. *Journal of Experimental Psychology: General, 119,* 115–130.

Nunberg, G. (1978). *The pragmatics of reference.* Bloomington: Indiana Linguistic Club.

Nunberg, G. (1979). The non-uniqueness of semantic solutions: Polisemy. *Linguistics and Philosophy, 3*(2), 143–184.

Pollio, H. R., Burns, B. C. (1977). The anomaly of anomaly. *Journal of Psycholinguistic Research, 6,* 247–260.

Popiel, S. J., & McRae, K. (1988). The figurative and literal uses of idioms, or all idioms are not used equally. *Journal of Psycholinguistic Research, 17*(6), 475–487.

Reagan, R. T. (1987). The syntax of English idioms: Can the dog be put on? *Journal of Psycholinguistic Research, 16*(5), 417–441.

Rumelhart, D. E. (1979). Some problems with the notion of literal meaning. In A. Ortony (Ed.), *Metaphor and thought* (pp. 78–90). New York: Cambridge University Press.

Ruwet, N. (1983). Du bon usage des expressions idiomatiques. *Recherches Linguistiques, 11,* 5–84.

Schweigert, W. A. (1986). The comprehension of familiar and less familiar idioms. *Journal of Psycholinguistic Research, 15*(1), 33–45.

Searle, J. (1975). Indirect speech acts. In P. Cole & J. L. Morgan (Eds.), *Syntax and semantics. Speech acts* (pp. 59–82). New York: Academic.

Searle, J. (1979). Metaphor. in A. Ortony (Ed.), *Metaphor and thought* (pp. 92–123). New York: Cambridge University Press.

Swinney, D. A., & Cutler, A. (1973). The access and processing of idiomatic expressions. *Journal of Verbal Learning and Verbal Behavior, 18,* 523–534.

Tabossi, P., & Cacciari, C. (1988). Context effects in the comprehension of idioms. In Cognitive Science Society (Ed.), *Proceedings of the Tenth Annual Conference of the Cognitive Science Society* (pp. 90–96). Hillsdale, NJ: Lawrence Erlbaum Associates.

Tannen, D. (1989). *Talking voices. Repetition, dialogue and imagery in conversational discourse.* Cambridge, England: Cambridge University Press.

Ullmann, S. (1962). *Semantics: An introduction to the study of meaning.* Oxford, England: Basil Blackwell & Mott.

Wasow, T., Sag, I., & Nunberg, G. (1983). Idioms: An interim report. In S. Hattori & K. Inoue (Eds.), *Proceedings of the XIIIth International Congress of Linguistics* (pp. 102–105). Tokyo: CIPL.

Winner, E. (1988). *The point of words. Children's understanding of metaphor and irony.* Cambridge, England: Cambridge University Press.

APPENDIX A

List of experimental idioms:

1. Back to the salt mines.
2. Bow and scrape.
3. Be dry behind the ears.
4. The fat is in the fire.
5. Go to bed with the chickens.
6. Have kittens.
7. Out of the hole.
8. Rap on one's knuckles.
9. Stick in one's throat.
10. Take the stump.
11. Throw oneself at someone's head.
12. Walk the chalk line.
13. Be behind the eight-ball.
14. Pay cash on the barrelhead.
15. Explode a bombshell.
16. Feel one's oats.
17. Grease the palm.
18. Lick one's boot.
19. Have one's ears pinned back.
20. Rest on one's oars.
21. Straw in the wind.
22. Take to the woods.
23. Throw one's hat in the ring.
24. Where the shoe pinches.
25. Be asleep at the switch.
26. The bottom drops out.
27. Darken one's door.
28. Fall down on the job.
29. Give her the gun.
30. Grease the wheels.
31. Make the feathers fly.
32. Polish the apple.
33. Show a clean pair of heels.

34. Take the bit in one's mouth.
35. Tell it to the marines!
36. Trip the light fantastic.
37. At one's heels.
38. Hose someone down.
39. Down the line.
40. Fan the breeze.
41. Go by the board.
42. Hard sledding.
43. The shoe is on the other foot.
44. Pour oil on troubled waters.
45. Stare in the face.
46. Take the starch out of someone.
47. Throw cold water on someone.
48. Be under the hammer.

APPENDIX B

List of experimental idioms used in their original Italian form, with their word-by-word translation and meaning:
Quasi-metaphorical idioms:

1. *Avere paura anche della propria ombra* (*be afraid of one's own shadow:* "be afraid by everything").
2. *Essere come due goccie d'acqua* (*be as two drops of water:* "be very similar").
3. *Essere noioso come una mosca* (*be as tedious as a fly:* "be tedious").
4. *Essere come cane e gatto* (*be like dog and cat:* "be enemies").
5. *Essere muto come un pesce* (*be as dumb as a fish:* "be silent and keep secrets").
6. *Essere in un mare di guai* (*be in a sea of troubles:* "be in many troubles").
7. *Dormire come un ghiro* (*sleep as a dormouse:* "sleep very soundly").
8. *Sentirsi come un animale in gabbia* (*feel as an animal in a cage:* "feel constrained, limited in one's freedom").
9. *Andare indietro come i gamberi* (*go backward as crayfishes:* "do not progress").

10. *Sentirsi come un pesce fuor d'acqua (feel as a fish outside the water:* "feel uneasy").

Transparent idioms:

1. *Costare un occhio della testa (cost an eye of the head:* "cost a lot of money").
2. *Piangere sul latte versato (cry over spilled milk).*
3. *Fare un buco nell'acqua (make a hole in the water:* "be unsuccessful").
4. *Cercare un ago in un pagliaio (look for a needle in a haystack).*
5. *Essere sulle nuvole (be among the clouds:* "be absent-minded").
6. *Affogare in un bicchier d'acqua (drown oneself in a glass of water:* "get lost over nothing").
7. *Fare ridere i polli (make chickens laugh:* "be socially unsuccessful").
8. *Chiudere bottega (close shop).*
9. *Non sapere che pesci prendere (not know which fish to catch:* "be very uncertain").
10. *Essere sulle spine (be on the thorns:* "be very anxious").

Opaque idioms:

1. *Darsi della arie (give oneself some airs:* "beast").
2. *Prendere per il naso (take someone by the nose:* "tease someone").
3. *Essere al settimo cielo (be at the seven sky:* "be in seventh heaven").
4. *Avere del sale in zucca (have some salt in the pumpkin:* "be intelligent").
5. *Rompere il ghiaccio (break the ice).*
6. *Toccare il cielo con un dito (touch the sky with a finger:* "be extremely happy").
7. *Mangiare la foglia (eat the leaf:* "understand a secret").
8. *Essere al verde (be at the green:* "be broke").
9. *Cadere dalle nuvole (fell from the clouds:* "be astounded").
10. *Tagliare la corda (cut the rope:* "escape").

3 Why Idioms Are Not Dead Metaphors

Raymond W. Gibbs, Jr.
University of California, Santa Cruz

Idioms suffer terrible indignities within linguistics, philosophy, and psychology. Compared to metaphors, which are thought to be "alive" and creative, idioms traditionally have been viewed as dead metaphors or expressions that were once metaphorical, but that have lost their metaphoricity over time. Scholars generally have assumed that idioms exist as frozen, semantic units within speakers' mental lexicons in the same way that long, perhaps ambiguous, words are represented mentally. Unlike comprehension of literal language, idioms presumably are understood through the retrieval of their stipulated meanings from the lexicon after their literal meanings have been rejected as inappropriate (Bobrow & Bell, 1973; Weinreich, 1969), or in parallel to processing of their literal meanings (Estill & Kemper, 1982; Swinney & Cutler, 1979), or directly without any analysis of their literal meanings (Gibbs, 1980, 1985, 1986).

My purpose in this chapter is to show that the dead metaphor view of idiomaticity is dead wrong. I argue that many idioms are very much alive metaphorically, and that speakers make sense of idioms because of the metaphorical knowledge that motivates these phrases' figurative meanings. This alternative conception of idiomaticity is important not only for our understanding of figurative language use and comprehension, but more significantly, because it illustrates the figurative nature of everyday thought. In the next section of this article, I discuss some of the reasons why scholars mistakenly assume that all idioms are dead metaphors. I then go on to describe why idioms are analyzable, and then I discuss empirical work that motivates why idioms mean what they do. Following this I show how metaphorical concepts influence people's understanding of idioms in different situational contexts. The concluding section presents my thoughts on the prospects for a psycholinguistic theory of idiom comprehension.

DEAD AND CONVENTIONAL METAPHORS

Scholars often treat idioms as dead metaphors because they confuse dead metaphors with conventional ones. For example, suppose we encounter a word like *gone* in an expression like *He's almost gone* to speak of a dying person. The traditional dead metaphor theory would claim that *gone* is not really metaphoric now, although it once may have been. *Gone* simply has come to have "dead" as one of its literal meanings. In a similar manner, the phrases *spill the beans* and *kick the bucket* are not viewed as metaphorical, though they at one time might have been quite figurative. *Spill the beans* simply has come to mean "reveal the secret," whereas *kick the bucket* now simply means "to die." Each of these idiomatic meanings presumably is listed as one of these phrase's literal meanings alongside their other literal meanings that are based on their compositional analyses, such as "tip over the beans" and "to strike your foot against the pail" (Green, 1989).

Because contemporary speakers have little understanding of the original metaphorical roots of phrases, such as *spill the beans* and *kick the bucket,* people are thought to comprehend idioms in the same way they know the meanings of individual words, as a matter of convention (cf. Lewis, 1969). For example, it is just an arbitrary fact of the language or a convention that we use the term *chair* to refer to *chairs* because we easily could have used any other word. This same arbitrariness of meaning is seen with idioms. Thus, it is conventional within our culture to greet someone by inquiring after the other person's health (e.g., *How are you?* or *How have you been?*), whereas in some other cultures it is conventional to greet someone by asking about the other person's gastronomic welfare (e.g., *Have you eaten?*) (Morgan, 1978). It is to some extent arbitrary whether or not a particular culture uses one form of greeting as opposed to another.

The meanings of idioms might be determined by such arbitrary conventions of usage. Thus, the expression *break a leg* to wish a performer good luck before a performance originated with the old superstition that it would be bad luck to wish someone good luck. Consequently, people started wishing their fellow actors good luck by wishing them bad luck (e.g., a broken leg). Over time the choice of *break a leg* has become rigidly fixed as a convention, one reason why similar phrases will not serve the same purpose (e.g., *fracture a tibia, I hope you break your leg*). Contemporary speakers may now understand that *break a leg* means "to wish someone luck" simply as a matter of convention without any awareness of why this phrase means what it does. It is for this reason that many idioms, such as *break a leg,* are considered to be dead metaphors.

Idioms are thought to have been metaphorical once because often we can trace back a phrase to its fully metaphorical uses in earlier stages of the language. Consider, for example, the phrase *fork in the road.* The word *fork* in this phrase has an established meaning just as it does in the phrase *knife and fork.* But we can well imagine that at an earlier time when the word regularly was applied only to the eating and cooking implement, people would use the word metaphorically in speaking of a place in which a road divided into two parts, much like the tines of an eating fork divide from its base into two or more separate directions. People do not necessarily make use of this earlier metaphorical mapping between eating implements and divided paths when understanding *fork in the road,* again suggesting that we normally interpret idioms as dead metaphors (Alston, 1964).

One problem with this analysis of *fork in the road,* as well as with many of our intuitions about the historical development of idioms, is that it happens to be wrong (Kronfeld, 1980). As it turns out, the original meaning of *fork* (from the Old English *forca* and Latin *furca*) is not the eating or cooking implement. This is a later sense, first recorded in the 15th century. The original sense seems to be the agricultural implement (pitchfork), and this developed in Middle English into a more general sense: anything that forks, bifurcates, or divides into branches. Thus, *fork in the road* is not really a dead metaphor because it did not develop as a metaphoric extension of *eating fork* or of *pitchfork* for that matter. Rather, both *fork in the road* and *kitchen fork* are specific tokens of the general sense "anything that forks," which is a concept that is very much alive in our conceptual systems.

The misinterpretation about the development of idiomatic meaning illustrates how difficult it is for speakers using language in ordinary circumstances or even professionally reflecting about it to have valid intuitions about metaphoricity in diachronic processes. The closer we feel that a particular metaphor is dead, the harder it is to reconstruct the process through which the original metaphor was understood. Our intuitions may not be sufficient to determine that some idioms were once metaphorically alive, but now exist in a petrified state in the language.

Even words that appear to be classic examples of dead metaphors have vitally alive metaphorical roots. Sweetser (1990) demonstrated that in Indo-European languages, words meaning "see" regularly acquire the meaning "know" at widely scattered times and places. The dead metaphor view of idiomaticity provides no reason for why the same kinds of meaning change recur over and over again throughout the history of Indo-European languages. But one easily can explain such changes in terms of conceptual metaphors (Sweetser, 1990). In the case of *see* words, there is a widespread and ancient conceptual metaphor that KNOWING IS SEEING, which is part of the more general MIND-AS-BODY metaphor (Sweetser, 1990). Because the metaphor exists in the conceptual systems of Indo-European speakers, the conceptual mapping between seeing and knowing defines what Sweetser called a "pathway" for semantic change, so that as new words for seeing develop, they eventually extend their meanings to knowing. The KNOWING IS SEEING metaphor, along with most other conceptual metaphors, actually motivates why the language changes in regular ways that make sense to us as speakers.

Determining whether an idiom is dead or just unconsciously conventional requires, among other things, a search for its systematic manifestation in the language as a whole and in our everyday reasoning patterns (cf. Lakoff & Johnson, 1980). There are plenty of basic conventional metaphors that are alive, certainly enough to show that what is conventional and fixed need not be dead (Lakoff & Turner, 1989). Consider some of the many conventionalized expressions about love. In English, speakers talk of love in the following ways: *He was burning with love, I am crazy about her, We are one, I was given new strength by her love, The magic is gone, Don't ever let me go, She pursued him relentlessly,* and so on. One might be tempted to argue that each phrase represents some specific metaphor that is no longer part of our everyday thinking. Many scholars assume that what makes each of these expressions seem fairly literal is that each one no longer possesses any degree of metaphoricity. But there is a great deal of systematicity in these various expressions that reflects particular metaphorical ways that we often think about love. For instance, *I was given new strength by her love, I thrive on love, He's sustained by love,* and *I'm starved for your affection* reflect the metaphorical concept of love as some kind of nutrient. The LOVE AS NUTRIENT conceptual metaphor has as its primary function the cognitive role of understanding one concept (e.g., love) in terms of another (e.g., nutrients). Conceptual metaphors arise when we try to understand difficult, complex, abstract, or less delineated concepts, such as love, in terms of familiar ideas, such as different kinds of nutrients.

Theorists have not come to terms with the fact that much of ordinary language is metaphoric because they hold the belief that all metaphors that are conventional and seemingly literal must be dead and really not metaphors any longer. This position fails to distinguish between conventional metaphors, which are part of our live conceptual system (e.g., LOVE IS A NUTRIENT), and historical metaphors that have long since died out. The mistake derives from an assumption that things in our cognition that are most alive and most active are those that are conscious. On the contrary, those that are most alive and most deeply entrenched, efficient, and powerful are those that are so automatic as to be unconscious and effortless (Lakoff & Johnson, 1980). Our understanding of love as a nutrient is active and widespread, but effortless and unconscious. Part of the evidence that conventional metaphors exist as live aspects of cognition is their occurrence in novel, poetic creations. The conceptual metaphor LOVE IS A NUTRIENT is beautifully elaborated upon in a poem titled "I drank a liquor never brewed" by Emily Dickinson:

> I drank a liquor never brewed
> From tankards scooped in pearl.
> Not all the Frankfort berries
> Yield such an alcohol.
>
> Inebriate of air am I
> And debauchee of dew,

Reeling through endless summer days
From inns of molten blue.

When landlords turn the drunken bee
Out of the foxglove's door,
When butterflies renounce their drams,
I shall but drink the more,

Till seraphs swing their snowy hats
And saints to windows run
To see a little tippler
From the manzanilla come!

These lines instantiate in spectacular ways some of the rich set of entailments that arise from the metaphorical mapping of nutrients onto love. If conceptual metaphors, such as LOVE IS A NUTRIENT, did not exist in our conceptual systems, then we could not understand novel, poetic language that makes use of them or even less creative phrases such as *I'm drunk with love*. In a similar fashion, our understanding that many idiomatic phrases have the figurative meanings they do is due to our ability to conceptualize experience in a metaphorical manner. The fact that idiomatic expressions, such as *spill the beans, blow your stack, pop the question,* and so on have highly conventionalized meanings does not in any way imply that these phrases are metaphorically dead.

IDIOMS ARE NOT NONCOMPOSITIONAL

The argument that the figurative meanings of idioms are not dead but metaphorically conventional suggests that people somehow have insight into the meanings and lexical makeup of these phrases. This idea seems contrary to any view that idioms are dead metaphors or that idioms are noncompositional because their individual word meanings do not contribute to the overall figurative meanings of these phrases (e.g., the words in *kick the bucket* do not appear to contribute to this phrase's figurative meaning of "to die"). The noncompositional nature of idioms suggests why idioms cannot undergo various syntactic operations without loss of their nonliteral meanings. For example, *John kicked the bucket* cannot be passivized into *The bucket was kicked by John* and still retain the meaning that John died (cf. Gibbs & Gonzales, 1985). Furthermore, the dead metaphor view of idioms also seems consistent with the observation that idioms appear to be lexically frozen. Thus, *John kicked the bucket* cannot be altered lexically into *John kicked the pail* without disrupting its figurative meaning. In general, the frequent use of idioms with their noncompositional, figurative meanings makes their nonliteral interpretations highly conventional and lexicalized (Heringer, 1976), one reason why idioms appear to be understood directly without analysis of their literal meanings (Gibbs, 1980, 1985, 1986; Ortony, Schallert, Reynolds, & Antos, 1978). Because the link between a idiom and its figurative meaning is conventionalized in the sense of being arbitrary, most speakers should have little ability to recognize why idioms have the meanings they do.

Part of the problem with most scholarly accounts of idiomaticity is that they limit their discussion to only a small number of idiomatic phrases. There is plenty of discussion of classic phrases such as *kick the bucket,* but less consideration has been given to the wide range of expressions that are generally idiomatic. The failure to consider the complete range of idioms results in incomplete theoretical generalizations about the nature of idiomaticity. Recent research, for instance, has shown that the individual words in many idioms systematically contribute to the overall figurative interpretations of these phrases, contrary to the noncompositional view of idioms (Fillmore, Kay, & O'Connor, 1988; Gibbs & Nayak, 1989; Lakoff, 1987; Langacker, 1986; Nunberg, 1978). For example, the results of linguistic analyses and various experimental work in psycholinguistics have shown that American speakers know that *spill the beans* is analyzable because *beans* refers to an idea or secret and *spilling* refers to the act of revealing the secret. Similarly, in the phrase *pop the question,* it is easy to discern that the noun *question* refers to a marriage proposal when the verb *pop* is used to refer to the act of uttering it. Idioms such as *pop the question, spill the beans,* and *lay down the law* are "decomposable" because each of their components obviously contributes to their overall figurative interpretations. Other idioms whose individual parts do not contribute individually to the figurative meaning of the idiom are semantically "nondecomposable" (e.g., *kick the bucket, shoot the breeze*) because people experience difficulty in breaking these phrases into their component parts (Gibbs & Nayak, 1989; Nunberg, 1978). A third group of idioms was viewed as decomposable, but abnormally so because their individual components have a different relationship to their idiomatic referents than do "normally" decomposable idioms. For example, we can identify the figurative referent in the idiom *carry a torch* only by virtue of our knowledge of torches as conventional metaphors for descriptions of warm feelings. Similarly, we understand the hitting of certain buttons in *hit the panic button* as a conventional metaphor for how we act in extreme circumstances. Each of these abnormally decomposable idioms differs from normally decomposable idioms, such as *button your lips,* whose components have a more direct relation to their figurative referents.

The analyzability of an idiom does not depend on that word string being literally well formed (Gibbs & Nayak, 1989). For instance, *pop the question* is literally anomalous but semantically decomposable. All that matters for an idiom to be viewed as decomposable is for its parts to have meanings, either literal or figurative, that contribute independently to the phrase's overall figurative interpretation. The analyzability of an idiom is really a matter of degree depending on the salience of its individual parts. Many idiomatic expressions exhibit intermediate degrees of analyzability. For instance, many speakers view the phrase *play with fire* as being less decomposable than *pop the question* because the meaning that *play* contributes to *play with fire* is not as salient as the meaning that *pop* contributes to *pop the question*. The more salient some word is within an idiom, the more likely that the word shares the same *semantic field* as does its idiomatic referent. Thus, when speakers judge that the idiom *let off steam* is analyzable or decomposable, they essentially are finding some relationship between the components *let off* and *steam* with their figurative referents "release" and "anger." This relationship between an idiom's words and their figurative referents is not arbitrary, but is based on active metaphorical mappings between different source and target domains that structure much of our experience. For example, the noun *steam* and the concept of anger are part of the same semantic field because anger is understood metaphorically, in part, in terms of heat and internal pressure (Gibbs & O'Brien, 1990; Lakoff, 1987; Lakoff & Johnson, 1980). This metaphorical motivation for idioms is discussed further later.

People's intuitions about the analyzability of idioms play an important role in determining these phrases' syntactic productivity (Gibbs & Nayak, 1989), lexical flexibility (Gibbs, Nayak, Bolton, & Keppel, 1989), ease of comprehension (Gibbs, Nayak, & Cutting, 1989), and ease of learning (Gibbs, 1987, 1991). For example, most linguistic discussion on the syntactic deficiencies of idioms provides little motivation as to why some idioms are productive and others not. Syntactically productive idioms are those that retain their figurative meanings when seen in a variety of syntactic constructions, whereas unproductive idioms are "frozen" in that they lose their figurative interpretations when syntactically altered.

The hypothesis examined in several recent studies was that people's intuitions about the syntactic versatility of idioms are affected by the analyzability or decomposability of these figurative phrases (Gibbs & Nayak, 1989). Results from a variety of experiments demonstrated that normally decomposable idioms (e.g., *pop the question*) were found to be much more syntactically productive than semantically nondecomposable idioms (e.g., *chew the fat*). Abnormally decomposable idioms were not found to be syntactically productive because each part does not by itself refer to some component of the idiomatic referent, but only to some metaphorical relation between the individual part and the referent. Thus, readers rarely accept a passivized construction such as *A torch for Sally was carried by Jim* as having a recognizable idiomatic meaning. These findings suggest that the syntactic versatility of idioms is not an arbitrary phenomenon, perhaps due to unknown historical reasons (Cutler, 1982), but can be explained at least partially in terms of an idiom's semantic analyzability. In a similar manner, the lexical flexibility of some idioms can be explained in terms of semantic analyzability (Gibbs, Nayak, Bolton, & Keppel, 1989). Thus, the decomposable phrase *pop the question* was found to better retain its figurative meaning when changed lexically (e.g., into either *burst the question* or *pop the request*) than did the nondecomposable phrase *kick the bucket* when lexically altered (e.g., into *boot the bucket* or *kick the pail*).

The analyzability of idioms also plays an important role in their immediate, "on-line" interpretations. Because the individual components in decomposable idioms contribute systematically to the figurative meanings of these phrases, people may process idioms in a compositional manner where the semantic representations of each component are accessed and combined according to the syntactical rules of the language. For example, the phrases *lay down* and *the law* serve as cues to the retrieval of the figurative meaning for *lay down the law* because each of these components has an independent meaning contributing to the entire idiom's nonliteral interpretation. On the other hand, a strict compositional analysis of semantically nondecomposable idioms (e.g., *kick the bucket, chew the fat, go for broke*) provides little information about the figurative meanings of these expressions. Consequently, readers or listeners subsequently might have to recover the directly stipulated meanings of nondecomposable phrases from the mental lexicon, a process that requires additional processing effort.

A series of reading-time studies provided some support for these hypotheses (Gibbs, Nayak, & Cutting, 1989). The results of these experiments showed that people took significantly less time to process decomposable idioms than to read the nondecomposable expressions. Both normally and abnormally decomposable phrases took less time to process than their respective literal, control phrases (e.g., *pop the question* versus *ask the question*), but nondecomposable idioms actually took longer to process than their respective literal controls (e.g., *chew the fat* versus *cook the fat*). These data suggest that people attempt to do some compositional analysis when understanding idiomatic phrases. When an idiom is decomposable readers can assign independent meanings to its individual parts and quickly will recognize how these meaningful parts combine to form the overall figurative interpretation of the phrase. These processing differences in the comprehension of decomposable and nondecomposable idioms do not imply that readers have no directly stipulated figurative meanings for decomposable idioms. Instead, it appears that the analyzability of decomposable idioms provides a very useful source of information that facilitates people's recognition that an idiomatic word string is meant to have a figurative interpretation. One explanation for the commonly observed finding that idioms are processed more quickly than literal phrases is that these studies primarily employ idioms that are more analyzable than nondecomposable (cf. Gibbs, Nayak, & Cutting, 1989).

One of the most debated issues in the research on idiom comprehension concerns the role that literal meaning plays in people's understanding of these figurative phrases. Previous research has demonstrated that readers do not need to analyze first the literal meaning of an entire idiom phrase before determining its nonliteral interpretation (Gibbs, 1980, 1985, 1986; Gibbs & Gonzales, 1985; Ortony et al., 1978; Swinney & Cutler, 1979). However, people may process the literal meanings of the individual words simultaneously to determining the overall figurative interpretation of these phrases (Cacciari & Tabossi, 1988). One might assume that the compositional analysis that people perform on idioms is based on the literal meanings of their individual words. Decomposable idioms might be easier to comprehend than nondecomposable phrases because the literal meanings of decomposable expressions directly contribute to these phrases' figurative meanings. On the other hand, processing the literal meanings of semantically nondecomposable idioms should be uninformative and might interfere with people's comprehension of these phrases.

This possibility about the role of literal meaning in idiom comprehension raises two significant issues. First, there is the problem of specifying the literal meanings of the individual words in idioms. Consider the idiomatic phrase *over my dead body*. What are the literal meanings of the individual words in this expression? The preposition *over* has over 100 related senses that are motivated by different metaphoric and metonymic principles (Brugman & Lakoff, 1989). It is unclear which of these meanings is literal, nor is it clear which of these meanings actually is activated when the phrase *over my dead body* has been understood. Most psycholinguistic models that assume that the literal meanings of words are activated during idiom processing fail to specify exactly what these meanings are or how such meanings are used in determining the figurative interpretations of idioms. Without some specification of what literal meaning is in general, or what constitutes the literal meanings of individual words, it seems premature to posit that people automatically process idioms by analyzing the literal meanings of its individual words. Again, I argue that people recognize that most idioms are at least partially compositional because their individual components have independent meanings. But this does not imply that these individual word meanings are literal or context-free. Instead, people at least appear to recognize that the individual parts of idioms have some figurative meanings that contribute to the overall nonliteral interpretations of idiomatic phrases.

A second issue regarding literal meaning and idiom processing concerns the fact that many idioms are literally ill-formed or opaque, such as *by and large, in the know, crack a joke,* and *promise the moon*. Literally ill-formed idioms violate selectional restriction rules. For instance, the idiom *swallow his pride* is literally ill-formed or anomalous because it violates the selection restriction that the verb *swallow* only occurs in sentences with noun phrases referring to some physical object. Most linguistic analyses assume that expressions that do not possess well-defined literal meanings must receive their interpretations by stipulation in the lexicon (Dowty, Wall, & Peters, 1982). But many ill-formed idioms are normally decomposable (e.g., *pop the question, perish the thought*), whereas many semantically nondecomposable idioms are literally well formed (e.g., *chew the fat, hit the sauce, give the sack*). If people perform a compositional analysis on an idiom based on its entire literal meaning, then people should process literally well-formed idioms faster than they do ill-formed expressions.

However, the data from Gibbs, Nayak, and Cutting (1989) clearly demonstrate that this is not the case. Participants in these studies actually took less time to understand ill-formed idioms than they did literally well-formed expressions. It appears that understanding idioms only requires that people assign figurative meanings to the parts of idioms; there is no need to analyze automatically each expression according to its entire literal interpretation. This seems especially likely given people's extreme familiarity with many idiomatic expressions. Thus people ordinarily attempt to perform some sort of compositional analysis, although not necessarily a literal analysis, when comprehending idiom phrases to attach meanings to these phrases' specific parts (Gibbs, Nayak, & Cutting, 1989). It is important to restate this point. The figurative meanings of idioms may be based on their internal compositional semantics even though this does not mean that idiomatic meaning is based on what scholars normally assume is literal meaning. Contrary to the popular conception that the literal meaning of a phrase or sentence is its compositional meaning, many phrases have compositional meanings that are based on the figurative meanings of their individual parts.

WHY IDIOMS MEAN WHAT THEY DO

There is substantial experimental evidence, then, that the meanings of idioms can be motivated partially in that speakers recognize some, often figurative, relationship between the words in idioms and their overall figurative interpretations. Earlier I suggested that the words in analyzable idioms share the same semantic field as do their figurative referents. The parts of idioms refer to different knowledge domains, many of which are conceptualized in terms of metaphor. People may recognize tacitly that the metaphorical mapping of information between two conceptual domains actually motivates why idioms mean what they do. For example, the idiom *John spilled the beans* maps our knowledge of someone tipping over a container of beans to a person revealing some previously hidden secret. English speakers understand *spill the beans* to mean "reveal the secret" because there are underlying conceptual metaphors, such as the MIND IS A CONTAINER and IDEAS ARE PHYSICAL ENTITIES, that structure their conceptions of minds, secrets, and disclosure (Lakoff & Johnson, 1980). Even though the existence of these conceptual metaphors does not predict that certain idioms or conventional expressions must appear in the language, the presence of these independent conceptual metaphors by which we make sense of experience provides a partial motivation for why specific phrases (e.g., *spill the beans*) are used to refer to particular events (e.g., the revealing of secrets).

Linguistic analyses of idioms provide some grounds for believing that idioms do not exist as separate semantic units within the lexicon, but actually reflect coherent systems of metaphorical concepts. For example, the idiomatic phrases *blow your stack, flip your lid, hit the ceiling, get hot under the collar, lose your cool,* and *get steamed up* appear to be motivated by the conceptual metaphor ANGER IS HEATED FLUID IN A CONTAINER, which is one of the small set of conceptual mappings between different source and target domain that form part of our conceptualization for anger. But is there any evidence that metaphors such as ANGER IS HEATED FLUID IN A CONTAINER are really conceptual and not, more simply, generalizations of linguistic meaning? Much of my work in the past few years has been devoted to exploring the possibility that idioms make sense in the ways that they do precisely because they are motivated by conceptual knowledge that is metaphorical. Thus, idioms like *blow your stack* and *flip your lid* make sense to us as referring to the idea of getting very angry in a way that phrases like *run to the store* or *mow the lawn* would not. The dead metaphor view suggests no reason for why some idioms seem so appropriate in having the meanings they do. After all, if the meaning of a phrase is truly dead, then people should not believe that any particular ways of talking about something like anger, such as *hit the ceiling* or *blow your stack,* seem so reasonable in a way that *mow your lawn* or *go to the store* do not.

One way to uncover speakers' tacit knowledge of the metaphorical basis for idioms is through a detailed examination of speakers' mental images for idioms (Gibbs & O'Brien, 1990; Lakoff, 1987). Consider the idiom *spill the beans.* Try to form a mental image for this phrase and then ask yourself the following questions: Where are the beans before they are spilled? How big is the container? Are the beans cooked or uncooked? Is the spilling accidental or intentional? Where are the beans once they have been spilled? Are the beans in a nice, neat pile? Where are the beans supposed to be? After the beans are spilled, are they easy to retrieve?

Most people have definite responses to these questions about their mental images for idioms. They generally say that the beans were in some pot that is about the size of a person's head, the beans are uncooked, the spilling of the beans is accidental, the spilled beans are all over a floor and are difficult to retrieve. This consistency in people's intuitions about their mental images is quite puzzling if one assumes that the meanings of idioms are determined arbitrarily. Gibbs and O'Brien (1990) used people's descriptions about their mental images for idioms as a way of discovering some of the metaphorical knowledge that motivates the meanings of idiomatic phrases. We examined people's mental images for groups of idioms with similar figurative meanings, such as about revelation (e.g., *spill the beans, let the cat out of the bag, blow the lid off*), anger (e.g., *blow your stack, hit the ceiling, flip your lid*), insanity (e.g., *go off your rocker, lose your marbles, bounce off the walls*), secretiveness (e.g., *keep it under your hat, button your lips, keep in the dark*), and exerting control (e.g., *crack the whip, lay down the law, call the shots*). Participants were asked to describe their mental images for these idioms and to answer questions about the causes, intentionality, and manner of actions in their mental images for these phrases.

We expected a high degree of consistency in participants' descriptions of their mental images for idioms with similar meanings because of the constraints conceptual metaphors (e.g., the MIND IS A CONTAINER, IDEAS ARE PHYSICAL ENTITIES, and ANGER IS HEAT) impose on the links between idiomatic phrases and their nonliteral meanings. If people's tacit knowledge of idioms is not structured by different conceptual metaphors, there should be little consistency in participants' responses to questions about the causes and consequences of actions within their mental images of idioms with similar nonliteral interpretations.

People had little difficulty with the mental imagery task. Most of the report's participants gave for their mental images of idioms contained rich details. For instance, one individual reported that her mental image for *call the shots* was as follows: "An army sergeant standing in front of a line of soldiers all of whom are faced in the same direction and when the sergeant shouts very loudly the soldiers all commence firing their rifles." Overall, participants' descriptions of their mental images were remarkably consistent for different idioms with similar figurative meanings. Across the five groups of idioms we studied, 75% of participants' mental images for the different idioms described similar general images. These general schemas for people's images were not simply representative of the idioms' figurative meanings, but captured more specific aspects of the kinesthetic events with the images. For example, the anger idioms such as *flip your lid* and *hit the ceiling* all refer to the concept of "getting angry," but participants specifically imagined for these phrases some force causing a container to release pressure in a violent manner. There is nothing in the surface forms of these different idioms to tightly constrain the images participants reported. After all, lids can be flipped and ceilings can be hit in a wide variety of ways, caused by many different circumstances. But our participants' protocols revealed little variation in the general events that took place in their images for idioms with similar meanings.

Participants' responses to the questions about the causes and consequences of the actions described in their images were also highly consistent (over 88% when averaged across both the different probe questions and the five groups of idioms). Consider the most frequent responses to the probe questions for the anger idioms (e.g., *blow your stack, flip your lid, hit the ceiling*). When imagining anger idioms, people reported that pressure (i.e., stress or frustration) causes the action, that one has little control over the pressure once it builds, its violent release is done unintentionally (e.g., the blowing of the stack), and that once the release has taken place (i.e., once the ceiling has been hit, the lid flipped, the stack blown), it is difficult to reverse the action.

Why are people so consistent in their intuitions about the causes and consequences of the actions described in their mental images for idioms? We argued that people are limited in the kinds of images they create for idioms because of very specific conceptual knowledge that is mostly metaphorical. For example, the participants' images for the anger idioms are based on folk conceptions of certain physical events. For anger, people use their knowledge about the behavior of heated fluid or vapor building up and escaping from containers (ones that our participants most frequently reported to be the size of a person's head). Thus, people's metaphorical mapping of knowledge from a source domain (e.g., heated fluid in a container) onto target domains (e.g., the anger emotion) helps them conceptualize in more concrete terms what is understood about the target domain of anger. Various specific entailments result from these general metaphorical mappings, ones that provide specific insight into the causes, intentionality, manner, and consequences of the activities described by stacks blowing, lids flipping, and ceilings being hit. Our argument is that the metaphorical ways in which we partially conceptualize experiences, such as anger, actually provide part of the motivation for why people have consistent mental images, and specific knowledge about these images, for idioms with similar figurative meanings.

Of course, any consistency in people's mental images for idioms with similar figurative meanings might be due not to the constraining influence of conceptual metaphors, but, more simply, to the very fact that these phrases share near identical meanings. Thus, people are constrained in their mental images for *blow your stack, flip your lid, hit the ceiling,* and so on because they all mean "to get very angry," not because they are motivated by similar conceptual metaphors. The figurative meaning "to get angry" by itself does not convey much information about the causes and consequences of the actions described in people's mental images so we did not feel this alternative hypothesis carried much weight. A set of follow-up studies showed that knowing the figurative meaning of an idiom (e.g., "getting angry") does not by itself account for why people have such systematic knowledge of their images of idioms (e.g., *blow your stack* or *flip your lid*). Asking people to imagine "to get very angry" produces, not surprisingly, a wide variety of mental images. Most importantly, though, our participants showed very little consistency in their responses to the questions regarding causation, intentionality, manner, and consequences about the actions in their mental images for paraphrases of the idioms. Furthermore, people were much less consistent in their mental images for literal phrases (e.g., *blow your tire*) than for idioms (e.g., *blow your stack*) because they do not possess the same degree of conceptual knowledge about their images for literal phrases as they do for idiomatic expressions.

The results of these mental imagery studies support the idea that the figurative meanings of idioms are motivated by various conceptual metaphors that exist independently as part of our conceptual system. Traditional theories of idiomaticity have no way of accounting for these imagery findings because they assume that the meanings of idioms arise from metaphors that are now dead.

CONCEPTUAL METAPHOR AND IDIOM
INTERPRETATION

Most of our concepts referring to ideas about anger, love, insanity, and revelation are not structured by a single conceptual metaphor, but are organized partially by a variety of metaphorical mappings. For example, our conceptualization of love is structured by various conceptual metaphors, such as LOVE IS A JOURNEY, LOVE IS A NUTRIENT, and LOVE IS WAR, each of which gives rise to different entailments about our love experiences (Kovecses, 1986). Similarly, anger is not just understood in terms of a heated fluid in a container, but also can be conceptualized in terms of ANGER IS ANIMAL BEHAVIOR and ANGER IS INSANITY. The mere existence of these independent conceptual mappings does not predict necessarily that certain idioms or conventional expression should exist as part of the language. But we can easily find examples of idioms that appear to be motivated by different conceptual metaphors. For instance, the idioms *blow your stack* and *bite your head off* both express extreme degrees of anger. However, *bite your head off* makes sense because people can link the lexical items in this phrase to the conceptual metaphor ANGRY BEHAVIOR IS ANIMAL BEHAVIOR. An animal jumping down a victim's throat is similar to someone shouting angrily. On the other hand, people understand the figurative meaning of *blow your stack* through the conceptual metaphor ANGER IS HEATED FLUID IN A CONTAINER where a person shouting angrily has the same explosive effect as does the top of a container blowing open under pressure.

Psycholinguistic research has shown that people's knowledge of the metaphorical links between different source and target domains provides the basis for the appropriate use and interpretation of idioms in particular discourse situations (Nayak & Gibbs, 1990). Participants in one study were asked to read stories that reflected different conceptual metaphors about a particular emotion concept. One pair of stories is presented here, each of which conceptualizes anger in different ways. The first is as follows:

Mary was very tense about this evening's dinner party.
The fact that Bob had not come home to help was making her
fume. She was getting hotter with every passing minute.
Dinner would not be ready before the guests arrived.
As it got close to five o'clock the pressure was really
building up. Mary's tolerance was reaching its limits.
When Bob strolled at ten minutes to five whistling and
smiling, Mary
   blew her stack
   bit his head off

This story was written to prime the metaphorical mapping ANGER IS HEAT-ED FLUID IN A CONTAINER by depicting Mary's increasing anger in terms of increasing pressure and heat. The use of phrases such as *very tense, making her fume, getting hotter, the pressure was really building up,* and *reaching its limits* are specific references to this mapping. Another story primed a different conceptual metaphor, ANGER IS ANIMAL BEHAVIOR:

> Mary was getting very grouchy about this evening's dinner party.
> She prowled around the house waiting for Bob to come home to help.
> She was growling under her breath about Bob's lateness.
> Her mood was becoming more savage with every passing minute.
> As it got closer to five o'clock Mary was ferociously angry with Bob.
> When Bob strolled in at 4:30 whistling and smiling, Mary
>> *bit his head off*
>> *blew her stack*

Participants in this study were asked to read each story and rate the appropriateness of each final phrase given its preceding story context. The results indicated that readers' judgments about the appropriateness of an idiom in context are influenced by the coherence between the metaphorical information depicted in a discourse situation and the conceptual metaphor reflected in the lexical makeup of an idiom. Thus, participants gave higher appropriateness ratings to *blew her stack* in a story that described the woman's anger as being like heated fluid in a container whereas *bit his head off* was seen as more appropriate in a story that described the woman's anger in terms of a ferocious animal. Even though two idioms may have highly similar figurative meanings, this does not imply that their meanings are identical because of the different conceptual metaphors that motivate their figurative interpretations. The phrase *bite his head off* implies that the angry person is demonstrating her anger in a more deliberate, intentional manner than is the case with the phrase *blow her stack*. This conclusion about differences in the meanings of similar idioms is significant because it provides some motivation for why some idioms seem especially appropriate to use in some situations but not others. The traditional dead metaphor view provides no explanation for the context-sensitivity of idioms other than to suggest that the use of idioms is an arbitrary matter of convention. The conceptual view of idiomaticity suggested here offers a motivated reason for why idioms mean what they do and are used in specific kinds of discourse situations.

Another consequence of the conceptual view of idiomaticity is that idioms should not be identical in meaning to their literal paraphrases. Contrary to the dead metaphor view, which assumes that the meanings of idioms are arbitrary for speakers and can be represented mostly in short phrases or even single words (Palmer, 1981), idioms have rather complex interpretations. For example, phrases such as *spill the beans* can not be paraphrased simply as meaning "to reveal a secret" in the way that most idioms dictionaries do (cf. Boatner, Gates, & Makkai, 1975; Long & Summers, 1979). The mapping of source domains such as containers onto minds results in very specific entailments about the act of revealing a secret. Thus, the act of revealing a secret usually is seen as being caused by some internal pressure within the mind of the revealer, the action is thought to be done unintentionally, and the action is judged as being performed in a forceful manner (Gibbs & O'Brien, 1990). One interesting possibility is that people actually draw these inferences about the act of revealing a secret each time they comprehend the idiom phrase *spill the beans*. However, people might be less likely to draw such inferences about causation, intentionality, and manner when comprehending literal paraphrases of idioms, such as *reveal the secret*. Literal phrases, such as *reveal the secret*, are not motivated by the same set of conceptual metaphors as are specific idioms such as *spill the beans*. For this reason, people do not view the meanings of *spill the beans* and *reveal the secret* as equivalent despite their apparent similarity.

I have recently tested this hypothesis about the nonequivalence of idioms and their literal paraphrases in a series of experiments (Gibbs, 1990, 1992). Participants read stories that described different human events, such as revealing secrets, getting angry, losing control of themselves, and so on. These stores contained information about the causes of the event, the intentionality of the action performed by each story's protagonist, and the manner in which the actions were performed. Some stories depicted this information in a manner that was consistent with the entailments of particular conceptual metaphors (the no-violation contexts). Presented next is an example of a no-violation story:

John heard some interesting gossip about Paul and Mary.
Even though Paul and Mary were married to other people,
they had recently started having a passionate affair.
John was very surprised when he found out about the affair.
So John called up another friend who knew Paul and Mary
and accidentally blurted out what he knew.
The friend commented to John that he had really
   spilled the beans.
      (or)
   revealed the secret.

Note that each of the entailments about the cause, intentionality, and manner in which a secret is revealed is stated explicitly and correctly in this story. Each of these entailments arises from the conceptual metaphors the MIND IS A CONTAINER and IDEAS ARE PHYSICAL ENTITIES (Gibbs & O'Brien, 1990).

Now consider a story from one of the violation conditions in which one of the original entailments (Intentionality) has been altered:

John heard some interesting gossip about Paul and Mary.
Even though Paul and Mary were married to other people,
they had recently started having a passionate affair.
John was very surprised when he found out about the affair.
John fully intended never to say a word to anyone.
One day he was talking to someone who knew Paul and Mary,
when John purposefully said something about what he knew.
The friend commented to John that he had really
    spilled the beans.
      (or)
    revealed the secret.

The empirical question was whether people understand idioms and their literal paraphrases in different ways depending on whether a story context is consistent or inconsistent with the specific entailments of the conceptual metaphors that motivate the meanings of those idioms. In the first study, participants simply rated the appropriateness of each final phrase given the preceding story. A second experiment measured the speed with which idioms and their paraphrases were processed in different contexts.

The results showed that the participants rated the idioms (e.g., *spill the beans*) and their literal paraphrases (e.g., *reveal the secret*) as being equally appropriate in the no-violation story contexts. However, the participants judged idioms as being less appropriate in the different violation conditions than they did literal paraphrases in these same contexts. Literal paraphrases are not constrained by conceptual metaphors in the way idioms are limited. Consequently, phrases such as *reveal the secret* were seen as appropriate in most story contexts regardless of the cause of the revelation, the intentionality of the act, or the manner in which it is done. This was not the case for *spill the beans*. Data from the reading-time experiment showed that idioms took longer to process when they were read at the end of violation contexts than in the no-violation stories, whereas the literal paraphrases were roughly as easy to process in the violation stories as in the no-violation conditions.

These findings demonstrate that idioms are not equivalent in meaning to their simple literal paraphrases. Idiomatic phrases have very specific figurative meanings that result from the entailments of the underlying conceptual metaphors that motivate their figurative interpretations. Literal phrases, such as *reveal the secret,* are not motivated by the same conceptual metaphors and consequently are less specific in meaning. In general, these data provide further evidence against the idea that idioms are dead metaphors and equivalent in meaning to their putative, literal paraphrases.

CONCLUSION

The dead metaphor view has dominated the study of idiomaticity in linguistics, philosophy, and psycholinguistics. By assuming that idioms are simple dead metaphors, figurative language researchers have had reason to neglect idioms in favor of other tropes, such as metaphor, that appear to be more creative or alive. But research in the cognitive sciences over the past few years clearly has demonstrated the fatal difficulties with the dead metaphor view of idiomaticity. Many idioms are not simple dead metaphors that are noncompositional in meaning. Nor are the figurative meanings of many idioms arbitrarily stipulated and listed as simple, literal paraphrases in the mental lexicon. Instead, idioms are partially compositional and their rich figurative meanings are motivated by the metaphorical knowledge people possess of the domains to which idioms refer. These metaphorical mappings between source and target domain knowledge often are conventionalized in the sense that they are so much a part of our everyday cognition as to be unconscious and automatic. Such figurative mappings provide part of the link between the lexical makeup of idioms and their figurative meanings such that many idioms make sense in having the meanings they do. Furthermore, the context-sensitive use and interpretation of idioms, at least, is due primarily to the recognition that many idioms are motivated by different metaphorical mappings that exist independently in our conceptual systems.

The conceptual view of idioms presented here offers a reasonable alternative to the traditional, dead metaphor view of idiomaticity. It is important to realize, however, that the dead metaphor and conceptual views of idiomaticity should not be seen as competing theories. Many idiomatic phrases very well could be dead or have meanings that are determined arbitrarily as matters of convention. At the same time, there exist a wide range of idioms that are extragrammatical, such as *by and large, all of a sudden,* and *take advantage of,* that resist a conceptual analysis. My argument, though, is that many, perhaps thousands of idioms profitably can be understood as being motivated partially by figurative schemes of thought, ones that are very much alive and part of our everyday thinking and reasoning. The scholarly study of idioms no longer can afford to view these phrases as a homogeneous class of linguistic items that differ from literal language, that differ from metaphor, and that resist standard grammatical analysis. Idiomatic language is remarkably complex and each phrase demands its own analysis in terms of its syntactic, semantic, pragmatic, and conceptual properties.

Previous experimental work on idiom comprehension in psycholinguistics has tended to emphasize issues such as whether literal meanings contribute to idiom processing, whether context facilitates recognition of idiomatic meanings, and whether the frequency or familiarity of idioms plays significant roles in how these phrases are learned and understood. The theoretical models that have been examined in these earlier empirical studies generally assume that there is, or should be, a single answer to the question of how idioms are understood. I believe that this assumption is seriously wrong. As we learn more about the complexity of idiomatic phrases, it seems increasingly likely that no single theory or model can account for all kinds of idioms and all kinds of discourse situations (both conversational and literary). Instead, different sources of linguistic and nonlinguistic information are evaluated during processing that contribute to people's immediate understanding of what speakers mean when they use idiomatic phrases. This idea suggests, for example, that listeners do not always instantiate specific conceptual metaphors that motivate an idiom's meaning when understanding some phrase in conversation. Similarly, people may not always analyze the literal word meanings of idioms during comprehension. There will be occasions when people do tap into an idiom's conceptual foundation. Readers also might process the individual word meanings when they attempt to comprehend certain kinds of idioms. But it is a mistake to assume that some types of analyses will occur each and every time someone encounters an idiomatic expression. The complexity of idioms leaves us, at present, with no other alternative than to embrace the plurality of theories that have been proposed to account for different aspects of idiomatic language.

The study of idioms is significant not only in terms of understanding how people learn and comprehend figurative language, but also because idiomaticity reveals some dramatic insights into the relationship of language and thought. The prevailing view of mind holds that thought and language are inherently literal, and that both can be characterized in objective terms. My work on idiomaticity advances the idea that the traditional view of mind is mistaken because human cognition is shaped fundamentally by various processes of figuration. It seems clear now that idioms do not represent the graveyard of metaphorical thought. Instead, our use and understanding of idioms attests to the continuous process of poetic thinking.

ACKNOWLEDGMENTS

Preparation of this chapter was supported by Grant MH42980 from the National Institute of Mental Health and by a Faculty Research Grant from the University of California, Santa Cruz.

REFERENCES

Alston, W. (1964). *The philosophy of language.* Englewood Cliffs, NJ: Prentice-Hall.
Boatner, M., Gates, J., & Makkai, A. (1975). *A dictionary of American idioms.* New York: Baron's Educational Series.
Bobrow, S., & Bell, S. (1973). On catching on to idiomatic expressions. *Memory & Cognition, 1,* 343–346.

Brugman, C., & Lakoff, G. (1989). Cognitive topology and lexical networks. In G. Cottrell, S. Small, & M. K. Tanenhaus (Eds.), *Lexical ambiguity resolution* (pp. 477–508). Stanford, CA: Morgan.

Cacciari, C., & Tabossi, P. (1988). The comprehension of idioms. *Journal of Memory and Language, 27,* 668–683.

Cutler, A. (1982). Idioms: The older the colder. *Linguistic Inquiry, 13,* 317–320.

Dowty, D., Wall, R., & Peters, S. (1982). *Introduction to Montague grammar.* Dordrecht, Netherlands: Reidel.

Estill, R., & Kemper, S. (1982). Interpreting idioms. *Journal of Psycholinguistic Research, 9,* 559–568.

Fillmore, C., Kay, P., & O'Connor, M. (1988). Regularity and idiomaticity in grammatical constructions: The case of *let alone. Language, 64,* 501–538.

Gibbs, R. (1980). Spilling the beans on understanding and memory for idioms in conversation. *Memory & Cognition, 8,* 449–456.

Gibbs, R. (1985). On the process of understanding idioms. *Journal of Psycholinguistic Research, 14,* 465–472.

Gibbs, R. (1986). Skating on thin ice: Literal meaning and understanding idioms in conversation. *Discourse Processes, 9,* 17–30.

Gibbs, R. (1987). Linguistic factors in children's understanding of idioms. *Journal of Child Language, 14,* 569–586.

Gibbs, R. (1990). Psycholinguistic studies on the conceptual basis of idiomaticity. *Cognitive Linguistics, 1,* 417–451.

Gibbs, R. (1991). Semantic analyzability in children's understanding of idioms. *Journal of Speech and Hearing Research, 34,* 613–620.

Gibbs, R. (1992). *What do idioms really mean? Journal of Memory and Language, 31,* 385–406.

Gibbs, R., & Gonzales, G. (1985). Syntactic frozenness in processing and remembering idioms. *Cognition, 20,* 243–259.

Gibbs, R., & Nayak, N. (1989). Psycholinguistic studies on the syntactic behavior of idioms. *Cognitive Psychology, 21,* 100–138.

Gibbs, R., Nayak, N., Bolton, J., & Keppel, M. (1989). Speakers' assumptions about the lexical flexibility of idioms. *Memory & Cognition, 17,* 58–68.

Gibbs, R., Nayak, N., & Cutting, C. (1989). How to kick the bucket and not decompose: Analyzability and idiom processing. *Journal of Memory and Language, 28,* 576–593.

Gibbs, R., & O'Brien, J. (1990). Idioms and mental imagery: The metaphorical motivation for idiomatic meaning. *Cognition, 36,* 35–68.

Green, G. (1989). *Pragmatics and natural language understanding.* Hillsdale, NJ: Lawrence Erlbaum Associates.

Heringer, J. (1976). Idioms and lexicalization in English. In M. Shibtani (Ed.), Syntax or semantics: The grammar of causative constructions (Vol. 6, pp. 205–216). New York: Academic Press.

Kovecses, Z. (1986). *Metaphors of anger, pride, and love.* Amsterdam, Netherlands: John Benjamins.

Kronfeld, X. (1980). Novel and conventional metaphors: A matter of methodology. *Poetics Today, 2,* 13–24.

Lakoff, G. (1987). *Women, fire, and dangerous things.* Chicago: Chicago University Press.

Lakoff, G., & Johnson, M. (1980). *Metaphors we live by.* Chicago: Chicago University Press.

Lakoff, G., & Turner, M. (1989). *More than cool reason: A field guide to poetic metaphor.* Chicago: University of Chicago Press.

Langacker, R. (1986). *Foundations of cognitive grammar* (Vol. 1). Stanford, CA: Stanford University Press.

Lewis, D. (1969). *Convention.* Cambridge, MA: Harvard University Press.

Long, T., & Summers, D. (1979). *Longman dictionary of English idioms.* London: Longman.

Morgan, J. L. (1978). Two types of convention in indirect speech acts. In P. Cole (Ed.), *Syntax and semantics: Vol. 9. Pragmatics* (pp. 261–280). New York: Academic.

Nayak, N., & Gibbs, R. (1990). Conceptual knowledge in the interpretation of idioms. *Journal of Experimental Psychology: General, 119,* 315–330.

Nunberg, G. (1978). *The pragmatics of reference.* Bloomington: Indiana University Linguistics Club.

Ortony, A., Schallert, D., Reynolds, R., & Antos, S. (1978). Interpretating metaphors and idioms: Some effects of context on comprehension. *Journal of Verbal Learning and Verbal Behavior, 17,* 465–477.

Palmer, F. (1981). *Semantics,* Cambridge, England: Cambridge University Press.

Sweetser, E. (1990). *Semantic structure and semantic change: A cognitive semantic linguistic study of modality, perception, speech acts, and logical relations.* Cambridge, MA: Cambridge University Press.

Swinney, D., & Cutler, A. (1979). The access and processing of idiomatic expressions. *Journal of Verbal Learning and Verbal Behavior, 18,* 523–534.

Weinreich, U. (1969). Problems in the analysis of idioms. In J. Puhvel (Ed.), *Substance and structure of language* (pp. 23–81). Los Angeles: University of California Press.

4 The Comprehension and Semantic Interpretation of Idioms

Giovanni B. Flores d'Arcais
Max-Planck-Institute for Psycholinguistics, Nijmegen, The Netherlands

This chapter deals with the comprehension of phrasal idioms. As is pointed out in several chapters in this book, idiomatic expressions represent a broad range of linguistic phenomena, ranging from lexical idioms, such as *rail at,* to phrasal idioms such as *to kick the bucket.*

Although most idioms are phrases constructed according to syntactic well-formedness principles, a few contain syntactic violations, such as *by and large.* Throughout this chapter, I am concerned only with phrasal idioms. Thus, for the present purpose, an idiom can be defined as a phrasal unit whose meaning is not obtainable from its syntactic components on the basis of Frege's phrasal principle of compositionality.

An idiom can represent a simple or a complex lexical unit, which in several cases can be taken to be synonymous with a single word (e.g., *to pull someone's leg* means "to tease"), or can be expressed with a whole proposition (e.g., *to take the bull by the horns* means "to attack a problem without fear").

A phrasal idiom thus typically consists of a verbal phrase with a verb and a noun phrase (NP) (*to kick the bucket*). These expressions have acquired a particular status, in the sense that the complete idiom has a given meaning that is not equal to the meaning of the parts as they are combined in the idiomatic expression. In this sense, the "literal meaning" of the idiom, whenever available, usually has little or nothing to do with the idiomatic meaning. To attempt to make a syntactic decomposition of an idiom means generally to lose the idiomatic meaning of it.

In this chapter I first summarize some of the properties of the idiomatic phrases, then briefly mention the main theories on the comprehension of idioms, and discuss some issues concerning idiom interpretation. The last part of the chapter reviews a number of experiments carried out as contributions toward a theory on the process of comprehending idiomatic phrases.

In the next sections, I first discuss a few important properties of idioms, which in turn is useful for the ensuing discussion of the comprehension processes.

SOME IMPORTANT PROPERTIES OF IDIOMS

Frozenness and Flexibility

Idioms differ to the degree to which they can tolerate morphological and syntactic operations. Parts of some idioms can be quantified, modified, or even omitted, lexical elements can be inserted at various points, clauses can be embedded in idiomatic phrases, and so forth. The degree to which this is possible depends on the degree of frozenness of an idiom. To say, for example, "the bucket was kicked by John" is syntactically perfectly possible, but the passivization operation destroys the idiomatic meaning for the original expression. Certain morphological and syntactic operations are allowed for virtually all idioms (e.g., insertion of an auxiliary in the phrase; cf. "he has kicked the bucket" vs. "he kicks the bucket"), whereas others are possible only with certain ones.

The extent to which an idiom can undergo syntactic and morphological operations while at the same time retaining its idiomatic meaning can be expressed in terms of the number and types of grammatical operations that an idiom is capable of tolerating. This degree can indicate the amount of frozenness of an idiom. Idioms can be classified on the basis of their degree of frozenness, from very frozen to very flexible. A kind of frozenness hierarchy has been proposed by Fraser (1970). In this hierarchy, an idiom at a given level of such a hierarchy, capable of tolerating a given operation, also can tolerate all operations that are allowed by idioms "below" that level.

Transparency and Opacity

A second important distinction among idioms concerns the degree of their *transparency*. Idioms can be more or less opaque, or, conversely, more or less transparent. In transparent idioms, such as *to leave the cat out of the bag*, the literal meaning is available, whereas in an opaque idiom such as *to take a leak* the literal interpretation is no longer available or has never been or is not even possible. Most opaque idioms are fossils in which the literal meaning is no more than a philological curiosity.

The two dimensions just considered, frozenness and flexibility on the one hand, and opacity and transparency on the other, represent continuous and not true dichotomies between two extreme and discrete values. An idiom can be more or less frozen on the one hand, and more or less opaque on the other. Moreover, the two dimensions are likely to be not completely independent.

Opaque idioms tend to be more frozen, although this tendency to covary seems rather weak.

The Point of Idiom Uniqueness

One of the questions asked in the present chapter concerns the moment in which an idiomatic phrase is recognized. In order to give an answer to this question, we have to know at what point it is possible to recognize the idiom. At which point does an idiom become an idiom?

Consider the following sentence with two different endings: In the discussion about the financial situation, it became apparent to John that his arguments were weak, and that he was going to lose {money/face}. It is clear that the phrase *to lose face* takes its idiomatic character only at the end of the sentence. It is unlikely that the recognition of the idiom exemplified here can take place before this point is reached in the sentence. In other cases, it is possible that an idiomatic phrase be identified at the beginning or before its completion. For example, except in very specific contexts, the idiom *to take the bull by the horns* is likely to be identified once the phrase "the bull" has been read or heard.

We thus can introduce an important notion, namely of the *point of idiom uniqueness,* which is the point at which the idiom becomes uniquely identifiable. For every idiomatic phrase, there must be a point at which the phrase can be interpreted only as an idiom. For many idiomatic phrases this point will be the last word of the idiom.

Depending on the familiarity of the idiom and especially on the context, the point at which the reader/listener is able to correctly interpret the idiom may not coincide with the point of idiom uniqueness, but in some cases can precede it. Consider, for example, the idiom *to spill the beans* (meaning "to violate a secret"). Without context, the point of idiom uniqueness is given by the word *beans.* However, with a previous context introducing the theme of the violation of a secret, the meaning of the idiom is likely to become available at the word *spill.* I would like to call the point at which the meaning of the idiom is retrieved by the reader/listener as the *point of idiom recognition,* which, depending on the presence of a context and on the familiarity of the idiom, can precede the point of idiom uniqueness.

The point at which the idiomatic meaning is retrieved suggests a parallel to the point of sentence disambiguation. In fact, many idiomatic phrases can be considered like ambiguous structures to which two alternative meaning interpretations can be assigned. There is, however, a basic difference with situations of syntactic ambiguity: While for syntactic ambiguities the two alternative interpretations require two alternative parsing operations that produce two different grammatical structures, the two interpretations of an idiom, the literal and the idiomatic one (when both are possible), are normally consistent with the same syntactic analysis. In most cases, moreover, the two meanings, the one corresponding to the idiomatic and the one corresponding to the literal reading of the phrase, are not incompatible with each other—being related to each other by some form of metaphorical extension.

Syntactic Parsing and Idiomatic Analysis

An idiomatic phrase normally is presented as part of a larger sentence structure. Whether each idiom is represented in the mental lexicon as a separate unit or not, an idiomatic phrase presents a syntactic structure on its own, and various morphological and syntactic operations are allowed in the idiomatic phrase. There is no reason to assume that, when an idiomatic phrase is encountered, normal syntactic parsing normally is suspended or will not take place. Because the linguistic processor cannot be sure about the nature of the idiom until at some point within the idiomatic phrase itself—normally until a point of "idiom uniqueness"—it is unlikely that the parser will be waiting for a whole "multi-word lexical entry" to be retrieved before resuming syntactic analysis.

The meaning of each sentence is obtained as a result of the operations of a lexical processor and of a parser. The construction of the meaning of any sentence can be taken to be based on the principle of compositionality. The phrase "a big dog" is interpreted as some composite of the meaning of *big* and of the meaning of *dog*. But although the meaning of the phrase "to kick the ball" is composed on the basis of one of the meanings of *kick* and one of the meanings of *ball*, the meaning of *to kick the bucket* is not instantiated compositionally. Thus, we face a particular problem. A phrasal idiom is embedded in a sentence, and normally the reader/listener does not know that the phrase ahead will be an idiom until a certain critical point—usually well into the idiomatic phrase—is reached. Thus, syntactic parsing should take place normally at least up to a given point in the sentence. When a listener hears the sentence ". . . and then he kicked . . . .", he or she does not yet know what the next NP is going to be, so normal syntactic analysis should take place at least up to the point where the full idiomatic expression is available, or when enough of it is available to allow an unique identification.

Thus, on the one hand an idiomatic phrase should be subject to normal syntactic analysis, but on the other hand the result of parsing would be an interpretation that is the literal one, based on the principle of compositionality, whereas the idiomatic character of the idiomatic phrase is not compositional, and the meaning of the idiom is not instantiated on the basis of the joint operations of the parser and of the lexical processor.

The Lexical Status of Idioms and Their Representation in the Mental Lexicon

We have seen that the meaning of an idiomatic phrase is not to be reconstructed from the meaning of the elements that compose it. What, then, is the structure of this meaning? How are idioms represented in the mental lexicon? Three different answers can be given to these questions: (a) Idioms can be listed in the mental lexicon as multiword lexical entries; (b) idioms are not listed as such, but are reconstructed on the basis of the idiomatic meaning starting from the entry of one or more of the content words that constitute the idiom; and (c) the meaning of the idiom would not be represented as such at all, but would be computed each time on the basis of the lexical units and of the phrasal structure by some process of metaphor construction.

The first alternative (a) has taken the form of the *idiom list* hypothesis, which was proposed within linguistics by Weinreich (1966). According to this hypothesis, in addition to the "normal" dictionary entries the lexicon would contain a list of idioms. A normal dictionary entry would be made up of a set of phonological, syntactic, and morphemic features, together with a sense description. The idiom list would contain a string of morphemes of various length, together with the meaning associated with it. In order to take this hypothesis seriously, we have to assume double listing for words that are part of an idiom. These would be listed in the normal dictionary entry list and also in the idiomatic list. Of course, the idiomatic list hypothesis is also consistent with the idea that each of the entries of the mental lexicon that are part of an idiom would have a "pointer" to the idiomatic meaning, much as in many dictionaries there is a special entry under one of the main words of the idiom.

According to the second alternative (b), the idiom would not be listed as separate entry, but would be reconstructed on the basis of one or more of its individual lexemes, which would be characterized by appropriate pointers to the idiomatic meaning.

The third alternative (c) is that idioms are not listed nor reconstructed, but computed every time they are met, via processes of analogical inference. The process of idiom comprehension then would be equivalent to the process of the comprehension of a metaphor.

Notice that it is by no means necessary that only one hypothesis holds. As we will see, it is perfectly possible to expect differences in the representation and in the availability of idiomatic phrases characterized by different levels of familiarity. Highly familiar idioms are likely to be represented as a unitary entry in the mental lexicon, whereas for infrequent and unknown idioms, especially opaque ones, it is rather unlikely that such a unitary representation is available. New idioms are likely to be treated by the listener/reader as a metaphor.

The three hypotheses have taken different forms in the literature (see, e.g., Cacciari & Glucksberg, 1991, for a review; see also other chapters of this book), and are not discussed further in this chapter.

THE COMPREHENSION OF IDIOMATIC EXPRESSIONS

Much as for other forms of figurative language, during the last 15 or 20 years a number of psycholinguistic studies have been dedicated to the processes of comprehension of idiomatic expressions. Most psycholinguistic studies of idioms have been concerned with one, or both, of the following questions. The first is whether the reader or listener retrieves both the literal and the idiomatic meaning of the idioms, or only the idiomatic, whereas the second question asks which of the two is computed first. After initial evidence in favor of the "literal first" hypothesis (Bobrow & Bell, 1973), or the "both meanings are computed in parallel" hypothesis (Swinney & Cutler, 1979), the bulk of recent evidence (see, e.g., Gibbs, 1984, 1986; Schweigert, 1986) seems to indicate that the idiomatic meaning is accessed directly, at no extra costs, and that the literal meaning may not even be recovered. On the other hand, these conclusions take diverse forms depending on the degree of frozenness of the idiom and on the type of idiom studied (see Gibbs, 1986). Some of this work is reported in other chapters of this book, so no attempt is made here to review it. Rather, in this chapter, I ignore these two questions altogether, and instead look directly at some of the features that are likely to characterize the process of idiom comprehension.

The Process of Idiom Comprehension

Before introducing some experimental work, I would like to propose a few assumptions on the process of idiom comprehension, which have guided the empirical studies discussed in this chapter:

Assumption 1: The comprehension of an idiom does not require a special processing mode. An assumption underlying much psycholinguistic work on idioms is that literal and idiomatic meaning are computed separately yielding two alternative interpretations. This assumption may not hold. Most words and most utterances are characterized by a whole range of senses or meanings, including "metaphoric" meanings. When talking about a person, the adjective *warm* usually indicates a property of character or personality, and only in specific contexts it is used to indicate temperature of the body. Thus, the so-called idiomatic meaning of a word within an idiom is likely to be obtained much as the other senses of the word. All senses or meanings can be taken to become available during comprehension, and the "idiomatic" sense becomes available when the idiom is interpreted as such. This assumption relates to the following one.

Assumption 2: Lexical access is obligatory for individual words even within idioms. As recent evidence has shown (e.g., Cacciari & Tabossi, 1988), individual lexemes always are accessed during language comprehension, even when they are part of an idiom. Thus individual words can facilitate the access of words related in meaning, independent of the fact that they are part of an idiom or not. The existence of priming effects of single words of an idiomatic phrase on words related to their literal meaning (e.g., Tabossi & Cacciari, 1988) does not constitute definitive evidence for the claim that a literal interpretation of the idiomatic phrase is entertained during sentence comprehension, but certainly supports the notion of an obligatory access, in the mental lexicon, to the single lexemes that constitute the idiom.

Assumption 3: Syntactic analysis is obligatory. Recent work on human parsing has shown that the syntactic structure of any sentence is computed for any string (see, e.g., Frazier, 1987). Syntactic computation is assumed to proceed in an automatic way (see Flores d'Arcais, 1982). Although a syntactic analysis is per se not necessary to understand the meaning of the idiom, the human parser always would analyze it fully. This claim has been tested in one of the experiments reported in this chapter.

Let me now briefly sketch how I propose that idiomatic phrases be understood within a sentence context. The underlying claim here is that the process of language comprehension does not differ whether the sentences contain an idiomatic phrase or not:

1. The *syntactic parser* analyzes the input strings and produces a grammatical structure with a given representation.

2. The *lexical processor* accesses the lexical items in the mental lexicon and delivers a meaning representation of the individual words. These two components can be taken to be modular, with the lexical processor feeding to the parser the results of its analysis.

3. *Semantic analysis* is made on the basis of the syntactic structure obtained and the appropriate lexical units associated with their meaning.

4. The results of the processes of these various components are taken and evaluated at the level of a *message* or *thematic interpretation* unit. Such a unit has been proposed as a feature characterizing several recent psycholinguistic models, with various terms used to identify it (e.g., *thematic processor;* Ferreira & Clifton, 1986; Frazier, 1987; Rayner, Carlson, & Frazier, 1983). Its function is essentially to collect, compare, and interpret evidence available from the linguistic components.

5. Even when the sentence contains an idiomatic phrase, according to the present view the syntactic parser and the lexical processor would work "normally" throughout the process of analyzing the input, the parser yielding a syntactic structure upon which the appropriate lexical representations computed by the lexical processor would be inserted. At the point of idiom identification, the lexical processor should retrieve the unique lexical representation of the idiom and its corresponding meaning. Thus, some conflict could arise at this point, in principle but not necessarily, between the syntactic processor and the lexical processor. The interpretation available so far to the message or thematic interpretation unit could become inconsistent with the new information sent by the lexical processor. This inconsistency may result in some processing difficulty. It is likely that such difficulty is only present with nonfamiliar idioms.

Highly familiar ones would become immediately available even at the lexical level and would not constitute any problem. Because most metaphors are understood without many difficulties, unfamiliar idioms also should present no problems for understanding. On the other hand, an idiom could be computationally more complex because of a possible conflict between the operation of different processing components, the lexical processor, the syntactic parser, and the semantic analyzer.

The Problems

The points discussed in the previous section lead to a series of questions, to which the present work has tried to offer some answers. A first question is to some extent related to the issue frequently asked in psycholinguistic experiments, namely whether the literal meaning is computed during the comprehension process. Whether the literal meaning is computed or not, there could be a need of additional computational effort required to comprehend an idiomatic phrase as compared to the comprehension of a nonidiomatic phrase. If the literal meaning is computed during idiom comprehension—be it before or in parallel with the idiomatic meaning—one should expect additional computational effort for comprehending an idiom. But even if the literal meaning is not computed, an idiom could be computationally more complex because of the possible conflict between the operations of the different processing components.

A second question concerns a possible difference between well-known and poorly known idioms. Highly familiar, frequently used items might be listed in the lexicon, whereas the comprehension of idioms with low familiarity and that are used rarely might require a full computation. An adequate psycholinguistic model of comprehension of idiomatic phrases should account for this possible difference.

At the intersection of the two previous questions, a third one emerges. The problem whether the literal meaning is computed or not during idiom comprehension is probably not appropriate without further specification. For very familiar idioms it seems very unlikely that the literal interpretation is computed. For unfamiliar idioms, on the other hand, the story looks different. Highly familiar idioms should not produce any processing problems. Low-familiarity idioms should present some difficulty, when the reader/listener is not yet in the conditions of finding out whether the phrase that she or he is reading is an idiom. Therefore, additional processing problems could arise at the moment a literal interpretation becomes no longer possible, namely at the point of idiom uniqueness, and more strongly when the context is rather neutral. So, one can expect some difficulty in processing low-familiarity idioms at the point of idiom uniqueness.

A fourth question, related to the assumption of an obligatory, automatic action of the human parser, is whether full analysis of the grammatical structure of the incoming string is taking place even when the sentence being understood includes a highly familiar idiomatic phrase that could be recovered as a multiword unit in the mental lexicon, without any need of syntactic analysis of its internal structure. This hypothesis has been tested in an experiment by using a word-by-word reading task, reported later. The assumption based on the present hypothesis is that inspection times for words at critical points in the string should be longer, and that this should be the case for the point of idiom uniqueness of unfamiliar idioms.

A fifth question, mentioned earlier in the present discussion, concerns the semantic analysis of rarely used or completely unknown idioms. According to a number of available theories on idioms in linguistics and psycholinguistics, idioms are listed in the lexicon, and are not computed. Whereas metaphoric expressions would be comprehended by various inferential processes, idioms would be searched in the lexicon as multiword lexical units. If this position is true, then every time a new idiom is met, it should act as a completely unknown word, and the listener/reader would be requested to use the context to make up some meaning for the phrase, or use some external source such as a dictionary or a human informant. However, because most idioms—except for extremely opaque ones—bear some semantic or pragmatic relation to the intended meaning, listeners/readers should be in the condition of interpreting unknown idioms and often obtain a plausible or not too inappropriate interpretation. This assumption has been tested in the last two studies reported in this chapter.

THE STUDIES

The present chapter reports on five different studies. A first study included a number of rating and scaling experiments designed to obtain information about familiarity and about the point of idiom uniqueness for a large number of idiomatic phrases. The second study tested the assumption that idiomatic phrases that, according to the list hypothesis, could be stored as multiword lexical units, and therefore could be interpreted as such, still undergo full syntactic analysis. A third study tested the hypothesis that highly familiar idioms are recognized easily without any need for computing the literal meaning, whereas low-familiarity idioms require additional processing effort. A fourth and fifty study tried to find out how people interpret unknown idioms and which principles they may use in assigning such an interpretation.

Study 1: Ratings of Properties of Idiomatic Phrases

The purpose of this study was to obtain some indications of a number of properties of a large sample of Dutch idioms. This study was carried out with a large number of subjects in different sections, and the details of the study are not reported here. The data obtained, besides being interesting in their own right, were used for the selection of the materials for the following studies reported in the present chapter.

Two hundred Dutch idiomatic phrases were chosen as the basis material for our study. They were submitted in various sets for different tasks to a total of 294 subjects, with the request to perform a number of tasks.

Definition of Meaning.   The first task for the subjects was to give a definition of the meaning of each of the idioms. The definitions given then were evaluated by two judges on a 3-point scale as (1) correct, (2) partially correct or somewhat related to the "dictionary meaning" of the idioms, or (3) completely incorrect. The average scale values of the idioms computed over all subjects gave an indication of the availability or knowledge of the meaning of the idioms.

Familiarity.   A second rating task consisted of giving an estimate of the frequency with which the subject thought a given idiom would be used in the language, by using a 7-point scale from "very frequently used" to "never used." This yielded for each idiom a "subjective frequency" or "familiarity" score.

Use of Literal Meaning.   In a third task, subjects were requested to answer the question whether in making an interpretation of the meaning of an idiom they thought that they had retrieved the "literal" meaning of the idiom. Following the answer to this question, the subject had to express on a 5-point scale the degree of confidence of having retrieved the literal meaning. The answers to these questions provided an indication of the extent to which the idiomatic meaning of idioms might be accessed via a literal interpretation. The values based on this task also were taken as a rough estimate of the degree of transparency of an idiom.

The Point of Idiom Uniqueness.   In a fourth task, subjects were requested to indicate for each idiom the point, that is, the word, at which the idiom becomes uniquely defined.

Results.   The definitions given and the ratings provided in the first place a number of details about properties of the idioms, which were used as a basis for the other studies. The full results of these ratings are reported elsewhere (Flores d'Arcais, in preparation). Some specific results are also of interest here.

On the basis of the definitions given in Task 1, the idioms were divided into two categories, namely the "well known" (high proportion of correct definition) and "not known" (incorrect definitions). Not surprisingly, "knowledge" and "familiarity" were highly correlated ($r = .78$). Correlations coefficients between the average scale values thus obtained for the various idioms were computed separately for the well-known idioms, and for the unknown ones. For the well-known idioms, the correlation between knowledge and use of the literal interpretation was $-.81$, whereas for the unknown idioms the correlation between the same variables was $-.30$ (both coefficients are significantly different from 0). Thus, when an idiom is well known, the reader does not think that he or she uses the literal meaning in order to understand it, whereas when the idiom is not well known, literal interpretation, according to the subjects' evaluation, is likely to be used in many cases. Furthermore, for well-known idioms, the most familiar ones are somewhat unlikely to be interpreted literally (correlation between familiarity scale values and use of literal meaning in interpretation $r = -.23$, $p < .05$), whereas for unknown idioms familiarity and use of literal meaning do not correlate at all ($r = .02$).

Study 2: Syntactic Processing During Comprehension of Idiomatic Phrases

If idiomatic phrases are stored in memory as multiword lexical units, as the list hypothesis claims, then syntactic analysis of the phrasal structure of the idiom in principle should not be necessary for comprehending the idiom. The present experiment tested the hypothesis that syntactic analysis is an obligatory, automatic process that does not depend on the particular structure being processed and that is insensitive to the lexical properties of the phrasal structure being processed. If an idiom is recognized at an early point, further analysis of the idiomatic phrase is in principle no longer necessary to understand the meaning of the phrase. Thus, a full syntactic analysis of the idiomatic phrase would not be required. If this is true, then a highly familiar idiom, which can be recognized early, could be understood without the need of a full syntactic analysis, whereas a nonfamiliar idiom would be understood only after a full grammatical analysis. Thus, the experiment investigated the question of whether syntactic analysis of the idiomatic phrase continues even when the idiom has been recognized and the appropriate idiomatic meaning has been assigned to it.

To what extent is syntactic analysis performed during comprehension of the sentences containing idioms? An answer to this question was sought in an experiment, in which readers were requested to detect syntactic violations in sentences containing phrasal idioms of high or low familiarity.

Material. Twenty-four sentences containing idiomatic phrases (12 highly familiar and 12 unfamiliar idioms) and 60 filler sentences constituted the material of the present experiment. In 50% of the presentation each sentence contained a grammatical violation, such as the following:

1. Violation of gender agreement between article and noun. For example, instead of the appropriate idiom *in hetzelfde schuitje,* the phrase presented included the masculine/feminine article *dezelfde.*

2. Concordance singular plural: *Twee vlieg in een klap* instead of *twee vliegen in een klap*.

Subjects and Procedure.   20 students at the University of Leiden took part in the experiment. The sentences were presented on a computer display one word at a time, in a left to right sequence with each word displayed occupying a different position as in a normal printed sequence. However, each word was presented and remained on the display only 250 ms and then disappeared. The end of the sentence was signalled by a period that could be accompanied by an asterisk to signal to the subjects to make a decision whether the sentence was correct or contained some violations.

Results.   The results, proportions of successfully detected violations in high- and low-familiarity idiomatic phrases, are summarized in Table 4.1. In both cases, there is the same probability of hitting a violation. The latencies for the correct responses were significantly different for familiar and unfamiliar idioms: Correct reports of grammatical violations took significantly shorter with highly familiar than with unfamiliar idioms [$F(1, 23) = 4.96, p < .05$].

Discussion.   The absence of any difference in the rate of detection of syntactic violations in high-familiarity and low-familiarity idioms can be interpreted by assuming that in both cases syntactic analysis is taking place. We had expected a lower proportion of detection of violations after the point of idiom recognition for high-familiarity items, under the assumption that once the idiom has been recognized, the reader no longer would pay attention to the surface structure of the rest of the phrase. Instead, syntactic violations still are detected, thus allowing the conclusion that syntactic analysis of the phrasal string that constitutes the idiom goes on even when the high-familiarity item has been recognized. This result is consistent with work by Cacciari and Tabossi (1988), which also has

TABLE 4.1
Proportion of Error Detection and Average Response Latencies (ms)
for Correct Detection of Syntactic Violations in High-
and Low-Familiarity Idioms

	Idiomatic Phrases		
	High Familiarity	Low Familiarity	Significance Difference
Proportion Errors	.28	.31	Not significant
Average Latencies (Correct Responses)	1278	1102	$p < .05$

shown that syntactic analysis is carried out automatically, whenever an input string is given for comprehension.

Study 3: Word-By-Word Reading of Sentences
Containing Idiomatic Phrases

As we already have discussed, if comprehending idiomatic phrases requires additional processing, because of the need of computing first a literal and then an idiomatic representation, or the necessity of constructing two interpretations in parallel, as several of the models in the literature alternatively suggest, then we should expect increasing processing loads with idiomatic phrases as compared with nonidiomatic ones. According to our previous discussion, however, we do not expect this to be the case for familiar idioms, for which no extra processing load should be expected. On the other hand, low-familiarity idioms might produce some processing problems when the reader/listener is at the point in which these can be uniquely identified as idioms. This should be more the case for the idioms embedded in a neutral context. Thus, in an appropriate experiment we predict some processing difficulty for the low-familiarity idiomatic phrases at the point of idiom uniqueness, especially when a neutral context does not offer previous cues for the appropriate idiomatic interpretation of the phrase. Furthermore, opaque, nonfamiliar idioms should produce more processing difficulty than transparent ones.

Thus the present experiment tested the hypothesis that highly familiar idioms do not produce any processing difficulty, whereas unfamiliar idioms should yield some processing difficulty at the points of idioms uniqueness. As an indication of processing difficulty we took the time of inspection of each word in a word-by-word reading task.

On the basis of the norms obtained in the first study summarized previously, I chose a number of highly familiar and unfamiliar idioms. For each of the two categories I selected a number of transparent and a number of opaque idioms. For each of the experimental idiomatic phrases, I had available an indication of the point of idiomatic uniqueness, obtained on the basis of the ratings of a number of subjects, as previously reported. These words were taken as the critical points for the measurement of reading latencies in the present experiment. This material was used in a self-paced reading experiment, in which sentences containing the idioms were presented one word at a time on a display, under subject's control. The intervals between the pressing responses of the subject were measured and recorded.

Material.   Twenty-four idiomatic phrases, 12 familiar and 12 very unfamiliar ones, of which respectively 6 were transparent and 6 very opaque, constituted the experimental material. They were embedded in neutral, literal or idiomatic context sentences. Seventy-two filler sentences were intermixed with these 24 sentences containing idioms. Twenty-four of these fillers were matched sentences with identical syntactic structures and very similar contents to the sentences containing idioms. The sentences were presented on a display one word at the time, under subjects' control.

Subjects and Procedure.   Twenty-four students at the University of Leiden took part in the experiment as volunteer paid subjects. The types of context sentences and the idioms contained were rotated in such a way that each subject received two sentences of each type and a subject would never see an idiomatic phrase in two different contexts. The subjects sat in front of the display at a distance of about 70 cm, and received the sentence one word at the time by pressing a key. The words of the sentence were displayed on the screen from left to right, and remained visible until the end of the sentence. Some of the sentences required two lines on the display.

Results.   The results, mean inspection times for the critical word, averaged over the "idiomatic point of uniqueness" word and the following word, are presented in Table 4.2. The analysis of variance yielded a very significant effect of familiarity [$F(1,11) = 8.12, p < .01$, by subjects, and $F(1, 11) = 5.32, p < .05$ by items]. Inspection times at the point of idiom uniqueness were virtually the same for familiar items and for control words, which were part of non-idiomatic phrases. Unfamiliar idioms, on the other hand, required significantly longer inspection times.

The interaction between familiarity and transparency was significant, [$F(1, 23) = 8.39, p < .01$] but this effect was mainly due to the unfamiliar items. Opaque unfamiliar idioms require significantly more inspection time than do transparent ones [$F(1, 5) = 6.79, p < .05$]. The interaction between type of context sentence and familiarity was significant only for the unfamiliar idiomatic phrases. As compared with the latencies for the control words, reading a phrase

TABLE 4.2
Mean Inspection Times (ms) Per Word for Familiar
and Unfamiliar Idiomatic Phrases in Idiomatic and Neutral Context,
Averaged Over the Word That Was Judged as Point of Idiom
Uniqueness and the Word Following It

| | Idioms | | | | |
| | Familiar | | Unfamiliar | | |
Context Sentence	Transp.	Opaque	Transp.	Opaque	Control
Idiomatic	423	435	527	549	417
Neutral	432	441	556	586	

containing a familiar idiom does not slow down the reading rate. So, neutral contexts induce longer inspection times, but more so for opaque idioms.

Discussion.   When a reader encounters the critical word of an idiom—the point of idiomaticity—she or he slows down with respect to a control in an equivalent string word only if the idiom is unfamiliar, and more so with a neutral context. This suggests that encountering a familiar idiom does not require any additional computation, and that processing goes on in the same way as with a sentence containing a nonidiomatic phrase of the same structural complexity of the idiomatic one. On the other hand, when the critical, idiomatic word of an unfamiliar idiom is met, the reader slows down his or her reading pace, thus indicating the need for assigning an alternative interpretation to the sentence at the point of idiomaticity.

Thus, the data show that readers, not surprisingly, have more difficulty in interpreting unknown idioms, whereas they do not seem to have any difficulty in interpreting a known idiom more than any other part of the sentence. When the context biases the idiomatic meaning, an unfamiliar idiom is understood better, but still is more difficult than a well-known idiom.

To conclude, we have obtained evidence for the notion that familiar idioms are processed without any problem. On the other hand, nonfamiliar idioms, especially when opaque and especially when embedded in a neutral context, do offer some processing problems. It seems reasonable to argue that this material is comprehended in its literal sense up to the point when this is no longer possible. At this point, some extra computation seems to be required.

Thus the data here reported bring us to the following conclusion. Familiar idiomatic phrases are understood directly, without any additional effort, and probably without the need of computing the literal interpretation. This, however, does not seem to be the case for nonfamiliar idioms, for which additional computational work seems to be required, and this especially when the context does not give any cue as to the presence of an idiomatic meaning of a critical string.

Study 4: Semantic Interpretation of Familiar and Unfamiliar Idioms

In this study, we presented the subjects with a number of idioms and requested that they choose, out of four alternatives, the phrase that correctly paraphrased the meaning of the idioms.

Material.   Forty-eight idioms, chosen in such a way as to cover the whole range of both the knowledge and the familiarity scales as determined in Study 1, constituted the material of this study. For each idiomatic phrase four alternative paraphrases were made. One of these alternatives corresponded to the correct (dictionary definition) interpretation of the idiom; the others were chosen from the erroneous definitions produced by the subjects of the study to be reported in the next section, or, in a few cases, created by the experimenter and two colleagues.

Subjects and Procedure.   Fifty students of the University of Leiden were given a booklet containing the 48 idioms with four alternatives each. The task was to choose the paraphrase that best corresponded in meaning to the meaning of the idiomatic phrase.

Results.   For highly familiar idioms, the proportion of correct choices was very high, (.87) whereas for low-familiarity idioms the proportion of correct choices was much lower, (.39) but still significantly different from chance ($p < .001$). The correlation between the proportion of choices of the correct alternative and the knowledge score of the idioms, obtained in Study 1, turned out high, $r = .85$, $p < .001$.

Discussion.   The subjects of this judgement study were in most cases capable of selecting the appropriate paraphrase for familiar idioms. On the other hand, they also performed better than by chance, even with unfamiliar idioms.

It is not surprising that familiarity with an idiom correlates highly with the correct interpretation. The fact that unknown idioms are assigned a correct paraphrase in a better-than-chance fashion suggests that people are capable of using the semantic information present in the string in order to reach a solution. What kind of strategies or principles do people use in searching for an interpretation of an unknown and opaque idiomatic phrase? This question was at the basis of the following study.

Study 5: Production of Paraphrases for Unknown Idiomatic Phrases

One of the questions asked in the present study concerned the semantic interpretation of unknown or poorly known idioms. What kind of interpretation can people provide when they meet an unknown idiom, or one that is very unfamiliar or difficult to remember? What kind of principles do people use in trying to make sense out of these idioms?

In the experiment here described we gave our subjects a number of unfamiliar idioms, with the request to provide in each case a paraphrase. We then analyzed the paraphrases trying to isolate the principles that our subjects might have used in producing them.

Material.   Sixty-four idiomatic phrases, 32 familiar and 32 unfamiliar ones (as indexed by the results of Study 1 previously reported), constituted the material of the present study. Within each of these two categories, 16 were rather transparent and 16 were rather opaque idioms. Together with this material, a total of 66 filler sentences were presented, some having a metaphoric figurative meaning, some only a literal meaning.

Subjects.   The subjects were 80 students of the University of Leiden who participated in this study in groups, and performed the task required together with another task, unrelated to the present one.

Procedure.   The idioms were printed (without context) on a booklet with appropriate space for the subject to provide an answer. Each page contained 10 phrases, and the order of the pages of the booklet was varied to ensure at least some randomization of the material.

Classification of the Responses.   The responses were evaluated first on the basis of their correctness. The evaluation consisted of matching the paraphrase with the dictionary meaning. This work was done by four judges, and in most cases the evaluation did not present any problem. The incorrect interpretations were classified independently by the four judges on the basis of a number of categories created by the judges themselves while sorting the responses. These categories then were pooled and after discussion given one single label. The paraphrases then were sorted and assigned to one of these categories. When multiple classification was possible, as in a few cases, the paraphrase given was discussed among the judges and the classification was based on a forced choice between the two possible categories. Attribution of the paraphrases to the categories thus created was in most cases completely unproblematic. In a few cases some discussion was required and in about 4% of the cases the paraphrases were based on very idiosyncratic principles, could not be classified clearly, or, finally, disagreement remained among the judges.

Results.   The proportion of paraphrases that closely matched the meaning of the idiomatic phrases was very high for the familiar idioms (.91) and significantly lower (.34) ($p < .001$) for the unfamiliar ones. For the further analysis, only the responses to the unfamiliar idioms were taken into consideration. The proportions of the different types of interpretations given are summarized in Table 4.3. The paraphrases given by the subjects can be taken to be based on one of the following principles:

1. Analogy: The idiomatic phrase is interpreted by analogy to a known idiom, which contains a word or a constituent of a familiar idiom. For example, consider the idiom *op zijn duim fluiten* (*to whistle in his thumb,* meaning "not being able to obtain what one wants"). A few subjects gave an interpretation by analogy to the idiom *uit zijn duim zuigen* (*to suck his thumb,* which means "to find out something").

Table 4.3
Proportions of the Different Types of Interpretations
Given to the Unfamiliar Idioms

Interpretation Made on the Basis Of:						
Correct	Analogy	Semantic Prop. One Word	Metaphoric Extension	Literal Meaning	Others	Non Class.
.34	.17	.18	.12	.11	.04	.04

2. Use of semantic properties of one of the words of the idiom, mostly one of the nouns, without considering the whole phrase. Take, for example, the idiom *uit de paardepoten komen* (*to come from the legs of the horse,* which is rather opaque and means "to go away"). Some interpretations given were of the following type: (a) "to originate from the country, from the farm" (horse as a farming animal); (b) "to run fast" (horse as a fast-running animal).

3. Metaphoric extension of the action or state described in the phrase: Consider as an example of this operation the idiom *voor twee ankers liggen* (to lie at two anchors, meaning "to be well taken care of"). The interpretations classified under this category were of the type (a) "not being able to move away" (two anchors keep you tight); or (b) "to have doubts, to be uncertain" (the existence of two identical alternatives makes the choice difficult).

4. Literal meaning: The interpretation given was close to the literal meaning. The subjects were not able to figure out any idiomatic interpretation.

5. Other: In this category we classified a number of responses that were very idiosyncratic, in the sense that the subjects seemed to create them without reference to any obvious principle, or gave a paraphrase that to all judges seemed completely arbitrary.

Discussion.   When presented with an unfamiliar idiom, and asked to give an interpretation, people seem capable of giving paraphrases that in several cases are appropriate and often closely match the conventional meaning of the idiom. The interpretations proposed are obtained through familiar idioms or a metaphoric analysis. Semantic information, which constitutes the meaning of the lexical units that are part of the idiomatic phrase, is used to construct an often appropriate or plausible interpretation.

GENERAL DISCUSSION

The studies summarized in this chapter have tried to analyze some of the processes that people bring to the interpretation and comprehension of an idiomatic phrase. The evidence obtained allows the following conclusions:

First, the input seems to undergo full syntactic analysis: Even very familiar idiomatic phrases, which in principle could be recognized after the first few component words, and do not require a syntactic analysis in order to be understood, seem to be parsed completely, much as any other linguistic string for which syntactic analysis is the normal and necessary route to obtain an interpretable structure.

Second, the results of one of the experiments reported indicated that there is a clear difference in processing between well-known familiar idioms and new, unfamiliar ones. Although the first normally are processed without any additional effort, the comprehension of an unfamiliar idiomatic phrase may require some additional computational effort.

Third, an unknown idiomatic phrase is given an interpretation based on a number of principles. Some of these have been isolated as evidence for the processes that bring one to a meaningful interpretation.

In summary, it can be concluded that processing idiomatic phrases may present some computational problems only when the idioms are very or completely unfamiliar. The interpretations given to these idioms are very often appropriate or at least close to their conventional meaning. In order to reach such interpretations, the language user adopts a number of strategies that are based on simple principles, some of which have been put in evidence by the work here described.

ACKNOWLEDGEMENTS

Part of the work here summarized has been supported by a grant of the C.N.R. of Italy to the author.

REFERENCES

Bobrow, S., & Bell, B. (1973). On catching on to idiomatic expressions. *Memory & Cognition, 1,* 343–346.

Cacciari, C., & Glucksberg, S. (1991). Understanding idiomatic expressions: The contribution of word meanings. In G. B. Simpson (Ed.), *Understanding word and sentence* (pp. 217–240). Amsterdam, Netherlands: North Holland.

Cacciari, C., & Tabossi, P. (1988). The comprehension of idioms. *Journal of Memory and Language, 27,* 668–683.

Ferreira, F., & Clifton, C. (1986). The independence of syntactic processing. *Journal of Memory and Language, 25,* 348–368.

Flores d'Arcais, G. B. (1978). The perception of complex sentences. In W. J. M. Levelt & G. B. Flores d'Arcais (Eds.), *Studies in the perception of language* (pp. 155–185). Chichester, England: Wiley.

Flores d'Arcais, G. B. (1982). Automatic syntactic computation and use of semantic information during sentence comprehension. *Psychological Research, 44,* 231–242.

Flores d'Arcais, G. B. (in preparation). *The comprehension of familiar and unfamiliar idioms.* Manuscript in preparation.

Fraser, B. (1970). Idioms within a transformational grammar. *Foundations of Language, 6,* 22–42.

Frazier, L. (1987). Sentence processing: A tutorial review. In M. Coltheart (Ed.), *Attention and performance XII: The psychology of reading* (pp. 559–586). Hillsdale, NJ: Lawrence Erlbaum Associates.

Gibbs, R. W. (1984). Literal meaning and psychological theory. *Cognitive Science, 8,* 275–304.

Gibbs, R. W. (1986). Skating on thin ice: Literal meaning and understanding idioms in conversation. *Discourse Processes, 9,* 17–30.

Rayner, K., Carlson, M., & Frazier, L. (1983). The interaction of syntax and semantics during sentence processing: Eye movements in the analysis of semantically biased sentences. *Journal of Verbal Learning and Verbal Behavior, 22,* 358–374.

Schweigert, W. A. (1986). The comprehension of familiar and less familiar idioms. *Journal of Psycholinguistic Research, 15,* 33–45.

Swinney, D. A., & Cutler, A. (1979). The access and processing of idiomatic expressions. *Journal of Verbal Learning and Verbal Behavior, 18,* 523–534.

Tabossi, P., & Cacciari, C. (1988). Context effects in the comprehension of idioms. In Cognitive Science Society (Eds.), *Proceedings of the Tenth Annual Conference of the Cognitive Science Society* (pp. 90–96). Hillsdale, NJ: Lawrence Erlbaum Associates.

Weinreich, V. (1966). Problems in the analysis of idioms. In J. Puhivel (Ed.), *Substance and structure of language* (pp. 23–81). Los Angeles: University of California.

II

ACQUISITION AND
PROCESSING OF IDIOMS

5 The Acquisition of Idioms and the Development of Figurative Competence

M. Chiara Levorato
Università di Padova, Italy

> *We can play the game too, and drop our cover. I agree that there's*
> *nothing under sun so awful as a clichè, since, love it or leave it, it's all*
> *the same cup of tea.*
> —*Umberto Eco, La bustina di Minerva*, L'Espresso

LITERAL AND FIGURATIVE LANGUAGE

In the present chapter, which investigates idioms from a developmental perspective, it is assumed that the ability to comprehend and produce idiomatic expressions is inseparable from the development of figurative language. Let me thus begin with an analysis of some of the problems inherent in the very definition of figurative language and of the criteria that differentiate it from literal language. This analysis is not meant to be complete or detailed, but serves to introduce a thesis that is central to this work: That is that the development of children's ability to produce and understand idioms depends on the development of the same linguistic abilities on which figurative language as well as language in general are based.

There is much controversy in psycholinguistics as to the validity of the distinction between figurative and literal language (Dascal, 1987; Gibbs, 1984, 1989). One of the weak points of this debate is that the criteria that are used to differentiate literal and figurative language have not yet been identified definitively. I limit myself to an analysis of three characteristics of figurative language that are important for its acquisition. The first characteristic is a gap between the speaker's words and his or her communicative intentions. A typical example of

101

this is irony, where the intended meaning can be the exact opposite of the explicit meaning. Another criterion that could distinguish literal from figurative language is the latter's conventionality: It departs from its original meaning, the literal one, and acquires new meaning by means of strongly held conventions. Idioms are perfect examples of this, because according to convention the meaning of an idiom is idiomatic, not literal. Clear evidence of this can be found in research where it has been proven that subjects took less time to process the figurative meaning of an idiom than the literal meaning (Swinney & Cutler, 1979), or that in any case recognition of the idiomatic meaning came first (Gibbs, 1980; Gibbs & Gonzales, 1985; Gibbs & Nayak, 1989; Gibbs, Nayak, Bolton, & Keppel, 1988). The third difference between literal and figurative language is that figurative language is generally more dependent on the context than literal language is. Actually, figurative expressions derive their meaning from context to an extent that varies with the degree of the conventionality of the expression.

There is no doubt these three characteristics play a crucial part in a child's acquisition of figurative language, though they each may be debated on several grounds. First, concerning the say-mean distinction, it should be noted that speakers usually do not communicate explicitly what they really mean: In any communicative act linguistic production is based to a great extent on the assumption that the listener will make all the inferences necessary in order to get at the meaning intended by the speaker. Second, concerning conventionality, in numerous linguistic forms that strictly speaking may not be considered figurative, the meaning is linked to culturally determined conventions, as for instance in the case of indirect speech acts. As for the third characteristic, literal language also can be context-dependent, because it is difficult to conceive of any expression existing outside a linguistic and extralinguistic context. However, the criteria that I have just discussed must be taken into account in studying the process of the acquisition of figurative language in children. In fact, children have difficulty understanding (a) that a distinction may exist between what is said and what is meant, (b) that the conventional meaning may differ from the literal one, and (c) that one needs to make use of all the available contextual information (the linguistic and nonlinguistic context as well as the relevant world knowledge) to identify the exact meaning of an expression.

Assuming that, for the aforementioned reasons, as well as others that I do not have the space to elaborate on here, the distinction between literal and figurative language does have heuristic value and therefore should not be neglected, my next question concerns the possible consequence of such a distinction. I hope to demonstrate the inaccuracy of any model for the acquisition of figurative language that considers this acquisition to be a special competence, and to show, on the contrary, that this acquisition is linked very closely to the development of cognitive processes in general. The prevalent position for some time has been that figurative language must involve different processing from that involved in literal language. Even if the linguistic distinction between literal and figurative language may be valid (and even if the speaker may be aware of it at some level), the processes underlying the comprehension and production of each type of language are not necessarily different. In the literature a number of reasons are given for this, to which I add the following:

1. The idea that different processing could be activated for different, although still linguistic, stimuli goes against the principle of economy on which cognitive functioning is based.

2. Differentiated processing would require some kind of mechanism to determine whether and when a given expression should be received in its literal meaning, and therefore undergo a normal processing, or whether it requires special processing, but such a mechanism seems highly implausible.

3. There is so much figurative language present in normal conversation that a special processing would have to be almost as frequent as so-called normal processing. (According to the estimates of Pollio, Barlow, Fine, and Pollio, 1977, an average of about four figures of speech are produced in every minute of speech.)

4. Nonliteral language where a discrepancy exists between what is said and what is meant can take a great variety of forms, ranging from expressions that are clearly figurative (e.g., proverbs, metaphors, idioms, and similes) to expressions in which the discrepancy is more subtle (such as irony and indirect speech acts).

5. It seems more appropriate to analyze the literal–figurative dimension in terms of a "fuzzy" category with some cases that are more typical than others.

6. Figurative language also includes expressions that are not figurative in themselves, but become figurative in a given linguistic context.

Taken together, these observations lead us first to limit the distinction between literal and figurative language, and second, to emphasize the existence of many different typologies. That both figurative and literal language include a wealth of forms is a fact that plays an important role in our model for the acquisition of figurative competence (Levorato & Cacciari, 1992) in which the ability to process figurative language occurs in parallel with and as a function of a more general ability to process language.

That a connection does exist between the acquisition of figurative language and general linguistic development is undeniable. My goal here is to put to good use some of the theoretical tools that have proven so productive in the study of children's language for a better understanding of the phenomenon of figurative language. The connection between the development of figurative language and more general aspects of the child's development has begun to be recognized. In his fine book on metaphor and irony, Winner (1988), for example, proposed a model for the development of these two forms of figurative language that is based on children's acquisition of world knowledge and on the growth of the ability to make inferences about the communicative intentions of the speaker. Though idiomatic expressions are conventional and not creative, unlike metaphor and irony, I believe that they are not acquired by associating form with meaning, but rather are acquired together with the development of skills that allow the child to comprehend language as a whole, that is to create a semantic representation of the linguistic information. These skills include coding, making inferences, activating world knowledge, using imagination and creativity, finding out the communicative intention of the speaker, activating metalinguistic knowledge and knowledge relating to the different kinds of discourse or text, and so on. In the course of the child's development, these processes and skills are ever more subject to a tendency or need to search for the greatest possible degree of coherence among all the linguistic and nonlinguistic information processed at a given moment and all other relevant information and previous knowledge.

With this, we touch on a crucial aspect of the acquisition of the ability to deal with figurative language, which we can define as *figurative competence*. Figurative competence is not acquired all at once, but is pieced together in the course of linguistic development and only can be acquired in full by a thoroughly competent speaker. In its most mature form it involves various linguistic skills, including: (a) the gradual broadening of word meaning, its position in a given semantic domain, and its paradigmatic and sintagmatic relations; (b) the ability to understand the dominant, peripheral, and polisemous meanings of a word, and also the ability to perceive the relationship between a given meaning and other related meanings; (c) the ability to suspend a purely referential strategy; (d) the ability to understand the figurative uses of a word and the relationship between the literal meaning and the figurative meaning; (e) the ability to process large amounts of language, such as a text or a dialogue sequence, in order to identify the meaning of ambiguous or unknown expressions; and (f) the ability to use figurative language productively in the creation of new figures of speech by means of the lexical and syntactic transformation of preexisting figures of speech.

I present here a very rough outline of the role that the skills and abilities listed earlier play in the development of figurative competence, particularly in the comprehension of idioms. In the conclusion of this chapter, after a report of the results of several experiments, I provide a more complete analysis of the processes and mechanisms through which figurative competence is acquired.

IDIOM COMPREHENSION

The study of the psychological processes involved in an adult's or a competent listener's use of idiomatic expressions is a radically different matter from studying the developmental processes involved in the acquisition of the necessary skills for such use. The reason for this difference lies in the very nature of idioms. Although these expressions originally described a particular situation literally, their use has been extended to a greater and ever more varied range of situations and they have lost their literal character, which has caused them to become highly conventionalized. The frozen quality of such expressions results in their being processed by adults, or by those who have acquired them, primarily through their figurative meaning. It could be said, intuitively, that because *to kick the bucket* means "to die," no one would ever think, in the appropriate context, that it might mean "to kick the pail." Nevertheless, idiomatic expressions often have a "literal" meaning that is different from the figurative meaning, and it is just this fact of having two meanings that reinforces the tendency in children to go no further than the processing of the literal meaning. The literal strategy, which consists of applying only lexical and morphosyntactic competence to the decoding of the literal meaning, is not only the preferred strategy and the one that is adopted first, but, especially in very young children, is the only strategy available.

Expressions that are relatively context-free for adults, such as idioms, can be processed correctly by children to the extent to which they can put to use all the contextual information available for the recognition of the nonliteral meaning.

The few studies that have investigated the role of context among children are unanimous in finding that it does aid the comprehension of figurative meaning (Ackerman, 1982; Cacciari & Levorato, 1989; Nippold & Tarrant Martin, 1989). However, this finding generally has not been backed up by much theoretical analysis. One question in particular remains to be answered, and that is the problem of establishing how and why an appropriate and sufficiently complete context should lead to the comprehension of idiomatic expressions not previously known to the child. I would like to try to answer this question with the following hypothesis: Context operates if the child is able to take all the linguistic information surrounding the figurative expression and search it for those clues that might lead to the idiomatic interpretation. Thus context provides background information for an hypothesis about the idiom's meaning, it aids the memory search for information that could serve to define the figurative meaning, and it provides the material for the appropriate inferential processes.

If we look at the role of context in adult comprehension of idioms we see that it functions quite differently for children. Whereas adults retrieve the idiomatic meaning first and only subsequently instantiate the interpretation of the idiom with the linguistic context (Kemper, 1986) or, even if they integrate the idiomatic meaning with the linguistic context parallel to the retrieval of the idiomatic meaning, the integration does not depend on the contextual information, children, on the other hand, analyze the figurative expression at the same time as the linguistic context and need the contextual information to grasp the idiomatic meaning. The processes involved—from inference to the activation of the required world knowledge—though not specific to the processing of idiomatic expressions, are especially necessary in the comprehension of idioms, because the principle of compositionality can not be applied in the same simple and linear way as for literal language (Fraser, 1970; Katz & Postal, 1963).

As already mentioned, one important element of figurative competence is the ability to use all the linguistic information available in the context in order to form a coherent semantic representation in which the semantic field established by the context will be consistent with the meaning given to the idiom. The primary characteristic of any type of text or discourse is *coherence,* because that is what determines its status as a text or discourse rather than a simple phrasal sequence. The comprehension process, which is based on the assumption that what is read or heard must be coherent, has its principle object in the identification of the main point of a text or discourse, and the creation of a semantic representation that will mirror the coherence of the text. In the comprehension of idioms, coherence is a key factor. The introduction of an idiomatic expression abruptly changes the subject of a text, and if the interpreter goes no further than a literal analysis, the coherence of the text is in jeopardy. The interpreter then must take the comprehension process a step further and submit the linguistic information to semantic processing that will allow for the reestablishment of coherence. In the more advanced stages of linguistic development the awareness of a semantic gap automatically may activate strategies, in particular the figurative strategy, for reestablishing coherence. However, there must be present a need for coherence in the text before the child will be able to arrive at this figurative strategy.

Comprehension should not be considered as an all-or-none process, but as a process that can occur at different depths or levels depending on various factors: the demands set by the task, the previous knowledge of the interpreter, his or her goals, and the extent of the acquisition of the ability to process language—the factor most relevant in a developmental study. A mere perception of some sense of the message is inadequate for a comprehension at a deeper level, involving a consideration of ambiguities, inferential steps, and nuances of meaning (Mistler-Lachman, 1972). In the first developmental stages every word or short sequence of words is submitted to a semantic/syntactic analysis, and the meanings that result from this analyses simply are juxtaposed in a semantic representation that consists of a collection of barely related items. Later the child acquires the ability to process linguistic data in ever more complex ways, so that the products of a semantic/syntactic analysis of short segments of text are subjected to further analyses with a view to integrating all the partial meanings into a global semantic representation (Levorato, 1988). One of the main features of this global representation is the degree to which the different semantic elements cohere. Thus, if a passage containing figurative expressions undergoes a superficial processing, the semantic representation created from it could include elements that do not cohere among themselves. As the children develop, however, they begin to search for coherence among the codified items of information, and acquire a greater ability to subject information to complex processing. Though it is difficult to say which comes first—the search for coherence or the growth of an ability to perform complex processing of linguistic material—it is possible, however, to hypothesize that the need to find coherence within one's own mental contents, or among the products of one's own processing, develops in parallel with the ability to carry out those analyses that allow for the creation of a coherent representation.

A STUDY OF THE ROLE OF CONTEXT

I now describe the experiments that test our model of comprehension of idioms as dependent on the ability to interpret their meaning within the linguistic context. Our hypothesis was that comprehension would be better when the children could make use of contextual information in order to figure out what the idiomatic expression meant. In Experiment 1,[1] the children's comprehension of idioms was studied under two conditions: (a) with idioms embedded in a linguistic context consisting of a short narrative, and (b) with idioms presented alone and out of context. Because previous studies had shown that children have difficulty in explaining the meaning of a sentence, comprehension was evaluated by means of a multiple-choice test (MCT).

Eight common idioms were selected, all of them having both a figurative and literal meaning (e.g., *to break the ice*), and for each idiom a story was prepared following a simple problem-solving narrative formed by a setting with characters, an initial event, and a solution. The last sentence of the story contained the idiomatic expression. For each story an MCT was prepared in which a question about the meaning of the idiom was followed by three possible answers: (a) the idiomatic meaning (idiomatic answer), (b) a paraphrase of the literal meaning (literal answer), and (c) a sentence that expressed a meaning different from both (a) and (b) but plausible in the context (associate answer). Both (a) and (c) made sense according to the semantic content of the story, whereas the literal answer expressed a semantic content not congruent with the story. Subjects were first and fourth graders. The following is an example of a story and of an MCT presented with it:

> A little boy named Paul moved to another town. It was winter so he had to change school. His mother suggested that he should try and get to know his new schoolmates. Once at school he lent them his crayons and that helped to break the ice.
>
> What did Paul do when he broke the ice?
>
> (a) He made friends with his schoolmates.
> (b) He broke a piece of ice.
> (c) He told his mummy everything.

---

[1]For more details, see Cacciari & Levorato (1989).

As Table 5.1 shows, more idiomatic answers were chosen when the idiom was presented in context, because in fact the linguistic content of the story facilitated comprehension of the idiom. Literal answers were chosen very rarely when the idiom was presented in a story context and were almost totally absent among the older children. In the no-context condition the literal answers were much more frequent, but it should be kept in mind that the literal answers were not incorrect, because the idioms used in this study did have a literal meaning. Older children chose more idiomatic answers than did younger ones. These results confirm that the linguistic context in which the idiom is embedded plays a significant role in the acquisition of the ability to comprehend figurative meaning.

Associate answers were chosen more often by younger children, irrespective of the presence or absence of a context. Although further investigation about associate answers is necessary, we can say tentatively that sometimes young children are able to reject a literal interpretation but are not able to identify the appropriate idiomatic meaning.

The stories provided for context had the effect of showing that the literal interpretation did not make sense at all and that it was incongruent with any expectation formed on the basis of previous information. Moreover, the context provided the necessary semantic background to interpret the idiom correctly. One might ask at this point what would happen if the linguistic context pointed less obviously to a figurative interpretation and to some extent did justify a literal interpretation. This was the focus of an experiment in which stories presented to children contained a reference to an object, event, or situation semantically related to the literal meaning of the idiom. The aim of the second experiment was to make the literal interpretation less implausible (though of course the figurative interpretation was still the correct one), to determine to what extent children might be fooled by this type of context and whether or not they would choose literal answers more frequently than in the first experiment. The hypothesis was that if context represents an important source of information for the interpreter in identifying figurative meaning, a context that is not incoherent with a literal interpretation would produce fewer idiomatic answers than a context in which the literal interpretation does not make sense. For the sake of brevity, we refer to the

TABLE 5.1
Percentage of Idiomatic, Literal, and Associate Answers in the
Idiomatic Context Condition and in the No-Context Condition,
for the Two Age Groups

Age	Idiomatic Context			No Context		
	Idiomatic	Literal	Associate	Idiomatic	Literal	Associate
7 yrs.	59,1	18,6	22,3	21,2	56,8	22
10 yrs.	87,5	3,7	8,8	51,1	40,1	7,8

story used in the first experiment as the *idiomatic context* and those used in the second experiment as the *literal context*.

Stories with the same eight idioms as in the first experiment were presented to children of the same age as those in the first experiment and followed by an MCT in which the idiomatic and literal answers were the same as for the first experiment, whereas the associate answers were appropriate to the new context.

Table 5.2 shows the percentage of idiomatic, literal, and associate answers chosen by children with the literal context condition. In this experiment, as in the first, the older children chose more idiomatic answers than did the younger ones, as was predictable. It is to be noted that even when a literal context was used, idiomatic answers were still more frequent than when the idiom was presented completely out of context (see Table 5.1). The percentage of associate answers that resulted in this experiment confirms the developmental trend of the previous experiment: This type of answer was chosen more often by younger children than by older ones. This result provides us with another indirect confirmation of the role of context in comprehension: As the percentage of children who chose associate answers was equal under the no-context as well as the context conditions (both idiomatic and literal), we can presume that this choice is typical of children who are not disposed to use the context to understand the idiom; that is the younger ones.

If we look at the percentage of idiomatic answers for figurative expression presented in an idiomatic story as compared with a figurative expression in a literal story, it becomes clear that the semantic content preceding the idiom does play a role in inducing figurative, that is, idiomatic answers. In fact, the percentage of idiomatic answers is higher in the idiomatic context, and this difference is statistically significant. In both linguistic contexts the children were able to some extent to use the global meaning of the story to choose the most plausible answer, though under the literal context condition it was more difficult for them to reject a literal interpretation.

The two experiments described so far produced very clear and coherent results that strongly support our hypothesis regarding the role of context. There are still some questions that remain unanswered. One might wonder legitimately, for instance, whether the results of the MCT might not overestimate the real ability

TABLE 5.2
Percentage of Idiomatic, Literal, and Associate Answers
in the Literal Context Condition, for the Two Age Groups

Age	Literal Context		
	Idiomatic	Literal	Associate
7 yrs.	51,3	28,7	20
10 yrs.	72,5	17,5	10

of the children to understand figurative language. Moreover, this task does not give any evidence of what interpretive strategies are used by children to understand the language addressed to them. The performance might differ if the children were presented with another kind of task. The ability to process figurative language is a complex competence involving many different skills that vary with the cognitive and linguistic demands of the situation. This was the issue we intended to address in the third experiment.

The same stories as in Experiment 1 were presented to the children but the idiom was incomplete, and the task was to complete the expression. The aim was to study the strategies used by the children in a task of this nature, especially when they did not yet possess the idiomatic lexicon necessary for producing the exact words of the idioms. Our hypothesis was that it would be possible to distinguish strategies determined by figurative competence even prior to the lexicalization of figurative expressions in their conventional form, and that such a competence would be linked to a global processing of the entire text in which the expression is embedded.

The children tested in this experiment were third and fifth graders; they were older than those in the previous two experiments, because we assumed that a production type of task would be more difficult than would a comprehension task.

The stories used in the first experiment (idiomatic context) were modified by deleting a part of the idiomatic expression, beginning with the second constituent after the verbal phrase. For instance, in the case of the story of Paul who went to a new school, the last sentence was: "Once at school he lent them his crayons and that helped to break the . . . ," so the completion of the narrative was not fully open to any possibility but only to a small set of possibilities.

The subjects were presented with the eight incomplete stories and were asked to complete them with the word or words they felt were most appropriate.

The children produced three types of answers, the first of which was an idiomatic completion in which the exact wording of the idiom was used.

The second type of answer was a literal completion in which the children merely adapted the words of the story rather than performing semantic analysis. The completions in this group were mostly of two types. In the first type of literal completion, the child saw the objects mentioned in the preceding part of the text as possible referents to the idiom. For example, for the story presented earlier in the discussion of Experiment 1, some children write "to break the crayon," with the result that the text was not totally incoherent and the completion did make some sense—in fact, crayons that are lent out might be broken—but these completions were clearly not products of a deep semantic processing of a text as a whole. In a story about a boy who had trouble fitting in with a new group of classmates, the breaking of a crayon is irrelevant. The listener, on hearing a story with such an ending, would judge it somewhat out of place because of the gap between the expectations created by the text and the contents of the last sentence.

In the second type of literal completion the child chose a concrete referent that suited the verbal form of the idiom and that in everyday, although literal, language was the most likely nominal sintagm for that verb. For example, with the idiom *to fall from the clouds* (the idiomatic meaning is "to be astounded") a common completion was *stairs,* which is easily associated with the verb *to fall.* Moreover, in Italian *stairs* agrees with *clouds* in gender and number (both are feminine) and therefore follows the same preposition linked with its article (*dalle*) that was the last word of the story before the ellipsis. As for the coherence, it is to be noted that in this example the existence of stairs are not altogether implausible on the ship of a captain who has lost his way (but would be less so if he were the captain of an airplane!). However, if we consider the general meaning of the text with this completion, the lack of proportion in this interpretation between the main goal of the character (to find his way again) and the result (he falls down the stairs) becomes obvious.

Both types of literal completion confirm that the strategy used was that of searching in the lexicon of the story for clues that would lead to a completion, and that the words chosen for the completions represented concrete referents. Thus, the inability to perceive a figurative use of the language seems to be associated with a lack of ability to understand the general meaning of a text and with a highly concrete mode of thinking.

The third type of answer was figurative completions, those that gave appropriate expression to the meaning of the idiom, the action, or the mental state of the character to whom the idiom referred, without the child's knowing the idiomatic expression. This produced expressions not canonical in Italian, such as "to break the fear" or "to break the shyness" (instead of *to break the ice*) or "to fall from surprise" (instead of *to fall from clouds*). With these completions the children produced metaphorical expressions and showed that they were not insensitive to the figurative potential of the language. Furthermore, they were able to go beyond a strictly literal use of the language in order to fulfill certain communicative aims. These children understood that the expression to be completed had to provide the information coherent with the global meaning of the text. Thus, it seems that the inferential process of looking for the appropriate completion is determined by the child's knowledge of the main features of the story, as for example, in the story of the new school, where the relevant fact is whether the boy achieved his aim in lending his crayons. Here we see that what is involved is the child's ability to process linguistic information.

It appears that the strategies of children who made literal completions and those of children who made figurative ones can be differentiated not only by their ability to use figurative language, but also by their overall cognitive and linguistic skills, and in particular by their ability to make the appropriate inferences from the available linguistic information, either by means of a complex semantic processing, or through the use of appropriate general knowledge.

TABLE 5.3
Percentage of Idiomatic, Literal, and Figurative
Completions Produced by 8 Years and 11 Years
of Age. (Total Does Not Reach 100%,
Because of Some Nonclassifiable Answers)

Age	Completion Task		
	Idiomatic	*Literal*	*Figurative*
8 yrs.	14	39.2	41.2
11 yrs.	40	26.9	26.2

Table 5.3 gives the percentages of the three types of completions. Idiomatic responses were much more common among the older children, who had acquired idiomatic expressions through their greater exposure to adult language and were able to produce them when they were provided with the beginning of an idiom. Literal completions were more common, on the other hand, among young children, as were the figurative completions, which also made up a consistent number of the responses of the older children (about one fourth of the total).

The figurative completions provide us with proof of a consistent and systematic strategy not evident in earlier studies and not disclosed by the experiments that used the MCT. This strategy tends to disappear as the children develop and they acquire the exact wording of the idioms. These figurative completions prove the existence of a figurative competence that comes before the acquisition of the specific idiomatic expressions and that (a) is the basis for the figurative use not only of idiomatic expressions but of language in general, and (b) precedes the conventionalizing phase.

One last consideration regards the difference between the three experiments, particularly between the multiple-choice task and the completion task. The former was useful for measuring the effect of independent variables such as the age of the subject and the informativeness of the context; however, it revealed less about the strategies the children used spontaneously. The completion task proved to be suitable for eliciting the strategies that the children presumably also used in nonexperimental situations. Although the children tested this way were a year older than the others, a comparison still can be made between the results of the tasks (see Tables 5.1 and 5.3). It is to be noted that the idiomatic responses were much more frequent with the MCT, a result that is in line with the findings of other studies about the relationship between comprehension and production in figurative language (Ackerman, 1982; Gibbs, 1986; Honeck, Sowry, & Voegtle, 1978; Prinz, 1983; Vosniadou & Ortony, 1983; Winner, Engel, & Gardner, 1980). The phenomenon of a gap between comprehension and production has been commented on often in the literature about linguistic development. Nevertheless, because the comprehension and the production tasks were presented to different groups of children with varying ages, their relationship is dealt with later.

ARE IDIOMS ACQUIRED BY ROTE?

A study of the acquisition of idiomatic expressions that aims at drawing up a developmental model of their comprehension must take into account all the factors involved. Thus, I now investigate in greater depth the comprehension and the production of idioms in relation to one factor that appears to affect the performance of children: the degree of their familiarity with an idiomatic expression. In studying this variable, especially in comparison with and in relation to other variables, we can judge more accurately the validity of the hypothesis that idioms may be acquired by rote. However, even if it were true that the familiarity was a factor in acquisition (as Schweigert, 1986, observed among adults), some form of figurative competence would be necessary for an understanding of the meaning of an idiom, given that context can convey so many variations in meaning.

In the following experiments, we compared the role of context with the role of familiarity, defined as the frequency with which an idiom appears in the language addressed to children.[2] If the ability to understand the figurative meaning of an idiomatic expression does depend on the acquisition of the wider cognitive and linguistic abilities discussed earlier, then, presumably, the frequency of an idiom would not play an important role in the process of identifying the idiomatic meaning. A confirmation of this hypothesis would mean that idioms cannot be treated like nondecomposable long words and cannot be learned by rote. However, because we could not exclude that familiarity might have some effect, either in itself or in combination with other factors, the object of this study was to find out if there were conditions under which the familiarity factor might operate, in what way this occurred, and whether familiarity interacted with other variables.

Along with the degree of familiarity, the variables considered in this study were the age of the subjects, the type of context surrounding the idiom (idiomatic context vs. literal context), and the type of task performed (comprehension vs. production).

A preliminary survey was conducted in order to establish how familiar the children were with certain idiomatic expressions. In this survey, elementary school teachers were asked to evaluate the frequency of occurrence of 85 different idiomatic expressions in the language the children encountered in school textbooks, in everyday conversations, and on television. On the basis of the

---

[2]For more details, see Levorato and Cacciari (1992).

teachers' evaluations, we chose for the experiment five of the most common idioms and five of the least common idioms (from now on referred to as familiar and unfamiliar idioms).

Two stories were prepared for each idiom, each story ending with an idiomatic expression that expressed the story's conclusion. In the first story, which we refer to as the idiomatic context, the literal interpretation was inappropriate because of the incongruence between the semantic field of the linguistic context and the semantic field of the idiom. In the second story, hereafter the literal context, a literal interpretation also would have been possible because the literal meaning related to objects or events in the context, although the idiomatic interpretation was still the most appropriate one. Three responses also were prepared for each story and presented in a multiple-choice task. They consisted of an idiomatic interpretation, a paraphrase of the literal interpretation, and a response that differed from the first two and was plausible in the context (associate answer).

The subjects of the experiment, children from the first and fourth grades, listened to the stories and then were asked to perform the multiple-choice task.

The results of this experiment are shown in Table 5.4. The age of the subjects had an effect on the idiomatic responses, the older children choosing them more often than the younger children did. These responses were also more frequent in the idiomatic context than in the literal context. Familiarity was not a significant factor in the choice of idiomatic responses. From this we conclude that the choice of an idiomatic response is determined by the child's ability to process the linguistic information surrounding the idiom and to identify the most plausible response in a given context. This ability depends on the age of the child, and therefore on his cognitive and linguistic development.

In the case of the literal responses, with fewer literal responses in the idiomatic context, it is clear that context played an important role. However, the literal responses were more common with unfamiliar idioms. Looking at the results for both idiomatic and literal responses as a whole, we find confirmation, especially among older children, of the role of the linguistic context in activating a figurative strategy based on an analysis of the linguistic information presented

TABLE 5.4
Percentage of Idiomatic, Literal, and Associate Choices,
for Familiar and Unfamiliar Idioms, in Idiomatic (IC) and
Literal Context (LC), Irrespective of the Age Factor

	Familiar		Unfamiliar	
	IC	LC	IC	LC
Idiomatic Answers	57	40	51	38
Literal Answers	14	30	24	42
Associate Answers	29	30	25	20

by the story. This explains why the idiomatic responses increase and the literal responses decrease when the linguistic context is semantically incompatible with a literal interpretation of the idiom. However, the fact that the children could be fooled by the literal context into choosing a not entirely inappropriate literal response implies that they had not completely acquired and systematically applied the figurative strategy, especially in the case of unfamiliar idioms. Though we do not have an adult sample available, we assume that when figurative competence is fully developed, the listeners choose the figurative interpretation whenever possible, basing the choice on their belief that whoever produced the message would not have intended to create any ambiguity and would not have meant a figurative expression to be interpreted literally. There is evidence in the literature that adults are influenced much the same way as the children in our study. In a study that had reading time as its dependent variable (Kemper, 1986), an unfamiliar idiom in a context with little information was read more slowly than a familiar idiom in an information-rich context. Thus, when the on-line processes in adults are examined, familiarity tends to enhance the effect of context. The same seems to happen with young children: In a literal context, unfamiliar idioms are interpreted literally more frequently than are familiar idioms. Further proof is needed, but the results of our research so far confirm that the frequency of occurrence of an idiomatic expression does have an impact, in that those children who do not make use of a systematic figurative strategy fall more easily into the trap of accepting the literal interpretation when the idiom is unknown to them than when they already have had some occasion to associate it with a figurative meaning.

As regards the associate responses, the results of this study agree to a striking extent with the results of the first study. These responses, that is, were influenced only by the factor of age, in that they were more common among the younger children. At this point we are fairly confident that the tendency to choose these hybrid responses—which are not literal and are closer to a figurative interpretation without being quite appropriate—does not relate to the child's familiarity with the idiom or to whether or not the linguistic information surrounding the idiom tends to trick the subject into a literal interpretation. The only factor operating for these choices is age, that is, the level of the child's linguistic and cognitive development. The most plausible interpretation here is that associate responses were chosen by children who were beginning to use a figurative strategy, but were not yet able to analyze the text and extract the semantic interpretation most appropriate to the context. This interpretation establishes two phases in the acquisition of idioms. In the first phase, children can and do use nonliteral strategies, although they are not yet able to process all the linguistic information completely in order to arrive at the most coherent interpretation of the idiom—and therefore they tended to choose the associate answers in our experiments. In the second and later phase, children have acquired fully the ability to process linguistic information and so are able to create a fully integrated and coherent semantic representation—typified by the idiomatic response in our experiment.

These points are taken up again later when we discuss the developmental sequence and the cognitive and linguistic skills that lead to figurative competence and make up its substratum. Now let us turn to some important points concerning the relationship between the comprehension and the production of idiomatic expressions. In the experiment described next, we investigated the relative effects of age and familiarity in a kind of production task, that is, a completion task, and because the subjects did both a multiple-choice and a completion task we were able to examine the relationship between comprehension and production.

The material used in the experiment consisted of the same stories used in the preceding experiment, but with part of the idiom left incomplete—the second element after the verb. The subjects of the experiment were children attending the second and fifth grades of elementary school. Each child performed the completion task individually, and then a week later, after hearing the complete story again, did an MCT.

In the completion task the same three categories of responses—idiomatic, literal, and figurative—were produced by the children as in the previous experiment on production. Table 5.5 gives the percentages of the three different responses at the two age levels and for the two degrees of familiarity. The number of idiomatic completions differed significantly according to the degree of familiarity, as familiar idioms were completed correctly more often than were unfamiliar idioms. They also differed according to age, because older children produced more than younger children.

Literal completions occurred more frequently among the younger children and were more common when the idioms were unfamiliar. Thus, idiomatic and literal completions were perfectly complementary, because they were both affected by the same factors—age and familiarity—but in opposite ways.

Figurative completions were more common with unfamiliar idioms, and furthermore were produced more often by older children than by younger children, although only when the idioms were unfamiliar. When the idioms were familiar, figurative completions were less common for both age groups.

TABLE 5.5
Percentage of Idiomatic, Literal, and Figurative Completions
for Familiar and Unfamiliar Idioms, According to the Two Age Groups

Age	Familiar			Unfamiliar		
	Idiomatic	Literal	Figurative	Idiomatic	Literal	Figurative
8 yrs.	62	22	16	3	65	32
11 yrs.	82	6	12	3	47	50

In conclusion, the frequency of occurrence of an idiomatic expression in the language addressed to children, which did not prove to be a significant factor in a preceding experiment that evaluated comprehension, turned out to be a crucial factor in a production task. This does not mean that children are able to use idiomatic expressions spontaneously in their conversation, but simply that they can produce appropriate completions when part of a familiar idiom is presented to them in context. With unfamiliar idioms younger children tended to produce literal completions more often than did older children, and the older children, in turn, produced more figurative completions. This serves to confirm that as they develop, children become progressively more skilled at perceiving the figurative possibilities of language. Though the results of the productionlike task are very clear, further investigation is needed into the way in which frequency of use interacts with other variables such as type of linguistic context, general level of world knowledge, and expertise in a given field.

As described earlier, a week afterward the children were given an MCT in which the story was presented with the complete idiom and the children had to choose among the three responses: idiomatic, literal, and associate.

I do not take too much time to analyze these results because the comprehension task has been discussed already in connection with the preceding experiment. Now, I focus on the differences between the children's performances in the production task and their performances in the comprehension task. The aim of this comparison was two-fold. First, I wanted to check our hypothesis as to the different degrees of complexity of the two tasks, and second, I wanted to verify the hypothesis that a production task helps children to comprehend a text at a far deeper level than when they have done an MCT.

The first hypothesis was confirmed by the number of idiomatic responses produced by the children in the production as compared with those produced in the comprehension tasks, and especially by those cases in which a nonidiomatic completion was followed by an idiomatic response. The fact that emerges most clearly is that for both age groups and for both familiar and unfamiliar idioms, a very high percentage of children made the "transition" from nonidiomatic completions to idiomatic responses in the MCT. This confirms that the MCT is an easier task for the children. However, it also indicates that MCTs should be used with some caution and in conjunction with other tasks in experiments of this nature, because they could overestimate the real figurative competence of children.

Our second hypothesis about the effect of a production task in inducing comprehension strategies was tested by comparing the children's performances in the MCT of the present experiment with the performances of the children in the preceding experiment in which they had not been subjected to the completion task.

Table 5.6 shows the percentages of the different responses (idiomatic, literal, and associate) of the children in both the preceding experiment (7 and 10 years

TABLE 5.6
Percentage of Idiomatic, Literal, and Associate Choices
in the MCT in the Previous Experiment (7 and 10 Years Old)
and in the Present One (8 and 11 Years Old)

Age & Task	Idiomatic	Literal	Associate
7 yrs: only MCT	36.5	29.5	34
8 yrs: MCT + Completion	70.8	17.2	12
10 yrs: only MCT	56.5	25.5	18
11 yrs: MCT + Completion	80	14.5	5.5

old) and the present experiment (8 and 11 years old). The comparisons involve familiar and unfamiliar idioms in both literal and idiomatic context. The most interesting comparison concerns the 7-, 8-, and 10-year-old children. The 7- and 10-year-olds took part only in the MCT, whereas the 8-year-olds also did the completion task. In comparing the 7- and 10-year-olds, a natural developmental tendency can be observed in which the number of literal responses decreased with age and the number of idiomatic responses increased. However, if we compare the 8- and 10-year-olds, this tendency is not present and an inverse trend may even be detected. Not only did the 10-year-olds not perform better than the 8-year-olds, but they actually produced an average of 18.7% fewer idiomatic responses.

These comparisons lead us to the conclusion that children tend to produce many more idiomatic responses when they go from a production task to a comprehension task. The very fact of having first done the production task made the children more inclined to choose idiomatic responses in the comprehension task. Thus, the children tended not only to choose more idiomatic responses than they would have been able to produce themselves, but they also chose more idiomatic responses when they had already had a chance to submit the linguistic information to the deep-level comprehension processing required by the completion task. Further research will have to verify whether or not it is simply the fact of being presented twice with the text that brings about such a marked improvement in the children's performances. The most likely hypothesis for this is that the completion task, because it is more demanding, forces the children to try to create a mental representation of the text that is both logical and coherent. In other words, they must search for some idea of what the story is about. In relation to age, and so to their level of linguistic development, the children may or may not carry out the task well, identifying the correct idiomatic completion in the case of familiar idioms, or in the case of unfamiliar idioms producing figurative or literal completions. In any case, in the course of the experiment the children seem to have acquired a greater capacity for recognizing the appropriate response when it was presented together with other, less appropriate responses. The interpretation that best accounts for all the results presented so far is that the children's ability to carry out these experimental tasks correlates closely with their linguistic ability in general and especially with the ability to elaborate semantic information and achieve the global coherence. The value of the results of the aforementioned comparisons should not be underestimated, either in reference to a theory of the development of figurative competence or to experimental methodology. It seems clear, in fact, that performing a more demanding task first and then a simpler task afterward did have some effect on the results of the latter. Further research is needed to ascertain how general this tendency is and whether analogous consequences would result if the easier task were to precede the more difficult task.

CONCLUSION: TOWARD A MODEL FOR THE DEVELOPMENT OF FIGURATIVE COMPETENCE

The results of the experiments reported previously are proof that the acquisition of idioms by children is far from a simple matter of passively learning conventional expressions, but is, on the contrary, a process involving complex linguistic and cognitive skills. There seems to be little recognition of this fact among those who study the language of children to judge by the research on the subject, which has not been abundant up to now (Ackerman, 1982; Cacciari & Levorato, 1989; Gibbs, 1987; Lodge & Leach, 1975; Nippold & Tarrant Martin, 1989; Prinz, 1983). In the model for the development of figurative competence that I propose, the acquisition of figurative competence is tied to the development of a whole series of linguistic skills that give the child an ever greater control over his or her communicative possibilities. This linguistic development could be said to start with a nominal realist phase, when an object and its name are viewed as one and the same thing, and it could be said to have concluded with metalinguistic competence, which involves reflection about language itself. Very young children, as we know, believe that language is motivated and not conventional; that is to say, the name of an object derives from that object, is intrinsic to it, and does not come from any agreement between speakers of the language. For example, if the "sun" were to change its name, children believe that it would lose its heat at well (Piaget, 1923). Osherson and Markman (1985) found that young children will accept that the name of an object can be changed, but believe that the properties of the object will change with the name. They also may believe that the name has the same properties as the object so that, for example, the name for a train must be long like a train. In terms of the development of figurative competence, this phase of total identification of an object with its name without the mediation of meaning can be thought of as Level O.

Later, the name ceases to be part of the object and begins to take on the character of a symbolic substitute. One of the first steps of this evolution is the overcoming of nominal realism. Meaning becomes of primary importance because the child is now aware that the name refers to a meaning. The acquisition of this awareness is linked to the discovery that the same linguistic label can be given to various referents (as is the case for polysemous linguistic units), and that the same referent can be designated by various linguistic labels. The cognitive substratum to this discovery is the growth of a conceptual system and the rapid speeding up and expansion of categorization processes. This point in the child's evolution, which could be termed Level 1, still is characterized by a prevailing tendency to apply a literal strategy in the processing of text or discourse.

This tendency to apply a literal strategy in comprehension can be broken down into the following aspects: (a) a tendency to conceive of meaning as the mere sum of the meanings of the component words, (b) a tendency to submit the linguistic information to shallow processing, (c) a tendency to be misled by the imaginative contents of figures of speech, and (d) a tendency to consider only the concrete elements of an expression. These tendencies reinforce each other and keep the child to a primitive concept of language, which is overcome only as the child proceeds along a parallel course of linguistic and cognitive development.

Level 2 of the development of figurative competence is characterized by the important fact that the child now can go beyond purely literal strategies and a purely referential and literal use of the language. In this phase we see context and inferential processing being used to arrive at meaning and coherence. Our experimental results about the role of context for the semantic interpretation of idioms are crucial for an understanding of the interpretive strategies used by children at this level. As discussed earlier, there is a greater tendency to select an idiomatic response when the idiom is presented in an idiomatic context than when it is presented out of context. This indicates that at a certain age children are able to perceive the incongruency of a literal interpretation with the contextual information surrounding an idiom. When the context cannot assimilate a given expression, the child then activates interpretative strategies that go beyond the literal. This phase could be defined as the phase of *suspended literalness*, because the child now is able to make use of information that would not have been available to him or her from a simple literal analysis. This phase corresponds with the last phase of cognitive pendulums in the linguistic realization (Nelson & Nelson, 1978). After a period of primitive forms of overgeneralization or narrow interpretation of language followed by a period in which names are used according to rigid and inflexible rules of strict association between name and referent, finally children learn to accept a more flexible and open approach in which linguistic labels are used to form analogies and metaphors. For example, they might say "this is like a dog." Now the child realizes that a discrepancy can exist between an expression and its meaning. The linguistic awareness thus acquired, although rudimentary, allows the child to perceive that such a discrepancy should not be interpreted as a communicative error or as a semantic anomaly. This induces the child to activate inferential processes that will resolve the anomaly and reestablish semantic coherence. This phase also is characterized by the ability to process semantic information, allowing the child to make use of the context as background information for hypotheses about the appropriate interpretation of the idiomatic expression. Thus, the child's arrival at Level 2 of the development of figurative competence—which our data indicate happens at approximately age 7 or 8 years—is the consequence of general linguistic development, and particularly of the acquisition of the ability to deal with semantic information. This is not acquired all at once, but is a slow and gradual process. Older children are better able than younger children to make use of contextual information, and at the same developmental level, different contextual information can facilitate to a greater or lesser degree the identification of idiomatic interpretation.

The next level, Level 3, is characterized by the children's discovery of the arbitrary nature of language, which then leads them to realize that language does not always need to be literal. Although a communicative event was what induced the child at Level 2 to activate strategies other than the literal, at Level 3 the child could be said to have acquired a kind of general rule that tells him or her not to depend too much on the surface form of a linguistic expression for meaning. This implies an ability to use language for the most diverse communicative purposes, and also means that, given a communicative need, the child is able to think up various linguistic ways to accomplish this, the literal approach figuring as but one of many options. The acquisition of figurative language, and with it the ability to produce and comprehend metaphors, similes, proverbs, and idioms, is only one of the consequences of this development. According to our interpretation of the experiment data, children who produced figurative completions had reached this phase. Their strategy, in fact, is characterized by a lack of interest in the literal aspects of the linguistic information and by the consequent attribution of priority to the meaning rather than to the significant. Compared with the preceding level, here there is a much more marked tendency to use the significant as a clue that might lead to the discovery of meaning. With the awareness of nonliteral language possibilities, meaning has become such a crucial element for communication that it detaches itself from the significant, which only serves as an aid in the search for meaning. To this is added the realization that the communicative intentions of the speaker are what count and that the speaker is free to use any means he or she wishes to express those intentions. In cognitive terms, the child's thinking at this point is losing the concreteness typical of children under 9 or 10 years of age. What stands out here is the fact that the child now realizes that the relationship between word and referent, as well as that between significant and meaning, is a relationship of one to many; that is, a given meaning can be communicated by many different expressions. From this the child also may arrive at the realization that some expressions are more effective than others in communicating a given meaning.

Level 4, in fact, is the concrete realization of all the potential developed in the preceding three levels. With a sufficient system of knowledge the child can link expressions to information and concepts already acquired and so may acquire conventionalized expressions such as idioms, frozen metaphors, formulaic expressions, and so on. Those children who produced idiomatic completions in our studies based their responses on their knowledge of familiar expressions. Because the prerequisite for acquiring these expressions in their standard form is the ability to identify the appropriate meaning in a given context, this level is seen as the logical successor to Level 3. Regarding the variables studied in our experiments, it could be said that if Levels 2 and 3 are the most strongly influenced by the context, Level 4 is the one most influenced by familiarity: The acquisition of the idioms depends on the extent to which they are encountered in appropriate contexts. The acquisition of some idiomatic expressions is possible even before this level, if the child is exposed to them enough, but Level 4 normally and logically comes afterward because Level 3 provides the meanings to which the figurative expressions then can be applied.

Level 4 has a limitation, however, which is that expressions are understood and produced as indivisible units, as formulas that are applied in a fixed way and that cannot be modified according to circumstance. This holistic approach does not allow the child to analyze the parts of an expression.

The complete acquisition of figurative competence comes only with Level 5, which is characterized by the ability to reflect on the meaning of a figurative expression and on the relationship between the significant and the meaning. The linguistic awareness characteristic of this level could be spoken of as metacomprehension: Language now can be "analyzed" in order to understand the relationship between communicative intentions and surface expression. The interpreter is able to reconstruct meaning by making semantic inferences about the elements of the idiom and by referring to his or her background knowledge. The strategies for interpreting figurative meaning and the inferential processes can be employed both with and without the aid of context.

At its most mature, this level represents the skills, as far as figurative language is concerned, of a truly competent speaker. Regarding idiomatic expressions, these skills can be described as follows: the ability to break down an idiom into its component parts and to make semantic inferences about these; the ability to comprehend idiomatic expressions even when they have been subjected to lexical substitution or syntactic and lexical variations; and the ability to generate new idioms by means of syntactic and lexical variations on existing idioms. In conclusion, at this level the interpreters' linguistic awareness makes it possible for them to use figurative language for diverse purposes in which the communication depends on the awareness of a special, intimate register full of tacit references and allusions (e.g., an idiomatic expression spoken with ironic intent, or an idiom changed in order to give hyperbolic expression to a given idiomatic meaning as in the expression *to burn a candle at three ends*). This new competence allows for the productive use of figurative language for a number of various figures of speech. Our data about Level 5 are still incomplete, but research is being undertaken to investigate the concept of idioms as creative linguistic forms that can be modified, and for which the meaning of each of the constituent words in both the on-line comprehension and the interpretation is accessed and plays a role in the overall comprehension of the idiom (Cacciari & Glucksberg, 1990).

The development of figurative competence parallels the transition from a limited linguistic competence in which language is concrete, referential, literal, and characterized by nominal realism, to a complete linguistic competence in which language use is supported by metalinguistic competence. This evolution is characterized by succession of phases in which the significant and the meaning are given more or less importance. The first change is from a tendency to make use of real life in order to acquire language to a tendency to use language to amplify the world knowledge (especially the social world). We could define this change as a shift from a search for the significant to a search for meaning (though at the beginning of this process words are not real significants so much as signals). In the beginning, in fact, the child uses linguistic labels to accompany his practical knowledge of the world. Thus, small children will typically ask adults for the names of objects they encounter in their exploration of reality. Later those names lose their character as extensions of the things they denote, and a new phase begins in which the child is searching for what lies behind the names (or between the names and the things)—in other words, the meaning. This phase sees the creation of a semantic system that will allow the child to recognize that an entity belongs to a conceptual category. Regarding figurative competence, the phases in which meaning has priority coincide with Levels 1, 2, and 3, which are characterized by the progressive development of interpretive strategies for polisemic, ambiguous, or figurative terms; the child at Level 1 applies very limited and elementary inferential processes, which become gradually more complex until at Level 3 an awareness of nonliteral possibilities of language opens up new interpretive possibilities in the search for an appropriate meaning. At Level 4, where the significant is conventionalized, and Level 5, where metalinguistic awareness is attained, the significant—and with it the surface forms of language—return to the forefront and have priority: The interpreter realizes the conventional and arbitrary nature of language and has acquired the ability to reflect on language and its uses. Interpretive strategies also are used along with syntactic and lexical strategies, to alter the significant according to particular communicative needs and to establish the relationship between the significant and the meaning.

In my opinion, the acquisition of idioms, although it may appear to be a "trivial" phenomenon in linguistic development, is fully a part of that development. With respect to other forms of figurative language that are less conventionalized, such as metaphors, idioms are peculiarly suitable for the study of the development of figurative competence. Although metaphors can be mastered already at Level 3 (when the use of the interpretive strategies is quite advanced), because there is an explicit relationship between the expression and the speaker's intention, the mastering of idioms comes at a later stage because of their conventional nature.

The model presented here is characterized by a developmental sequence in which each level gives way to and at the same time prepares the way for the following level, which in its turn incorporates all the abilities acquired at the preceding levels. However, this model does not exclude some variations to the sequence. An inversion is possible, especially regarding the temporal relationship between Levels 3 and 4 due to specific learning experiences. A key role is played therefore by the systems of knowledge that are available at each stage of development and that assist in the transition from one level to the next. It is also possible that a child may be at different levels at the same time according to the extent of his or her knowledge relating to a particular semantic domain and the linguistic expressions connected with it. For example, a child who is interested in baseball may develop expertise in the use of expressions relating to baseball much more quickly than a child who does not play baseball. This does not mean that the only factors are expertise and experience, because in fact structural constraints do exist that limit that range of variability within one individual and among individuals. A child obviously cannot reach Level 3 before she or he is able to carry out inferential processes of some complexity. Nor can a child reach Level 5 if his or her thinking is still tied to the concrete.

Idioms, and consequently comprehension, may vary in complexity with respect to various factors. Two main aspects need to be considered: the cognitive aspect and the linguistic aspect. The former involves the semantic content of idiom, so that, for example, idioms that represent concrete actions are presumably less difficult to understand, at least for children, than idioms that represent emotions or mental states, and among the latter those referring to basic emotions differ from those referring to complex cognitive states. The linguistic aspect may include the morphosyntactic or semantic elements. Only one study, that by Gibbs (1987), has examined the relationship between linguistic factors such as semantic transparency and syntactic frozenness and the ability of the child to understand and explain the meaning of idiomatic expressions. His results seem to indicate that children are able to carry out inferential processes to make the meaning of a transparent idiom compatible with the semantic field of the context. This suggests that research is needed not only into the effects of context in itself, but also its effects in relation to other variables. Syntactic frozenness refers to the degree to which an idiom will tolerate variations in its syntactic form, such as the transformation of an active verb into a passive verb, the insertion of adverbs, and so on. The most important result of Gibbs' investigation was that this variable played a role in the comprehension of idioms only for the kindergarteners and first graders, but not for third and fourth graders. In fact, younger children understood syntactically frozen idioms better than flexible idioms. The reason for this, according to Gibbs, is that syntactically frozen idioms are always recognized in their standard form and so are acquired before flexible idioms. To a certain extent this result confirms the importance of frequency of idioms in their acquisition, as it may influence the extent to which the child perceives the need to deal appropriately with such problematic linguistic input.

Idioms have apparent literal meanings that do not make sense in the linguistic context in which they appear. If the children could verbalize in Gricean terms the problem they encounter with the comprehension of idioms, they might ask themselves, "How am I to resolve this obvious violation of the rule that language must be relevant, one of the most pervasive rules of linguistic communication?" The obvious inadequacy of a literal interpretation leads the child to treat the figurative expression as if it were in quotation marks, sustained, that is, by a communicative intention that we could call "so to speak," in which the speaker intends to communicate something other than the literal meaning. An idiomatic expression creates a situation that could be compared in a certain sense with symbolic play. In symbolic play a real object stands for something other than itself, and the players assign to it a meaning that suits their intentions (Piaget, 1951). Similarly, an idiom is treated as a piece of language that stands for some meaning other than that on the surface. The relationship between significant and meaning is not the conventional one, but a deviation from the conventional that is legitimized by the speaker's intentions.

The analogy between the "pretence" as it applies to symbolic play and the "so to speak" as it applies to idioms goes beyond the pragmatic. In the same way that the relationship between significant and meaning in symbolic play does have some motivation, because a certain formal similarity is necessary between the object used as a symbolic substitute and that which it represents, so too for idioms a certain similarity exists, though it is not always immediately apparent, between the surface form—the significant—and the figurative meaning. There is a reason why the idiom *to bring coals to Newcastle* has come to mean what it does, and does not mean the same as an idiom such as *to kick the bucket*. So too, this latter idiom is appropriate to describe a quick death and not drawn-out death throes, because the act of kicking takes only an instant. Thus the literal meaning may be more relevant in the comprehension of idioms than sometimes has been thought, as numerous recent studies have observed (Cacciari & Glucksberg, 1990; Cacciari & Tabossi, 1988; Gibbs, Nayak, & Cutting, 1989; Glucksberg, McGlone, & Cacciari, 1990). In this regard we note some interesting reasons provided by fifth graders when asked to explain certain idioms. For instance, for the idiom *to be in seventh heaven* ("to be very happy"), an explanation was, "If heaven is as wonderful as everyone says, just think what seventh heaven must be like"; or for *to break the ice* a child said, "It's hard to break the ice and the more time passes, the harder it gets"; or for *to have your head among the clouds* ("to be absent-minded") an answer was, "You can't be up among the clouds and have both feet on the ground at the same time. . . . The ground is the real world, while the clouds are your fantasies."

The child, of course, is not alone in facing the task of discovering the meaning of new expressions, because adults do participate in this process. But meaning never can be created by the simple association of a proposition with particular semantic information. This cannot be an automatic process for various reasons; first, and somewhat paradoxically, because the high degree of conventionality of idiomatic expressions make them quite flexible semantically so that their meaning may vary with the context. From this point of view, idiomatic expressions can be seen as labels that refer to meanings slightly different one from another. In different contexts *to break the ice* might mean "to start a conversation," "to get over embarrassment," "to overcome suspicion," or "to start up a friendship." It seems that idioms contain a semantic core to which particular semantic elements can be associated more or less as accessories. The meaning of an idiom acquires ever more depth as it is perceived in different contexts: With the experience of ever more and different contexts the child is able to perceive the core information and the accessory elements or those that vary with the context.

There is another reason why the acquisition of idiomatic meaning necessarily must be a constructive process characterized by successive adaptations and corrections. Even if the child may learn the meaning by asking an adult, she or he still must find out how and when to use it. Children may learn that *to kick the bucket* means "to die," but they have yet to understand that this expression may be appropriate in referring to a cockroach on the floor and not to the teacher, nor to the death of Napoleon, or even worse, to the death of a hero (for whom it might be more appropriate to use the expression *to draw his last breath*), although it could be used in speaking of Nero, especially if one wanted to convey contempt. As with all language, idioms can be part of either a narrow or limited code, or a complex code. Idiomatic expressions are not limited, in fact, to the language of "popular" culture, but can be found in every sphere of human life and communication. Indeed, what makes their use so fascinating is the way they involve the imagination, make abstract meanings more concrete, add a wealth of meaning to simple concepts, and finally, make the commonplace conversation more interesting. Like poetic language, idioms express in few words what would require many more words to express in literal terms but, given their conventional nature they do not require complex creative strategies, such as those needed for poetic language. Nor can they be called neutral denotations, because in fact they bring about a mutual understanding between speaker and interpreter based on their shared participation in a communicative game.

REFERENCES

Ackerman, B. P. (1982). On comprehending idioms: Do children get the picture? *Journal of Experimental Child Psychology, 33,* 439–454.

Cacciari, C., & Glucksberg, S. (1990). Understanding idiomatic expression: The contribution of word meanings. In G. B. Simpson (Ed.), *Understanding word and sentence* (pp. 217–240). Amsterdam, Netherlands: Elsevier.

Cacciari, C., & Levorato, M. C. (1989). How children understand idioms in discourse. *Journal of Child Language, 16,* 387–405.

Cacciari, C., & Tabossi, P. (1988). The comprehension of idioms. *Journal of Memory and Language, 27,* 668–683.

Dascal, M. (1987). Defending literal meaning. *Cognitive Science, 11,* 259–281.

Fraser, B. (1970). Idioms within a transformational grammar. *Foundations of Language, 6,* 122–142.

Gibbs, R. (1980). Spilling the beans on understanding and memory for idioms in context. *Memory and Cognition, 8,* 148–146.

Gibbs, R. (1984). Literal meaning and psychological theory. *Cognitive Psychology, 8,* 191–219.

Gibbs, R. (1986). Skating on thin ice: Literal meaning and understanding idioms in conversation. *Discourse Processes, 9,* 17–30.

Gibbs, R. (1987). Linguistic factors in children's understanding of idioms. *Journal of Child Language, 14,* 569–586.

Gibbs, R. (1989). Understanding and literal meaning. *Cognitive Science, 13,* 243–251.

Gibbs, R., & Gonzales, G. P. (1985). Syntactic frozenness in processing and remembering idioms. *Cognition, 20,* 243–259.

Gibbs, R., & Nayak, N. P. (1989). Psycholinguistic studies on the syntactic behavior of idioms. *Cognitive Psychology, 21,* 100–138.

Gibbs, R., Nayak, N. P., Bolton, J. L., & Keppel, M. (1988). Speakers' assumptions about the lexical flexibility of idioms. *Memory & Cognition, 17*(1), 58–68.

Gibbs, R., Nayak, N. P., & Cutting, C. (1989). How to kick the bucket and not decompose: Analyzability and idiom processing. *Journal of Memory and Language, 28,* 576–593.

Glucksberg, S., McGlone, M., & Cacciari, C. (1990, November). *Understanding idioms: The psychology of allusion.* Paper presented at the 31st annual meeting of the Psychonomic Society, New Orleans.

Honeck, R. P., Sowry, B., & Voegtle, K. (1978). Proverbial understanding in a pictorial context. *Child Development, 49,* 327–331.

Katz, J. J., & Postal, P. M. (1963). Semantic interpretations of idioms and sentence containing them. *Quarterly Progress Report of the Research Laboratory of Electronics, MIT, 70,* 275–282.

Kemper, S. (1986). Inferential processes in the comprehension of idioms. *Metaphor and Symbolic Activity, 1,* 43–56.

Levorato, M. C. (1988). *Racconti, storie e narrazioni. I processi di comprensione dei testi* [The processes of text comprehension]. Bologna, Italy: Il Mulino.

Levorato, M. C., & Cacciari, C. (1992). Children's comprehension and production of idioms: The role of context and familiarity. *Journal of Child Language, 19,* 415–433.

Lodge, L., & Leach, E. (1975). Children's acquisition of idioms in the English language. *Journal of Speech and Hearing Research, 18,* 521–529.

Mistler-Lachman, J. L. (1972). Levels of comprehension in processing of normal and ambiguous sentences. *Journal of Verbal Learning and Verbal Behavior, 11,* 614–623.

Nelson, K. E., & Nelson, K. (1978). Cognitive pendulums and their linguistic realization. In K. E. Nelson (Ed.), *Children's language* (Vol. 1, pp. 223–287). New York: Gardner.

Nippold, M. A., & Tarrant Martin, S. (1989). Idiom interpretation in isolation versus context. A developmental study with adolescents. *Journal of Speech and Hearing Research, 32,* 58–66.

Osherson, D., & Markman, E. (1975). Language and the ability to evaluate contradictions and tautologies. *Cognition, 3,* 213–226.

Piaget, J. (1955). The language and thought of the child. New York: Meridian Books. (Original work published 1923).

Piaget, J. (1951). *Play, dreams and imitation in childhood.* New York: Norton.

Pollio, H., Barlow, J., Fine, H., & Pollio, H. (1977). *Psychology and the poetics of growth.* Hillsdale, NJ: Lawrence Erlbaum Associates.

Prinz, P. M. (1983). The development of idiomatic meaning in children. *Language and Speech, 3,* 263–272.

Schweigert, W. (1986). The comprehension of familiar and less familiar idioms. *Journal of Psycholinguistic Research, 15,* 33–45.

Swinney, D. A., & Cutler, A. (1979). The access and processing of idiomatic expressions. *Journal of Verbal Learning and Verbal Behavior, 18,* 523–534.

Vosniadou, S., & Ortony, A. (1983). The emergence of the literal-metaphorical-anomalous distinction in young children. *Child Development, 54,* 154–161.

Winner, E. (1988). *The point of words: Children's understanding of metaphor and irony.* Cambridge, MA: Harvard University Press.

Winner, E., Engel, M., & Gardner, H. (1980). Misunderstanding metaphor: What's the problem? *Journal of Experimental Child Psychology, 30,* 22–32.

6 Ill-Formedness and Transformability in Portuguese Idioms

Teresa Botelho da Silva
University of Cambridge

Anne Cutler
MRC Applied Psychology Unit

Idioms are usually defined by their property of semantic eccentricity; they are meaningful strings whose meaning is not a direct function of the meanings of their components. In linguistics and psycholinguistics, the main problem posed by idioms is the necessity (in grammatical analysis and comprehension) of treating the string as a unit rather than decomposing it into its parts. The syntactic behavior of idioms has been important to this problem principally because of variability among idioms in the extent to which they maintain their idiomaticity under syntactic transformation.

Treating an idiomatic string as a unitary item has loomed large as a problem because so many idioms are, in principle at least, susceptible to a parallel literal reading. Buckets can be kicked, beans spilled, and ice broken in the real, as well as the idiomatic, world. Indeed, much of the literature on the processing of idioms has focused on the question of whether the literal meaning of an idiom is activated when the idiom is encountered; this question only has meaning, of course, for idioms with a literal counterpart.

Not all idioms have a literal counterpart, however. For semantic or syntactic reasons, a literal interpretation may be completely ruled out. We refer to such idioms as *ill-formed*. Semantic ill-formedness usually arises because of violations of selection restrictions among the idiom's components—it is difficult to see how one could literally *rack one's brains,* for example. Syntactic ill-formedness usually violates subcategorization restrictions; thus, only in the idiom can one be *in the know*, because elsewhere in the language *know* functions solely as a verb.

Perhaps because so much of the literature on idioms and idiom processing deals (as usual) exclusively with English, syntactic and semantic ill-formedness among idioms has received little attention. Indeed, idioms without a literal counterpart are often dismissed as accidental exceptions—on the grounds, for instance, that they contain a unique form (e.g., *eke out*), that they include forms that are fossilized survivors of originally free forms (e.g., *cast a slur on*), or that one of their components has lost one of its original meanings (e.g., *trip the light fantastic*). Some approaches to idiomaticity have even claimed that such collocations cannot be considered "proper idioms" exactly because they violate the condition of ambiguity, which in these approaches is considered to be a basic requisite of idioms. Thus, Weinreich stated that "ambiguity is an essential characteristic of true idioms" (1969, p. 44); he denied the status of idioms to collocations such as *cockles of the heart* or *spic and span* because they contain unique forms. Similarly, Makkai (1973) called such units "pseudo-idioms."

We agree that *spic and span* and *cockles of the heart* do not make strong claims to idiomaticity. But *rack one's brains* and *in the know* certainly do, and although they do not contain unique forms, by virtue of their ill-formedness they are not ambiguous. Therefore, on an ambiguity criterion such as that proposed by Weinreich, these phrases would necessarily have to be excluded from the realm of idiomaticity in English. To be sure, idioms without a literal counterpart are relatively uncommon in English. This is probably one reason why an ambiguity criterion has seemed defensible. If the source of ill-formedness is indeed quite often the presence of a unique form, then identifying ill-formedness with unique forms can be a practical step—by eliminating the latter, one also more or less eliminates the former. Another reason, of course, may be that dismissing the problem of ill-formedness simply facilitates clean elegant models of representation (e.g., Weinreich's polysemy-based model).

The problem is that ill-formed idioms are far more frequent in other languages, for instance French (Boisset, 1978) and German (Greciano, 1983). They are also, as we shall show, extremely frequent in Portuguese. In such languages, ill-formedness in idioms may much more often than not go beyond unique forms; thus, it can hardly be dismissed as irrelevant by decree.

ILL-FORMEDNESS IN PORTUGUESE IDIOMS

In this chapter, we discuss ill-formedness in Portuguese idioms, and describe a memory experiment in which this factor was manipulated. To establish the separate categories of semantic and syntactic ill-formedness, we present several examples of each. (For each idiom, we give the Portuguese base form, followed by a literal English translation, then a paraphrase of the meaning). Examples 1 to 6 are idioms for which a literal counterpart cannot be found for semantic reasons:

1. *Dar bocas* ("to give mouths" = to utter silly remarks).
2. *Meter medo a um susto* ("to scare a fright" = to be very frightening).

3. *Mandar à fava* ("send to the broadbean" = to send about one's business).

4. *Fazer trinta por uma linha* ("to make 30 by one line" = to misbehave).

5. *Fugir a boca para a verdade* ("to run away the mouth to the truth" = to be sincere without intention).

6. *Armar um pé de vento* ("to set a foot of wind" = to make a scene).

The ill-formedness exhibited by these idioms is of a semantic nature. Example 1 has a simple verb plus noun phrase (V + NP) structure; *dar* is a transitive verb and *bocas* is assigned the role of direct object. If one cannot literally "give mouths," it is not because *give* and *mouths* are syntactically incompatible, but because the semantic reading of the noun is not productive in association with the semantic reading of the verb.

Likewise, the violation in Example 2 is also semantic; the prepositional phrase (PP) *a um susto* is assigned the role of indirect object to a verb whose indirect object should be [+Animate], but *susto* (fright) can only be [−Animate].

In Example 3, we have a different type of semantic violation—the verb *mandar* (to send), in the sense used here, requires a directional locative complement that must be either [+Animate] or [+Place], as in *mandar à avó* (send to the grandmother) or *mandar ao mercado* (send to the market). *Fava* (broad bean) does not qualify as a semantically adequate locative complement. It is possible, of course, that the original phrase from which this idiom derives may have been quite regular, something like *mandar buscar favas* (send to fetch broadbeans).

In Example 4, *fazer* (to make, to do) is used with the odd Direct Object *trinta por uma linha* (thirty by one line) when it would require a [+Concrete] or a [+Activity] Direct Object. It could be argued that the object is actually *linha* (line), but then we would have a syntactic irregularity because the numeral qualifier *30* would demand a plural noun. In the present stage of the language, there is no such activity or object, but again it seems possible that it once designated some type of parlor game which has vanished from the memory of the speakers' community.

Example 5 presents a similar irregularity to that of Example 3. *Fugir* (to run away) usually demands a directional locative complement which has to be [+Concrete], either [+Animate] or [+Place]. *A verdade* (the truth) is neither; added to this we have the oddity of a [−Volitive] subject accompanying a verb whose meaning implies volition.

In Example 6, the irregularity is again in the Direct Object, which should be [+Concrete] but is not—although, of course, *pé* (foot) could be a concrete noun were it not qualified by *de vento* (of wind).

Thus, one can say that Portuguese offers varied examples of highly metaphorical idioms without a literal counterpart, clearly unambiguous, and with interesting semantic irregularities. Now consider the idioms in Examples 7 through 12, which present marked syntactic irregularity in comparison to standard Portuguese syntax; Mira Mateus, Brito, Silva Duarte, & Hub Faria, 1983):

7. *Levar X à certa* ("to take X to the certain" = to trick X).
8. *Fazer caixinha* ("to make little box" = to keep secret).
9. *Cair em si* ("to fall in oneself" = to become aware).
10. *Andar na boa vai ela* ("to go in the good goes she" = to be out on a spree).
11. *Ter pó a X* ("to have dust at X" = to dislike X intensely).
12. *Estar-se nas tintas para X* ("to be oneself [reflex.] in the inks for X" = not to care about X).

Example 7 is an instance of categorial irregularity. The structure of the idiom can be analyzed as:

13. V + X + PREP (LOC) + ART + ADJ

The verb *levar* is a transitive verb with a valency of three, usually taking a directional locative complement [PREP(loc) + NP] or [PREP(loc) + S]. The combination present in the idiom, [PREP(loc) + ADJ], is therefore ruled out. It is in the adjective *certa,* used in its feminine singular form, that the irregularity lies, as this seems to be performing the role of N in an NP, to the point of being preceded by DET (the definite article *a,* which appears in obligatory contraction with the PREP *a*), in its adequate inflexional form, singular feminine.

In Example 8, *fazer caixinha,* we have an example of an incomplete NP. The verb *fazer* (make or do) is a transitive verb, and the NP fills the role of direct object. The irregularity concerns the constituents of the NP. In Portuguese, the presence of DET before the N is compulsory in the NP if the N is in the singular and is a countable noun. The only exception to this rule occurs when the N designates an activity and, therefore, changes from countable to uncountable, allowing Example 14 but not Example 15, which is therefore marked * to signify unacceptability:

14. Eu detesto cinema ("I hate cinema").
15. *Ele comprou cinema ("He bought [a] cinema").

In Example 9, *cair em si,* the ill-formedness resides in the prepositional complement. The verb *cair* is an intransitive verb of movement, which generally requires a directional locative. The structure of this idiom makes the prepositional complement *em si* play the role of a directional locative; but in the case of the verb *cair* (fall), the referent of the locative cannot be identical to the referent of the subject—so Example 16 would be unacceptable:

16. A pedra$_1$ caiu na pedra$_1$ ("the stone$_1$ fell in/on the stone$_1$").

The PREP COMP (and its flexion) shows that the personal pronoun case used—the ablative—establishes an anaphoric relation with the subject, thus violating the requirements stated previously.

In Example 10, *andar na boa vai ela,* we again have an irregularity in the form of the prepositional complement. *Andar* generally takes a locative complement. In the present idiom, the structure of which is V+PREP(LOC)+ ART+ADJC+V+PRO, the phrase *na boa vai ela* is assigned this locative role. The problem rests on the fact that the preposition heading the locative is contracted with a DET, the definite article *a* (feminine singular), which should be preceding (as it is prepared to do by the agreement) an NP; but the NP is absent. This absent NP would contain the noun with which the adjective *boa* is prepared to agree (because it appears in its feminine singular). It cannot be claimed that *ela,* the personal pronoun (feminine singular), has taken the NP function in the new S node; pronouns cannot be determined by articles, nor do they take adjectives. It may be the case that there was once an N in the Prep Complement and that it came to be dropped, but it seems more likely that this is a case of combination of a process of fossilization of a question *ela vai na boa (vida)?* (Is she leading the good life?), which came to be used as an idiom with the subsequent dropping of the noun *vida.* This whole fossilized former question would then have taken the characteristics of a noun; that might explain why it cannot be pluralized (i.e., why Example 17 is possible but not Example 18):

17. *O Miguel e a Isabel andam sempre na boa vai ela* ("Miguel and Isabel go always in the good goes she" = Miguel and Isabel are always out on a spree).

18. **O Miguel e a Isabel andam sempre nos bons vão eles* "*Miguel and Isabel go always in the good go they."

The idiom in Example 11, *ter pó a X,* shows a very odd subcategorization irregularity and has the interesting syntactic structure of its literal paraphrase. The verb *ter* (have) only takes an indirect object if its direct object is a sense noun, as in the idiom's paraphrase *Ter ódio a X* ("have hate at X"). In the idiom, the object is not a sense noun but a common noun (dust) with which the verb *ter* remains a two argument verb, therefore not allowing an indirect object. An indirect object (X) is, nevertheless, obligatory and is headed by the preposition *a.*

Finally, in Example 12, *estar-se nas tintas para X,* we see another case of subcategorization irregularity caused by the combination of a reflexive pronoun with the verb *estar.* The reflexive pronoun is generally used only with transitive verbs in Portuguese, indicating that the action operates on the subject that performs it. The verb *estar* is used to indicate a temporary state of being in a place, mood, or condition (as opposed to the other verb which is translated by the English be, namely *ser*, which indicates a permanent state of existence); it is not a transitive verb, so a reflexive conjugation is ruled out. There are exceptions to this rule, involving verbs that indicate the subject's participation in an action of the affective type: *apaixonar-se* (fall in love), *zangar-se* (get angry). Verbs like *ficar* (stay), *ir* (go), *rir* (laugh), and *sorrir* (smile) can occasionally take a reflexive pronoun, in which case they also take on a new semantic reading. But the verb *estar* is not in either group and only in this idiom is it used with a reflexive. The case of the apparent parallel idiom *estar-se borrifando para X* ("be sprinkling oneself for X"), which means exactly the same, is in fact totally different because it uses a nonstandard construction that translates into the English present continuous.

These are only a few of many ill-formed idioms in Portuguese. Whereas in English ill-formed idioms, particularly syntactically ill-formed idioms such as *by and large* or *in the know,* are not the rule, in Portuguese such cases are much more common.

THE PSYCHOLINGUISTIC IMPLICATIONS OF ILL-FORMEDNESS

The mental processes involved in understanding idioms are the subject of a huge body of research, and rightly so, because the phenomenon of idiomaticity has important implications for models of the perception and production of language. If comprehension of a sentence consists, in the default case, of retrieving the meanings of individual words and combining them according to their grammatical relations, then any case in which the meaning of a string is not a direct function of such operations is obviously theoretically problematic (i.e., interesting).

Psycholinguistic interest in idiomaticity has focused upon three main aspects of the problem:

1. There is the issue of how idioms are represented in the mind, that is, whether they are stored as lexical chunks or processed as any other word string (e.g., Cacciari & Tabossi, 1988; Estill & Kemper, 1982; Swinney & Cutler, 1979).

2. There is the issue of access, the mechanism that makes a speaker opt for an idiomatic interpretation rather than for a literal interpretation when both are available (e.g., Gibbs, 1980, 1986; Ortony, Schallert, Reynolds, & Antos, 1978; Van Lancker & Canter, 1981).

3. There is the question of the processing of transformed versus untransformed idioms (e.g., Gibbs & Gonzales, 1985; Gibbs & Nayak, 1989;

Reagan, 1987); this, of course, also addresses the first problem (i.e., storage of idioms in the mind), because if idioms are stored as unitary lexical representations and are retrieved as such, then the introduction of syntactic transforms should increase processing demands and make the lexical representations less promptly available, whereas if idioms are processed as any other word string, there should be no systematic differences in the amount of processing needed for transformed versus untransformed idioms.

Semantic and syntactic ill-formedness are clearly relevant to these issues. On the one hand, the selection of an idiomatic meaning obviously faces no competition from a potential literal meaning for ill-formed idioms because, by definition, they have no literal counterpart. Therefore, they may serve as a useful control condition in investigations of how idiomatic meanings are accessed. On the other hand, the possibility exists that ill-formedness itself might serve as a signal that the incoming string is an idiom. This, in turn, might lead to the counterintuitive prediction that ill-formed idioms could actually, in some respects, be processed more easily than well-formed idioms—at least in languages in which idiom ill-formedness is common.

Indeed, although ill-formedness among English idioms has hardly been studied at all, there are indications of support for this prediction. Brannon (1975) compared English idioms with and without literal counterparts in several experiments in which subjects judged the grammaticality of sentences or judged whether or not two sentences had the same meaning. Among idioms without a literal counterpart, Brannon included several that we would describe as syntactically ill-formed (e.g., *out of whack, go bananas*); she found that idioms with a literal counterpart (e.g., *hit the bottle, down in the dumps*) took longer to process in these tasks than matched unambiguous sentences did, but idioms without a literal counterpart were processed faster than matched unambiguous sentences.

On the other hand, some semantically ill-formed idioms were included in experiments by Mueller and Gibbs (1987) and Gibbs and Nayak (1989), although their criteria for ill-formedness do not correspond exactly to the distinctions we outlined previously. Mueller and Gibbs (1987) reported that such ill-formed idioms were harder to process than well-formed idioms; thus, the processing effects of ill-formedness, in English at least, remain unclear.

Syntactic ill-formedness also interacts in an interesting way with the issue of syntactic transformability. In English, those idioms that are syntactically ill-formed, such as *in the know,* also tend to be syntactically frozen (Fraser, 1970); i.e., to allow no syntactic transforms; e.g., **The know was what he was in after talking with the boss;* cf. *The doghouse was what he was in once his wife found out.* In Portuguese, however, ill-formedness and transformability are not fully confounded. Although syntactically ill-formed idioms tend to be frozen to a greater extent than well-formed idioms (Botelho da Silva, 1989), this is not always the case. Some ungrammatical idioms allow transformations; as an example, *ter pó a X* can allow relative clause embedding, as in *O pó que a Beatriz tem à escola não tem razão de ser* ("the dust which Beatrice had at school had no reason to be"). If one can imagine a continuum of syntactic ill-formedness, at least in listener judgements, it is reasonable to suppose that transformed ill-formed idioms are even further along that continuum than their untransformed base forms, if only because of the very low frequency with which they might occur, hence their relative unfamiliarity to listeners (cf. Cutler, 1982; Reagan, 1987).

Gibbs and Gonzales (1985) made the interesting claim that the difficulty in processing transformed idioms should make them more memorable and hence easier to recall. This claim is based on their finding that in a cued-recall task, transformable idioms were recalled more accurately than frozen idioms; this finding contrasts interestingly with the results from a phrase-judgment task in which subjects made significantly faster acceptability judgments to the frozen idioms than to the transformable ones. If our speculation that ill-formedness could produce greater ease of processing has any foundation, and if, furthermore, transformability of an ill-formed idiom only acts to increase ill-formedness, then we might actually expect the pattern which Gibbs and Gonzales found (for well-formed idioms) to be reversed with ill-formed idioms: Transformed idioms might prove easier to process and hence harder to recall.

So far, these speculations are just that; we cannot as yet provide an empirical confirmation or disconfirmation of their validity. At this point, we merely wish to draw attention to the potential usefulness of ill-formedness as a factor in psycholinguistic investigations of idiomaticity. Ill-formedness is not highly common among English idioms; this suggests that the relevant experiments should be carried out in other languages that allow the relevant contrasts and this, too, is a development that we would welcome.

In the next section, we report an initial study of the recall of idioms, in which we manipulated both ill-formedness and transformability. We were interested not only in the contribution of these factors to the probability of recall per se, but also in establishing exactly how transformed idioms are recalled (i.e., whether they are, in fact, recalled in their transformed form or, perhaps, in their base form without the transforms which were applied to them).

MEMORY FOR TRANSFORMED IDIOMS:
AN EXPERIMENT

The properties of Portuguese idioms allow a systematic test of whether ill-formedness affects the way an idiom is processed. When ill-formed idioms are comparatively rare and may differ systematically from well-formed idioms in structural characteristics (e.g., length), it is hard to institute a controlled test of the effects of ill-formedness. However, when ill-formed idioms are common, this variable can be added to the repertoire of idiom properties that have been sub-jected to psycholinguistic investigation.

In the experiment that we describe here, we also exploit a new methodology for the study of idiom processing. We assess the recall of idioms via an inci-dental-learning paradigm. Subjects were presented with the idiomatic (and con-trol) materials and asked to assess the acceptability of each string. After they had completed this task with the entire set of materials, they were given a surprise recall task. Our primary measure of interest was performance on this recall task.

The materials were 30 Portuguese idioms, 15 well-formed and 15 ill-formed (of which 10 were semantically ill-formed and 5 were syntactically ill-formed). Within each subset of 15, 10 were transformable; the other 5 were frozen idioms, and thus admitted of no transforms. All idioms were embedded in sentence contexts; for the 20 transformable idioms (10 of each type), two versions of each context were given—one where the idiom appeared untransformed, one where it appeared transformed. We constructed 20 nonidiomatic control sentences, 10 well-formed and 10 ill-formed. Each sentence contained a proper name or a noun

TABLE 6.1
Examples of Sentences Presented in the Experiment

	Well-Formed	*Ill-Formed*
Transformed Idioms	*No tribunal os pontos foram pos-tos nos is pelo juiz Monteiro.* (In court the dots were put on the i's by Judge Monteiro.)	*O pé de vento que o Artur ar-mou não teve razão de ser* (The foot of wind which Ar-thur set had no reason to be.)
Untransformed Idioms	*O polícia deu cabo do canastro ao ladrão de carros.* (The policeman destroyed the basket to the car thief.)	*O cabeleireiro tem pó às cli-entas que nunca sabem como querem o cabelo.* (The hairdresser has dust to clients who never know how they want their hair.)
Frozen Idioms	*No verão as crianças passam sempre pelas brasas depois do almoço.* (In summer, children always pass by burning coals after lunch.)	*Os motoristas estão-se nas tintas para os peões.* (Drivers are (reflex.) in the inks for pedestrians.)
Control Strings	*O gerente chegou ao banco muito atrasado para a reunião.* (The manager arrived at the bank very late for the meet-ing.)	*O Pedro vai nunca pescar neste lago.* (Pedro goes never fishing in this lake.)

denoting a profession; these were intended for use as recall prompts. Table 1 contains examples of the sentences presented to subjects, and the full set of idioms tested appears in the Appendix.

The transforms that we used were the following: (a) relative clause embedding, (b) insertion, (c) active nominalization, (d) passivization, (e) clefting, and (f) permutation. These were not systematically manipulated; only one operation was applied to each idiom. In a previous study (see Botelho da Silva, 1989), a hierarchy of operations, analogous to that established by Fraser (1970) for English, was established for Portuguese; in this hierarchy, the operations we used were ordered as shown earlier, with relative-clause embedding producing the highest proportion of "acceptable" judgments and permutation the lowest. Interestingly, this study produced a contrast with Fraser's hierarchy, in that it was not necessarily the case that acceptability at a given level of the hierarchy implied acceptability at lower levels. We note that Gibbs and Gonzales (1985) also found that mean acceptability ratings for transformed idioms produced by a group of subjects did not correspond to the intuitive hierarchy proposed by Fraser and did not always pattern in a strictly hierarchical order. In the present study, we deliberately chose transformed constructions across a range of acceptability because of the nature of the subjects' ostensible primary task in the acquisition phase of the experiment—acceptability judgment.

Two sets of materials were constructed, differing only in which version of a transformable idiom appeared in each set; for each such idiom, its untransformed version appeared in one set and its transformed version in the other (with grammaticality, of course, counterbalanced across sets).

Fourteen native speakers of Portuguese took part in the experiment; seven received each materials set. The subjects were tested individually and the 50 sentences of each set were randomized separately for each subject. Subjects read each sentence aloud from a card and then judged it as "perfectly correct," "possible," or "impossible" in the Portuguese language. After the 50 sentences had been judged, the subjects were asked to write down as much as they could recall of the entire set of sentences. They were told to write down full sentences where they could, but also any parts of sentences they could recall, and they were given unlimited time for this task. Recall prompts were given for (randomly chosen) sentences of which no part had been recalled (but a maximum of four recall prompts was given to each subject).

The results can be exploited in several dimensions. We have data on how often a given idiom was recalled and the form in which it was recalled; we also have data on how acceptable subjects judged the idiom to be in the form in which it was presented. We can, therefore, look at recall per se as a function of grammaticality and transformability. We can look at recall in the light of acceptability, and we can look at how idioms are recalled, again as a function of the variables we manipulated.

Effects of Ill-Formedness and Transformability on Recall

For a measure of recall per se we counted any recognizable version of the target string, irrespective of syntactic form or paraphrase. The clearest finding from this analysis was that idioms were recalled more often than control strings— 19.29% of idioms overall were recalled in comparison with 7.14% of control strings. This difference was significant [χ^2 (1) = 20.06; p < .001].

Surprisingly, however, grammaticality had no effect on probability of recall. There were 40 instances of recall of well-formed idioms (19.05%) and 41 of recall of ill-formed idioms (19.52%), an insignificant difference. Among the ill-formed idioms, there was again no significant difference in the probability of recall between the semantically and the syntactically ill-formed set.

Transformability also had no effect, with the probability of recall for frozen and transformable idioms virtually identical.

Transformation, in contrast, had a strong effect: The probability of recall for untransformed idioms (37%) was almost twice as high as for transformed idioms (21%). This difference is significant [χ^2 (1) = 8.35; p < .01].

Acceptability and Recall

As in the preceding study (Botelho da Silva, 1989), the acceptability ratings from these subjects were lower for transforms of ill-formed idioms than for transforms of well-formed strings, in accordance with the tendency of ill-formed idioms towards syntactic frozenness. There was, however, no discernable indication in the results of a systematic relationship between recall probability and rated acceptability.

How are Idioms Recalled?

When we examined the precise form in which subjects recalled the idioms, we found the most surprising result of this study. When transformed idioms were recalled (remember that this happened in only 21% of cases), they were more often than not recalled without the transforms which had been applied to them. Only in one third of such cases were they recalled as they had been heard, another one tenth were paraphrased, and the majority were recalled in their base form.

This pattern held equally true for ill-formed idioms, both semantically and syntactically, and for well-formed idioms.

The frequency of paraphrase in comparison with exact recall was low for untransformed transformable idioms and for frozen idioms, and showed no relation with well-formedness. By comparison, an interesting pattern was revealed in recall of the control strings. More than half of recall instances of these involved paraphrase, and paraphrase was much more likely for well-formed strings than for ill-formed strings. This presumably reflects the long-known fact that the form of linguistic material is less well recalled than the content. Consider, however, the fact that idioms resisted this tendency to a considerable extent (for all un-transformed idioms, only 20% of recall instances involved paraphrase, compared with over 50% of recall instances for control strings). We suggest that this indicates closer connection between form and content in the case of idiom strings and is just what would be expected if idioms are being processed as, in some sense, unitary items.

CONCLUSION

Our experiment constitutes only a pilot study but it offers some very interesting implications for further research—although these are not necessarily the implications we were expecting when we undertook the study! Of our two original aims, the first was to investigate the role of ill-formedness in idiom processing. We found none; ill-formed and well-formed idioms produced very similar recall results. However, even this negative result has potential implications; if it proves reliable and parallels results from other processing tasks, it would argue against processing models which predict different processing costs for idioms which have to be distinguished from a literal counterpart versus idioms which don't (see Cutler, 1983, for further discussion of this issue). Our second aim was to explore incidental learning methodology as a tool for investigating idiom processing; our results suggest that this methodology could prove extremely useful.

We hope others will follow up and extend our results on recall for idioms presented in transformed form; our subjects tended to detransform such items and recall the base form instead. We suggest that this finding is very consistent with a view of idioms as unitary lexical items, and, along with our finding that idioms were more resistant to paraphrase than were control strings, lends support to lexical-unit models of idiom representation (e.g., Swinney & Cutler, 1979).

Finally, our failure to find advantages for transformable idioms in ease of recall contradicts Gibbs and Gonzales' (1985) prediction to this effect; indeed, our failure to find effects of well-formedness could also be construed as contrary to a prediction that idioms which require differential amounts of processing will produce differential recall results. Note also that we found better recall for untransformed idioms, which suggests that if the transforms we used increased the amount of processing necessary for understanding, then the increased processing certainly did not lead to increased recall probability.

Este estudo é só uma gota no oceano, mas talvez contribua para descobrir o fio da meada deste fenómeno linguistico que se tem provado um osso bem duro de roer.

REFERENCES

Boisset, J. H. (1978). *Idioms as linguistic conventions*. Unpublished doctoral dissertation, University of Florida, Gainesville.

Botelho da Silva, T. (1989). *Processing of frozen idioms*. Unpublished master's dissertation, Cambridge University, Cambridge, England.

Brannon, L. L. (1975). *On the understanding of idiomatic expressions*. Unpublished doctoral dissertation, University of Texas, Austin.

Cacciari, C., & Tabossi, P. (1988). The comprehension of idioms. *Journal of Memory and Language, 27,* 668–683.

Cutler, A. (1982). Idioms—The colder the older. *Linguistic Inquiry, 13,* 317–320.

Cutler, A. (1983). Lexical complexity and sentence processing. In G. B. Flores D'Arcais & R. Y. Jarvella (Eds.), *The process of language understanding* (pp. 43–79). Chichester: Wiley.

Estill, R. B., & Kemper, S. (1982). Interpreting idioms. *Journal of Psycholinguistic Research, 11,* 559–568.

Fraser, B. (1970). Idioms within a transformational grammar. *Foundations of Language, 6,* 22–42.

Gibbs, R. W., Jr. (1980). Spilling the beans on understanding and memory for idioms in conversation. *Memory and Cognition, 8,* 149–156.

Gibbs, R. W., Jr. (1986). Skating on thin ice: Literal meaning and understanding idioms in conversation. *Discourse Processes, 9,* 17–30.

Gibbs, R. W., Jr., & Gonzales, G. (1985). Syntactic frozenness in processing and remembering idioms. *Cognition, 20,* 243–259.

Gibbs, R. W., Jr., & Nayak, N. P. (1989). Psycholinguistic studies in the syntactic behavior of idioms. *Cognitive Psychology, 21,* 100–138.

Greciano, G. (1983). Signification et denotation en allemand—La semantique des expressions idiomatiques [Signification and denotation in German: The semantics of idiomatic expressions]. *Recherches Linguistiques, 9.* Université de Metz.

Makkai, A. (1973). *Idiom structure in english.* The Hague, Netherlands: Mouton.

Mira Mateus, M. H., Brito, A. M., Silva Duarte, I., & Hub Faria, I. (1983).*Gramática da Lingua Portuguesa* [Grammar of the Portuguese Language]. Coimbra: Almedina.

Mueller, R., & Gibbs, R. W., Jr. (1987). Processing idioms with multiple meanings. *Journal of Psycholinguistic Research, 16,* 63–81.

Ortony, A., Schallert, D., Reynolds, R., & Antos, S. (1978). Interpreting metaphors and idioms: Some effects of context on comprehension. *Journal of Verbal Learning and Verbal Behavior, 17,* 465–478.

Reagan, R. T. (1987). The syntax of English idioms: Can the dog be put on? *Journal of Psycholinguistic Research, 16,* 417–441.

Swinney, D. A., & Cutler, A. (1979). The access and processing of idiomatic expressions. *Journal of Verbal Learning and Verbal Behavior, 18,* 523–534.

Van Lancker, D., & Canter, G. J. (1981). Idiomatic versus literal interpretations of ditropically ambiguous sentences. *Journal of Speech and Hearing Research, 24,* 64–69.

Weinreich, U. (1969). Problems in the analysis of idioms. In J. Puhvel (Ed.), *The substance and structure of language* (pp. 23–81). Berkeley: University of California Press.

APPENDIX

Well-Formed Idioms

1. Bater a bota ("to beat the boot" = to die).

2. Andar de vento em popa ("to go with the wind in the stern" = to go very well).

3. Passar pelas brasas ("to pass by the burning coals" = to take a nap).

4. Ir a nove ("to go at nine" = to move very quickly).

5. Baixar a bolinha ("to lower the little ball" = to quiet down).

6. Estar nas suas sete quintas ("to be in one's seven farms" = to feel very happy).

7. Pôr o carro à frente dos bois ("to put the cart before the oxen" = to change the natural order of things).

8. Dar cabo do canastro de ("to destroy the basket to" = to spank).

9. Pôr no prego ("to put in the nail" = to pawn).

10. Apalpar o terreno ("to feel the ground" = to ponder before taking action).

11. Puxar a brasa à sua sardinha ("to pull the burning coal to one's sardine" = to defend one's interests).

12. Pôr os pontos nos is ("to dot the i's" = to settle matters).

13. Dar o nó ("to give the knot" = to get married).

14. Perder a cabeça ("to lose the head" = to get out of control).

15. Fazer uma fita ("to make a film" = to create a scene).

Ill-Formed Idioms

Syntactically Ill-Formed

1. Estar-se nas tintas ("to be [reflex.] in the inks" = to be indifferent).

2. Cair em si ("to fall inside oneself" = to become aware).

3. Dar o dito pelo não dito ("to give the said by the not said" = to change one's position).

4. Ter pó a X ("to have dust at X" = to hate X).

5. Pôr-se a pau ("to put oneself at stick" = to be on the alert).

Semantically Ill-Formed

6. Dar à lingua ("to give to the tongue" = to chatter continuously).

7. Esticar o pernil ("to stretch the spindle-shank" = to die).

8. Meter os pés pelas mãos ("to put the feet through the hands" = to blunder).

9. Mandar à fava ("to send to the broadbean" = to send away, to dismiss).

10. Armar um pé de vento ("to set a foot of wind" = to make a scene).

11. Dar à luz ("to give to the light" = to give birth to).

12. Dar a mão a palmatòria ("to give the hand to the ferrule" = to recognize a mistake).

13. Dizer cobras e lagartos de ("to say snakes and lizards of" = to speak ill of).

14. Fazer trinta por uma linha ("to make 30 by one line" = to misbehave).

15. Escangalhar-se a rir ("to destroy oneself laughing" = to laugh heartily).

7 The Activation of Idiomatic Meaning in Spoken Language Comprehension

Patrizia Tabossi and Francesco Zardon
University of Ferrara and University of Bologna, Italy

As pointed out by most authors in this volume, idioms are multifaceted objects, whose study requires various viewpoints and different methodological approaches. They are not only complex, but also in many respects elusive, to the point that it is probably a useless exercise to try and define them (Dascal, 1987; Fernando, 1978). Several aspects contribute to render the characterization of these expressions a challenging task. Typically, idioms are assumed to be strings of words whose semantic interpretation cannot be derived compositionally from the interpretation of their parts. According to this characterization, however, *break the ice* is as good an idiom as *switch off* or *by accident,* even though our intuition suggests different degrees of "idiomaticity" of these expressions.

Syntactic behavior does not show any higher homogeneity: It is well known, for instance, that idioms vary widely in "frozenness" (Fraser, 1970). Thus, *lay down the law* accepts most syntactic operations, whereas an expression of identical syntactic structure such as *blow off steam* accepts none.

Similarly, although the semantic interpretation of some idioms appears to be completely unrelated to the meanings of their component words (e.g., *kick the bucket*), the meanings of others can be inferred at least to some extent from their elements (e.g., *carry a torch*). These differences probably underlie the seemingly contradictory theoretical claims presented by current research on idioms. On the one hand, there are those who stress the aspects of semantic opacity of these expressions (Katz, 1973). On the other hand, an increasingly popular view posits some level of compositionality in the comprehension and production of idioms (Cacciari & Glucksberg, 1990; Gibbs & Nayak, 1989; Wasow, Sag, & Nunberg, 1983).

Related to the issue of semantic opacity/transparency is the question of how

145

idioms fit in the distinction between literal and figurative language, provided that this distinction is tenable (Rumelhart, 1979). Here the difficulty arises from the fact that some idioms share numerous characteristics with figurative expressions, in particular with metaphors (Gibbs & O'Brien, 1990; Lakoff, 1986). Other idioms, however, are so conventional and frozen to make it hard to appreciate the difference between them and actual individual words: Leaving aside orthography, how do expressions such as *nonetheless* and *by and large* differ from each other?

Given these great diversities, it is not surprising that the scope of most studies on idioms is often rather limited, with theoretical claims and empirical findings typically being restricted only to some subset of those expressions, or to some specific aspects of the many processes involved in their comprehension (or both). The work presented here is no exception, and the admittedly partial approach it takes is one that looks at idioms from the standpoint of spoken language processing, focusing on the question of when during comprehension do idiomatic meanings become available.

Even within this perspective, there are many questions one may ask. One issue often tackled in this area concerns ambiguity. Many idioms, in fact, are ambiguous between a literal and a figurative interpretation. *Break the ice,* for instance, can refer either to the crushing of frozen water or to the smoothing of a difficult social interaction. This has led to a concentration of research efforts on investigations of which of the two meanings becomes available first to the listener: the literal, which has to be computed, or the figurative, which is pre-stored in memory and only needs to be retrieved. This line of research, which has a long tradition (Gibbs, 1980; 1986; Ortony, Schallert, Reynolds, & Antos, 1978; Swinney & Cutler, 1979; see also Colombo, chapter 8 of this volume), has produced two influential theories of idiom processing.

According to the lexical representation hypothesis, idioms are stored in the lexicon as long, morphologically complex words, and are identified as any other lexical items. During comprehension, the process of recognition of an idiom starts at the beginning of the string, in parallel with the computation of its literal meaning. However, because computing is a longer process than retrieving, the idiomatic meaning of the string becomes available before its literal one (Swinney & Cutler, 1979).

The other view on idiom comprehension assumes that the computation of the literal meaning of an idiom does not run in parallel with the process of recognition of its figurative meaning. Rather, it occurs after that process, and is started only when the idiomatic meaning fails to integrate into context (Gibbs, 1980; 1986).[1]

A somewhat different approach has been taken by Cacciari and Tabossi

---

[1]Gibbs recently has modified his views (cf. chapter 3 in this book). His previous positions nevertheless have been reported here and elsewhere in the chapter because they are very influential in the area of idiom processing.

(1988), who investigated the semantic activation of unambiguous idioms, that is, idioms that do not have a literal meaning (e.g., *shoot the breeze*). The expressions they used were verbal idioms of two types: predictable and nonpredictable. Here predictability refers to people's propensity to complete the initial fragment of a string idiomatically. Thus, *to be in seventh* is completed by most people as *to be in seventh heaven,* although a literal continuation is possible. In contrast, *to break the* tends to be completed literally rather than as *to break the ice.* Accordingly, the former idiom, unlike the latter, is considered to be predictable.

In three cross-modal lexical decision experiments Cacciari and Tabossi (1988) found different patterns of results depending on whether or not the idiomatic strings were predictable. When the idioms were predictable, subjects were faster at performing a lexical decision task to a target presented at the offset of the string when the target was figuratively rather than literally related to the idiom. However, when the idiom was not predictable, subjects were faster on the literally related target, whereas the idiomatically related target did not differ from the control. Only sometime after the offset of the string, the idiomatically as well as literally related target were responded to significantly faster than was the control.

In order to explain these findings, and contrary to the view that idioms are represented mentally as separate lexical entries (Estill & Kemper, 1982; Glass, 1983; Mueller & Gibbs, 1987; Swinney & Cutler, 1979)—henceforth, the lexical view, the authors proposed that the meanings of idioms, at least verbal ones, are associated with configurations of words. These words are the same that are processed during literal language comprehension, and each takes part in all the idiomatic configurations in which it occurs. According to this hypothesis, the processing of an idiomatic string takes place literally, until sufficient information in the string renders it recognizable as an idiom. Only at this point, referred to as the idiom key, is the idiomatic meaning activated. Thus, this view is in contrast with what usually is assumed by current models of lexical processing, according to which the activation of the meaning of a word occurs soon after its onset along with the activation of the meanings of other words sharing the same onset (Marslen-Wilson, 1987; McClelland & Elman, 1986). The notion of key, which is discussed further at the end of the chapter, intuitively reflects the point in a string at which one becomes aware of the possibility of being presented with an idiom, and is specified operationally in Cacciari and Tabossi (1988) by means of the following procedure: People are requested to complete an increasingly longer idiom fragment, and the point at which the majority of them complete the fragment idiomatically can be considered its key. This point, according to the configuration hypothesis, is predictive of when the meaning of the idiom becomes active.

Admittedly, various factors may speed up the activation of idiomatic meanings. A sentential context, for example, can direct one's comprehension of a fragment toward its idiomatic completion, rendering the activation of its meaning faster (Tabossi & Cacciari, 1988). Likewise, pragmatic incongruency may provide important cues to idiom comprehension. The occurrence of *kicked* in the context of an old and sick man, for instance, renders the literal action of kicking rather more implausible than the figurative kicking of the bucket, possibly speeding up the activation of this meaning. Also, it is well known that people may be biased toward idioms when presented with them in the context of other similar expressions (Bobrow & Bell, 1973).

But although linguistic and extralinguistic factors may facilitate the semantic activation of an idiomatic string, none of these cues is essential to it. In fact, one common observation is that idioms are easy to understand; and indeed, many ambiguous idioms appear to be both more commonly used and more quickly understood in their figurative rather than in their literal interpretation (Cronk, 1990; Gibbs, 1986). Thus, one tenet of this hypothesis is that at least in the absence of contextual biases, the semantic activation of an idiom does not take place until after its key, whose position in the string determines therefore when during the processing of the idiom its meaning becomes available.

Although consistent with the findings in Cacciari and Tabossi (1988), this assumption was not tested directly in that study. Accordingly, the main goal of this chapter is to explore further the notion of key, attempting to provide some direct evidence for the role that it may play on the activation of idiomatic meaning during language processing.

EXPERIMENTAL EVIDENCE: EARLY
VERSUS LATE KEY POSITION

The idioms selected for the first cross-modal lexical decision experiment were all well-known Italian expressions with two main characteristics. First, they were verbal idioms with two content words after the verb; second, the first content word was sufficient to prompt the idiomatic completion of the strings. In other words, the first content word was the key of these expressions.

The selected idioms, each embedded in a sentence, were presented auditorily to the subjects paired with a visual target that was related semantically to their meaning, as illustrated in the following example:[2]

Finally, Silvio had succeeded in setting his mind at rest
RESIGNED

---

[2]Experiments 1 and 2 were conducted with Italian subjects and Italian materials, which are listed in the Appendix along with their corresponding English translations. Because most of the Italian idioms have no exact English equivalent, in the text the examples are English idioms with similar characteristics to those employed in the study.

The subjects listened to the sentences and performed a lexical decision task on the visual targets paired with each idiom. The targets were presented at one of three positions: after the verb (e.g., *setting*), after the first content word (e.g., *mind*), and after the second content word (e.g., *rest*). Differences in the subjects' reaction times (RTs) to decide that the targets were words in the three positions were taken to reflect the state of activation of the idiomatic meanings at those points.

It was predicted that if the position of the key influences the activation of meaning of an idiom during comprehension, here, where the key is the first content word, idiomatic meaning should be already available soon after it. Hence, RTs to the targets at the first and second content word should not differ from each other and both be faster than at the verb.

EXPERIMENT 1

Method

Subjects. Thirty undergraduates volunteered to participate in the experiment, which lasted about 35 min. None had participated previously in an experiment of this type.

Materials and Design. Twelve verbal idioms containing two content words following the verb were selected. Their syntactic structure was V (NP) (PP),[3] where at least one of the components in parentheses was present.

These idioms were all well-known expressions in the language. This was established by asking 15 subjects to paraphrase a list of idiomatic expressions, including the ones used here. These were paraphrased correctly by at least 95% of the subjects.

In order to establish the position of the key in the idioms, 15 independent judges were asked to complete increasingly longer fragments of a list of idiomatic strings. In the case of the selected expressions, 90% of the judges completed the string idiomatically after the presentation of the first content word that was assumed to be the key of the idioms in this experiment.

Each idiom was embedded in a sentence that was constructed to provide as little contextual information as possible. In addition, for each idiom, a word related to its meaning was selected for use as visual target in the experiment (see Appendix).

Besides the test materials, filler materials also were prepared. They consisted of 96 "formal" and 12 "colloquial" sentences. The latter, which were obtained

---

[3]V means verb; NP means noun phrase; PP means prepositional phrase.

by using colloquial lexical items but did not contain idiomatic expressions, were devised in order to avoid the test sentences being noticed by the subjects as strange or awkward in the experimental situation. Each of the 108 filler sentences, which were approximately of the same structure and length as the test sentences, was paired with a visual target that had no relation with either the overall meaning of the sentences or any of their individual words.

Out of the 96 formal sentences, half were paired with target visual words, whereas the remaining 48 formal sentences in addition with the 12 colloquial ones were paired with targets that were legal pseudowords.

All 120 sentences (12 test and 108 filler) were recorded by a male speaker on one channel of a tape recorder. There was a 5-s interval between sentences. A 1,000 Hz pulse, placed automatically on the other channel of the tape and inaudible to the subjects, caused a word to be displayed on the screen of an Apple microcomputer for 1,500 ms. It also started a digital timer, which either stopped when the subjects pressed the space bar or reset automatically after 5 s.

In the filler sentences the pulse occurred 100 ms after the offset of one word chosen in such a way as to cover the entire range of positions within sentences (i.e., beginning, middle, end).

All the experimental sentences were recorded three times, so that for each of them the pulse could be placed in three positions: 100 ms after either the verb, the first content word, or the second content word.

Pulses were placed 100 ms after word offsets rather than at their exact end in order to maximize the probability of the idiomatic meaning being detected at each position, because there is reason to believe that the activation of an idiom may be a slow process, and its meaning may require sometime after string offset before becoming detectable (Cacciari & Tabossi, 1988).

In order for the same idiom to be presented only once to each subject, three lists of sentences were constructed, each containing only one version of each test sentence. Each list contained all 12 idioms: 4 with the pulse after the verb, 4 after the first content word, and 4 after the second content word. In addition to the test sentences, each list also included the 108 filler sentences, thus yielding a total of 120 sentences. One set of 120 visual targets (12 idiomatic, 48 filler word, and 60 nonword targets) was paired with the three lists of sentences.

Each list of sentences, together with the paired set of targets, was divided in three blocks of 40 trials each. Trials were counterbalanced across blocks, and occurred in a quasi-random order, with the constraint that no more than three target words or nonwords appeared in a row.

An equal number of subjects was assigned randomly to one of the experimental lists. Within each list, subjects acted as their own controls.

Procedure.   Subjects were tested individually. They sat in a sound-attenuated room in front of an Apple microcomputer monitor connected to a stereo tape recorder. They were instructed to perform a lexical decision task to strings of letters that would appear on the monitor while listening to a sentence. They were told to press the space bar of the keyboard with their dominant hand if the visual target was a real word and to do nothing otherwise. After 10 practice trials, one of the three experimental lists was presented to each subject. Reaction times to lexical decisions were recorded.

The subjects were informed that they should pay attention to the sentences because at the end of the test session they would be asked questions about them. Immediately after the end of the experimental session, the subjects were given 20 sentences, each printed on a card, half of which had been presented in the experiment. The other half was derived from the sentences the subjects actually heard. The subjects' task was to decide which sentences were old and which were new. The mean percentage of correct recognitions was 73%, and none of the subjects recognized less than 60% of the sentences.

Results and Discussion

In order to reduce variability, data points above or below 2 standard deviations (SDs) from the mean RTs to each target were excluded from the analyses. These data, together with errors, accounted for 3.33% of all responses. Table 7.1 shows the mean RTs and SDs for the correct responses under the three experimental conditions.

There was a reliable main effect both in the analysis by subjects [$F(2, 58)$ = 5.34, MSe 3,174; p = .007] and in the analysis by materials [$F(2, 22)$ = 4.77, MSe 1,670; p = .02]. Planned nonorthogonal comparisons showed that RTs to the targets were faster after the first content word than after the verb, whereas RTs after the first and the second content word did not differ significantly from each other: V versus W1, $F(1, 58)$ = 5.64, p = < .05; W1 versus W2: $F(1, 58)$ = 0.70, n.s.).

In agreement with the predictions, the findings suggest that in those idioms in which the key is the first content word, meaning is already active after that word. Unfortunately, this pattern of results is also compatible with the view that idioms

TABLE 7.1
Mean RTs and SDs for Correct Lexical Decisions
to Targets in the Three Positions: V (Verb),
W1 (First Content Word), and W2 (Second Content Word)
in Experiments 1 and 2

	V	W1	W2
Experiment 1	672	638	626
	(96)	(78)	(74)
Experiment 2	637	631	605
	(69)	(81)	(78)

are represented mentally as lexical items. If idioms are represented in the same way as words, in fact, they also should be processed in a comparable way, and hence have their meanings activated early during identification, in analogy with what happens in lexical processing.

The configuration and the lexical alternatives lead, however, to different predictions in the case of idioms that, unlike those in Experiment 1, have their key later than the first content word, toward the end of the string. According to the lexical view, the time course of activation of the meanings of these expressions should not be different from that of the idioms in Experiment 1. In both cases, meaning should be activated very early on in the string, in analogy with what happens in lexical processing. According to the configuration hypothesis, however, the further down in the string an idiom key is, the later will its meaning be activated. Hence for idioms whose key occurs later than in the idioms in Experiment 1, activation also should be found later, and not be already available at the first content word. The prediction was tested in a further experiment. This was analogous to the previous one, except that idioms used here had their key at the second content word rather than at first, as in the following example:

In the end, the man hit the nail on the head.
ACCURATE

The predictions were as follows. If the activation of the meaning of an idiom does not occur until its key has been processed, in this experiment no facilitation to the targets should be observed before the second content word. Hence, RTs to the targets should be faster in this position than in the other two positions, which should not differ from each other. Alternatively, the notion of key does not play a role in the meaning activation of an idiom. In this case, idiomatic meaning activation should be initiated already after the first content word, and RTs to the target at this point therefore should be significantly faster than after the verb, where it is presumably too early for idiomatic meaning to be active and prime the target.

EXPERIMENT 2

Method

Subjects. A total of 27 undergraduates volunteered for the experiment, which lasted about 35 min. As in Experiment 1, none had participated previously in an experiment of this sort.

Materials and Design. A new group of 12 familiar idioms was chosen. These idioms had the same syntactic structure as those in Experiment 1. Also they had two content words following the verb. Their key, however, occurred later than in the previous group. This was established on the basis of the same pretest reported in Experiment 1, but the criterion for selection differed, in that none of the new idioms was completed idiomatically after the first content word. In fact, 90% of the judges failed to complete idiomatically the whole strings prior to the second content word. Thus this word was taken to be the key of these expressions (see Appendix). The filler materials were the same as those used in Experiment 1, and so was the design.

Procedure.   The procedure was the same as in the Experiment 1. In the memory task, the mean of correct recognitions was 75%, and none of the subjects had a performance below 60% correct identifications.

Results

The mean of errors was 2.16%. The mean RTs of correct responses in the three experimental conditions and related SDs are reported in Table 7.1. Analyses of variance, both by subjects and by materials, showed a reliable main effect of target position: $F1(2, 52) = 3.71$, MSe 2,155; $p = .03$; $F2(2, 22) = 3.34$, MSe 1,161; $p = .054$.

Planned nonorthogonal comparisons showed no significant difference between RTs after the verb and after the first content word, which were both reliably slower than RTs after the second content word: V versus W1, $F(1, 52) = 0.26$, n.s.; W1 versus W2, $F(1, 52) = 4.23$, $p = .04$.

The data indicate that the meaning of an idiom is not activated until very late during the processing of that expression, in agreement with the prediction of the configuration hypothesis for those expressions whose key, as in this experiment, is toward the end of the string.

ACTIVATION AND KEY

Taken together, Experiments 1 and 2 suggest that the notion of key does play a role in determining idiomatic meaning activation. In fact, the point of activation of an idiom during its processing depends on the characteristics of the string: When its key occurs early, its meaning is also activated early (Experiment 1); when the key is later, so too is activation (Experiment 2).

These findings also support the hypothesis that the meaning of an idiom is not activated soon after its onset; rather it is triggered only after sufficient information is available to the listener to signal the presence of an idiom. Only after such a point—that is, after the key—does the idiomatic meaning become available.

It might be argued that this interpretation of the results is unwarranted. In fact, although indicating differences in the semantic activation of the two groups of idioms at the first and at the second content word, the data fail to show that there is no activation for either group at the verb. This point is crucial. Let us suppose, in fact, that such activation exists, and RTs after the verb are not a baseline, but reflect the initial semantic activation of idiomatic meaning. In this case, findings in Experiments 1 and 2 simply would indicate differences in the speed at which semantic activation builds up in the two groups of idioms, actually supporting the lexical view that predicts early activation for all idiomatic expressions.

Two arguments run against this interpretation. First, the differences between verb and first and second content word in Experiment 1 (34 ms and 46 ms, respectively), and between verb and second content word in Experiment 2 (32 ms) are typical of the range of differences observed between primed and unprimed conditions in cross-modal lexical decision studies (Swinney, 1979; Tabossi, 1988; Zwitserlood, 1989). Also, evidence to the effect that idiom meanings are not yet active at the verb comes from Swinney (1982), who reported a cross-modal study on the time course of activation of expressions such as *see the light,* where he found the idiomatic meaning active at the end of the string, but not at verb offset.

The present findings are therefore difficult to reconcile with the view that idioms are processed as long words. In the field of lexical processing, it generally is agreed that semantic information is activated before the identification of a word (Marslen-Wilson, 1987). As soon as a word fragment is available, the meanings of various words compatible with the perceptual input up to that point are activated, and subsequent perceptual information is used to select among the active competing meanings the one associated to the actual stimulus word.

Many aspects of these processes are still under debate, including the question of what is the perceptual information used to initiate word recognition, or what are the words whose meanings are activated during early phases of the process (Bard & Shillcock, in press; Lahiri & Marslen-Wilson, 1991; Luce, 1986; Noteboom, 1981; Salasoo & Pisoni, 1985). However, it commonly is accepted that more than one meaning is activated after the initial fragment of a spoken word and this process of multiple activation occurs early, before word recognition. Hence, if the lexical view of idiom representation and processing is correct, halfway through the expressions one ought to find their meaning always active, and no difference should be observed between idioms in Experiments 1 and 2.

Perhaps one way of reconciling the present data with a lexical hypothesis of idiom processing would be to explain the pattern of results in this study as due to the different uniqueness or recognition points of the idioms in Experiments 1 and 2. In lexical processing, uniqueness point refers to the point at which on the basis of perceptual information a word diverges from any other in the language, whereas recognition point indicates the point at which a word can be discriminated from the other competing candidates, taking into account contextual as well as sensory constraints. Thus, it might be claimed that the notion of key of an idiom corresponds to the uniqueness point of a lexical item, or perhaps to its recognition point, and has in idiom processing the same role that uniqueness and recognition point have in word processing. Here, it is well known that the earlier is the uniqueness point in a lexical item, the sooner this is recognized. Moreover, recognition may be anticipated further in an appropriate context: There the selection of a word meaning for contextual integration may take place before its uniqueness point. Analogously, idiom meanings were activated sooner in Experiment 1 than in Experiment 2 simply because the key, which according to this argument corresponds to their uniqueness or recognition point, occurred earlier in the former group of expressions than in the latter.

It should be noted, however, that although similar to both the uniqueness point and the recognition point of a word, the key of an idiom cannot be characterized in the same way as either of these notions. In fact, the uniqueness point of a word in a language is determined by the lexicon of that language. Although *pow-* can be completed as *powder, power,* or *pow-wow, powd-* can be completed only as *powder:* /d/ is accordingly the uniqueness point for that word because no other words in English have *powd-* as their initial fragment. This is not the case with the key of an idiom, which may occur at a point where the perceptual input still could have a literal completion. *To be in seventh,* for instance, could be completed equally well with *position* or *heaven.* In fact, most of the predictable idioms in Cacciari and Tabossi (1988) were of this sort.

Likewise, although the recognition point of a word can precede its uniqueness point, because contextual factors intervene along with perceptual factors to determine word identification, the key of an idiom is not established contextually, and there is some evidence that predictable strings are completed idiomatically even in contexts that do not rule out literal completions. "The tennis player was in seventh . . . ," for instance, is usually completed as "The tennis player was in seventh heaven," even though "The tennis player was in seventh position" is an equally good completion (Cacciari & Tabossi, 1988). Thus, the key of an idiom seems to correspond exactly neither to the uniqueness nor to the recognition point of a lexical item, and it is therefore unlikely that its role in idiom processing can be reduced simply to the role of either notion in word recognition. Furthermore, even if the key of an idiom did correspond to word uniqueness or recognition point, these notions still would not explain the pattern of results. Both recognition and uniqueness point, in fact, refer to the point in time where, in isolation or in context, a word diverges from all its alternatives. According to the multiple activation hypothesis of lexical processing, however, the meaning of a word is activated, along with other lexical meanings, before either point. Yet, in contrast to what seems to be the case with lexical processing, the present findings indicate that semantic activation of an idiom occurs late in the string, and how late may depend on factors such as the location of the key, for which there is no obvious correspondence in the processing of individual lexical items.

But how can a key be characterized? Although this notion, as noted earlier, can be operationalized easily, its theoretical specification is less simple. The difficulty—or at least part of it—stems from the fact that as already pointed out, a key does not seem to have any formal property: It does not correspond to a point after which the language offers no other acceptable possibility than complete the string idiomatically; it has no special syntactic role, nor does it necessarily mark a syntactic or semantic anomaly.

Perhaps the best way of specifying an idiom key is in probabilistic terms, as the point in the string after which the probability of the fragment to continue idiomatically is very high, even though a different, literal completion still may be possible. Probability here refers to language use. Thus, although both *build castles* and *hit nails* can refer to perfectly reasonable actions, in actual use the first expression tends to be employed in the context of *building castles in the air*, whereas the latter often is used with reference to hammers, picture frames, and the like. There is no intrinsic necessary difference between those idioms, but in many varieties of contemporary English the former fragment is far more predictive of the occurrence of an idiom than the latter, and people seem to be sensitive to this factor while processing those expressions.

Admittedly, this characterization is at best incomplete. It fails to capture the fact, for instance, than an idiom key not only indicates a point in the string, but often is the most important part of the idiom. A common observation, in fact, is that not all elements in an idiomatic expression seem to contribute equally to its comprehension, some parts being more crucial than others. This is illustrated by the fact that many idioms (e.g., *break the ice*) retain their meaning even with some lexical changes (e.g., *crack the ice*), but there are words that cannot be substituted without loss of meaning (e.g., *break the frozen water*).

But although partial, probability does seem to have a role in the characterization of an idiom key. In fact, it has some similarities with the transitional probability used by behaviorists to describe linguistic behavior, when this was treated as a stochastic process (Shannon & Weaver, 1949). Within that framework, the transitional probability of a word is the probability of occurrence of that word, given the preceding words. Clearly, at the beginning of a sentence, almost if not all words can occur, but as more and more information comes in, the possible continuations offered by the language, and by discourse and knowledge constraints become increasingly limited, up to a point where only one possibility is left (Attneave, 1959). The critiques to this approach are not only well known, but are part of the foundations of cognitive psycholinguistics (Chomsky, 1957, 1959). However, the notion of transitional probability seems to capture one characteristic of an idiom key: Namely, it does not reflect any formal property of idioms, but the fact that when certain words co-occur in the language very frequently they are part of an idiom.

The importance of a factor such as use on idiom processing also is suggested by a number of studies that have looked at their frequency and familiarity (Cronk, 1990; Popiel & McRae, 1988; Schweigert, 1991). Popiel and McRae, for instance, had their subjects rating how familiar they were with a list of ambiguous idioms, and how frequently those expressions occurred in their literal and figurative meaning. The results indicated that among familiar idioms, some often are used both literally and figuratively, but others occur almost exclusively in their figurative meaning.

That frequency factors may play a role in how early idiomatic meanings are activated during language processing is not surprising, given the well-established and robust effects of frequency in almost all domains of language comprehension. What is specific of the way in which frequency—and hence probability—is considered here is that it refers not to a single element, but to the co-occurrence of items in a sequence of elements, namely the idiom string.

In conclusion, from the perspective of language processing, the empirical evidence presented in this study appears to support the view that the meaning of an idiom is not activated as that of a word. Rather, processing an idiomatic string is probably not very different from processing proverbs, song lyrics, or poems. Just like what happens with idioms, in fact, it is most improbable that when listening to "La nebbia . . ." or "La nebbia agli . . .", anyone who has attended Italian schools activates anything besides the individual words in the string. However, if the next word is *irti,* a long-known poem suddenly pops up from memory, and she or he can do nothing but get ready for the worst.[4]

ACKNOWLEDGMENTS

This research was supported by Fondi 60% Grant No. 9000107 and CNR No. 892361. We would like to thank Cristina Cacciari, Corrado Cavallero, Sam Glucksberg, and Donia Scott for their helpful comments and suggestions.

REFERENCES

Attneave, F. (1959). *Applications of information theory to psychology.* New York: Holt, Rinehart & Winston.

Bard, E. G., & Shillcock, R. C. (in press). Competitor effects during lexical access. In G. T. Altmann & R. C. Shillcock (Eds.), *Spoken language processing.* Hillsdale, NJ: Lawrence Erlbaum Associates.

Bobrow, S., & Bell, S. (1973). On catching on to idiomatic expressions. *Memory & Cognition, 1,* 343–346.

Cacciari, C., & Glucksberg, S. (1990). Understanding idiomatic expressions: The contribution of word meanings. In G. B. Simpson (Ed.), *Understanding word and sentence* (pp. 217–240). Amsterdam, Netherlands: Elsevier.

Cacciari, C., & Tabossi, P. (1988). The comprehension of idioms. *Journal of Memory and Language, 27,* 668–683.

Chomsky, N. (1957). *Syntactic structures.* The Hague, Netherlands & Paris: Mouton.

Chomsky, N. (1959). A review of B. F. Skinner's "verbal behavior." *Language, 35,* 36–58.

---

[4]The unforgettable poem is *San Martino* by Giosue' Carducci.

Cronk, B. (1990). *Familiarity and likeliness for figurative and literal meanings of idioms.* Poster presented at the 2nd annual convention of the American Psychological Association, Dallas.

Dascal, M. (1987). Defending literal meaning. *Cognitive Science, 11,* 259–281.

Estill, R. B., & Kemper, S. (1982). Interpreting idioms. *Journal of Psycholinguistic Research, 11,* 559–568.

Fernando, C. (1978). Towards a definition of idiom, its nature and function. *Studies in Language, 2*(3), 313–343.

Fraser, B. (1970). Idioms within a transformational grammar. *Foundations of Language, 6*(1), 22–42.

Gibbs, W. R. (1980). Spilling the beans on understanding and memory for idioms in context. *Memory & Cognition, 8,* 149–156.

Gibbs, W. R. (1986). Skating on thin ice: Literal meaning and understanding idioms in conversation. *Discourse Processes, 9,* 17–30.

Gibbs, W. R., & Nayak, N. P. (1989). Psycholinguistic studies on the syntactic behavior of idioms. *Cognitive Psychology, 21,* 100–138.

Gibbs, W. R., & O'Brien, J. E. (1990). Idioms and mental imagery: The metaphorical motivation for idiomatic meaning. *Cognition, 36,* 35–68.

Glass, A. L. (1983). The comprehension of idioms. *Journal of Psycholinguistic Research, 12,* 429–442.

Katz, J. J. (1973). Compositionality, idiomaticity and lexical substitution. In S. R. Anderson & P. Kiparsky (Eds.), *A festschrift for Morris Halle* (pp. 357–376). New York: Holt, Rinehart & Winston.

Lahiri, A., & Marslen-Wilson, W. D. (1991). The mental representation of lexical form: A phonological approach to the recognition lexicon. *Cognition, 38,* 245–294.

Lakoff, G. (1986). The meanings of literal. *Metaphor and Symbolic activity, 1*(4), 291–296.

Luce, P. (1986). *Neighborhoods in the mental lexicon.* Unpublished doctoral dissertation, Indiana University, Bloomington.

Marslen-Wilson, W. D. (1987). Functional parallelism in spoken word recognition. In U. Frauenfelder & L. K. Tyler (Eds.), *Spoken word recognition* (pp. 71–102). Cambridge, MA: MIT Press.

McClelland, J. L., & Elman, J. L. (1986). The TRACE model of speech perception. *Cognitive Psychology, 18,* 1–86.

Mueller, R. A., & Gibbs, R. W. (1987). Processing idioms with multiple meanings. *Journal of Psycholinguistic Research, 16,* 63–81.

Noteboom, S. D. (1981). Lexical retrieval from fragments of spoken words: Beginnings versus endings. *Journal of Phonetics, 9,* 407–424.

Ortony, A., Schallert, D. L., Reynolds, R. E., & Antos, S. J. (1978). Interpreting metaphors and idioms: Some effects of context on comprehension. *Journal of Verbal Learning and Verbal Behavior, 17,* 465–477.

Popiel, S. J., & McRae, K. (1988). The figurative and literal uses of idioms, or all idioms are not used equally. *Journal of Psycholinguistic Research, 17*(6), 475–487.

Rumelhart, D. E. (1979). Some problems with the notion of literal meaning. In A. Ortony (Ed.), *Metaphor and thought* (pp. 78–90). New York: Cambridge University Press.

Salasoo, A., & Pisoni, D. B. (1985). Sources of knowledge in spoken word identification. *Journal of Memory and Language, 24,* 210–231.

Schweigert, W. A. (1991). The muddy waters of idiom comprehension. *Journal of Psycholinguistic Research, 20,* 305–314.

Shannon, C. E., & Weaver, W. (1949). *The mathematical theory of communciation.* Urbana: University of Illinois Press.

Swinney, D. A. (1979). Lexical access during sentence comprehension: (Re)consideration of context effects. *Journal of Verbal Learning and Verbal Behavior, 14,* 645–660.

Swinney, D. A. (1982). The structure and time course of information interaction during speech comprehension: Lexical segmentation, access, and interpretation. In J. Mehler, E. C. T. Walker, & M. Garrett (Eds.), *Perspectives on Mental Representation* (pp. 151–167). Hillsdale, NJ: Lawrence Erlbaum Associates.

Swinney, D. A., & Cutler, A. (1979). The access and processing of idiomatic expressions. *Journal of Verbal Learning and Verbal Behavior, 18,* 523–534.

Tabossi, P. (1988). Accessing lexical ambiguity in different types of sentential contexts. *Journal of Memory and Language, 27,* 324–340.

Tabossi, P., & Cacciari, C. (1988). Context effects in the comprehension of idioms. In Cognitive Science Society (Eds.), *Proceedings of the Tenth Annual Conference of the Cognitive Science Society* (pp. 90–96). Hillsdale, NJ: Lawrence Erlbaum Associates.

Wasow, T., Sag, I., & Nunberg, G. (1983). Idioms: An interim report. In S. Hattori & K. Inoue (Eds.), *Proceedings of the XIIIth International Congress of Linguistics* (pp. 102–105). Tokyo: CIPL.

Zwitserlood, P. (1989). The locus of the effects of sentential-semantic context in spoken-word processing. *Cognition, 32,* 25–64.

APPENDIX

The following lists are the test sentences and targets for Experiments 1 and 2 in Italian, translated word by word into English and with the meanings of the Italian idioms. In most cases, these do not have an English equivalent, so in order to respect the form of the idiomatic expression in Italian the translation into English is necessarily stilted.

Experiment 1

1. Finalmente, Silvio era riuscito a mettersi il cuore in pace.
   —RASSEGNATO
   Finally, Silvio had succeeded in setting his heart at rest.
   —RESIGNED

2. Al lavoro ogni giorno saltava la mosca al naso a qualcuno.
   —IRRITABILE
   At work every day it jumped the fly to the nose of someone. (someone was upset)
   —IRRITATED

3. Giovanna, che era una nuova impiegata, prendeva a pesci in faccia tutti.
   —MALE
   Joan, who was a new clerk, took with fishes in the face everybody. (ill-treated everybody).
   —BAD

4. Alla fine, si scoprì che l'opera dello scrittore non era farina del suo sacco.
   —TRUFFA

At the end, it was discovered that the work of the writer was not flour of his bag. (his own work)
—CHEAT

5. Improvvisamente, il senatore americano passò dalle stelle alle stalle.
—PEGGIO
Suddenly, the American senator went from stars to stables. (lost importance)
—WORSE

6. Per alcuni è naturale lavare un'offesa col sangue.
—VENDETTA
For someone it is natural to wash an offence with blood. (kill the offenders)
—REVENGE

7. Come sempre, Cristina tirava acqua al suo mulino.
—VANTAGGIO
As usual, Christine pulled water to her mill. (pursued her interest)
—ADVANTAGE

8. Dopo il colloquio col direttore, Luca aveva un diavolo per capello.
—RABBIA
After the meeting with his boss, Luc had a devil each hair. (was furious)
—FURY

9. Tutti sapevano che la ragazza diceva pane al pane.
—SINCERA
All knew that the girl used to say bread to the bread. (talked the truth)
—SINCERE

10. Secondo l'opinione degli amici, Giovanni era in una botte di ferro.
—SICURO
According to the opinion of his friends, John was in a barrel of iron. (was on the safe side)
—SAFE

11. Claudio toccava il cielo con un dito ogni volta che usciva con Milena.
—FELICE
Claude touched the sky with a finger (was happy) everytime he went out with Milena.
—HAPPY

12. La fidanzata pensava che a Marco desse di volta il cervello.
—PAZZO
The girlfriend thought that to Marc the brain turned. (was mad)
—MAD

Experiment 2

1. Nel romanzo, il personaggio principale faceva l'avvocato del diavolo.
   —POLEMICO
   In the novel, the main character was the devil's advocate.
   —POLEMIC

2. L'anziana signora aveva il cuore in gola quando vide entrare gli sconosciuti.
   —PAURA
   The old lady had the heart in the throat (was frightened), when she saw strangers come in.
   —FEAR

3. La madre si accorse che il figlio aveva le mani bucate.
   —SOLDI
   The mother noticed that the son had the hand pierced. (was a spendthrift)
   —MONEY

4. Alla cena, Maria vide con stupore che c'era un pesce fuor d'acqua.
   —IMBARAZZO
   At the dinner party, Mary saw with surprise that there was a fish out of water.
   —EMBARRASSMENT

5. Lo scolaro mise una mano sul fuoco che il suo compagno non mentiva.
   —SICURO
   The boy put a hand on the fire (swore) that his schoolmate did not lie.
   —SURE

6. Il bambino sapeva benissimo quale era il cavallo di battaglia della sua cantante favorita.
   —SUCCESSO
   The child knew very well which was the warhorse of his favorite singer.
   —SUCCESS

7. Nel film, il protagonista aveva una spada nel cuore.
   —DOLORE
   In the movie, the main character had a sword in the heart. (pain)
   —PAIN

8. Sandro si ricordava ancora di quando vedeva il sole a scacchi.
   —PRIGIONE
   Sandy still remembered when he used to see the sun in checks. (was in jail)
   —JAIL

9. Stefano sapeva che finchè non era verde per la bile, il padre taceva.
—ARRABBIATO
Steve knew that until he was green for the bile (was furious), the father kept silent.
—ANGRY

10. L'insegnante mostrò quale era la punta di diamante della sua classe.
—MIGLIORE
The teacher showed which was the diamond point in her class.
—BEST

11. Secondo la signora, era la pietra dello scandalo della famiglia la causa di tutto.
—CATTIVO
According to the woman, it was the stone of the scandal (the culprit) of the family the cause of everything.
—BAD

12. La sola cosa spiacevole della vacanza fu la spina nel fianco delle difficoltà economiche.
—PROBLEMA
The only unpleasant thing in the vacation was the thorn in the side (aching pain) of the financial problems.
—DIFFICULTY

8 The Comprehension of Ambiguous Idioms in Context

Lucia Colombo
University of Padova, Italy

The study of the identification and comprehension of ambiguous idiomatic strings, like *kick the bucket,* shares many of the issues that are involved in the study of lexical ambiguity, and as such is important for understanding the processes involved in sentence comprehension. Ambiguous idioms in fact can be assigned either a literal interpretation, based on the compositional meanings of its constituents, or a figurative meaning, which has been learned and associated with the whole string. Some of the crucial questions that have been asked in the study both of ambiguous words, and of ambiguous idioms, concern problems like the following: Is there an automatic exhaustive activation of meanings or a context-dependent preactivation? At which point in time does activation of each meaning occur? Is selection of the appropriate meaning immediate or delayed?

Because of their relevance to the study of ambiguous idiomatic expressions, the main models of lexical ambiguity are described briefly. The two main views that have been proposed to describe the temporal course of activation of meanings in ambiguous words are the *exhaustive access* model and the *selective access* model. According to the first, all meanings are activated automatically independent of context bias and of meaning dominance, and selection of the appropriate meaning is made in a later stage (Onifer & Swinney, 1981; Seidenberg, Tanenhaus, Leiman, & Bienkowski, 1982; Swinney, 1979; Tanenhaus, Leiman, & Seidenberg, 1979). According to the selective access model, context can preactivate one meaning (Simpson, 1981; Tabossi, 1988; Tabossi, Colombo, & Job, 1987; Van Petten & Kutas, 1987). When one of the meanings is dominant with respect to the others, because of its frequency of occurrence, it will be active earlier independently of context, whereas the secondary meanings need preactivation by contextual features to become active. A variation of this model, the *reordered access* model, was proposed by Duffy, Morris, and Rayner (1988) and Rayner and Duffy (1986). According to the latter model, the effect of context and dominance is to make the biased meaning available earlier, rather than to selectively preactivate it.

Although the selective access and the reordered access models localize the effect of context before or during semantic activation, another model was proposed by Rayner and Frazier (1989; see also Frazier & Rayner, 1990), the *integration* model, in which it is claimed that all meanings are activated automatically independent of context, and the effect of context is located during the process of integration. Ease of integration, together with dominance of meaning, account for the rapidity with which a meaning is selected and the nonsuitable meaning is discarded. The interesting feature of this model is that it allows the assumption of an automatic activation of meanings, and at the same time it accounts for the effect of dominance and context.

The roles of context and of the availability of meanings during the temporal course of activation and integration are also important to the study of the comprehension of ambiguous idioms. This becomes apparent when examining the models that have been proposed to explain the comprehension of idiomatic expressions.

Quite opposing views are represented in the two models called the *idiom list* hypothesis and the *direct access* hypothesis. According to the *idiom list* hypothesis (Bobrow & Bell, 1973), idioms are represented in a special list in the lexicon and are retrieved from this list only after the literal interpretation has failed to match the context.

More recently, Gibbs and collaborators (Gibbs, 1986; Gibbs & Gonzales, 1985) conducted a series of experiments showing that idioms can be accessed directly, and the literal interpretations need not be computed. According to Gibbs, idioms are stored in the normal lexicon, and the ease with which they are accessed (as single words) depends on their degree of "frozenness." This term has been used to indicate the extent to which idiomatic expressions can undergo syntactic transformations without changing the figurative meaning (Fraser, 1970). When the words of the idiom are connected strongly, they are more likely to be treated as single units. Once the idiomatic meaning becomes active, the literal interpretation that was being constructed is inhibited (Gibbs, 1980, 1986). Gibbs suggested that the context in which the idiomatic expression is encountered can be used to activate the idiom directly.

This suggestion is in contrast both with the idiom list hypothesis, which claims that the literal interpretation is always the first to be available, and with the view held by Swinney and Cutler (1979), the *lexical representation* hypothesis. According to the latter, idioms are represented as large words, and as such they are activated as soon as enough perceptual information has been extracted. No matter how biasing is the context, according to this model both the idiomatic and the literal meanings of the phrase are activated simultaneously. The lexical representation hypothesis is analogous to that proposed in the exhaustive access model. The underlying idea is that lexical access is an autonomous process, which takes place automatically, independently of other higher level processes and before selection of the meaning appropriate to the context occurs.

Applied to the processing of idioms, the exhaustive access model predicts that when an idiom is encountered, both its interpretations are accessed simultaneously. However, ambiguous idioms are not completely comparable to ambiguous words because the retrieval of meanings in the case of ambiguous words include operations at a level not higher than lexical access. In the case of idioms, retrieval of the idiomatic meaning indeed may be limited to lexical access, if the assumption holds that idioms are represented as single words. However, the computation of the literal meaning involves both lexical access of the single words, and a structural and interpretative analysis at the sentence level. Performing these operations may require different time courses, as it appears, for instance, from the experiments reported in the literature (Gibbs, 1980; Glass, 1983; Ortony, Schallert, Reynolds, & Antos, 1978; Swinney & Cutler, 1979), which show that comprehension of the figurative meaning of the idiom is faster than comprehension of the literal meaning. For instance, deciding whether a sentence is meaningful or not is faster for idiomatic expressions, as compared to normal, literally interpreted phrases (Swinney & Cutler, 1979), and is faster for more frozen (that is, less suitable to transformations without a change in meaning) than less frozen idioms (Gibbs & Gonzales, 1985).

The reason why different time courses probably are implicated might lie precisely in the fact that if idioms are represented as single words, the meaning associated with each of them is already stored, or precomputed, whereas a literal interpretation must be constructed through inferences or the computation of relations among the single words. One possibly could claim that at the beginning of the idiomatic phrase only the literal interpretation has started. By the time the last word begins, however, enough information may have accumulated to allow activation of the idiom, and access to its stored meaning. By this time, processing of the literal interpretation already may have stopped and decayed. This interpretation has received support by experiments using the cross modal priming paradigm (Cacciari & Tabossi, 1988; Swinney, 1981).

In Swinney's (1981) experiment, neutral context sentences containing an idiomatic expression (e.g., *kick the bucket*) were presented auditorily; target words were presented visually, either at the offset of the first word of the idiom or at the offset of the last word. He found that at the end of the first word (*kick*) only the literal meaning was activated, whereas at the end of the idiom only the target related to the figurative meaning was facilitated.

Swinney's (1981) results are inconsistent with the lexical representation hypothesis in two ways: first, because they show that the figurative meaning is not activated automatically from the beginning of the idiom, as suggested by the lexical representation hypothesis. More important, the literal meaning does not appear to be activated at the end of the idiom, in contradiction with the view holding a simultaneous activation of literal and figurative meanings. Swinney's results also suggest that a triggering context is not necessary for the activation of the idiomatic meaning to take place, because it appears to be activated even in a neutral context.

A similar result was found by Cacciari and Tabossi (1988) with predictable idioms that were unambiguous, that is, idioms that cannot be understood literally but that can be interpreted literally before the last word is encountered (e.g., *shoot the breeze*). However, when unpredictable idioms were used there was no evidence of activation of the figurative meaning when the last word had just been heard. Only after 300 ms from the offset of the idiom was there evidence of facilitation for reaction times to the target related to the figurative meaning. In these experiments the context was neutral. When a biasing context was provided (Tabossi & Cacciari, 1988), both the literal meaning of the last word of the idiom and the figurative meaning were primed at the offset of the final word of the idiom. These results are particularly striking because the idioms used by Cacciari and Tabossi did not have a literal interpretation after the last word and suggest that at least the literal meaning of the single words, if not the structural literal interpretation, always is activated automatically. It is another matter, of course, to decide whether the literal interpretation of the whole string is initiated even in contexts biasing the figurative interpretation of an idiom, or when idioms with no literal interpretation are processed.

One of the main characteristics of idioms, which has been considered critical for their definition (Chomsky, 1980; Fraser, 1970), is that the figurative meaning cannot be derived from a compositional interpretation of the literal meanings of the single words that compose the idiom. If it is assumed that literal meanings are activated automatically and that the language processor proceeds with the construction of a structural interpretation and an elaboration based on compositional meanings, then whether a figurative meaning is activated and the moment in which it is activated may depend on several factors. Thus, it is crucial to determine what factors are responsible for triggering the activation of its figurative meaning.

The aim of the present chapter is to investigate the effect of context on the processing of ambiguous idioms. In the first experiment a cross-modal priming paradigm was used. A sentence containing an idiom and biasing either its literal or its figurative interpretation was presented auditorily; at the offset of the last word of the idiomatic phrase a target word was presented visually, related either to the literal meaning of the last word of the idiom (*kick the bucket, pail*) or to its figurative interpretation (*kick the bucket, die*). When either the literal or the figurative meaning of the idiomatic expression has been retrieved, lexical decision on a target word related to the accessed meaning should be facilitated, with respect to the lexical decision made on a control word. If facilitation with respect to the control word is obtained from target words related to both meanings, then it may be concluded that both the literal meaning of the last word of the idiom and the figurative meaning have been retrieved simultaneously.

In the present experiment two groups of subjects were used. One group was presented with the context that biased only the literal reading of the idioms, the second group with the context biasing the figurative meaning. Subjects who always were presented with idioms in the literal reading should be less likely to show an effect of expectations about figurative expressions. Thus, priming of the idiomatic meaning should not appear in the literal bias context, and if it does, then it would be even stronger evidence that the figurative meaning is activated automatically. If, on the other hand, an effect of context occurs, it should be manifested as a differential facilitation for targets related to either one of the readings, as a function of context.

EXPERIMENT 1

Method

Subjects.   Two groups of 20 subjects each were tested, all of them students of psychology at the University of Padua.

Material.   In the first phase of the selection 63 idiomatic phrases and 64 nonidiomatic phrases of about the same length were presented to 31 subjects, with the task of writing down the first word that came to their mind after reading the phrase. The aim of the task was to select ambiguous items, that is, items with the literal meaning as frequent as the figurative. This was ascertained by checking whether the associated word was related to either of the two meanings. For instance, if the words associated to the idiomatic phrase *kick the bucket* were *pail* or *water,* they were considered to be related to the literal meaning. If the associated words were *die* or related words, then the meaning implied was the figurative one. On the basis of the association task, and of the author's judgment, 16 items were selected that had equally plausible literal and figurative meanings. The items were of about the same length in words.

Two words were paired to each idiom, related to either its literal or its figurative meaning, to be used as target words in the lexical decision task. The target relative to the literal sense was associated or related semantically to the last word of the idiom, whereas the target relative to the figurative meaning was related to the meaning of the whole expression. In addition, two control target words were selected, matched for length and frequency to the respective related target. The mean frequency of the target words was 44, 19, 38, and 20 (on a count of 500,000; Bortolini, Tagliavini, & Zampolli, 1972) for, respectively, targets related to the literal meaning, targets related to the figurative meaning, and the respective controls.

To verify that the targets relative to the figurative meaning could be primed by the idiomatic expression, 15 subjects were tested in a priming experiment. Subjects were presented with the 16 idioms selected in the first phrase plus 5 new idiomatic expressions, plus 11 nonidiomatic phrases of the same length as the idioms. These phrases served as primes in a lexical decision task. The target words were formed by the 32 words relative to each idiom, plus 16 nonwords. Two lists were made. Each list included 16 target words, either related or unrelated to each idiom, plus 16 pronounceable nonwords. Every subject saw all the priming idioms only once, and the correspondent targets either were related to the figurative meaning or were the appropriate controls. The results showed that the idioms effectively primed the related targets, with respect to the controls: The mean reaction times (RTs) were 556 and 606 ms for related and control targets, respectively [$F'(1, 14) = 11.5, p < .01$ by subjects, $F''(1, 15) = 6.8, p < .02$ by items].

Two sentences were constructed for each idiomatic expression, one biasing the literal meaning, the other biasing the figurative meaning (see Appendix). An attempt was made to avoid, as far as possible, including words in the sentences that were associated to the related target, so that the bias toward one type of meaning was produced at the interpretive level of analysis of the sentence, not by lexical preactivation.

Two tapes were formed. Each tape included, in a different order, 16 sentences containing the idiomatic expressions, either in the literal or the figurative context bias version, randomly intermixed with 25 filler nonidiomatic sentences. Each tape was preceded by eight sentences for practice. Four lists of visual targets were paired with each tape. Each list included 16 experimental target words, 8 filler words, 17 filler pronounceable nonwords, plus 4 words and 4 nonwords to be used as practice. The 16 experimental target words included four words literally related to four different idioms, four words figuratively related, and eight control words, all relative to different idioms, so that every subject was presented with each idiom only once, paired with a target word in one of the different experimental conditions. The two groups of 20 subjects were assigned randomly to the two experimental conditions determined by the type of bias produced by the sentence context, literal or figurative. Within each group of 20 subjects, four subgroups were determined by the association with one of the four lists of targets.

Procedure

The sentences were recorded with a Revox B77 tape recorder by a male speaker with a normal intonation. The tapes then were digitalized by means of a digit-to-analog converter, and the resulting output was analyzed to find the exact offset of the last word of the idiom. A pulse of about 5 volts was located in correspondence with the offset. The tape recorder was connected to an Apple IIe microcomputer that produced the display of the target word on the computer screen and recorded RTs and errors.

The subjects were seated in front of the computer screen, with their right and left fingers resting on the 9 and 5 buttons of the computer console, and listened to the sentences through the headphones. Subjects were instructed to listen to the sentences carefully for comprehension, and that they would be given a list of sentences for a recognition test at the end of the session. They also were told to look at the screen where a string of letters, either word or nonword, sometimes would appear. As soon as they detected it, they had to make a lexical decision, pushing the relative buttons, as fast and as accurately as possible. When the experiment was finished, the subjects were presented first with the recognition test, and then with a list containing the idioms used in the experiment. They had to mark those items they were unfamiliar with or did not know the meaning of. This procedure of checking the familiarity of the idiomatic meanings was followed in all of the experiments in the present chapter.

Results and Discussion

An analysis of the protocols of the recognition test showed that subjects had understood the task correctly, listening for comprehension, as instructed. The data consisted of mean RTs of correct responses. Outliers that were +2 standard deviations (SDs) from the mean for each subject (2.2% for the literal context group, 1.5% for the idiomatic context group) were substituted by the mean per subject through all conditions. RTs exceeding 1,400 ms were cut off (.9% for the literal, .6% for the idiomatic group). Also the data relative to the idioms that were not known to the subjects were discarded (3.1% for the literal, 1.8% for the idiomatic group). Finally, 1.5% of the data for the literal group and .9% for the idiomatic group were cut off due to failure of the equipment.

Mean response times for the two types of context are shown in Table 8.1. An analysis of variance (ANOVA), with one between-subject (context) and two within-subject factors, type of prime-target relation (literal, figurative), and type of target (experimental, control), was carried out on the RT data. In the analysis by subjects, the significant factors were type of relation, $F'(1, 38) = 4.05, p < .05$, and type of target, $F'(1, 38) = 15.10, p < .001$. The interaction between the two factors was also significant, $F'(1, 38) = 5.69, p < .05$.

In the analysis by items, context was not significant, $F''(1, 30) = 2.84 \ p < .10$, and neither was type of relation, $F''(1, 30) = 1.07$. The factor type of target was significant, $F''(1, 30) = 12.7, p < .001$. The interaction between type of target and type of relation was not significant, $F''(1, 30) = 1.95$.

The data relative to the group that was presented with the literal context were analyzed separately. RTs to experimental targets, that is targets related to either the literal or figurative sense of the idioms, were facilitated with respect to RTs to the control condition [$F'(1, 19) = 7.6 \ p < .05; F''(1, 15) = 9.6, p < .01$]. The

TABLE 8.1
Mean Lexical Decision Times and Error Percentage
(in Parentheses) in Experiment 1

	Context			
	Literal		Figurative	
Type of Target	Experim.	Control	Experim.	Control
Prime-target Relation				
LITERAL	639 (0)	716 (.6)	692 (0)	760 (.6)
FIGURATIVE	708 (1.5)	732 (0)	725 (.6)	774 (.6)

interaction between type of prime-target relation and type of target was signifi-cantly by subjects, $[F'(1, 19) = 4.7, p < .05; F''(1, 15) = 2.4, p > .1]$, showing that only the 77-ms facilitation for targets related to the literal meaning of the idioms (*kick the bucket-pail*) was significant as tested by the Newman–Keuls statistics ($p < .001$), whereas the difference between targets related to the figur-ative reading of the idiom and its control did not reach significance. The other significant result from the ANOVA related to the factor type of prime-target relation $[F'(1, 19) = 8.5, p < .01; F''(1, 15) = 2, p > .1]$, which showed that literally related targets were faster than figuratively related targets. Error rate was very low, 2.2% of the total set of data.

The data relative to the idiomatic context group also was subjected to the same analyses. As for the former group, the factor type of target was significant $[F'(1, 19) = 7.5, p < .05; F''(1, 15) = 5.7 p < .05]$, but the interaction this time did not approach significance. The rate of errors was 1.8%.

The lack of a significant interaction between context, type of relation, and type of target in Experiment 1 indicates that priming can be obtained for targets related to both the literal and the figurative meaning of the idiom. The priming effect for the figuratively related target words is smaller, independent of the influence of context. In fact, when analyzed in the literal context condition only, this priming effect failed to reach significance. This result could be due just to lack of power. It also could be explained assuming that the activation of the idiomatic meaning takes more time, with respect to the activation of the literal meaning, and so has not reached asyntote when priming is measured at the offset of the idiom. The bias offered by the idiomatic context could be sufficient to speed up activation.

Another possibility cannot be discounted. That is, targets related to the literal meaning of the noun were associated to it, whereas targets related to the figur-ative meaning were related semantically to the figurative interpretation of the whole idiom. Semantic relations seem to produce more fragile priming effects than do associative relations (Colombo & Williams, 1990; Lupker, 1984).

The fact that in the literal context, RTs to targets related to the figurative meaning were facilitated, although to a smaller degree, seems to be in opposition to the findings of Cacciari and Tabossi (1988). In their experiments, when unpredictable idioms were used in neutral contexts, there was no evidence supporting the view that the figurative meanings of idioms had been activated immediately. Only after 300 ms was there evidence of priming for the figurative meaning. Although the context was neutral, the idiomatic reading of the phrase was the only one possible, because the idioms did not have a literal interpretation. Therefore the idiomatic interpretation had to become active at some point. Thus, it appears that the language processor first had considered the literal interpretation of the idiomatic phrase, and had rejected it only when it did not produce a plausible or meaningful interpretation. However, with more predictable idioms the figurative meaning was activated, whereas the literal word meaning was not.

A possible explanation for the inconsistency of the present results with those obtained by Cacciari and Tabossi (1988) is in terms of idiosyncratic differences among idioms. Perhaps the idioms used in Experiment 1 of the present study, although they have a literal interpretation, are quite common in their idiomatic reading, which was therefore available relatively quickly. Another difference between the two studies is in the relative proportion of filler sentences and idiomatic sentences (16 to 25 in the present experiment, 12 to 60 in Cacciari & Tabossi). The higher proportion of sentences containing idioms in the present study may have created an expectation that activated the idiomatic meaning, even though it was not biased by the context.

The present results also can be explained in terms of an interpretation that locates the effect of facilitation on the integration process that occurs after word recognition, rather than on processes occurring before the presentation of the target. Facilitation of the target word could be produced by its rapid integration in the ongoing mental representation being constructed. It has been suggested that the lexical decision task is particularly sensitive to postaccess integration processes (Balota & Lorch, 1986; Colombo & Williams, 1990; Forster, 1981; Lupker, 1984; Seidenberg, Waters, Sanders, & Langer, 1984). Judgment of whether a string of letters is a meaningful word or not is claimed to be sensitive to the presence of a semantic relation between prime and target, so that it becomes easier to respond when the target word is easily integratable into the former context. On this account, facilitation of target words depends on the ease of constructing a representation congruent with the preceding information. When the figurative sense of the idiom is activated, even in the literally biased context, it might constitute a local context against which the target word is integrated, and capable therefore of producing facilitation.

The target words related to the literal meaning appeared to be activated independently of context. As Gibbs (1986) rightly pointed out, however, this fact does not imply necessarily that the literal interpretation of the sentence as a whole is being constructed. The process of constructing the literal interpretation of a sentence is a more complex process compared to that of retrieving a meaning stored in memory, as seems to be the case with idioms. Thus, one very well might argue that, although the literal interpretation always is initiated, it is abandoned as soon as the idiomatic meaning is retrieved and found to be congruent with the context. Moreover, there is another reason why facilitation of literally related targets cannot be taken as evidence in favor of the contextually independent construction of literal meanings. Namely, facilitation could be attributed to backward priming (Koriat, 1981; Seidenberg et al., 1984; Van Petten & Kutas, 1987). As prime words and literally related target words were associated, and were presented at 0 Stimulus Onset Asynchrony (SOA), backward priming might well have occurred. Therefore, the present results are inconclusive with respect to the problem of whether the literal interpretation always is computed.

EXPERIMENT 2

In Experiments 2 and 3 the course of activation of the idiomatic meaning, and of its integration with the context, was investigated in a self-paced reading task. In this task, sentence segments of different lengths are presented on a screen and the subject has to press a button when she or he has completed reading the segments. RTs are assumed to reflect processes involved in both identification and semantic activation of single words, and in higher level comprehension processes. The use of this paradigm should allow examination of the time course of activation of both the literal and the figurative meaning.

It was assumed that, while the segments of the sentence accumulate, a structural interpretation is constructed. If, at presentation of the idiom, the figurative meaning has been activated, two incompatible interpretations would be active, and the language processor has to select one of them. Decisions on which interpretation to select, and when to operate the selection, may depend on several factors. One of these factors is context. If the context is neutral, the language processor might decide to delay selection until disambiguating information is provided. Or, it might select immediately which interpretation is more likely on the basis of frequency of occurrence (e.g., how often an idiom is used in the figurative sense). When the context is biasing one interpretation, then an immediate selection can be made (Frazier & Rayner, 1990; Rayner & Frazier, 1989).

If in the condition where the context is biasing the figurative meaning information that is not congruent with the context is provided after the idiom is presented, a potential garden path is created. Thus, if a delay is found in encountering this incongruous information, this should be evidence that selection of the idiomatic interpretation already had been made.

Let us consider the following example: "The man was going to kick the bucket, that was on the kitchen floor."

In this example the idiom is followed by a relative pronoun as subject of a verb phrase (e.g., ". . . kick the bucket, that was . . ."). There are two possible referents to the pronoun. One is the noun of the idiom, the second is the whole phrase, considering the verb as a nominal. In the latter case, in Italian, the relative pronoun is preceded most often by the article *the* when it refers to a whole phrase. Therefore the favored referent in the example should be the noun of the idiom. This could be intended in the literal or in the figurative meaning. Some idiomatic expressions, although not each to the same extent, would allow a pronoun to refer to the figurative meaning of its noun. Indeed several authors (Cacciari & Glucksberg, 1991; Gazdar, Klein, Pullum, & Sag, 1983; Gibbs & Nayak, 1989; Wasow, Sag, & Nunberg, 1983) argued that some idioms are subject to internal modification by adjectives or relative clauses, which can apply to the whole idiom or to a part, and claimed that the meaning of an idiom can be a compositional function of its parts, which are not intended literally however. This view has led to the formulation of the *idiom decomposition* hypothesis (Gibbs & Nayak, 1989; Gibbs, Nayak, & Cutting, 1989).

In Experiments 2 and 3, the context of the sentences biased either the literal or idiomatic meaning or was neutral. The idiom always was followed by a relative clause in all of the contexts. The relative clause was formed by the relative pronoun (*che*, "that"), plus a verb followed by either a noun phrase, a prepositional phrase, or an adverb, which completed the verb phrase introduced by the relative pronoun, as in the following example: ". . . break the ice, that was in the fridge." The relative pronoun referred to the literal meaning of the last word of the idiom, which was always a noun. The prepositional phrase "in the fridge" contributed to the specification of the literal sense of the noun of the idiom, and consequently also of the relative pronoun. If, at presentation of the relative clause, the idiomatic meaning has been activated and integrated, reading the successive segments containing the literally related clause should produce a situation similar to that created by a garden path, where the language processor has to reconsider alternative interpretations to that formerly biased by the context. The garden path thus should produce a delay in reading times. If, on the other hand, the figurative meaning had not been activated, or already had been suppressed, no delay would be expected on the postidiom region.

Sentences were presented visually, divided into segments of different length, formed by one or more words. The first critical segment was formed by the idiomatic phrase, the second by a relative pronoun as subject of the relative clause, and the third by a verb phrase. The segments corresponding to the idiom and the region postidiom were formed by the same words, as shown in Examples 1 and 3. In Experiment 2 the context was either ambiguous, or biasing the literal meaning of the idiom, as shown, respectively, in Examples 1 and 3:

1. It looked/like/the man/was going/to kick the bucket/that/was on the kitchen floor/.

2. It looked/like/the man/was going/to hit the bucket/that/was on the kitch-en floor/.
3. The man/was enraged/and/in an outburst/he kicked the bucket/that/was on the kitchen floor/.
4. The man/was enraged/and/in an outburst/he hit the bucket/that/was on the kitchen floor/.

In the control condition, the verb of the idiom was substituted by another verb in order to form a phrase with a meaning similar to that of the literal meaning of the idiom, but which could not be intended idiomatically (Sentences 2 and 4). Reading times for the idiomatic string versus the control string were compared in the two contexts.

The predictions depend on whether it is assumed that, besides activation of the meanings, integration and selection also occur during the time interval between presentation of the critical segment and the pressing of a button. The predictions also may depend on the relative time course of activation of the two possible interpretations.

If the figurative meaning, being associated to the whole phrase, is activated automatically, one might not expect any lengthening in reading times due purely to activation, but only to the further operations of integration and selection of meanings. It can be assumed that these operations are carried out immediately only when incompatible interpretations are active. This assumption is consistent with one made by Frazier and Rayner (1990) in a study where the processes involved in the resolution of meaning, as opposed to sense ambiguity, was investigated. In the first type of ambiguity the meanings are unrelated (i.e., "river bank" vs. "money bank"), whereas in the second the two meanings are to some extent related (i.e., "newspaper," "magazine" vs. "publisher"). According to the data found by Frazier and Rayner, the language processor seems to employ different strategies in the two cases. In the resolution of meaning ambiguity the processor has to decide between incompatible interpretations, but when the meanings are related, as is the case for sense ambiguity, the two interpretations may be to some extent compatible.

The selected idioms were understandable and plausible in both the literal and the figurative interpretation. Considering first the idiom region, when the idiom is in a neutral context, if both the literal meaning and the figurative meaning are activated almost simultaneously one would expect a delay in reading times with respect to the control condition, due to the necessity of a selection between incompatible interpretations.

When the context biases the literal interpretation, even if the idiomatic meaning has been activated, the language processor may select immediately between the alternative interpretations. Thus, a lengthening of reading times with respect to the control condition would be expected in the idiom region, due to the selection process. However, if the idiomatic meaning has not been activated, or has been activated too late, when the literal interpretation already has been confirmed, no difference would be expected between the experimental and the control conditions.

It is assumed that if the figurative interpretation is selected, when the relative clause is encountered (second and third segments) a garden path occurs. Thus, reading times in this region should give information about whether the figurative meaning has been activated, and when. Longer RTs in the postidiom region with respect to the control condition were expected in the sentences with a neutral context, showing that the figurative meaning has been activated. If a delay is found in the literal bias context, this would indicate that the figurative meaning becomes active independent of context.

Method

Subjects.   Twenty-eight students of the University of Padua volunteered as subjects in the experiment.

Material.   Sixteen idiomatic phrases were selected for the experiment. They were all ambiguous idioms formed by a verb phrase and a noun phrase, with a plausible and meaningful literal interpretation, beside the figurative one. Nine of the 16 idioms had been used in Experiment 1; the remaining idioms were changed because of the experimental condition's constraints, by which they had to be modified by a relative clause.

Each idiom was preceded either by a neutral context or by a context biasing the literal interpretation, forming the experimental condition of context bias. Moreover, a control condition for each type of context was created, in which the verb of the idiom was changed with a synonym, or quasisynonym, so that the idiomatic meaning was not retained. The frequency of the verbs in the two conditions was matched (72 for the verb of the idiom, 68 for the control verb). Thus, two factors were manipulated, context (neutral vs. literal bias) and type of string (idiom vs. control). The sentences are listed in the Appendix.

For each idiomatic phrase there were four experimental conditions, for a total of 64 test sentences. The sentences were assigned to four lists. In each list each idiom appeared once in only one of the four experimental conditions. A set of 49 filler sentences was added to each list. None of the fillers contained idiomatic phrases. The order of the idioms was fixed within a list, but was different between the lists. Each subject was presented with a list containing the 16 experimental and 49 filler sentences, for a total of 65 sentences.

The sentences were presented in segments of different length in order not to create an expectation for a particular type of chunk (word or phrase). The critical segments, on which the analyses had to be carried out, were the following: the idiom phrase, the relative pronoun, the region following the pronoun. These segments were exactly the same in all four conditions, except for the changing of the verb of the idiom in the control conditions.

Procedure

Sentences were displayed with a self-paced technique. Segments (one- to four-words long) were displayed in the center of the screen of a monitor commanded by an IBM computer, and remained there until the subject pressed the plus button on the numeric keypad. The software for executing the experiment and analyzing the data was the MEL (Micro Experimental Laboratory). In the instructions given to the subjects particular emphasis was placed on sentence comprehension. Subjects were told that they would be asked questions about the sentences, to ensure that they were reading for understanding. After each segment was displayed, subjects read it and pressed a button as soon as they thought they had understood. After the final segment appeared a blank was displayed. At random intervals, fixed within a list, a pause was made and the experimenter asked a question about the immediately preceding sentence. The data relative to these questions were not analyzed, as subjects were almost totally correct. RTs were recorded, from the appearance of each segment on the screen, to the pressing of the plus button.

Results and Discussion

The data consisted of mean RTs for critical segments. Data relative to idioms for which the idiomatic interpretation was unknown to a subject were discarded (6.7%). Also, 3.2% of the data were missing because of a failure of the equipment. Separate ANOVAs were carried out on the mean RTs of the three critical segments, with two factors, two levels each (neutral vs. literal context; idiom vs. control).

None of the factors, or interactions, was significant. For the first segment the mean reading times were respectively 862, 898, 866, and 880 ms, for the neutral sentences containing the idiom, for their controls, for the literal sentences containing the idiom, and their controls (all $Fs < 1$). For the second segment (the relative pronoun) the factor context was not significant, $F < 1$, the factor idiom versus control was marginally significant, $F(1, 27) = 4.15$, $p = .051$, and so was the interaction with context, $F(1, 27) = 3.5$, $p > .05$. Mean RTs for the relative pronoun were 638, 716, 671, and 661, respectively. An analysis of the simple main effects showed that RTs for the relative pronoun were shorter in the sentences containing an idiom in the neutral context, with respect to the control, $F(1, 27) = 5.56$ $p < .05$.

For the third and final segment (containing the remaining part of the relative clause) reading times were 949, 978, 897, and 911 ms, and no factor was significant.

According to these data, there is no evidence for activation of the figurative meaning in either the literally biased context, because no delay was found in reading the idiomatic string with respect to the control, or in the neutral context. The only evidence of an effect of the presence of an idiom was in the faster RTs for the relative pronoun region when the idiom followed a neutral context, in exactly the opposite direction to what would be expected if the language processor were facing a garden path, a result that does not have an obvious interpretation. If this result reflected the fact that the idiomatic interpretation had been retrieved and integrated, then longer RTs should have been found at least in the final region, where a literal interpretation clearly is required.

Considering all three segments, these results suggest that the language processor has a preference for the literal reading of idiomatic expressions when no figurative bias is given. It is worth pointing out that in this experiment the idiomatic phrases never were biased by an idiomatic context, because if such a bias had been given, the sentences would have become implausible when the relative clause, referring to the literal meaning of the noun of the idiom, was presented. Given the lack of any significant effect in the expected direction, and therefore the weakness of a conclusion based on a null result, the claim that the figurative meaning was not activated should be qualified by a result showing that indeed, when the idiomatic meaning is activated, a garden path occurs, with a consequent delay in RTs.

EXPERIMENT 3

In Experiment 3, two types of sentence contexts were manipulated, a literal context and an idiomatic context. The literally biased sentence formed a plausible sentence, whereas the sentence with a figurative bias became implausible when the relative clause was encountered, as shown in Examples 5 and 6:

5. Giovanni was so enraged that he wanted to hit something and he kicked the bucket, that was on the kitchen floor.
6. The rich old man was very ill, and his inheritor was hoping that he kicked the bucket, that was on the kitchen floor.

When the context is disambiguating, if the processor computes both the literal and the figurative interpretation, the ambiguity could be resolved immediately. In the condition where the context is biasing the literal interpretation of the idiom the sentence is plausible, and there is no garden path. This condition therefore was used as a control for both the idiom region and the region following the idiom. If the context biases the idiomatic meaning, a garden path must occur when the relative clause is encountered. Thus, it is expected that reading times for the postidiom region should be faster in Example 5 than in 6.

In order to distinguish the longer reading times due to the effect of implausibility, from those due to a garden path, a third condition was created. The noun of the idiom was replaced by another noun that did not form an idiomatic expression, but made the sentence implausible (Example 7).

7. The rich old man was very ill, and his inheritor was hoping that he kicked the pail, that was on the kitchen floor.

In the sentence fragment ". . . kicked the pail, that was on the kitchen floor," the implausibility starts when the word *pail* is presented, given the preceding context. At this point, if there is an effect of implausibility, there should be a delay with respect to the corresponding segment in Examples 5 and 6, where the noun of the idiom is perfectly acceptable as a continuation in both contexts. However, the effect of implausibility should be smaller with respect to a garden-path condition, because the language processor can decide immediately that the sentence is implausible, and does not have to consider alternative interpretations.

Method

Subjects.   Thirty students of the University of Padua volunteered as subjects.

Material.   To the set of idioms used in Experiment 2, two more idioms were added, in order to balance the number of items within each condition. The critical regions were formed by the idiom and the postidiom regions, and were modified with respect to Experiment 2. The idiomatic phrase was divided into two segments. The first segment was formed by the verb of the idiomatic verb phrase (*kick*), the second segment by the noun phrase following the verb (*the bucket*). This modification with respect to the presentation conditions of Experiment 2, where the idiom had been presented as a single segment, was made in order to control for differences in activation of the different parts of the idiom. It also made it possible to verify whether a delay would be found in the control condition, as the implausibility was made apparent by the noun of the verb phrase. The third segment included a relative pronoun as subject, and its verb, whereas the fourth segment was formed by a prepositional phrase or an adverb and ended the sentence. The four segments formed the critical regions on which analyses of reading times were performed.

Eighteen nouns were selected to substitute for the nouns of the idioms in the control condition. They were comparable to the nouns of the idioms for frequency and length, (mean frequency = 41.8 for the idiom noun, 32.6 for the control; mean length = 6 for the idiom noun, 5.3 for the control.) The 18 idioms were inserted in sentences with a literal or an idiomatic bias, for a total of 54 test sentences. Three lists were created, each containing an equal number of test sentences (18) plus 53 filler trials. In each list each idiom appeared in only one of the three experimental conditions.

Because sentences in this experiment could be plausible or implausible, some of the filler sentences used in Experiment 2 also were made implausible, in order to have an equal number of plausible and implausible sentences within each list. Thus, each subject was presented with 71 sentences.

Procedure

The procedure was similar to that used in Experiment 2, except for the following changes. The self-paced reading task was modified by the introduction of a secondary task. Subjects were asked to perform the self paced reading task, pressing a button with the index finger of their right hand, and to decide as quickly as possible whether the sentence made sense, pressing a button for a "yes" response and another for a "no" response, with the index and middle fingers of their left hand. The buttons used in the sentence decision task were different from the button used for self-paced reading.

Once again, reading for comprehension was stressed particularly, however no comprehension tests were given. Subjects were required to make the plausibility decision as fast as possible, and in order to do that, they were told that they had to read and understand the segments as soon as they were presented.

Results

For the reading times, separate analyses were carried out for each of the four segments in the three experimental conditions. RTs for idioms that were unknown to subjects in their figurative interpretation were discarded (6.6% of the data). Also RTs for sentences incorrectly classified were removed (16%) and were analyzed as errors. Mean RTs are displayed in Table 8.2.

The ANOVA on the first and second segments, corresponding to the verb and to the noun of the idiom, respectively, showed that there was no significant difference in reading times, $F(2, 58) = 1.29$, $F(2, 58) = 1.69$, respectively (see Table 8.2).

The analysis on the third segment showed a marginally significant effect, $F(2, 58) = 2.57$, $p < 1$. T tests on the means showed that the difference between the idiomatic test sentence and the literal sentence was significant, ($p < .05$). Finally, the analysis on the last segment was significant, $F(2, 58) = 4.36$, $p < .05$. T tests showed that the RTs to the final region in the idiomatic context condition differed from RTs in both the idiomatic control condition and literal context condition, $p < .05$. The latters did not differ from each other. Item analyses were not significant for any segment.

An analysis also was carried out on the mean RTs to decide whether the sentence was plausible or implausible. Mean RTs were 609 ms for the idiomatic context condition, 586 ms for the control condition, and 680 ms for the literal context condition. The difference were not significant, $F(2, 58) = 2.5$, $p < 1$. Also the analysis by items showed a marginal effect, $F(2, 34) = 2.48$, $p < .1$.

TABLE 8.2
The Mean Reading Times for the Idiom (First Two Rows) and the
Postidiom Regions (Third and Fourth Rows), the Mean Reaction
Times for Correct Plausibility Decisions, and Error Percentage
(in Parentheses, Fifth Row) for the Different Experimental
Conditions in Experiment 3

	Idiom. Context Experimental	Idiom. Context Control	Literal Context
1 idiom	679	673	657
2 idiom	756	697	710
1 postidiom	719	689	678
2 postidiom	762	706	712
Plausibility decision	609 (3.3)	586 (3.3)	680 (9.6)

In the analysis of errors, it was found that there was a significant trend for errors to occur more frequently in the literal context condition, $F(2, 58) = 14$, $p < .001$. Error percentages were 3.3% for the idiomatic context, 3.3% for the control condition, and 9.6% for the literal context condition. T tests on the means showed that the literal context condition was significantly different from the other two conditions, which did not differ from each other ($p < .01$).

To interpret the present results it is necessary to assume that the most likely referent for the relative pronoun is the noun of the idiom, rather than the idiom as a nominal. Because this assumption is crucial, it was advisable to have some empirical grounds to support it. Thus, a test was carried out on the material of Experiment 3 to verify the probability that the relative pronoun was interpreted as referring to the literal meaning of the noun of the idiom, to its figurative meaning, or to the whole phrase as a nominal. The sentences of Experiment 3 were divided into two lists. One list contained 18 sentences, half of which were formed by the idioms in the figurative context and half by the idioms in the literal context. In the second list the order was reversed, so that subjects saw all the items only once. Two more lists were constructed, containing the same idioms preceded by a neutral context, plus filler sentences in which the noun of the idiom had been substituted by another noun, as in the control condition of Experiment 3. The sentences ended immediately after the relative pronoun, and subjects were asked to provide a meaningful completion. Four groups of 10 subjects each were used, randomly assigned to one of the lists.

The data for four sentences were lost due to an error of the experimenter. The completions were scored according to the following categories. The first category included completions where the relative pronoun referred to the literal meaning of the noun. For the second and third categories the relative pronoun referred to the figurative meaning of the noun, or to the whole phrase, respectively. The fourth category consisted of completions that were paraphrases of the meaning of the idiom, or other types of nonrelevant completions.

It was found that, for the sentences biasing the idiomatic meaning of the idiom, 51% of completions were formed by clauses in which the relative pronoun referred to the figurative meaning of the noun of the idiom, 17% by clauses referring to the literal meaning, and 9% by clauses referring to the idiom as a whole. The fourth category (nonrelevant completions) included 23% of the completions. For control sentences, where the noun of the idiom has been replaced by another noun to form a control condition, completions in terms of the literal meaning of the noun were 95.5%; the remaining completions belonged to the category of paraphrases or other nonrelevant completions. For sentences with a neutral context, 60% of the completions referred to the literal meaning of the noun, 2.5% to the whole idiom, 7% to the figurative meaning of the noun, and the remaining were classified as paraphrases or other.

Clearly, these results show that subjects tended to assign the noun of the idiom rather than the whole phrase as a referent to the relative pronoun. Moreover, when the bias of the context constrains a figurative interpretation, subjects tried to make a meaningful completion by proposing an interpretation of the relative clause that is congruent with the context, and refers to the figurative meaning. In contrast, when the context is neutral the preferred referent was the literal meaning of the noun.

Reference to the noun occurred more easily when idioms are transparent. For instance, for the idiom *break the ice* the connection between literal and figurative meaning is quite transparent, and 80% of the completions in the present test were formed by phrases referring to the figurative meaning of the noun, 10% to the literal meaning of the noun, none to the idiom as a whole. With nontransparent idioms, like *mangiare la foglia* ("to eat the leaf"), meaning something like "to grasp the deceit," no reference to the literal or figurative meaning of the noun was given.

Discussion

The results of Experiment 3 show that, when the context biases the idiomatic meaning, RTs in both the ambiguous region and in the postambiguity region increase. Such increase is only marginally significant for the ambiguous region. This might be due to variability in the extent to which the figurative meaning is activated and integrated with the context. In contrast, no difference is found for the two conditions in the first part of the idiom (first segment). Apparently, the idiomatic meaning is not activated at such an early test position, or, alternatively, there is no cost to the activation.

The occurrence of a garden path in the postidiom region shows that the idiomatic meaning has been activated and integrated in the context, but only in the biasing context, when a reanalysis of the interpretation has been required. When the context is neutral, as was the case in Experiment 2, there is no lengthening of reading times in the ambiguous region, nor is there any evidence of the occurrence of a garden path in the postidiom region. Moreover, no lengthening of RTs for the ambiguous region appears when the context is biased toward the literal interpretation.

It is worth noting that no significant delay was found in the control condition of Experiment 3, relative to the literal condition. That is, processing the control noun, which made the sentence implausible, in the verb phrase did not take significantly longer with respect to the literal condition, in either of the three segments. It appears that when the implausibility is very obvious, the language processor immediately decides that the sentence is not plausible and this decision is not costly, in processing terms.

What seems to involve more complex decision processes, reflected in longer RTs, is the condition in which there is an ambiguity and two interpretations are possible, one on the basis of the context preceding the idiom, and the second on the basis of information following it. The language processor seems to prefer to maintain the interpretation that had been selected initially on the basis of the context (the figurative interpretation in the case of the idiomatic context). This fact is confirmed by the results of the completion test where 51% of the completions assigned the figurative meaning of part of the idiom as a referent for the relative pronoun, even at the cost of grammatical correctness in some cases. However, such preference only occurs when the context biases the idiomatic meaning. When the context is neutral the literal meaning of the noun is the preferred referent, as shown by the completions in which the pronoun was assigned a literally intended referent in 60% of the cases. Therefore, the construction of an interpretation of the relative pronoun in terms of the figurative meaning of the noun conflicts with the latter preference. This conflict is reflected in the RTs to the region immediately following the idiom.

Finally, when the whole relative clause has been read, its only possible interpretation, in terms of the literal meaning of the noun, compels the language processor to reconsider the given interpretation, which leads to a decision of implausibility. It is interesting to note that the RTs to the sentence classification task do not reflect any differences. Presumably, the decision about the plausibility of the sentence is made before the end of the sentence. However, even more interesting, a higher number of errors has been found in the literal context condition with respect to the other two, despite the fact that it required a positive response. It appears that the presence of an idiom increases the probability of making an error in a literally biased sentence. This fact suggests that the idiomatic meaning is active at the time of the sentence classification, and interferes with the judgment. Perhaps, the fact that the effect of this activation is only manifest in the pattern of errors during sentence classification reflects a delayed activation, due to postperceptual processes. Alternatively, it could be that the idiomatic meaning has been activated during the presentation of the sentence, but only on some trials, and to an extent not detectable in selfpaced reading.

One more point to consider relates to the fact that in an idiomatic context the idiom can be perceived as modified by a relative clause referring to the figurative meaning of one of its part (the noun). This is in agreement with the suggestion that the figurative interpretation can be constructed, to some extent, on the basis of the different components of the idiom (Gazdar et al., 1983; Gibbs & Nayak, 1989; Gibbs et al., 1989; Wasow et al., 1983). This view is in opposition to the idea that the idiomatic meaning is a stored representation directly associated with the whole phrase, and might hold particularly for certain types of idioms, like *break the ice,* so-called "analyzable-transparent" in the classification proposed by Cacciari and Glucksberg (1991). For these types of idioms the construction of an idiomatic interpretation may involve similar processes to those required to form an interpretation of unambiguous nouns in selecting the sense appropriate to the context. For instance, the action of "breaking," rather than being applied to a physically concrete domain, is mapped onto an abstract domain that defines a metaphorical connotation of the concept of "coldness" implied by the idiom.

The results of Experiments 2 and 3 suggest that with ambiguous idioms the presence of a biasing context is a necessary condition for activation of the figurative meaning to occur. This result is in opposition with that found in Experiment 1 where a different experimental paradigm had been used. In that experiment, priming was found for both the figurative and the literal meaning independent of context. A similar conflict was found elsewhere in the literature, with respect to ambiguous words. Data provided by the cross-modal priming paradigm (e.g., Onifer & Swinney, 1981; Swinney, 1979) showed a different pattern from those obtained using the eye fixations methodology (Rayner & Frazier, 1989). As has been noted in the discussion of Experiment 1, performing a lexical decision task in the cross-modal priming paradigm can involve mechanisms that are peculiar to the specific experimental situation, and so may be different from those involved in another situation, requiring a different task. Thus, it could be that priming effects are magnified in the priming paradigm, and by the decision mechanism involved in lexical decision. In self-paced reading (and may be also in normal reading) concepts may be activated just very briefly, and to a smaller extent, not sufficient to be detected. If this is the case, the priming paradigm, especially when the lexical decision is used, is more appropriate to investigate how concepts are represented and related, rather than the processes involved in reading and listening.

CONCLUSION

Several factors are involved in the comprehension of idioms. One of these factors, already pointed out by Cacciari and Tabossi (1988), is predictability. This factor itself presumably involves several components, which now are considered.

An important component may be frequency of occurrence of an idiomatic expression, that is, how frequently the idiom has been encountered, or how strong is the connection between the string of words forming an idiom and its associated meaning. The contribution of this factor is likely to vary, in view of the fact that idioms can be subject to syntactic operations. Thus, as the superficial form of the string is not always the same, the availability of the stored meaning is likely to vary. Thus the hypothesis of an automatic activation should be modulated, considering the relative strength of the connection between an orthographic or phonological form, word or phase, and its semantic representation as predictor of the automaticity of the process involved. If there is a strong connection, the meaning is more likely to become available, and in a shorter time (Cohen, Dunbar, & McClelland, 1990).

Another important component involved in the comprehension of idioms is the degree of frozenness (Gibbs & Gonzales, 1985). Related to this aspect is the syntactic form in which the idiom is expressed. Syntactic cues, like presence or absence of articles, are certainly critical to determine the probability that an expression is interpreted as an idiom, rather than literally. Moreover some idiosyncratic aspects of idioms also could be important. For instance, some idiomatic expressions make reference to events that would be unlikely if intended literally, as, for instance, in the case of idioms like *lose face,* or, in Italian, idioms like *avere il pollice verde* ("to have a green finger").

Context is obviously one of the most relevant variables to consider when studying the comprehension of idiomatic expressions. In particular, it seems critical, especially when ambiguous idioms are involved, to understand whether and how context interacts with other factors to determine the point at which the idiomatic meaning is activated and integrated. A distinction that may be useful in this respect is that of local and global context. To illustrate this distinction a few words are necessary. The meanings of single words in a phrase or sentence interact both locally and globally. They must be combined locally in order to define a semantic domain (see Examples 8, 9, & 10) where the context contributes to the selection of the particular sense of the word *run,* that is, a concrete sense involving a physical and spatial movement as in 8, a concrete spatial sense with no real movement involved as in 9, or an abstract sense as in 10. At the global level the meanings of the single words must be integrated to form an interpretation at the whole sentence level:

8. The train ran through the country.
9. The scar ran through his face.
10. The business ran efficiently.

Thus, local context determines cohesion and integration of lower level constituents, like the phrase in which a word is included. Global context determines and is linked to higher level elaborative processes, like interpretation of the whole sentence.

To illustrate the relevance of this distinction between local and global levels consider the following examples. An ambiguous idiom, like *break the ice*, can have a meaningful interpretation at the local level. However, an interpretation of the opaque unambiguous idiom *shoot the breeze* based on the compositional meanings of its words would not be meaningful, unless used in a peculiar sense. Alternatively, in a context biasing the idiomatic meaning of *kick the bucket* ("die") (e.g., "The old man had been sick for a long time and finally he kicked the bucket") the literal interpretation, possible at the local level, would not be meaningful, or at least not very plausible, at the global level. Lack of a successful integration of the interpretation constructed at the local level with the global context therefore could act as a triggering device for the activation of the figurative meaning.

Finally, one more factor to consider is transparency. As pointed out earlier, a transparent idiom may require different processing strategies from those required by an opaque idiom. Similarly, Frazier and Rayner (1990) showed that the language processor uses different strategies to deal with words having different meanings or different senses. If this is the case, constructing an idiomatic interpretation might not, or not always, involve the simple activation of a stored meaning, at least for transparent idioms, because it would be a compositional function of the figurative meaning of its words, and the language processor would have to use different strategies with different types of idioms. Such a view was suggested by Gibbs et al. (1989) and is consistent with their results.

In conclusion, the study of the processes involved in the comprehension of idiomatic expressions appear to be central to the understanding of the human language processor.

ACKNOWLEDGMENTS

The preparation of this chapter was supported by a CNR grant in 1988 to the author. The data for the first experiment were reported at the Joint Conference of the Experimental Psychological Society, the Società Italiana di Psicologia and the Società Italiana di Neuropsicologia held in Padua, April 1986. The data for the second and third experiments were reported at the Second Workshop on Language Comprehension held in Aix-en-Provence, April 1991. I wish to thank Sandro Bettella for his invaluable aid with technical problems and programming, Emanuele Tressoldi for helping run the subjects in Experiment 1, and the Department of Electrotechnical Engineering of the University of Padua for technical support in the preparation of the stimulus material for Experiment 1. I am also grateful to Robert Pierce for editing the paper.

Address correspondence to: Lucia Colombo, Dipartimento di Psicologia Generale, P.zza Capitaniato, 3, 35139 Padova, Italy. Email address: PSICO04 @IPDUNIVX.UNIPD.IT

REFERENCES

Balota, D. A., & Lorch, R. F. J. (1986). Depth of automatic spreading activation: Mediating priming effects in pronunciation but not in lexical decision. *Journal of Experimental Psychology: Learning, Memory, and Cognition, 12*(3), 336–345.

Bobrow, S., & Bell, S. M. (1973). On catching on to idiomatic expressions. *Memory & Cognition, 1,* 343–346.

Bortolini, U., Tagliavini, C., & Zampolli, A. (1972). *Lessico di frequenza della lingua italiana contemporanea* [Lexicon of the frequency of the contemporary Italian language]. Milano, Italy: Garzanti.

Cacciari, C., & Glucksberg, S. (1991). Understanding idiomatic expressions: The contribution of word meanings. In G. B. Simpson (Ed.), *Understanding word and sentence* (pp. 217–240). Amsterdam, Netherlands: Elsevier.

Cacciari, C., & Tabossi, P. (1988). The comprehension of idioms. *Journal of Memory and Language, 27,* 668–683.

Chomsky, N. (1980). *Rules and representations.* New York: Columbia University Press.

Cohen, J. D., Dunbar, K., & McClelland, J. L. (1990). On the control of automatic processes: A parallel distributed processing account of the Stroop effect. *Psychological Review, 97*(3), 332–361.

Colombo, L., & Williams, J. (1990). Effects of word- and sentence-level contexts upon word recognition. *Memory & Cognition, 18*(2), 153–163.

Duffy, S. A., Morris, R. K., & Rayner, K. (1988). Lexical ambiguity and fixation times in reading. *Journal of Memory and Language, 27,* 429–446.

Forster, K. I. (1981). Priming and the effects of sentence and lexical contexts on naming time: Evidence for autonomous lexical processing. *Quarterly Journal of Experimental Psychology, 33A,* 465–495.

Fraser, E. (1970). Idioms within a transformational grammar. *Foundations of Language, 6,* 22–42.

Frazier, L., & Rayner, K. (1990). Taking on semantic commitments: Processing multiple meanings vs. multiple senses. *Journal of Memory and Language, 29,* 181–200.

Gazdar, G., Klein, E., Pullum, G. K., & Sag, I. A. (1983). *Generalized phrase structure grammar.* Hertfordshire, England: Basil Blackwell.

Gibbs, R. (1980). Spilling the beans on understanding and memory for idioms in conversation. *Memory & Cognition, 8,* 449–456.

Gibbs, R. (1986). Skating on thin ice: Literal meaning and understanding idioms in conversation. *Discourse Processes, 9,* 17–30.

Gibbs, R. W., & Gonzales, G. P. (1985). Syntactic frozenness in processing and remembering idioms. *Cognition, 20,* 243–259.

Gibbs, R. W., & Nayak, N. (1989). Psycholinguistic studies on the syntactic behavior of idioms. *Cognitive Psychology, 21,* 100–138.

Gibbs, R. W., Nayak, N., & Cutting, C. (1989). How to kick the bucket and not decompose: Analyzability and idiom processing. *Journal of Memory and Language, 28,* 576–593.

Glass, A. L. (1983). The comprehension of idioms. *Journal of Psycholinguistic Research, 12*(4), 429–442.

Koriat, A. (1981). Semantic facilitation in lexical decisions as a function of prime target association. *Memory & Cognition, 8,* 587–598.

Lupker, S. J. (1984). Semantic priming without association. *Journal of Verbal Learning and Verbal Behavior, 23,* 709–733.

Onifer, W., & Swinney, D. A. (1981). Accessing lexical ambiguities during sentence comprehension: Effects of frequency of meanings and contextual bias. *Memory & Cognition, 9,* 225–236.

Ortony, A., Schallert, D., Reynolds, R., & Antos, S. (1978). Interpreting metaphors and idioms: Some effects of context on comprehension. *Journal of Verbal Learning and Verbal Behavior, 17,* 465–477.

Rayner, K., & Duffy, S. A. (1986). Lexical complexity and fixation times in reading: Effects of word frequency, verb complexity, and lexical ambiguity. *Memory & Cognition, 14*(3), 191–201.

Rayner, K., & Frazier, L. (1989). Selection mechanisms in reading lexically ambiguous words. *Journal of Experimental Psychology: Learning, Memory, and Cognition, 15*,(5), 779–790.

Seidenberg, M. S., Tanenhaus, M. K., Leiman, J. M., & Bienkovski, M. (1982). Automatic access of the meanings of ambiguous words in context: Some limitations of knowledge-based processing. *Cognitive Psychology, 14*, 489–537.

Seidenberg, M. S., Waters, G. S., Sanders, M., & Langer, P. (1984). Pre- and postlexical loci of contextual effects on word recognition. *Memory & Cognition, 12*, 315–328.

Simpson, G. B. (1981). Meaning dominance and semantic context in the processing of lexical ambiguity. *Journal of Verbal Learning and Verbal Behavior, 20*, 120–136.

Swinney, D. (1979). Lexical access during sentence comprehension: (Re)consideration of context effects. *Journal of Verbal Learning and Verbal Behavior, 18*, 645–660.

Swinney, D. (1981). Lexical processing during sentence comprehension: Effects of higher order constraints and implications for representation. In T. Myers, J. Laver, & J. Anderson (Eds.), *The cognitive representation of speech* (pp. 601–609). Amsterdam, Netherlands: North Holland.

Swinney, D., & Cutler, A. (1979). The access and processing of idiomatic expressions. *Journal of Verbal Learning and Verbal Behavior, 18*, 523–534.

Tabossi, P. (1988). Accessing lexical ambiguity in different types of sentential contexts. *Journal of Memory and Language, 27*, 324–340.

Tabossi, P., & Cacciari, C. (1988). Context effects in the comprehension of idioms. In Cognitive Science Society (Ed.), *Proceedings of the Tenth Annual Conference of the Cognitive Science Society* (pp. 90–96). Hillsdale, NJ: Lawrence Erlbaum Associates.

Tabossi, P., Colombo, L., & Job, R. (1987). Accessing lexical ambiguity: Effects of context and dominance. *Psychological Research, 49*, 161–167.

Tanenhaus, M. K., Leiman, J. M., & Seidenberg, M. S. (1979). Evidence for multiple stages in the processing of ambiguous words in syntactic contexts. *Journal of Verbal Learning and Verbal Behavior, 18*, 427–440.

Van Petten, C., & Kutas, M. (1987). Ambiguous words in context: An event-related potential analysis of the time course of meaning activation. *Journal of Memory and Language, 26*, 188–208.

Wasow, T., Sag, I. A., & Nunberg, G. (1983). Idioms: An interim report. In S. Hattori & K. Inone (Eds.), *Proceedings of the XIII International Conference of Linguists* (pp. 102–115). Tokyo: CIPL.

APPENDIX

Sentences biasing the literal (a) or the figurative (b) interpretation of the idioms (idioms are underlined in the figurative context) and target words, in parentheses (experimental control), used in Experiment 1. In italics are translations of the idioms or the English equivalents:

1a. Il bambino stava giocando nel prato e il suo compagno gli lanciò la palla che egli riuscì ad afferrare al volo, dopo una lunga corsa (uccello - ospite).

1a. The child was playing in the garden and his mate threw him the ball that he was able to catch on the flight, after a long run (bird - guest).

1b. Era così intelligente ed acuto che non aveva bisogno di lunghe spiegazioni, ma riusciva ad *afferrare al volo* le parti essenziali di un problema (idea - luce).

1b. He was so clever and sharp that he did not need long explanations, but could catch on the flight *(to grasp immediately)* the essential parts of the problem (idea - light).

2a. Per appendere un quadro, bisogna scegliere il punto sul muro in cui battere il chiodo, e poi dare dei colpi precisi (martello - omaggio).

2a. To hang a picture, one needs to choose the point on the wall where to hit the nail, and then strike accurately (hammer - present).

2b. Tutti gli amici gli ripetevano continuamente che doveva trovarsi un altro lavoro, e specialmente Luigi, il suo più caro amico, continuava a *battere il chiodo,* ma inutilmente (insistenza - preavviso).

2b. All his friends kept telling him that he ought to find another job, in particular Luigi, his dearest friend, kept hitting the nail, *(to insist)* with no result (insistence - notice).

3a. Il pacco era confezionato così accuratamente che dovette prendere la forbice per tagliare la corda che lo legava strettamente (spago - tasto).

3a. The parcel was so accurately prepared that he had to use the scissors to cut the rope that tied it so tightly (string - key).

3b. Il prigioniero pagò una somma enorme al guardiano della cella e riuscì a *tagliare la corda,* dopo molte peripezie (fuga - onda).

3b. The prisoner payed the warden a huge sum and succeeded in cutting the rope, *(to escape)* after many perils (flight - wave).

4a. Dopo aver dipinto l'inferriata con la vernice l'operaio aveva lasciato cadere delle macchie di colore dappertutto, e si trovò il pollice verde, perciò se lo dovette lavare (rosso - tardo).

4a. After he had painted the railing with the varnish the workman spilled the painting everywhere, and he discovered that his thumb was green, so he had to wash it (red - slow).

4b. Il balcone pieno di bellissimi fiori della casa di fronte è curato da una signora *con il pollice verde,* che conosco bene (piante - motivo).

4b. The balcony of the house opposite ours, which is full of beautiful flowers, is taken care of by a lady with the green thumb, *(to have a green finger)* whom I know well (plants - motive).

5a. Il giorno del suo compleanno tutti i suoi amici per festeggiarlo volevano tirargli gli orecchi (occhi - acqua).

5a. On his birthday all his friends wanted to pull his ears to celebrate (eyes - water).

5b. La mamma si alzò, lo guardò severamente e gli disse che doveva *tirargli gli orecchi* e lo mondò a letto senza cena (castigo - postale).

5b. His mother stood up, looked at him severely and told him that she ought to pull his ears, and sent him to bed without supper (punishment - postal)

6a. Quella palestra è molto attrezzata ma c'è poco spazio, l'altro giorno, mentre sollevavo un peso, urtai contro lo spigolo nell'alzare il gomito, e mi feci molto male (braccio - denaro).

6a. That gymnasium is very well equipped but there is not enough space, the other day while lifting weights, I bumped against the edge of a corner in raising the elbow and I hurt myself (arm - money).

6b. All'uscita dell'osteria ho visto il vecchio Giovanni che barcollava e stava per cadere, perchè si sa che gli piace *alzare il gomito* ogni tanto (vino - arma).

6b. Coming out of the pub I saw old John who was staggering and was going to fall, as it is well known that he likes to raise his elbow *(to drink too much)* every now and then (wine - weapon).

7a. A causa dell'incidente nell'autostrada si era prodotto un enorme ingorgo di traffico, ed era impossibile farsi strada, perciò siamo rimasti fermi parecchie ore (città - voce).

7a. Because of the accident in the motorway a huge traffic jam had formed, and it was impossible to make one's way, therefore we had to stop for several hours (town - voice).

7b. Non perde alcuna occasione per mettersi in mostra, quell'arrivista del mio collega cerca sempre di avere successo e vuole ad ogni costo *farsi strada,* anche in modo disonesto (ambizione - paesaggio).

7b. He doesn't miss any opportunity to make an exhibition of himself, that ambitious colleague of mine is always trying to be successful and wants to make his way at any cost, even dishonestly (ambition - landscape).

8a. Nel teatrino, i bambini si divertivano molto a vedere i buffi movimenti delle marionette, sospese ad un filo, e manovrate dall'abile artista (lana - data).

8a. In the puppet theater, the children enjoyed themselves looking at the funny movements of the puppets, hanging from a thread, and moved by the skilled artist (wool - date).

8b. L'esploratore durante il viaggio fu costretto ad affrontare numerose peripezie, e molte volte la sua vita fu *sospesa ad un filo* ma riuscì sempre a cavarsela (rischio - squadra).

8b. During the journey the explorer was compelled to face many perils, and many times his life hung by a thread but he managed to get out of the problems (risk - team).

9a. Dopo l'operazione Luigi si era molto indebolito e non riusciva neppure a camminare, fu quindi molto contento quando lentamente riuscì a fare il primo passo, e a ristabilirsi un po' (piede - conto).

9a. After the operation Luigi was very weak and couldn't even walk, therefore he was very happy when he slowly managed to take the first step, and feel better (foot - bill).

9b. Era da tempo che volevo conoscere quella ragazza così timida, quando la incontrai alla festa sapevo che dovevo *fare il primo passo,* e parlarle (approccio - ammasso).

9b. For a long time I've been wanting to know that girl so shy, when I met her at the party I knew I was supposed to take the first step and talk to her (approach - bulk).

10a. La medicina era così amara che il bambino non voleva ingoiarla, e gli sembrò di sputare veleno, da quanto cattiva era (mortale - cammino).

10a. The medicine tasted so bitter that the child refused to swallow it, and it seemed like he was spitting poison, because it tasted so bad (mortal - walk).

10b. Il successo e la bellezza della sua amica le facevano così rabbia che quando ne parlava sembrava *sputare veleno,* da quanto male ne diceva (invidia - agenzia).

10b. The success and the beauty of her friend made her so furious that when she talked about it it looked like she was spitting venom, so ill did she speak of her friend.

11a. D'estate siamo stati all'aperto di notte a guardare il cielo, e mi ha fatto vedere le stelle, e insegnato i loro nomi (luna - gara).

11a. In the summer we used to stay outside during the night to watch the sky, and he has made me see the stars, and taught their names (moon - game).

11b. Nell'autobus affollato, un signore mi ha pestato e mi ha fatto *vedere le stelle,* e allora l'ho insultato (dolore - affare).

11b. In the crowded bus a man stepped on my toes and made me see the stars *(to see the stars by daylight)* so I insulted him (pain - business).

12a. A giudicare dai numerosi buchi nel vecchio mobile in cucina, qualcosa lo rode, forse un tarlo (denti - riva).

12a. Judging from the many holes in the old kitchen cupboard, something is gnawing it, perhaps a wood-worm (teeth - shore).

12b. Giovanni mi sembra molto teso e preoccupato negli ultimi giorni, *qualcosa lo rode,* ma non so capire cosa (angoscia - assalto).

12b. Giovanni has been looking very tense and worried in the past few days, something is gnawing him, *(to be worried)* I do not know what (anguish - assault).

13a. La maestra a lezione spiegò che i serpenti e i rettili sono animali a sangue freddo (caldo - ricco).

13a. During the lecture the teacher said that snakes and reptiles are cold blooded animals (warm - rich).

13b. La situazione era molto complessa e richiedeva che lui avesse auto-controllo e agisse *a sangue freddo,* per poterla risolvere (calma - cambio).

13b. The situation was very complicated and required him to have self-control and to act in cold blood, to be able to get through (calm - change).

14a. Durante quella terribile estate dovette rimanere in città, e l'unico modo per sopportare il caldo era una doccia fredda, più volte al giorno (brividi - cresta).

14a. During that awful summer he had to stay in town, the only way to stand the heat was a cold shower, many times during the day (shiver - crest).

14b. La notizia imprevista arrivata ieri è stata *una doccia fredda,* e mi ha rovinato la giornata (delusione - perfezione).

14b. The unexpected yesterday news was a cold shower, *(nasty surprise)* it wasted my day (disappointment - perfection).

15a. Il clown per far ridere i bambini si fece portare una torta di panna montata, in cui voleva ficcare il naso, per poi lanciarla via (bocca - libro).

15a. To make children laugh the clown had a cream cake brought in, where he wanted to thrust his nose, and that he wanted afterward throw away (mouth - book).

15b. Il tuo amico mi ha fatto molte domande, mi sembra un tipo che *ficca il naso* anche dove non dovrebbe (curioso - affetto).

15b. Your friend asked me many questions, he looks like someone who thrusts his nose everywhere, even where he should not (curious - affection).

16a. Per preparare una buona granatina, si deve prendere l'apposito arnese per rompere il ghiaccio, altrimenti non viene bene (neve - pelo).

16a. To prepare a good granatina, one must take the right tool to break the ice, otherwise it doesn't come out properly (snow - hair).

16b. Il signore seduto nel treno si annoiava e si chiedeva come riuscire a far conversazione con il tizio seduto di fronte, ma non sapeva come fare a *rompere il ghiaccio* (iniziativa - testimone).

16b. The man who was sitting in the train was getting bored and was wondering how to start conversation with the guy sitting in front of him, but could not break the ice (initiative - witness).

Materials used in Experiment 2 (a - literal contexts, b - ambiguous contexts); in parentheses are the control words, in italics the English translation of the figurative meaning of the idiom, or the English equivalent:

1a. Per fare una granatina doveva rompere (spaccare) il ghiaccio che si era formato nel frigo.

1a. To make a granatina he had to break (crack) the ice that had formed in the fridge.

1b. Attratto dalla ragazza l'uomo cercava timidamente di rompere (spaccare) il ghiaccio *(to break the ice)* che si era formato sul vetro.

1b. Attracted by the girl the man was shyly trying to break (crack) the ice that had formed on the glass.

2a. All'arrivo della scatola prese la forbice per tagliare (rompere) la corda che legava il pacco.

2a. As the box arrived he took the scissors to cut (break) the rope that tied the parcel.

2b. Per il prigioniero era indubbiamente molto difficile tagliare (rompere) la corda *(to escape)* che legava il pacco.

2b. Undoubtedly it was very difficult for the prisoner to cut (break) the rope that tied the parcel.

3a. Era nella panna che il pagliaccio per far ridere ficcava (poneva) il naso che era bello rosso.

3a. It was in the cream that the clown, to make people laugh, thrusted (put) his nose that was very red.

3b. Ero stupefatta quando mi sono accorta dove ficcava (poneva) il naso *(to thrust one's nose)* che era bello rosso.

3b. I was astonished when I realized where he thrusted (put) his nose that was very red.

4a. Mentre faceva il bagno Giovanni voleva gettare (strizzare) la spugna che spruzzava dappertutto.

4a. While he was taking a bath Giovanni wanted to throw (squeeze) the sponge that was splashing everywhere.

4b. Ormai stanco a quel punto Giovanni voleva gettare (strizzare) la spugna *(to give up)* che spruzzava dappertutto.

4b. Now weary, at that point Giovanni wanted to throw (squeeze) the sponge that was splashing everywhere.

5a. Manovrata dall'abile artista la marionetta era sospesa ad (tenuta da) un filo che pendeva dal soffitto.

5a. Maneuvered by the skilled artist the puppet was suspended to (kept by) a thread that was hanging from the ceiling.

5b. Per tutto il tempo si era sentito sospeso ad (tenuto da) un filo *(to hang by a thread)* che pendeva dal soffitto.

5b. All time long he had felt suspended to (held by) a thread that hung from the ceiling.

6a. Talvolta osservando il cielo capita di vedere (guardare) le stelle che formano l'Orsa Maggiore.

6a. Sometimes watching the sky one happens to see (look at) the stars that form the Great Bear constellation.

6b. Girandosi improvvisamente quell'uomo mi ha fatto vedere (guardare) le stelle *(to see stars by daylight)* che formano l'Orsa Maggiore.

6b. Turning suddenly the man has made me see the stars that form the Great Bear constellation.

7a. Il falegname prese il pezzo di legno e si mise a battere (colpire) il chiodo che fissò al muro.

7a. The carpenter took the piece of wood and started hitting the nail that he fastened to the wall.

7b. Continuava a battere (colpire) il chiodo *(to insist)* che doveva fissare al muro.

7b. He kept hitting (striking) the nail that he had fastened to the wall.

8a. Il cavallo era troppo fiacco per tirare (spingere) la carretta che era piena di mattoni.

8a. The horse was too weak to pull (push) the cart that was full of bricks.

8b. La vecchia era sfinita e non ne poteva più di tirare (spingere) la carretta *(to drudge)* che era piena di mattoni.

8b. The old woman was worn out and done up with pulling (pushing) the cart that was full of bricks.

9a. Il medico chiese al paziente di stringere (far vedere) i denti che erano sottoposti alla cura.

9a. The doctor asked the patient to clench (let see) the teeth that were under treatment.

9b. Ai soldati fu raccomandato di stringere (far vedere) i denti *(to endure something)* che erano sottoposti alla cura.

9b. The soldiers were advised to clench (let see) the teeth that were under treatment.

10a. A causa di tutte le spese fatte voleva fare (vedere) i conti che si erano accumulati.

10a. Because of all the expenses that had been made he wanted to do (see) the accounts that had piled up.

10b. Con un cenno mi ha fatto capire di volere fare (vedere) i conti *(to reckon)* che si erano accumulati.

10b. With a sign he made me understand he wanted to do (see) the accounts that had piled up.

11a. Mi disse che aveva visto il gatto in cucina mangiarsi (ingoiare) il fegato *(to be worried)* che era la sua passione.

11a. He told me he had seen the cat in the kitchen eating (ingesting) the liver that he was very fond of.

11b. Lo aveva visto come si mangiava (ingoiava) il fegato *(to be worried)* che era la sua passione.

11b. He had watched how (he/she/it/) ate (ingested) the liver that he/she/it was very fond of.

12a. Mentre dipingeva si guardò le mani e si accorse di avere il pollice verde (rosso) che pulì sullo straccio.

12a. While he was painting he looked at his hands and realized he had the green (red) thumb that he cleaned with the rag.

12b. Guardando il suo bellissimo terrazzo aveva scoperto di avere il pollice verde, *(to have a green finger)* che pulì sullo straccio.

12b. Looking at his beautiful balcony he had discovered he had the green thumb that he cleaned with the rag.

13a. Il dottore per visitarlo gli ha chiesto di alzare (sollevare) il gomito che si era fratturato recentemente.

13a. To visit him the doctor asked him to raise (lift) the elbow that he had recently broken.

13b. L'altro giorno all'osteria con gli amici gli era capitato di alzare (sollevare) il gomito *(to drink too much)* che si era fratturato recentemente.

13b. A few days ago while he was at the pub with his friends he happened to raise (lift) the elbow that he had recently broken.

14a. Stefano era affamato e la mamma gli ha dato (offerto) del salame che gli è indigesto.

14a. Stefano was hungry and his mother gave (offered) him some salami that he cannot digest.

14b. È un tipo molto suscettibile e si è offeso perchè Giorgio gli ha dato (offerto) del salame *(to call someone an ass)* che gli è indigesto.

14b. He is a very susceptible guy and he got offended because Giorgio has given (offered) him some salami that he cannot digest.

15a. Il cacciatore per prendere la mira ha dovuto chiudere (coprirsi) un occhio che gli faceva male.

15a. To take aim the hunter had to close (to cover) an eye that ached.

15b. Per quella faccenda ha dovuto chiudere (coprirsi) un occhio *(to overlook)* che gli faceva male.

15b. Because of that affair he had to close (to cover) an eye that ached.

16a. Durante un brusco movimento della nave il capitano ha perso (rotto) la bussola che serve per navigare.

16a. During a rough movement of the ship the captain has lost (broken) the compass that is used for navigation.

16b. Dopo l'incidente Stefano ha perso (rotto) la bussola *(to lose one's head)* che gli avevo regalato.

16b. After the incident Stefano has lost (broken) the compass that I had given as a present to him.

Materials used in Experiment 3 (a - literal contexts, b - figurative contexts); in parentheses are the words for the control condition, in italics the English translation of the figurative meaning or the equivalent English idiom:

1a. Per fare una granatina doveva prendere l'apposito arnese per rompere il ghiaccio che era in frigo.

1a. To prepare a granatina he had to take the appropriate device to break the ice that was in the fridge.

1b. Dopo il litigio con la fidanzata Mario voleva parlarle ma non riusciva a rompere il ghiaccio *(break the ice)* che era in frigo (il piatto che era in frigo).

1b. After the row with her girlfriend Mario wanted to talk to her but could not break the ice (plate) that was in the fridge.

2a. All'arrivo della scatola l'uomo prese velocemente la forbice per tagliare la corda che legava il pacco.

2a. When the box arrived the man hurried to take the scissors to cut the rope that tied the parcel.

2b. Nonostante le guardie che gli sparavano il prigioniero era riuscito a tagliare la corda *(to escape)* che legava il pacco (il nastro che legava il pacco).

2b. In spite of the guards that fired at him the prisoner managed to cut the rope (ribbon) that tied the parcel.

3a. Era nella torta di panna che il pagliaccio per far ridere ficcava il naso che era molto lungo.

3a. It was in the cream cake that the clown, to make people laugh, thrust his nose that was very long.

3b. Quella donna voleva sempre sapere tutto di tutti e mi ha irritato scoprire dove ficcava il naso *(to thrust one's nose)* che era molto lungo (il dito che era molto lungo).

3b. That woman always wanted to know everything of everyone and it annoyed me to find out where she thrusted her nose (finger) that was very long.

4a. Nella vasca dove faceva il bagno il bambino voleva gettare la spugna che perdeva acqua.

4a. In the bathtub where he was bathing the child wanted to throw the sponge that spilled water.

4b. Deluso l'atleta aveva capito di non farcela a vincere e aveva deciso di gettare la spugna *(to give up)* che perdeva acqua (il secchio che perdeva acqua).

4b. The disappointed athlete had understood that he could not make it and had decided to throw the sponge (pail) that spilled water.

5a. Manovrata dall'abile artista la marionetta nel teatrino era sospesa ad un filo che pendeva dal soffitto.

5a. Maneuvered by the skilled artist the puppet in the little theater was suspended to a thread that hung from the ceiling.

5b. Dopo il terribile incidente la vita dell'esploratore era stata sospesa ad un filo *(to hang by a thread)* che pendeva dal soffitto (il cavo che pendeva dal soffitto).

5b. After the accident the explorer's life had been suspended to a thread (cable) that hung from the ceiling.

6a. Andrea una sera ha portato Maria in giardino e mostrando il cielo le ha fatto vedere le stelle che formano l'Orsa Maggiore.

6a. One evening Andrea took Maria in the garden and pointing to the sky he made her see the stars that form the Great Bear constellation.

6b. Quell'uomo in autobus mi ha dato un pestone così forte e mi ha fatto vedere le stelle *(to see stars by daylight)* che formano l'Orsa Maggiore (gli astri che formano l'Orsa Maggiore).

6b. The man in the bus stepped in my toes so heavily, and he made me see the stars (luminaries) that form the Great Bear constellation.

7a. Il falegname ha preso il pezzo di legno e si è messo a battere il chiodo che doveva fissare al muro.

7a. The carpenter took the piece of wood and started hitting the nail that he had to fasten to the wall.

7b. Quando vuole una cosa Sandro la chiede insistentemente e finchè non l'ha ottenuta continua a battere il chiodo che deve fissare al muro (il legno che deve fissare al muro.)

7b. When he wants something, Sandro asks with insistence for it and, until he has obtained it, he keeps hitting the nail (wood) *(to insist)* that he must fasten to the wall.

8a. Il cavallo è troppo magro per trascinare un grosso peso e non ce la fa a tirare la carretta che è mezza rotta.

8a. The horse is too thin to drag a heavy weight and cannot manage to pull the cart that is half broken.

8b. Quando gli ho chiesto se ce la fa a mantenere tutti i suoi figli ha risposto che è duro tirare la carretta *(to drudge)* che è mezza rotta (la canna che è mezza rotta).

8b. When I asked him if he can manage to support all his children he told me that it is hard to pull the cart (cane) that is half broken.

9a. L'infermiere chiese al paziente che doveva provare l'apparecchio di stringere i denti che gli facevano male.

9a. The nurse asked the patient that had to try the dental apparatus to clench his teeth that ached.

9b. Il soldato aveva paura ma il comandante aveva raccomandato di andare avanti e di stringere i denti *(to endure something)* che gli facevano male (i polsi che gli facevano male).

9b. The soldier was scared but the commander had advised to go ahead and to clench his teeth (pulse) that ached.

10a. Mi disse che aveva visto il gatto in cucina che si era arrampicato sul tavolo e si stava mangiando il fegato che gli piaceva molto.

10a. He told me that he had seen the cat in the kitchen that had climbed on the table and was eating the liver that he liked much.

10b. Per aver perso troppi soldi in borsa l'azionista era disperato e si stava mangiando il fegato *(to be worried)* che gli piaceva molto (il gelato che gli piaceva molto).

10b. Having lost too much money at the stock exchange market the share-holder was desperate and was eating the liver (ice cream) that he liked much.

11a. Martino pasticciando con i colori si era sporcato e guardandosi le mani aveva visto che aveva il pollice verde che pulì sullo straccio.

11a. Martino playing with the painting colours had got dirty and looking at his hands had seen that he had the green thumb that he cleaned on the rag.

11b. Vedendo le rigogliose piante che erano cresciute in casa sua la amiche le dicevano che aveva il pollice verde *(to have a green finger)* che pulì sullo straccio (rosso che pulì sullo straccio).

11b. Looking at the luxuriant plants that had grown in her house her friends told her that she had the green (red) thumb that she cleaned on the rag.

12a. Il dottore per visitare l'arto colpito in un incidente di lavoro gli chiese di alzare il gomito che era fratturato.

12a. To visit the limb injured in a work accident the doctor asked him to raise the elbow that had broken.

12b. Tutte le volte che va fuori con gli amici a cenare mangia troppo e poi gli succede di alzare il gomito che si era fratturato (il braccio che si era fratturato).

12b. Every time he dines out with his friends he eats too much and then he happens to raise the elbow (arm) *(to drink too much)* that had broken.

13a. Stefano non aveva mangiato a colazione ed era affamato e la mamma gli ha dato del salame che gli piace molto.

13a. Stefano had not eaten for breakfast and he was hungry and his mother gave him some salami that he likes very much.

13b. Stefano è molto suscettibile e si è offeso perchè la mamma lo ha sgridato e gli ha dato del salame *(to call someone an ass)* che gli piace molto (del gelato che gli piace molto).

13b. Stefano is very susceptible and he took offense because his mother scolded him and gave him some salami (ice cream) that he likes very much.

14a. Il cacciatore ha preso il fucile e per prendere la mira ha dovuto chiudere un occhio che era gonfio.

14a. The hunter took the gun and to take aim he had to close an eye that was swollen.

14b. Era stato fatto troppo chiasso attorno a quella vicenda e il giudice aveva deciso di chiudere un occhio *(to overlook)* che era gonfio (il naso che era gonfio).

14b. There had been too much rumor about that affair and the judge had decided to close an eye (nose) that was swollen.

15a. Durante un brusco movimento della nave il capitano ha perso la bussola che serve per navigare.

15a. During a rough movement of the ship the captain has lost the compass that is used for navigation.

15b. Da quando si è innamorato di quella ragazza Gino non capisce più niente, ha perso la bussola *(to lose one's head)* che serve per navigare (il timone che serve per navigare).

15b. Since he has fallen in love with that girl Gino does not understand anything anymore, he has lost the compass (rudder) that is used for navigation.

16a. Ieri Giulia è andata a passeggiare sulla riva del mare e ha preso un granchio che camminava sulla sabbia.

16a. Yesterday Giulia went for a walk on the seashore and she took a crab that was crawling on the sand.

16b. All'inizio Giulia pensava che Giuseppe fosse cotto di lei ma aveva preso un granchio *(to take a blunder)* che camminava sulla sabbia (una mosca che camminava sulla sabbia).

16b. At the beginning Giulia thought that Giuseppe was lovesick for her but she had taken a crab (fly) that was crawling on the sand.

17a. Il bruco dopo aver strisciato lentamente lungo il ramo aveva mangiato la foglia che era sulla pianta.

17a. Having slowing crawled along the branch the caterpillar had eaten the leaf that was on the plant.

17b. Avevo cercato di tenergli nascosta quella storia ma lui aveva mangiato la foglia *(to take the hint)* che era sulla pianta (l'insetto che era sulla pianta).

17b. I had tried to keep that story concealed but he had eaten the leaf (insect) that was on the plant.

18a. Il medico chiese al paziente che si lamentava di mostrare i denti che erano guasti.

18a. The doctor asked the patient that was complaining to show the teeth that were decayed.

18b. Mario era un tipo molto aggressivo e quando occorreva sapeva mostrare i denti *(to show one's teeth)* che erano guasti (la radio che era guasta).

18b. Mario was a very aggressive guy and when needed he could show the teeth (radio) that were decayed.

9

Syntactic and Semantic Processing During Idiom Comprehension: Neurolinguistic and Psycholinguistic Dissociations

Robert R. Peterson
Indiana University

Curt Burgess
University of California - Riverside

Research in psycholinguistics traditionally has been guided by the assumption that the comprehension of language involves the construction of increasingly abstract levels of representation over time. For example, in understanding an utterance, a listener initially may construct fairly shallow descriptions of the utterance's acoustic and phonetic form. These shallow representations, then, guide (or serve as input to) intermediate-level processors (e.g., lexical and syntactic processors) whose output, in turn, fuels higher level processing systems (e.g., those that determine the meaning of individual sentences, and build representations of the discourse as a whole). The adoption of this levels-of-processing framework has influenced significantly the kinds of theoretical issues that psycholinguists have tended to view as central to the field. Thus, researchers have been preoccupied with addressing such issues as the "psychological" reality of particular linguistic levels of representation, the temporal relationship among levels (i.e., whether levels of processing operate in strict temporal succession, or whether they operate in cascade), and the ways that a given level responds to ambiguous input (e.g., whether it computes a single interpretation or instead constructs multiple representations). One issue in particular, however, that has motivated an impressive amount of research over the past decade concerns the modular versus interactive nature of the various processing systems. This research specifically has sought to determine whether there is only bottom-up communication among processing levels (i.e., where information flows only from lower to higher processors), or whether, in addition, higher level processors sometimes can guide the operation of lower level systems. Thus, it is the nature of the dependencies that exist among processing levels that is at the heart of the modularity debate.

In the present chapter, we specifically consider the processing dependencies that exist between the syntactic and semantic systems. To investigate these dependencies, we have focused on the comprehension of idiomatic phrases (e.g., *kick the bucket*). Although these kinds of phrases generally have been ignored within the modularity debate, we argue that research on idiom comprehension may provide important insights into the processing relationships that exist between syntax and semantics. Idioms seem particularly well suited for this task because they often exhibit intriguing dissociations between these two levels of representation. That is, many idioms are structured in syntactically appropriate ways, although this structure cannot be used, in combination with the meanings of the idiom's individual words, to derive the idiom's figurative interpretation. For example, *kick the bucket* is a well-formed verb phrase, but its idiomatic meaning bears little relation to the phrase's syntactic structure. This lack of correspondence between levels creates something of a dilemma for the comprehension system: Whereas the syntactic processor could generate a structural description of an idiom in a straightforward manner, the semantic processor, if it used that description (in combination with the words of the idiom), would generate a literal interpretation of the idiom, even in contexts where the figurative interpretation was intended. Given this characteristic of idiomatic phrases, an important empirical question that needs to be addressed is whether (and how) the processing system might prevent an unintended literal interpretation from being computed. Two solutions to this problem seem possible, both of which have important implications for how the two processing systems might interact. First, the semantic processor simply could ignore the information being fed to it by the syntactic processor. If this possibility is correct, then it would suggest that the semantic processor is not obligatorily responsive to bottom-up syntactic input. Second, the semantic processor actively could signal the syntactic processor to cease ongoing structural analysis. According to this view, the operation of syntactic processing is dependent on both bottom-up and top-down (i.e., semantic) influences. Investigating how idioms are processed, therefore, may provide us with a truly unique vantage point from which we can observe the ongoing interactions among different linguistic systems.

The remainder of this chapter is organized into two main sections. In the first section, we briefly review some of the ways that researchers have thought about the syntactic and semantic character of idiomatic phrases. In addition, we present the results from a series of experiments that we recently have conducted that directly address the issue of syntactic/semantic dependencies in processing. Two specific questions were explored in these studies. First, we investigated whether the syntactic processor actually computes the structure of an idiom during comprehension. Second, we tested whether the semantic processor is compelled to derive the literal interpretation of the idiom, based on that structure. As noted earlier, answers to these questions can provide insight into the nature of the interactions that occur between the syntactic and semantic systems. In the second section of the chapter, then, we review some of the neurolinguistic literature on idiom comprehension. This research is particularly relevant to the issues being raised here because it has shown that there is, in fact, a neural dissociation between syntactic processing and the construction of figurative meaning. Specifically, it appears that, although syntactic processing tends to be a left hemisphere function, the comprehension of idiomatic phrases (and other kinds of figurative phrases as well) appears to be a specialization of the right hemisphere. Neural research, therefore, may give us important insights into how the comprehension system utilizes hemispheric asymmetries to deal with dissociations among processing levels. At the end of this second section we attempt to relate our experimental findings to neurolinguistic data, and suggest some experiments that would help to clarify the role that the two hemispheres play in idiom comprehension specifically, and in the interdependencies among levels of processing more generally.

IDIOMS, SYNTACTIC PROCESSING, AND LITERAL MEANING

There are a number of studies in the literature that have investigated the role of literal processing during the comprehension of idiomatic phrases. Unfortunately, these studies have not attempted to distinguish between syntactic and semantic analyses, and therefore they do not provide direct evidence regarding the nature of the dependencies that exist between these levels. Nevertheless, many of the models that have evolved in the idiom-processing literature make some specific claims that are (at least indirectly) relevant to the issue we are addressing in this chapter. First, we briefly describe some of these existing models, focusing specifically on the kinds of implications that they might have for the issue of syntactic/semantic dependencies. During this discussion, we develop three new models that more directly specify the relationship between syntactic and semantic processing during the comprehension of idiomatic phrases. We refer to these new models as the *syntactic dominance,* the *semantic dominance, and syntactic-semantic autonomy* models, respectively. Later in the chapter, we present a series of experiments that attempt to distinguish among these three candidates.

Swinney and Cutler (1979) argued that idioms are stored as single entries in the mental lexicon, and are retrieved in the same manner as any other lexical item (they refer to this view as the *lexical representation* hypothesis). Thus, according to this view, the comprehension of an idiom does not require that a compositional analysis be undertaken. Instead, the figurative meaning of an idiom can be retrieved directly (and holistically) from the lexicon. Swinney and Cutler assumed that the retrieval of an idiom's figurative meaning occurs in parallel with the computation of its literal meaning. Figurative processing, however, will tend to conclude more quickly than literal processing because the direct access of the figurative meaning is simpler than the compositional analysis required to derive a literal interpretation. In support of this claim, Swinney and Cutler demonstrated that subjects can make a judgment that an idiomatic phrase (e.g., *see the light*) is meaningful more quickly than they can make the same judgment about a phrase having only a literal interpretation (e.g., *get the light*).

Several researchers have argued that parallel access occurs not only for idioms presented in isolation, but also for idioms presented in contexts that clearly bias the idiom's interpretation (Estill & Kemper, 1982; Ortony, Shallert, Reynolds, & Antos, 1978). This claim generally has been based on demonstrations, like Swinney and Cutler's (1979), that idioms are no harder, and perhaps are easier to process than are literal phrases. The claim that the literal meaning of an idiom is retrieved even in contexts where it is inappropriate implies that literal processing is, in fact, obligatory. In terms of the issue of interlevel dependencies in processing, this view suggests that the semantic processor cannot ignore bottom-up input from the parser. That is, even in figuratively biasing contexts, the semantic processor apparently is compelled to assemble a literal interpretation of an idiomatic phrase based (in part) on the phrase's syntactic structure. For the purposes of future reference, we refer to this particular view of syntactic and semantic processing as the syntactic dominance model, reflecting the fact that output from the syntactic processor automatically guides the operation of the semantic processor; that is, the semantic processor is obligatorily responsive to structural input. Later, we contrast this model with two other possible models of syntactic/semantic dependencies.

In contrast to the Swinney and Cutler (1979) position, Gibbs (1986) argued that faster responses to idiomatic than to literal phrases could be accounted for by a serial rather than a parallel processing model. Specifically, he suggested that the meaning of an idiom always precedes literal processing, with the literal meaning being derived only if the figurative meaning is found to be anomalous given the immediate context. To provide evidence for this hypothesis, Gibbs presented subjects with short stories that ended with a sentence containing an idiomatic expression. The story was biased for either a literal or a figurative interpretation of the idiom. After reading the story, subjects were presented with a target sentence that paraphrased either the literal or figurative meaning of the idiom, or was unrelated to the idiom's meaning. The subjects' task was to decide if the target sentence was meaningful. Gibbs found that responses to figurative paraphrases were facilitated following literal contexts, thus suggesting that the idiomatic meaning had been retrieved even though it was contextually inappropriate. On the other hand, responses to literal paraphrases were not facilitated following figuratively biased contexts, suggesting that the literal meaning of the idioms had not been computed. Gibbs argued that these data demonstrate that the figurative meaning of an idiom is always computed, whereas the literal meaning is computed only if the figurative meaning is inappropriate.

An important implication of the Gibbs (1986) model is that the semantic processor can terminate literal processing of an idiomatic string. Although this claim is intriguing, there are a number of important questions regarding the termination process that are left unspecified in the model. For example, whereas Gibbs seems to imply that the figurative meanings of idioms can be retrieved without any analysis of their literal meanings, it is never made clear how the semantic system actually decides to abort literal processing. Of particular difficulty for the model is the fact that (literal) semantic interpretation appears to occur in rapid fashion during on-line comprehension, presumably proceeding on a word-by-word basis (Crain & Steedman, 1985; Marslen-Wilson, 1985; Marslen-Wilson & Tyler, 1980). Thus, in order for there not to be any literal interpretation of an idiomatic string, the termination of literal processing must occur immediately upon the presentation of the first word of the idiom (i.e., if termination did not occur immediately, then, contrary to Gibbs' claim, the first word of the idiom would be integrated rapidly, and literally, with the preceding text). It seems doubtful, however, that immediate termination could occur in all contexts. Consider, for example, the sentence "The man kicked the bucket." According to Gibbs' model, a listener, upon hearing the word *kicked* would terminate literal analysis of the sentence (i.e., would not integrate *kicked* with *the man*) and therefore would interpret the remainder of the verb phrase figuratively. The problem with this scenario is that there is no cue in the context to indicate that the rest of the sentence will continue idiomatically. Indeed, our intuition is that a sentence beginning with "The man kicked the" will turn out, more often than not, to be a literal statement (e.g., 'The man kicked the ball"), rather than a figurative assertion (e.g., "The man kicked the bucket"). Of course, it may be that the system suspends literal analysis any time a word is encountered that could be part of an idiomatic phrase. Such a strategy, however, would be terribly inefficient. Given that most words in the language can be part of some idiomatic phrase, this strategy would result in routine suspension of literal analysis, and hence, in tremendous delays in interpretation. As noted previously there is ample evidence in the sentence processing literature indicating that such delays in processing typically do not occur.

Thus, we disagree with Gibbs' (1986) claim that literal analysis always must await the evaluation of possible figurative interpretations of a given phrase. It is important to note, however, that we are not claiming that a full literal interpretation of an idiomatic phrase must be constructed in all contexts (as the syntactic dominance model proposes). That is, it seems logically possible that, under some circumstances, literal analysis, in fact, could be suspended. In particular, this potentially could occur when when an idiom is presented in a figuratively biasing context. For example, consider the sentence fragment, "The man was old and feeble and it was believed that he would soon kick. . . ." Intuitively, it seems that, in this context, one can recognize *kick* as being the beginning of the idiom *kick the bucket*. If the processing system in fact can retrieve the idiom at this point, then the successful integration of the meaning "die" into the developing representation of the sentence could signal the semantic processor to disregard the literal implication of the remainder of the phrase. Thus, if the sentence finished with the words *the bucket,* the meaning of those words, and their grammatical function, might not be considered by the semantic processor. Cacciari and Tabossi (1988) recently provided evidence consistent with this scenario. These researchers demonstrated that when subjects are biased to interpret the beginning of a phrase idiomatically, the final words of the phrase are not interpreted literally (or more specifically they showed, using a cross-modal priming procedure, that the final word of the idiom does not prime its literal associates).

Both Gibbs' (1986) and Cacciari and Tabossi's (1988) hypotheses contradict the claims of syntactic dominance model (as outlined earlier), because each proposes that the computation of literal meaning can be terminated. An important question remains, however, regarding the actual scope of this termination process. In particular, it is not clear which levels of processing (other than one computing the semantic structure of the sentence) might be aborted. Can the parser, for example, terminate its structural analysis of an idiomatic string once the figurative meaning of the idiom has been retrieved? We briefly describe two possible models that provide different answers to this question (we refer to these models as the semantic dominance model and the syntactic-semantic autonomy model, respectively). The models differ from one another specifically in terms of the type of top-down dependencies that they posit between semantics and syntax. Because each model posits that literal interpretation can be disabled, they both contradict the claims made by the syntactic dominance model.

According to the semantic dominance model, the semantic processor, upon retrieving the idiomatic meaning of an idiom, will integrate that meaning with the representation of the preceding text, and will signal the syntactic processor to discontinue further structural analyses. This model predicts, therefore, that neither a full structural description of an idiom, nor its literal interpretation, will be derived necessarily in a figuratively biasing context. Compared to the syntactic dominance model, the semantic processor in this model is more independent of syntactic processing because it does not interpret structural input automatically. In addition, in this model the semantic processor exerts more control over the syntactic processor because the establishment of a figurative interpretation of the idiom can inhibit further structural analyses. Such top-down influences make the model particularly compatible with interactive models of sentence processing (e.g., Altman & Steedman, 1988; Crain & Steedman, 1985; Taraban & McClelland, 1988).

The final model that we consider is similar to the semantic dominance model in that it proposes that the semantic processor can terminate its analysis of the literal meaning of an idiomatic phrase. However, in this model there is no feedback from the semantic to the syntactic processor, hence the termination of the literal analysis does not inhibit further syntactic processing (as it does in the

TABLE 9.1
Sample Sentence Primes and Targets from Experiments 1, 2, and 3

Sentence Primes	Targets					
	Exp. 1		Exp. 2		Exp. 3	
	Verb	Noun	"Verb"	"Noun"	Abstract	Concrete
Idiomatic Contexts						
The man was old and feeble and it was believed that he would soon *kick the*	grow	town	glatted	glatter	truth	shelf
The business was running quite smoothly so the manager warned the disgruntled secretary not to *rock the*	lend	shirt	ditted	ditter	guilt	pearl
Literal Context						
The soccer player slipped when tried to *kick the*	grow	town	glatted	glatter	truth	shelf
The only way the mother could get her baby to go to sleep was to lay him down and gently *rock the*	lend	shirt	ditted	ditter	guilt	pearl

semantic dominance model). We refer to this model as the syntactic-semantic autonomy model. This model predicts, therefore, that a full syntactic description of an idiom always will be derived, even though the idiom's full literal meaning will not necessarily be computed. In comparison to both the syntactic dominance and the semantic dominance models, this final model assumes the greatest degree of independence between the two levels of processing, because neither processor is obligatory responsive to the other's output. Of the models that we have considered, this model is the most compatible with modular models of sentence processing (Ferreira & Clifton, 1986; Rayner, Carlson, & Frazier, 1983).

Deciding which of the aforementioned three models (i.e., the syntactic dominance, the semantic dominance, and the syntactic-semantic autonomy models) best describes the nature of syntactic/semantic dependencies in on-line comprehension requires answering two specific questions. First, it must be determined whether the syntactic structure of an idiomatic phrase is necessarily computed in a figuratively biasing context. The syntactic dominance and the syntactic-semantic autonomy models propose that a full description is derived, whereas the semantic dominance model suggests that syntactic analysis is terminated during the course of processing an idiomatic phrase. The second critical question, then, is whether the full literal meaning of an idiom is computed obligatorily. The syntactic dominance model claims that it is, whereas the other models suggest that termination of literal analysis is possible. Overall, then, the three models make unique predictions with respect to these two questions (see Table 9.1 for a summary of these predictions), and thus they lend themselves to direct empirical test. In the next section, we briefly describe the results of a set of three experiments that we have conducted to distinguish among the models. In the first two experiments, we explored the syntactic processing of idiomatic phrases. In the final experiment, we tested whether the literal meaning of an idiom is computed in contexts that bias a figurative interpretation.

Syntactic Processing of Idiomatic Phrases

The nature of syntactic processing has received some attention in the idiom comprehension literature. For example, Gibbs and Gonzalez (1985) investigated how the processing of an idiom varies as a function of the idiom's syntactic frozenness (see also Reagan, 1987; Swinney & Cutler, 1979). Frozenness refers to the extent to which an idiom can undergo syntactic transformations and still retain its figurative meaning. Some idioms are extremely frozen and can undergo few transformations (e.g., "John kicked the bucket" can mean "John died," whereas "The bucket was kicked by John" cannot), whereas others are more flexible (or unfrozen), and can undergo several different transformations (e.g., both "Her father laid down the law" and "The law was layed down by her father" seem to mean that "Her father gave strict orders"). In addition to these extremes, idioms also can be intermediate in their level of syntactic flexibility (retaining their meaning under some, but not all, transformations). Thus frozenness appears to be a continuous rather than a strictly dichotomous dimension (Fraser, 1970; Gibbs & Gonzalez, 1985; Reagan, 1987).

Gibbs and Gonzalez (1985) argued that the more frozen an idiom is, the easier it is to process. This processing advantage might arise because, with increasing levels of frozenness, less syntactic analysis is required in order to derive the meaning of the idiom. This view of frozenness would seem to suggest that the three models that we have proposed might be too extreme in their views of syntactic processing. Rather than the all-or-none view taken by these models (i.e., the models propose that a full syntactic description either is, or is not, derived), it might be better to think of syntactic processing in more continuous terms, with idioms undergoing different degrees of structural analysis depending on their level of frozenness. It is important to note, however, that the discrete view that we have adopted is not necessarily incompatible with the continuous view outlined by Gibbs and Gonzalez. The apparent differences between the views arise because they focus on slightly different questions. In our models, we are interested in whether the syntactic processor automatically computes the structure of an idiomatic phrase, but we do not necessarily address the question of whether a full syntactic description is required to access an idiom's figurative meaning. In contrast, it is this latter question that is of specific interest to Gibbs. These two questions, however, are logically independent. For example, it might be that the syntactic processor obligatorily performs a complete structural analysis of an idiom (consistent with the syntactic-semantic autonomy model), even though idioms differ in the amount of structural analysis that is required to retrieve their figurative meanings. We return to this issue following the presentation of Experiments 1 and 2, and also address it in the second section of this chapter when we consider the neurolinguistic underpinnings of idiom comprehension.

To investigate the syntactic processing of idiomatic phrases, we (Peterson, Burgess, Dell, & Eberhard, 1989) used a sentence-priming procedure. Subjects were presented with auditory sentence primes that ended with incomplete idioms (e.g., *kick the* . . .). Sentences were biased for either a literal *(ball)* or idiomatic *(bucket)* noun completion.[1] Examples of each of these sentence types are given in Table 9.2. Immediately following the final word of each incomplete sentence, a visual target word was presented on a computer screen. Subjects were instructed to name the target word as quickly as possible, and their naming latencies were recorded. The target words were always semantically unrelated to the contexts. Critically, however, the syntactic appropriateness of the target word was manipulated. Specifically, on a given trial the target was either a noun (an appropriate completion) or a verb (an inappropriate completion; see Table 9.2 for examples of these targets). A number of studies in the literature have demonstrated that responses are faster (in both lexical decision and naming) to syntactically appropriate than to inappropriate targets (e.g., Goodman, McClelland, & Gibbs, 1981; West & Stanovich, 1986; Wright & Garrett, 1984). We used this syntactic priming effect as an indicator of ongoing structural analysis. We were specifically interested, then, in comparing the magnitude of priming between literally and figuratively biased sentence primes in order to determine if idiomatic strings undergo normal syntactic analysis. Thus, we were expecting that, for literally biased sentences, responses would be faster to the noun than the verb targets.[2] At issue, then, was whether a comparable effect occurs with figuratively biased sentences. If it does, then it suggests that the syntactic structures of idiomatic strings are derived during on-line comprehension (consistent with both

[1]Using a Cloze procedure, literal and idiomatic contexts were found to be equally constraining for their expected noun completions.

[2]A pilot study demonstrated that, in isolation, there was no difference in naming latency between the noun and verb targets. Similar results were found for the targets used in Experiments 2 and 3.

210 PETERSON AND BURGESS

TABLE 9.2
Empirical Predictions Made by the Three Models

Empirical Questions	Predictions		
	Syntactic Dominance Model	*Semantic Dominance Model*	*Syntactic-Semantic Autonomy Model*
Does an idiom undergo a full syntactic analysis?	YES	NO	YES
Is the literal meaning of an idiom computed?	YES	NO	NO

the syntactic dominance model and the syntactic-semantic autonomy model). If, however, the priming effect with figuratively biased sentences is eliminated or reduced (compared to the priming effect with literal sentences), it would suggest that there is a diminution of syntactic processing during the comprehension of idiomatic phrases (consistent with the semantic dominance model).

The results of Experiment 1 are shown in Fig. 9.1. As can be seen, verb targets were named more slowly than were nouns, and this pattern held for both literal and idiomatic sentence contexts. Critically, the magnitude of the priming effect was similar in the two contexts. In fact, the syntactic priming effect was numerically larger for the idiomatic sentences than for the literal sentences (29 ms vs. 16 ms, respectively), although this interaction was not statistically significant. These data clearly indicate, then, that there is no diminution of syntactic processing when figurative contexts are used. These results are consistent with the predictions made by the syntactic dominance and the syntactic-semantic autonomy models. Both of these models assume that the syntactic processor obligatorily parses an idiomatic phrase. In contrast, the results of Experiment 1 fail to support the semantic dominance model. In that model, parsing of an idiomatic string is discontinued once the phrase has been interpreted figuratively, and therefore the observed syntactic priming effect makes the model less tenable. However, it is premature to reject the model based solely on the results of Experiment 1 because the semantic dominance model assumes that parsing is terminated only if the literal meaning of the idiom no longer is being computed. Thus, disproving the model requires testing for the derivation of literal meaning. We directly address this issue in Experiment 3.

There is a possible criticism of the results from Experiment 1 that could qualify our conclusion that idioms undergo full syntactic analysis. Specifically, it is possible that the syntactic priming effect that was obtained in Experiment 1 is not a reflection of the syntactic incompatibility of the verb targets per se. Instead,

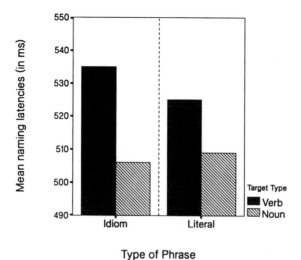

FIG. 9.1. Mean naming latencies as a function of the type of phrase and grammatical category of the target.

the priming effect might reflect facilitation in naming the nouns due to a bias in our materials that resulted in the nouns being related more semantically than the verbs to the general meaning of the sentences. To circumvent this potential problem, we replicated the findings of Experiment 1 using nonword targets that have suffixes primarily associated with a verb or a noun. For the "verb" nonwords, we used the suffix -ed, which is a salient inflectional marker for past tense. For the "noun" nonwords, we used the suffix -er, which is the derivational morpheme for agentive.[3] An example of a "verb" and a "noun" nonword are *glatted* and *glatter*, respectively (see Table 9.2 for additional examples). Thus, the -ed and -er nonwords functionally parallel the verb and noun targets used in Experiment 1. A syntactic priming effect would be reflected, therefore, by longer naming latencies to the -ed nonwords compared to the -er nonwords when they follow the sentence contexts that we used previously.

The results from this experiment are shown in Fig. 9.2. As in Experiment 1, a syntactic priming effect was found with both literal and figurative sentences. Moreover, the effect for figurative sentences was statistically larger than that for literal sentences (49 ms vs. 17 ms, respectively). Thus, the results from this experiment again support the conclusion that idiomatic phrases undergo a full

---

[3]Of course, the suffix -er also is used with comparative adjectives. However, the ambiguity in the interpretation of the -er suffix is not a problem in the present study, because both nouns and adjectives are syntactically appropriate continuations of our sentence contexts.

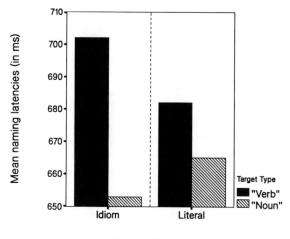

FIG. 9.2. Mean naming latencies as a function of the type of phrase and the type of nonword target.

syntactic analysis. Because the targets in this experiment were meaningless nonwords, the priming effects cannot be attributed to the semantic relations that held between the targets and sentence contexts.

In both Experiments 1 and 2, the syntactic priming effect for figurative primes was larger than the effect for literal primes, although this difference was statistically significant only in the second experiment. Why might such an effect occur? We assume that the representation of an idiom in memory includes information regarding both its meaning (i.e., that *kick the bucket* means "to die"), as well as its syntactic structure. When one encounters the idiom in a biasing context, it is likely that the mental representation of the idiom will be accessed relatively quickly (probably before one has been exposed to the entire idiom). The retrieval of the idiom will make available the idiom's syntactic structure, and thus will allow the comprehension system to project the upcoming structure of the remainder of the idiomatic phrase in a relatively determinate fashion. A literal phrase, because it does not have a preexisting mental representation, may be less efficient at generating specific syntactic expectations. Idioms, therefore, might make available syntactically relevant information more effectively than do literal phrases, and as a result they might be more susceptible to interference when syntactic violations occur.

As noted previously, Gibbs and Gonzales (1985) presented evidence suggesting that syntactically frozen idioms are easier to process than are unfrozen idioms. One possible explanation for this processing difference is that frozen idioms do not undergo a full syntactic analysis during comprehension. If this view is correct, then one might expect that frozen idioms would be the least susceptible to syntactic priming effects. However, the fact that we obtained, in Experiment 2, a larger syntactic effect for idioms as compared to literal phrases suggests that this possibility may not be correct. Even relatively unfrozen idioms tend to be less flexible syntactically than their literal counterparts, and hence one would have expected that the syntactic effect for idioms would have been smaller than the effect for literal phrases, regardless of the overall level of frozenness of the idioms.

To test directly whether frozenness affects the syntactic processing of idiomatic strings, we obtained frozenness ratings for each of our idioms. To do this, we gave subjects either the literal or idiomatic sentence from each of our sentence pairs, along with a syntactically transformed version of the sentence. The transformation was either the passive, where possible, or other movement of a noun phrase (NP) in cases where passivization was not grammatical. The subject rated how similar in meaning the original and transformed sentences were. A 5-point rating scale was used, with 1 being "very different in meaning" and 5 being "very similar in meaning." Overall, the mean rating for the idiomatic sentences was significantly lower than for the literal sentences (2.67 vs. 3.18, respectively). Thus, it is clear that the idiomatic phrases that we used are less flexible syntactically than are the corresponding literal phrases.

Based on the aforementioned ratings, we obtained frozenness scores for each of our idioms by subtracting the mean rating for each idiomatic sentence from the mean rating for its literal control. Thus, the larger the frozenness score, the greater the frozenness of the idiom (i.e., a large score indicates that the rating was relatively low for the idiom, relative to the rating for the idiom's literal control). The frozenness scores for the idioms ranged from $-.69$ to 3.00. We computed the correlation between the frozenness scores and the syntactic priming effects obtained for the idioms in Experiments 1 and 2. The correlations were $-.01$ and $-.08$, respectively. Neither of these correlations approached significance. Thus, frozenness did not affect the magnitude of the syntactic priming effect. Apparently, on-line syntactic expectations are not influenced by the degree of structural flexibility of a given idiomatic phrase. It is important to keep in mind, however, that this conclusion specifically applies to expectations of the final word of an idiom, presented in a strongly biasing sentence context. Perhaps frozenness might play a role at earlier points in the idiom, and in contexts that are less constraining.

In summary, we found a syntactic priming effect for idioms with both word and nonword targets. It appears, therefore, that the processing of idiomatic and literal strings is largely indistinguishable in terms of the syntactic representations that are derived.

Literal Interpretation of Idiomatic Phrases

In a final experiment, we addressed the question of whether the literal meaning of an idiomatic phrase is computed, even in a context biasing the idiom's figurative interpretation. As sentence primes, we used those idiomatic and literal sentences from the previous experiments that required a concrete noun as a completion. For example, in the literal context "The soccer player slipped when he tried to kick the . . . ," the completion must be literally "kickable," and so must be concrete. Target words in the experiment, then, were either unrelated abstract or concrete nouns (e.g., *truth* versus *shelf,* respectively; see Table 9.1 for further examples). We assumed that the semantic bias of the literal sentences would delay naming responses to the abstract nouns (relative to the concrete nouns). We refer to such an effect as *conceptual priming*. Of primary interest in this experiment, then, was whether figuratively biased sentences would show a similar priming effect. Consider for example the sentence context "The man was old and feeble and it was believed that he would soon kick the. . . ." Although the expected completion (*bucket*) is a concrete noun, the concreteness of the completion is essentially irrelevant to the idiom's figurative meaning per se. Thus, one would not expect to find a conceptual priming effect (i.e., slower responses to abstract than to concrete targets) with these sentences unless the literal meaning of the idiom was derived along with the idiom's figurative interpretation. The presence of conceptual priming therefore was used in Experiment 3 as an indicator of ongoing literal computation.

The syntactic dominance model claims that the semantic processor obligatorily must analyze the literal meaning of an idiom based on structural input from the syntactic processor. This model predicts, therefore, that conceptual priming should occur with idiomatic sentences. In contrast, the syntactic-semantic autonomy model assumes that a full literal interpretation of an idiom is not derived, even though its syntactic structure is computed. Thus, this latter model predicts that conceptual priming will not arise with idiomatic sentences. Recall that the semantic dominance model was incompatible with the results from Experiments 1 and 2 (because it predicts that syntactic analysis can be terminated once the figurative meaning of the idiom has been retrieved). Ruling out the model, however, requires demonstrating that the literal meaning of the idiom no longer was being considered at the time that target word was presented. Failure to find a conceptual priming in the present experiment therefore would serve as convincing evidence against this model.

The same cross-modal priming procedure that was used in the previous two experiments was used in Experiment 3. The results of the experiment are shown in Fig. 9.3. Overall, abstract targets were named significantly more slowly than concrete targets. However, this conceptual priming effect interacted with the type of sentence context. Although literal sentences showed a significant 21-ms effect, the priming effect was not significant for idiomatic sentences (the effect

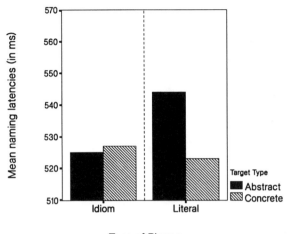

FIG. 9.3.   Mean naming latencies as a function of the type of phrase and concreteness of the target.

with idioms was only 2 ms, and it was in a direction opposite to that found with literal sentences). The pattern of data from Experiment 3 suggests, therefore, that the literal meaning of an idiomatic phrase is computed only in literally biasing contexts. When the context biases an idiomatic interpretation of the phrase, literal analysis appears to be terminated prior to the final word of the idiom.

The results from this experiment stand in sharp contrast to the pattern of results found in the first two experiments. In the prior experiments, idiomatic sentences showed syntactic priming effects that were as large as (if not larger than) literal sentences. In the present experiment, however, a conceptual priming effect was found for literal sentences only. Taken together, these results suggest that, by the final word of an idiomatic phrase, subjects continue to monitor the syntactic structure of the idiom, but do not compute a corresponding literal interpretation of the phrase. This dissociation between syntactic and semantic analyses serves as strong evidence in support of the syntactic-semantic autonomy model of processing. According to this model, the semantic processor terminates its analysis of the literal meaning of an idiomatic phrase once the figurative meaning of the idiom has been retrieved. There is, however, no feedback from the semantic to the syntactic processor in this model, hence the semantic processor cannot suppress directly further syntactic processing. Therefore, a full syntactic description of an idiom always will be computed, regardless of contextual constraints, and regardless of the status of ongoing literal processing. These results are compatible with modular views of parsing, which stipulate that the parser is insensitive to semantic and pragmatic contingencies (e.g., Frazier, Clifton, & Randall, 1983).

NEUROLOGICAL DISSOCIATIONS IN IDIOM COMPREHENSION

In the preceding section, we presented evidence suggesting that syntactic processing occurs during the comprehension of idiomatic phrases. We also demonstrated that, in a figuratively biasing context, the literal interpretation of an idiomatic phrase is not derived. This dissociation between syntactic and semantic levels of analysis is important, and will need to be accounted for by any complete model of idiom comprehension. Intriguingly, such dissociations have relevant parallels in the neurolinguistic literature. In this section of the chapter, we consider neurolinguistic studies of idiom comprehension, and attempt to relate that data to the priming data we presented in the last section. Our discussion focuses specifically on the nature of hemispheric asymmetries in the processing of literal and idiomatic language.

In the past decade we have attained a notable degree of neurolinguistic sophistication beyond the stereotype that (right-handed) humans are strongly lateralized for language in the left hemisphere and lateralized for visual/spatial processing in the right hemisphere. Although there is a consensus that language production is strongly left-lateralized, it is now less controversial to acknowledge that the right hemisphere possesses certain language comprehension abilities. There is an increasing amount of evidence that suggests that both the right and left hemispheres contribute to the comprehension of semantic relationships (Burgess & Simpson, 1988b; Chiarello, 1988a; Van Lancker, 1985). For example, both hemispheres show evidence of a basic semantic priming effect with words that are associatively and semantically related (e.g., *doctor-nurse;* Chiarello, 1985). In fact, the right hemisphere actually shows an advantage over the left hemisphere in priming for words that have weak or indirect semantic relations (e.g., *dull-moody, lawyer-nurse;* Burgess & Rosen, 1988; Chiarello, Burgess, Richards, & Pollock, 1990). Similarly, although dominant and subordinate meanings of ambiguous words show priming in either hemisphere, the subordinate meanings stay active longer in the right hemisphere (Burgess & Simpson, 1988a). Thus, it has become recognized increasingly that both hemispheres have contributions to make to the lexical/semantic processing required by the language comprehension system.

A more specialized account of hemispheric capability emerges, however, when we consider the language subsystems that underlie the processing of syntactic structure one the one hand, and figurative processing on the other. The domain of syntactic processing appears to be more clearly a left-hemisphere function. For example, patients with left-hemisphere damage seem unable to distinguish between such sentences as "The boy kisses the girl" and "The girl kisses the boy," a distinction that requires the coordination of the meaning of individual lexical units with the serial syntactic structure of the sentence (Gazzaniga & Hillyard, 1971; Heeschen & Jurgens, 1977). Syntactic comprehension difficulties with left-hemisphere-damaged patients are most pronounced when the context does not provide any semantic or discourse-level constraints for syntactic interpretation (Caplan & Hildebrandt, 1988; Caramazza & Berndt, 1978; Caramazza & Zurif, 1976).

Conversely, figurative language seems most impaired with patients who experience right-hemisphere brain damage. For example, these patients have difficulty appreciating the connotative relationships between words (Brownell, Potter, Michelow, & Gardner, 1984), making inferences (Beeman, 1990), understanding indirect speech acts (Foldi, 1987; Hirst, Le Doux, & Stein, 1984), appreciating humor (Bihrle, Brownell, Powelson, & Gardner, 1986; Wapner, Hamby, & Gardner, 1981), comprehending metaphors (Brownell, 1988), as well as understanding idiomatic phrases (Myers & Linebaugh, 1981).

An experiment by Van Lancker and Kempler (1987) directly explored the neural underpinnings of figurative and literal comprehension. These researchers had left-hemisphere-damaged (LHD) and right-hemisphere-damaged (RHD) patients select the appropriate line drawing (out of a set of four) that corresponded to either a single concrete noun *(bird)*, a sentence containing a figurative phrase ("He's turning over a new leaf"), or a novel literal sentence ("He's sitting deep in the bubbles"). For the idioms, one drawing was related to the literal interpretation of the idiom, whereas another was consistent with the idiom's figurative interpretation. The other two drawings depicted a scene that was either opposite in meaning to the idiom or was irrelevant. The drawings used with the novel literal sentences were somewhat different. All three of the distractors for these sentences involved some change in grammatical or thematic roles of the nouns (e.g., agent-patient reversal) or misassignment of adjective modification (e.g., the sentence "When the happy girl pushes, the angry boy swings" had a drawing of an unhappy girl pushing a boy). Correct performance on the literal sentences, therefore, required careful attention to the syntactic details of the sentences. A critical finding from the experiment was that there was an interaction between patient type and stimulus set. Specifically, LHD patients performed worse than RHD patients on the novel literal sentences (those that required detailed syntactic analysis), but outperformed the RHD patients on the figurative sentences. Apparently, left-hemisphere damage interferes significantly with syntactic analysis, but is less disruptive of figurative processing. Based on these results, Van Lancker and Kempler argued that syntactic analysis is not a necessary component of idiomatic interpretation. They suggested that the results are supportive of an "idiom-as-a-word" hypothesis or what we earlier referred to as the lexical representation hypothesis (Swinney & Cutler, 1979). According to this view, an idiom's meaning is directly (and holistically) retrieved from memory (presumably from the right hemisphere) without any consideration of the idiom's internal structure.

The claim that idiom comprehension does not require syntactic analysis has important implications for the data that we presented in Experiments 1 and 2. Recall that we demonstrated that the magnitude of syntactic priming that occurs with idiomatic strings is equal to (or even surpasses) that found with literal phrases. Van Lancker and Kempler's (1987) conclusions suggest, therefore, that the priming effects we observed may not be directly relevant to the retrieval of figurative meaning per se. Instead, the priming effects simply may reflect obligatory parsing of the idiomatic phrases by the left hemisphere. If this is correct, it potentially explains why we observed independence between syntactic and semantic analyses. Perhaps analysis of the figurative meaning of an idiom occurs in the right hemisphere, neurally dissociated from left-hemisphere parsing.

Although the idiom-as-a-word hypothesis is intriguing, there are, nevertheless, a number of empirical problems it faces. The first comes from Van Lancker and Kempler's (1987) own data. Recall that their experiment used a single-word condition in addition to the idiom and literal sentence conditions. Performance did not differ reliably between LHD and RHD groups in the single word condition and, critically, their performance in this condition was very close to that of intact control subjects. These data indicate, therefore, that the patients were capable of retrieving lexical items from memory. If an idiom truly is represented as a simple lexical item (as the idiom-as-a-word hypothesis suggests) then one would expect that the patients would be highly competent in comprehending these items as well. In particular, one would expect the LHD patients to perform in the idiomatic condition at roughly the same level as they did with single words, and at approximately the same level as normal subjects. This pattern did not occur, however. Although LHD patients outperformed their RHD counterparts, their performance was still significantly worse than the normal controls, and was worse than their own performance in the single-word condition. Clearly, then, idiomatic interpretation involves processing that is in some way more complex than a simple lexical representation view would propose. Perhaps the decrement in performance in the idiomatic condition by LHD patients resulted from their impoverished ability to analyze the idiomatic phrases structurally. If this claim (which is admittedly speculative) turns out to be correct, it would suggest, in contrast to the idiom-as-a-word hypothesis, that syntactic analysis is an important component of idiomatic processing.

A second important challenge to the idiom-as-a-word hypothesis comes from the results that we presented in Experiment 2. In that experiment, the priming effect for idiomatic phrases was significantly larger than that for literal phrases. We suggested that such a pattern might be expected to occur if the stored representation of an idiom contains information regarding the phrase's syntactic structure. Such information might be made available during the processing of the phrase, and then could be used by the parser to generate specific syntactic expectations. If the idiom-as-a-word hypothesis is correct, it become a mystery as to why the representation of an idiom would guide syntactic processing in this way. Presumably, syntactic information would be stored with an idiom only if that information were relevant to the idiom's retrieval. Thus, we suggest that our data support a view of idiom processing in which structural analysis contributes to successful comprehension. Further, given that we found no effect of syntactic frozenness on the magnitude of syntactic priming, it appears that syntactic analysis contributes to the comprehension of both frozen and unfrozen idioms.

Given this view, how might we account for Van Lancker and Kempler's (1987) finding that LHD patients (who presumably have impaired syntactic capabilities) performed better on idiomatic sentences than did RHD patients (who have intact parsers)? There may have been two factors that conspired to produce this result. First, it may be that the RHD patients had difficulty with the idiomatic strings due to particular processing biases of the left hemisphere. Specifically, the left hemisphere has been characterized as making rapid and inflexible commitments when interpreting lexical items (Brownell, Potter, Bihrle, & Gardner, 1986; Burgess & Simpson, 1988b; Chiarello, 1988b). Thus, RHD patients may have interpreted the initial words of the idiom literally, and, as a result, may have had trouble appreciating the figurative status of the remainder of the phrase. According to this view, then, the left hemisphere has difficulty with idiomatic phrases because it is "garden-pathed" away from a figurative interpretation during processing. The right hemisphere does not have this kind of trouble with idiomatic phrases because it tends not to make rigid interpretive commitments (Brownell et al., 1986; Burgess & Simpson, 1988b; Chiarello, 1988b). Note that this account of hemispheric asymmetries is qualitatively different from that given by the idiom-as-a-word hypothesis. According to that hypothesis, RHD patients have difficulty with idiomatic phrases because idiomatic entries in the lexicon occur only in the right hemisphere. The obvious problem with this argument is that there is no a priori account of why the left hemisphere is unable to represent idiomatic words. Our account, in contrast, focuses not on representational differences between the hemispheres, but instead on well-documented processing differences. As a result, our hypothesis fits more directly into extant neurolinguistic models of comprehension.

Although the aforementioned hypothesis accounts for the poor performance by RHD patients on the idiomatic phrases, we still must explain why the LHD patients (whose parsers apparently were impaired) were able to comprehend the idioms at a relatively high level (although at a level still below that of normal subjects). Research by Caramazza and Zurif (1976) may provide an answer to this question. These investigators demonstrated that, although LHD patients have difficulty interpreting sentences such as "The tiger is chasing a fat lion," they performed much better on sentences like "The bicycle that the boy is holding is broken." The critical difference between these sentences appears to be that, in the first, the subject and object noun phrases are reversible (in the sense that either pragmatically could be the agent of the verb), whereas in the second sentence the nouns are nonreversible (because *bicycle* is an inanimate object and thus can not serve as the agent of the sentence). These data suggest that the right hemisphere is adept at utilizing nonsyntactic cues to derive the structural relations among the components of a sentence. Perhaps such analyses were used by LHD patients in the Van Lancker and Kempler (1987) experiment to determine the structure of idiomatic phrases as well. Consider, for example, how the right hemisphere might analyze a sentence like "He kicked the bucket." Because the subject and object noun phrases of this sentence are literally nonreversible (i.e., *bucket* cannot be the agent of *kicked* because it is an inanimate noun), the right hemisphere presumably could determine the underlying literal structure of this sentence without syntactic mediation. The retrieval of this structure subsequently might allow access to the idiom's representation in memory (which itself contains the information that *bucket* is the underlying object of the phrase). According to this view, then, the right hemisphere sometimes might be able "bootstrap" its way to a figurative interpretation by first deriving a thematic representation of an idiomatic phrase. This bootstrapping hypothesis predicts that LHD patients might be particularly sensitive to the literal relations among the components of an idiomatic phrase. This prediction could be tested empirically using the conceptual priming paradigm that we outlined in Experiment 3. We would expect that LHD patients might show a robust conceptual priming effect for idiomatic phrases. Such a finding would contrast with the data from our (intact) subjects, who did not display conceptual priming when idiomatic phrases were presented. The bootstrapping hypothesis also predicts that LHD patients might be easily confused by idioms whose nouns are literally reversible.

In our experiments, we demonstrated that the syntactic structure of an idiom is obligatorily computed, even though its literal meaning is not always derived. How might we accommodate these findings within a neurolinguistic model of comprehension? We suggest the following processing scenario. When presented with linguistic input, both hemispheres attempt, in parallel, to map individual word meanings onto an evolving discourse representation. The kinds of information that they have available to them to perform this task differs, however. In particular, the left hemisphere can make use of syntactic constraints whereas the right hemisphere must build interpretations on the basis of nonstructural cues alone. We assume that, in general, the left hemisphere is more efficient at integrating information into the discourse model, and thus it will tend to control interpretation. However, because the left hemisphere tends to make rapid, and inflexible, commitments to particular interpretations (at the expense of alternative, more esoteric, possibilities), it sometimes will fail to appreciate some potential aspects of meaning. As noted previously, idiomatic meanings may be particularly problematic for the left hemisphere in this regard, because the left hemisphere may be biased to interpret the initial words of an idiom literally, and may be unable to recover from these initial commitments. Thus, in general, the left hemisphere may be biased to compute a literal interpretation of an idiomatic string, possibly even in figuratively biasing contexts. The fact that we found, in Experiment 3, that the literal meaning of an idiom was not fully computed in a biasing context implies, therefore, that the right hemisphere sometimes can usurp left-hemisphere interpretive processing, and can integrate idiomatic interpretations into the discourse representation.

What processing event might trigger the right hemisphere to contribute to discourse processing in this way? Perhaps as the left hemisphere is evaluating the literal meaning of an idiomatic string, it detects that the meaning is anomalous with the preceding (figuratively biased) context. The detection of anomaly, then, might cause an attentional shift from the left to the right hemisphere, as the system searches for an acceptable interpretation of the phrase. The shift in attention could make the figurative meaning available, and thus allow it to be integrated into the discourse representation. Successful integration, then, could create "closure" at the discourse level, blocking further attempts to map the meanings of the individual words of the idiom into the discourse model. As a result, literal processing in the left hemisphere might be aborted (accounting for the lack of a conceptual priming effect for idioms in our third experiment). Closure at the discourse level, however, might not disable lower level systems in the left hemisphere. Thus, parsing of the idiomatic phrase could continue, even after figurative integration is complete.

It is important to note that the views just discussed does not necessarily imply that retrieval of the figurative meaning of an idiom will occur only after the entire phrase has been evaluated literally by the left hemisphere. If detection of an anomaly occurs during processing of the initial words of the phrase, then retrieval and integration of the figurative meaning of the idiom could take place before the final words of the idiom are processed fully. Thus, the anomaly view is, in fact, compatible with data showing that the retrieval of idiomatic meaning occurs as fast as (or perhaps faster than) the derivation of a phrase's literal meaning (e.g., Ortony et al., 1978). It is important to note, however, that the anomaly view predicts that a delay in figurative processing could occur if the initial parts of the idiomatic phrase can be integrated literally into the preceding context (i.e., if there is no cue that the literal interpretation is incorrect). Cacciari and Tabossi (1988) recently presented evidence consistent with this prediction.

Although anomaly detection might contribute to idiomatic interpretation, it is probably not a necessary component. Consider, for example, the sentence context "The man was old and feeble and it was believed that he would soon kick. . . ." Intuitively, one assigns a figurative interpretation to *kicked* in this context, even though the literal meaning of the word is not, in any obvious way, anomalous with the preceding context. To account for this phenomenon, we suggest that the sentence context primes the idiom's representation in memory (in much the same way that a sentence context might prime a semantically related word), and thereby increases the speed by which the right hemisphere can retrieve the idiomatic representation. Early retrieval might allow the right hemisphere to integrate a figurative meaning into the discourse representation before the left hemisphere has had time to commit to a literal interpretation. This view suggests, therefore, that the two hemispheres compete with one another for the privilege of integrating their particular interpretations into a discourse structure. The competition, then, is of a "horse-race" variety, with the winner being the hemisphere that is the first to develop a contextually appropriate interpretation of the input. Under most circumstances, the left hemisphere wins this race easily. However, with idiomatic phrases presented in a biasing context, the right hemisphere sometimes can prevail as well.

Interestingly, the horse race model predicts that the detection of a literal anomaly can influence idiom processing as well. That is, according to the model, a figurative interpretation of an idiomatic phrase will be derived any time the right hemisphere can retrieve that interpretation before the left hemisphere can integrate words literally. Logically, such a right-hemisphere advantage could be obtained by either speeding up processing in the right hemisphere (e.g., priming the idiomatic meaning) or slowing processing in the left hemisphere. The detection of anomaly, in fact, may have this latter influence. That is, words that are literally anomalous with the preceding context will force a delay in integration in the left hemisphere, thereby providing time for the right hemisphere to retrieve a preferable (i.e., figurative) interpretation. The horse race model suggests, therefore, that context can have two mutually reinforcing effects on idiom comprehension. Specifically, context can both provide support for a figurative interpretation and, simultaneously, hinder literal integration (see McDonald & Carpenter, 1981, for a similar proposal).

SUMMARY

In this chapter, we have focused on interdependencies that exist between different linguistic processing systems during the course of understanding idiomatic speech. In the first section of the article, we explored specifically the processing relationship that exists between semantic and syntactic analyses, whereas in the final section we explored how these levels of processing might be coordinated across the two cerebral hemispheres. We demonstrated, in a set of three experiments, that the full syntactic structure of an idiomatic phrase is computed in a figuratively biasing context, even when the phrase's literal meaning no longer is being evaluated. These results serve as clear evidence in support of a processing distinction between syntax and semantics, and highlight the obligatory character of structural analysis per se. We presented a neural processing model, then, to account for these results. According to this model, the integration of a figurative meaning in the right hemisphere into a discourse representation blocks further semantic evaluation in the left hemisphere. Figurative integration, however, does not (or cannot) interfere with left-hemisphere parsing, perhaps because the right hemisphere is ill-equipped to communicate with the parser in such a fashion. Further research clearly is needed to elaborate on the role of semantic and syntactic analyses in the retrieval of figurative meaning. We believe that theoretical advancement will come most efficaciously, however, if considerations of hemispheric processing serve as a springboard for this research.

REFERENCES

Altman, G. T., & Steedman, M. (1988). Interaction with context during human sentence processing. *Cognition, 30,* 191–238.

Beeman, M. (1990). *Coherence inferencing and structure building in the cerebral hemispheres.* Unpublished doctoral dissertation, University of Oregon, Eugene.

Bihrle, A. M., Brownell, H. H., Powelson, J. A., & Gardner, H. (1986). Comprehension of humorous and non-humorous materials by left and right brain-damaged patients. *Brain and Cognition, 5,* 399–411.

Brownell, H. H. (1988). Appreciation of metaphoric and connotative word meaning by brain-damaged patients. In C. Chiarello (Ed.), *Right hemisphere contributions to lexical semantics* (pp. 19–31). New York: Springer-Verlag.

Brownell, H. H., Potter, H. H., Bihrle, A. M., & Gardner, H. (1986). Inference deficits in right brain-damaged patients. *Brain and Language, 29,* 310–321.

Brownell, H. H., Potter, H. H., Michelow, D., & Gardner, H. (1984). Sensitivity to lexical denotation and connotation in brain-damaged patients: A double dissociation? *Brain and Language, 22,* 253–265.

Burgess, C., & Rosen, A. (1988, April). *Priming of emotional words in the cerebral hemispheres.* Paper presented at the Fifth Annual Linguistic Studies Conference on Language and Communication, Syracuse, NY.

Burgess, C., & Simpson, G. B. (1988a). Cerebral hemispheric mechanisms in the retrieval of ambiguous word meanings. *Brain and Language, 33,* 86–104.

Burgess, C., & Simpson, G. (1988b). Neuropsychology of lexical ambiguity resolution: The contribution of divided visual field studies. In S. L. Small, G. W. Cottrell, & M. K. Tanenhaus (Eds.), *Lexical ambiguity resolution in the comprehension of human language* (pp. 411–430). Los Altos, CA: Morgan Kaufmann.

Cacciari, C., & Tabossi, P. (1988). The comprehension of idioms. *Journal of Memory and Language, 27,* 668–683.

Caplan, D., & Hildebrandt, N. (1988). Disorders of syntactic comprehension. Cambridge, MA: MIT Press.

Caramazza, A., & Berndt, R. S. (1978). Semantic and syntactic processes in aphasia: A review of the literature. *Psychological Bulletin, 85,* 898–918.

Caramazza, A., & Zurif, E. B. (1976). Dissociation of algorithmic and heuristic processes in language comprehension: Evidence from aphasia. *Brain and Language, 3,* 572–582.

Chiarello, C. (1985). Hemisphere dynamics in lexical access: Automatic and controlled priming. *Brain and Language, 26,* 146–172.

Chiarello, C. (Ed.). (1988a). *Right hemisphere contributions to lexical semantics.* New York: Springer-Verlag.

Chiarello, C. (1988b). Semantic priming in the intact brain: Separates roles for the right and left hemispheres? In C. Chiarello (Ed.), *Right hemisphere contributions to lexical semantics* (pp. 59–69). New York: Springer-Verlag.

Chiarello, C., Burgess, C., Richards, L., & Pollock, A. (1990). Semantic and associative priming in the cerebral hemispheres: Some words do, some words don't, . . . sometimes, some places. *Brain and Language, 38,* 75–104.

Crain, S., & Steedman, M. (1985). On not being led up the garden path: The use of context by the psychological parser. In D. Dowty, L. Kartunnen, & A. M. Zwickey (Eds.), *Natural language parsing* (pp. 320–358). Cambridge, England: Cambridge University Press.

Estill, R. B., & Kemper, S. (1982). Interpreting idioms. *Journal of Psycholinguistic Research, 6,* 559–568.

Ferreira, F., & Clifton, C. (1986). The independence of syntactic processing. *Journal of Memory and Language, 25,* 348–368.

Foldi, N. S. (1987). Appreciation of pragmatic interpretations of indirect commands: Comparison of right and left hemisphere brain-damaged patients. *Brain and Language, 31,* 88–108.

Fraser, B. (1970). Idioms within a transformational grammar. *Foundations of Language, 6,* 22–42.

Frazier, L., Clifton, C., & Randall, J. (1983). Filling gaps: Decision principles and structure in sentence comprehension. *Cognition, 13,* 187–222.

Gazzaniga, M. S., & Hillyard, S. A. (1971). Language and speech capacity of the right hemisphere. *Neuropsychologia, 9,* 273–280.

Gibbs, R. (1986). Skating on thin ice: Literal meaning and understanding idioms in conversation. *Discourse Processes, 9,* 17–30.

Gibbs, R., & Gonzalez, G. P. (1985). Syntactic frozenness in processing and remembering idioms. *Cognition, 20,* 243–259.

Goodman, G. O., McClelland, J. L., & Gibbs, R. W. (1981). The role of syntactic context in word recognition. *Memory & Cognition, 9,* 580–586.

Heeschen, C., & Jurgens, R. (1977). Pragmatic-semantic and syntactic factors influencing ear differences in dichotic listening. *Cortex, 13,* 74–84.

Hirst, W., Le Doux, J., & Stein, S. (1984). Constraints on the processing of indirect speech acts: Evidence from aphasiology. *Brain and Language, 23,* 26–33.

Marslen-Wilson, W. D. (1985). Speech shadowing and speech communication. *Speech Communication, 4,* 55–73.

Marslen-Wilson, W. D., & Tyler, L. K. (1980). The temporal structure of spoken language understanding. *Cognition, 8,* 1–71.

McDonald, J. L., & Carpenter, P. A. (1981). Simultaneous translation: Idiom interpretation and parsing heuristics. *Journal of Verbal Learning and Verbal Behavior, 20,* 231–247.

Myers, P. S., & Linebaugh, C. W. (1981). Comprehension of idiomatic expressions by right-hemisphere-damaged adults. In R. H. Brookshire (Ed.), *Clinical aphasiology: Conference proceedings, 1981.* Minneapolis: BRK.

Ortony, A., Shallert, D. L., Reynolds, R. E., & Antos, S. (1978). Interpreting metaphors and idioms: Some effects of context on comprehension. *Journal of Verbal Learning and Verbal Behavior, 17,* 465–477.

Peterson, R. R., Burgess, C., Dell, G. S., & Eberhard, K. (1989, March). *Dissociation of syntactic and semantic analyses during idiom processing.* Paper presented at the second annual CUNY Conference on Human Sentence Processing, New York.

Rayner, K., Carlson, M., & Frazier, L. (1983). The interaction of syntax and semantics during sentence processing: Eye movements in the analysis of semantically biased sentences. *Journal of Verbal Learning and Verbal Behavior, 22,* 358–374.

Reagan, R. T. (1987). The syntax of English idioms: Can the dog be put on? *Journal of Psycholinguistic Research, 16,* 417–441.

Swinney, D. A., & Cutler, A. (1979). The access and processing of idiomatic expressions. *Journal of Verbal Learning and Verbal Behavior, 18,* 523–534.

Taraban, R., & McClelland, J. L. (1988). Constituent attachment and thematic role assignment in sentence processing: Influences of content-based expectations. *Journal of Memory and Language, 27,* 597–632.

Van Lancker, D. R. (1985). Nonpropositional speech: Neurolinguistic studies. In A. W. Ellis (Ed.), Progress in the psychology of language (Vol. 3, pp. 49–118). Hillsdale, NJ: Lawrence Erlbaum Associates.

Van Lancker, D. R., & Kempler, D. (1987). Comprehension of familiar phrases by left- but not by right-hemisphere damaged patients. *Brain and Language, 32,*265–277.

Wapner, W., Hamby, S., & Gardner, H. (1981). The role of the right hemisphere in the apprehension of complex linguistic materials. *Brain and Language, 14,* 15–33.

West, R. F., & Stanovich, K. E. (1986). Robust effects of syntactic structure on naming. *Memory & Cognition, 14,* 104–112.

Wright, B., & Garrett, M. (1984). Lexical decision in sentences: Effects of syntactic structure. *Memory & Cognition, 12,* 31–45.

III MEANING AND STRUCTURE

10 Building Castles in the Air. Some Computational and Theoretical Issues in Idiom Comprehension[1]

Oliviero Stock
Jon Slack
IRST, Istituto per la Ricerca Scientifica e Techologica, Italy

Andrew Ortony
Institute for the Learning Sciences, Northwestern University

A successful natural language understander, be it a human or a machine, frequently is faced with the problem of making sense of linguistic expressions that do not necessarily mean what they say. There are many different kinds of expressions that have this property, some of which have received more attention in the research literature than others. There has been, for example, a great deal of work on the processes involved in the comprehension of indirect speech acts (e.g., Clark & Lucy, 1975; Gibbs, 1983) and there is an even larger literature on the comprehension of metaphorical uses of language (e.g., Ortony, in press). However, until recently, the comprehension of idioms has been studied less extensively, partly perhaps because there is a rather appealing and intuitive view of the nature of idioms that has the effect of depriving the question of how they are understood of any really interesting or problematic properties. We refer to this as the "idioms-are-big-words" view.

As recently as a decade ago research on idiom comprehension (e.g., Ortony, Schallert, Reynolds, & Antos, 1978; Swinney & Cutler, 1979) accepted quite uncritically the idioms-are-big-words view. Swinney and Cutler proposed a process model in which idioms are accessed from the lexicon in parallel with an attempt at literal interpretation. According to the model, familiar idioms are likely to be processed very quickly because as "long words" they do not require any deep linguistic analysis—they simply are recognized. From this view the comprehension of an idiom may be accompanied by some partial processing of

[1]This work has been carried on as part of MAIA, an experimental platform of the integrated AI project under development at IRST.

the literal meaning, but the literal meaning plays no role in the determination of the idiomatic meaning.

Consider the following examples:

1. The car John bought was a pig in a poke.
2. The ice was unexpectedly broken when John entered the room.

Example 1 is no problem for a language understander. There is an English idiom (or part of one) *pig in a poke,* which never occurs in any other form. So, for example, you may have bought a pig in a poke this morning but you cannot say that you bought a pig this morning in a poke (although you might well have bought a pig this morning in an auction). Similarly, the pig in a poke that John bought he presumably bought unwittingly, but he could not be said to have bought a pig unwittingly in a poke. The phrase *pig in a poke* simply cannot be manipulated in any way whatsoever, either lexically or syntactically. This means that it can be entered safely in the lexicon as a lexical item—a noun with its associated meaning.

One might take the position that the expression *pig in a poke* is in fact only part of an idiom—that the "real" idiom is the verb phrase "buy a pig in a poke." If one takes this view, then one has to deal with the possibility that not only can one "buy a pig in a poke," but that one might also get away with "selling a pig in a poke" as well as "getting a pig in a poke." In this case one would have to propose a small group of pig-in-a-poke idioms, some of which (certainly the first two cases) allow syntactic changes. For example, one can say "The pig in a poke that we're talking about I bought yesterday." Because there is no objective way to select between the two approaches, it seems preferable to take the noun phrase as the idiom and to specify in its representation the verb forms with which it can appear.

Wood (1986) defined idioms as fixed expressions that lie at the end of two continua: They are totally noncompositional and totally nonproductive. From the practical perspective of natural language understanding, such a definition is of limited utility. This is because if an expression is totally nonproductive (both lexically and syntactically), it is trivially easy for a natural language understander to process. Expressions such as *by and large* and *hither and thither* really can be handled using the idioms-are-big-words approach by simply putting them in the lexicon along with *pig in a poke.* The main problem for a natural language understander is to recognize that it is dealing with an idiom, and this problem is trivialized if the expression occurs always and only in a unique form: Simple pattern matching will solve it. If, on the other hand, the expression has some degree of flexibility, a simple pattern-matching mechanism will not suffice. From a practical perspective it is no solution to define away the problem by relabeling the computationally challenging cases so that they are no longer called idioms. Rather, we need to specify (preferably psychologically plausible) mechanisms for dealing with nonliteral uses of language—especially idioms and idiomlike expressions. Given this as the goal, the idioms-are-big-words approach is too limited in scope. There are just too many expressions that are not amenable to such an account for it to represent anything like a general solution to the idiom comprehension problem.

TWO THEORETICAL ISSUES

The approach one takes to the question of how idioms are understood depends to some extent on the solutions one adopts to some basic theoretical issues having to do with idioms. One of these concerns the question of whether some (or even most) idioms are based on underlying conceptual metaphors as, for example, Lakoff (in press), Nayak & Gibbs (1990), and Gibbs and O'Brien (1990) proposed. The other, related issue has to do with the question of why idioms have the linguistic properties that they have.

The question of the nature of the relationship between literal and idiomatic meaning is related to the general issue of compositionality in idioms. The non-compositionality criterion, which is used so frequently to characterize idioms, reflects the widespread belief that the meanings of individual constituents do not contribute their literal meanings to the meaning of an idiom as a whole (e.g., the meanings of *kick* and *bucket* play no role in the idiomatic meaning of the idiom *to kick the bucket*). There are reasons, however, to suppose that this is not always true. The extreme version of the rejection of this view can be found in, for example, the work of Glucksberg (e.g., 1990), who argued that the literal meanings of the constituents must make a contribution because they can be exploited in creative modifications of the conventional idiom. A more conservative reservation is based on the fact that there is a whole class of idioms for which noncompositionality is false, a class that Wood (1986) referred to as "metaphorical idioms." We have in mind here expressions such as "to cross [that] bridge when X comes to it." In expressions of this kind, the meaning in principle could be derived from the constituents by whatever process is employed ordinarily in understanding metaphors. In this particular case, for example, one readily could produce a more abstract representation of its meaning—something like "to engage in [that] activity when circumstances demand," and from that one could generalize further to some abstract notion such as postponement until necessary. Cacciari and Glucksberg (1990) referred to idioms of this kind as *analyzable* and *transparent*.

In general it seems plausible to suppose that for nonmetaphorical idioms—the kind that Cacciari and Glucksberg (1990) called analyzable and *opaque*—the apparent dissociation between the literal and idiomatic meaning is simply due to the fact that the connection is buried in the history of the language and the culture. Thus, for example, the relation between the literal and idiomatic meaning of *spill the beans* is still not arbitrary, at least not from a historical perspective, but it is generally unknown and inaccessible to native speakers of English in much the same way as is the connection between the original and modern meanings of the word *sinister*. Gibbs (Nayak & Gibbs, 1990) made much of the apparent dissociation, arguing that in fact very often such idioms are grounded in deep conceptual metaphors that motivate them and that explain why they mean what they do. We suspect, however, that Gibbs underestimated the importance of the historical underpinnings of idioms by investing in an account that imposes on many idioms a rational/cognitive basis that they do not really possess.

Gibbs' view appears to be that a particular idiom is contextually appropriate because different idioms refer to different (parts of) underlying conceptual domains. For example, Nayak and Gibbs (1990) wrote:

> Idioms are not discretely represented in the mental lexicon in such a way that the figurative meaning of each phrase is arbitrarily linked to each idiomatic word string. Instead idioms whose meanings are generated from the same conceptual metaphor may be linked together in a temporal sequence as part of a semantic field for each type of conceptual referent (anger fear joy etc.). . . . [This] systematic mapping is due to people's understanding of certain aspects of emotion concepts in terms of familiar concrete and well-structured concepts such as heat and animals. . . . These conceptual metaphors . . . are used to understand and perhaps create our conceptual knowledge of these abstract and less well-structured concepts. (p. 328)

We are skeptical about the role of such "conceptual metaphors" in understanding and creating (in this case emotion) concepts. If we wanted a psychologically plausible mechanism for understanding such concepts (and hence presumably for understanding language that embodies them), we would need on this account some sort of shared meaning representation for the idioms and their associated (metaphorically grounded) concepts. We think, however, that there are more parsimonious ways of building a natural language understander and that the kind of data that led Gibbs and his colleagues to their conclusions are compatible with other correspondingly parsimonious explanations. At the same time, the data are suggestive of other important facts.

The kind of findings that lead Gibbs (Gibbs & O'Brien, 1990; Nayak & Gibbs, 1990) to his view that (many) idioms have a metaphorical basis are that the choice among semantically equivalent idioms is context sensitive, in that subjects prefer idioms that are compatible with a primed underlying metaphor, and that different members of idiom families can be shown to relate to different parts of a complex concept. In general, findings of the first kind raise the possibility that subjects prefer consistency. If the context describes somebody as metaphorically "growling" in anger, then an idiom such as *bite X's head off* is preferred to one such as *blow one's top*. However, this preference might be simply the result of surface associative connections—people no doubt also would judge the word *bite* to be closer than the word *blow* to a prime like *growl*, even in a situation where no idioms and metaphors were involved at all. The second kind of finding shows that the related concept is complex but not that it is necessarily metaphorical in nature. So, for example, Nayak and Gibbs (1990, Experiment 2) found that some idioms from the same family (e.g., idioms having to do with anger) refer to different temporal parts of a typical anger sequence (e.g., something *gets on one's nerves* before *one blows one's top*, and later one may *cool down*). They take this as evidence against the traditional view that each of these idioms needs a "separately stipulated meaning" (which they propose is the same in each case, i.e., get angry; p. 320). We are not convinced by this line of reasoning. One easily could acknowledge that each of these idioms refers to something slightly different and one equally could admit readily that (most of) the difference has to do with the stage of a typical anger episode without drawing any counter intuitive or dramatic conclusions. We merely need conclude that *to get on one's nerves* means (something like) "to irritate one" (which is normally temporally prior to getting angry, or at least expressing anger), that *to blow one's top* means "to express strong anger," and that *to cool down* means "to (start the) return to normal after an expression of strong anger." All that follows from this is that if anybody oversimplifies by asserting that all three idioms mean "to get angry" they are wrong, but most native speakers know they have slightly different meanings anyway.

On the positive side, however, we think there is something important about the subtle variations between the meanings of different idioms in the same domain. For example, it commonly is said that *to kick the bucket* means "to die." But we think this is an oversimplification. One could not describe a convicted murderer who just had been given a lethal injection by a state executioner as having just *kicked the bucket*. The idiom seems to require death by (more or less) natural causes, and relatively suddenly too. But this means that the idiom carves out a certain piece of our knowledge about dying. It is as though it imposed constraints on the values of some of the parameters (e.g., method, cause, etc.) associated with dying. Such an account at least would explain why we have such idioms—they serve to specialize an existing concept in a way not specialized by an existing lexical item. (This is probably not always true, but it is probably often or even usually true).

Although semantic and discourse productivity are interesting phenomena we do not think that it is incumbent on a theory of idiom comprehension to account for them. Both Glucksberg (e.g., 1990) and Gibbs (1990) have proposed that the literal meanings of idioms do play some role in their comprehension. Glucksberg, in criticizing the process model of Swinney and Cutler (1979), argued that idioms do not behave like long words. For example, many idioms can survive lexical substitution. Glucksberg illustrated this by arguing that one can "crack the ice" rather than break it. However, he failed to notice two things that are relevant here. First is the fact that such lexical productivity, although occasionally possible, is certainly not the rule (one cannot "drop the beans" or "release the cat from the bag"). Second, even when it is possible, the range of substitutions is very restricted. For example, even if we grant the possibility of "cracking the ice," one cannot communicate the idiomatic meaning of *break the ice* using "fracture the ice" or "break the frozen water." Thus, if one were wedded to the idioms-are-big-words view, Glucksberg's objections would be relatively easy to deal with. One could argue first that there are two linguistically close realizations of some idioms (*break/crack the ice* or *cook/roast X's goose*), and second that the examples he offered exploit a metalinguistic strategy, namely, the use of a pun, the whole point of which is to say something ambiguous, where, in this instance one reading is somehow (e.g., syntactically, semantically, or pragmatically) defective. Our view of this is that such semantic and discourse productivity phenomena in fact exploit their own bizarreness—a speaker knows full well that there is something wrong with talking about "cracking the ice" and this very fact motivates his or her creative use of such an expression. At the same time we certainly agree that such creative linguistic acts depend critically on the availability of the literal meanings of the constituents of the idiom in order for them to be so exploited. The model we propose allows for the simultaneous availability of the literal meaning (at least up to a point), although it does not claim that the literal meaning plays an (active) role in the processing of the idiomatic meaning. Being available is not the same as making a contribution.

SYNTACTIC FLEXIBILITY

Having argued against the proposal that the semantic and discourse productivity of idiomatic expressions show that the literal meanings of their constituents play a role in their comprehension, we now want to argue that the degree of syntactic flexibility exhibited by idioms is related to the comprehension process. As we saw previously, some idiomatic phrases behave like big words and cannot be varied either syntactically or lexically. Other idioms, however, are quite flexible (Wasow, Sag, & Nunberg, 1982). So we can say "after the lunch break the air was cleared" as a syntactic variant of the idiom *to clear the air*. The degree of syntactic flexibility seems to be related strongly to the level of analyzability of an idiom (Gibbs & Nayak, 1989; Gibbs, Nayak, Bolton, & Keppel, 1989; Gibbs, Nayak, & Cutting, 1989); the more analyzable they are the more syntactic flexibility they exhibit. The levels of analyzability suggested by Cacciari and Glucksberg (1990) relate to the way in which the constituent parts of an idiom map onto their idiomatic referents. Idioms classified as analyzable and transparent have constituents that map directly onto their respective idiomatic referents. For example, in the idiom *pop the question,* the verb *pop* maps to its referent "suddenly ask" and the noun phrase "the question" maps to the "marriage proposal." This contrasts with the classification analyzable and opaque, where the relation between an idiomatic constituent and its referent is not semantic, but rather is in some sense indirect. For instance, in the idiom *spill the beans,* there is no direct semantic relation between *beans* and "secrets." Finally, idioms classified as nonanalyzable possess constituents that do not map onto the constituents of the idiom's referent. The constituent words *kick* and *bucket* in the idiom *kick the bucket,* for example, bear no relation to the idiomatic meaning "to die." Henceforth in this chapter, we refer to this relationship between the constituent words of an idiom and the constituents of the idiomatic meaning as the *referent mapping.*

We want to argue that idiom comprehension involves the recognition of the referent mapping associated the idiom and that the structure of the mapping determines the degree of syntactic and semantic flexibility the phrase exhibits. The differences is analyzability reflect the different types of data structures mapped by an idiom's referent mapping. For nonanalyzable idioms the underlying referent mapping merely takes word strings into word strings and no further structure is transferred. For analyzable idioms, on the other hand, the referent mapping takes constituent words into constituent words but in a structured manner. For instance, in our example *pop the question* the verb and object of the idiom map to the verb and object of its meaning, respectively. In other words, the referent mapping preserves the linguistic functional structure of the idiomatic phrase. The mapping can be thought of as carrying information from the surface form of an idiomatic phrase to the "deep" or semantic representation of the phrase. The additional information encoded in a syntactic variant of an idiom can be carried to the underlying meaning representation only if the corresponding referent mapping preserves it.

For a nonanalyzable idiom like *kick the bucket* the range of syntactic variation is minimal, allowing differences in tense such as *kicks the bucket* and *kicked the bucket,* but not passivization, "the bucket was kicked." The latter transformation would involve a restructuring of the word string, which is not permitted by the idiom's string-to-string referent mapping. Variations in tense are allowable because tense can be regarded as a global feature of the word string and in this sense is external to it. Information about the tense might be detected at the surface level by a morphemic analyzer and passed independently of the idiomatic word string to the underlying meaning structure. String-to-string referent mappings realize the idioms-as-big-words hypothesis in that the internal structure of the mapped strings is opaque to them. The referent mappings of analyzable idioms, on the other hand, map the linguistic functional structure of the strings.

In this approach it is necessary to distinguish two levels of linguistic representation involved in idiom comprehension. The first level is the surface representation of the idiomatic phrase encoded as a constituent tree. In the system we describe, this level of representation corresponds to the constituent structure built by the parser as it configures the semantic information associated with the constituent lexical elements. At this level, the parser is able to identify the word strings that comprise big word idioms.

The second level of representation encodes the predicate-argument structure, or functional structure, of the phrase. That is, how the main predicate of the idiom, generally the predicate associated with the verb, relates to its arguments such as the subject and object grammatical functions. This level of structure also encodes the predicate-argument structure of the idiom's underlying meaning. In our system, these two structures are stored as part of the lexical entries associated with the constituent lexemes of the idiomatic phrase. The referent mapping, binding the two structures, is encoded as a set of substitutions that replace the constituent elements with their corresponding referent elements in the semantic representation of the idiom.

In terms of this representational framework, the referent mappings of nonanalyzable idioms bind the surface level representation of the idiom directly to its associated meaning structure, whereas the corresponding mappings for analyzable idioms bind the idiom's predicate-argument structure to the equivalent structure for its semantic representation. Analyzable idioms permit syntactic flexibility because, under such variations, their representations remain unchanged at the level of predicate-argument structure. For example, the phrase "the beans were spilt by John" is interpretable because at the predicate-argument level of representation its structure, SPILL[subj(John), obj(the beans)], is the same as for the nonpassivized form of the phrase. Figure 10.1 depicts the referent mapping for this phrase, showing how the predicate-argument structure of the phrase is preserved by the substitutions that implement it. If the referent mapping did not distinguish this level of structure, analyzable idioms could not be recognized under such transformations. For nonanalyzable idioms, the predicate-argument structure of the idiom's referent meaning is retrieved as a whole by the idiom's surface-level word string.

It should be noted that we are not attempting to explain the origins of the different categories of referent mapping, that is, why the idiom *kick the bucket* is a word-string-to-word-string mapping, whereas for other idioms it preserves the

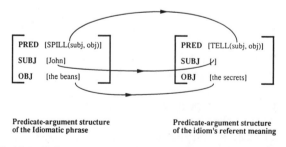

PRED [SPILL(subj, obj)]   PRED [TELL(subj, obj)]
SUBJ [John]   SUBJ [ ]
OBJ   [the beans]   OBJ   [the secrets]

Predicate-argument structure   Predicate-argument structure
of the Idiomatic phrase   of the idiom's referent meaning

FIG. 10.1   Referent mapping for the idiom *to spill the beans.*

linguistic structure. As we already have said, we believe these origins to be buried in the cultural history of a language. Instead, we want to claim that idiom comprehension corresponds to the recognition of the referent mapping underlying an idiom and that such mappings are encoded in the lexicon. If this is the case, then a computational model of idiom comprehension comprises a parsing mechanism for recognizing the referent mappings of idioms based on their lexical constituents.

PROCESSING IDIOMS

Before discussing our own approach to parsing idioms, we briefly mention some of the other approaches that have been taken. In some systems a simple preprocessor is dedicated to the recognition of idiomatic forms. This preprocessor replaces the group of words that comprise the idiom with the word or words that convey its meaning. In Augmented Transition Network (ATN) systems, especially if oriented toward a specific domain, particular sequences of arcs sometimes are inserted in the network which, if transited, leads to the recognition of a particular idiom (e.g., PLANES: Waltz, 1978). LIFER (Hendrix, 1977), one of the most successful applied systems, is based on a semantic grammar and within this mechanism, idiom recognition is implemented without considering the syntactic flexibility of idioms, that is, the possibility of changing the syntactic structure of the idiom while still preserving its figurative meaning.

PHRAN (Wilensky & Arens, 1980) is a system based entirely on pattern recognition. An interesting aspect of PHRAN is that it has a twin generator called PHRED (Jacobs, 1985) that reverses the process. PHRAN and PHRED share the same database of patterns (including single words at the same level). PHRAN normally proceeds deterministically, applying the two principles "when in doubt choose the more specific pattern" and "choose the longest pattern." The limits of this approach lie in its low capacity for generating various alternative interpretations in the case of ambiguity (although a nondeterministic implementation also was realized eventually and in running the risk of having too great a spread of nonterminal symbols (i.e., word's syntactic class) if the database of idioms is large. Work on idioms that takes a similar perspective and that pays particular attention to the problem of learning idioms is that of Dyer and Zernik (1986).

A more recent approach to processing idioms is that of van der Linden (1991). His original approach was based on a connectionist model similar to the one developed by Cottrell (1988) for the resolution of lexical ambiguity (van der Linden & Kraaij, 1990). The model consisted of four levels of units; the lowest level units encode form, the units on the next level encode syntactic discriminations, which activate units on the next, semantic, feature level. Finally, the semantic feature units activate relational nodes in the semantic network. In common with many connectionist models, excitatory links exist between levels and inhibitory links within levels. The meanings of idioms are encoded in the semantic network and a particular idiom is recognized when its unit emerges as the strongest competitor at this level, inhibiting the various nonidiomatic readings. One problem with this approach that van der Linden (1991) himself has identified is that it is computationally expensive, requiring extensive parallel processing resources. A more serious drawback, and one that is shared with other connectionist natural language models, is that the network must encode all the possible syntactic and semantic forms that a particular idiom might take. Such models have difficulty when they encounter a new form for an idiom because the information necessary to distinguish it from possible nonidiomatic readings is not represented within the network and hence is unable to contribute in support of the idiom's semantic network unit. For big word idioms this is not much of a problem, but for idioms that exhibit some degree of syntactic flexibility and for idioms in languages based on relatively free word order, this problem quickly becomes intractable. This type of reasoning led van der Linden (1991) to move toward a symbolic hierarchical model in which idioms are presented as part of a lexicon incorporating an *inheritance hierarchy*, very much in line with the approach we propose next.

Our approach is implemented in a system called WEDNESDAY 2 (Stock, 1989)—a system whose design was intended to be to some extent psychologically plausible in that it was inspired by empirical evidence from idiom comprehension studies (Cacciari, 1988; Swinney & Cutler, 1979). It is intended to be a flexible approach designed to integrate idioms into the lexicon simply as more information about particular words rather than as a separate list requiring special treatment as suggested by Katz (1973).

Because the processing of idioms in WEDNESDAY 2 exploits the basic mechanisms of the parser, it is helpful to understand the parser independently of idiom processing in the first place.

WEDNESDAY 2 is a nondeterministic parser that can explore different alternatives when in a given state and with a given data situation. So, on the one hand, it can commit itself to one particular choice, but on the other hand, it eventually might provide all of the possible interpretations of a sentence or of a fragment. If working with finite resources, and in particular if the basic apparatus is sequential, the problem of managing partial structures and the control of the process becomes crucial.

Representation of Linguistic Knowledge

The representation of linguistic knowledge in WEDNESDAY 2 is based on two distinct syntactic aspects often merged together in other approaches. One is the information carried by morphemes—information that is combined in word specifications. This includes local syntactic information and entities for which we use the metaphor of "impulses." The role of these impulses in parsing is to provoke the linking together of fragments of semantic information on the basis of syntactic constraints. Yet, technically speaking, they are expressed in a declarative form and it is the parsing processor that makes use of them. The other syntactic aspect is constituted by restrictions on the space where this linking can occur. Maintaining the previous metaphor, this means limiting the space where impulses "operate." This latter aspect is responsible for the structuring of the sentence into constituents. What is crucial for this approach is that the positions of elements inside a constituent and their functional aspects are not determined necessarily by the second component but depend on the information included in the lexicon. So it is possible to deal with a whole range of characterizations from rigid word-order languages, to languages in which only dependencies between particular parts of speech must hold, down to free word-order languages.

A word interpretation (there can be more than one interpretation for a word) includes a semantic interpretation and syntactic information of various kinds including subcategorization specifications that appear as alternative specifications in impulses. So an impulse basically specifies all the ways in which a given linguistic function is to find its value. It also includes measures of likelihood that are used to derive an overall measure of likelihood of a partial analysis. A particular indication (i.e., "main") is provided for the head element of the constituent at the semantic level.

The only other data that the parser uses are recursive (nonaugmented) transition networks that provide restrictions on search spaces where impulses can look for requested elements. In other words, these networks deal with the distribution of constituents. A particular kind of arc is designated to indicate that only the occurrence of something expected by preceding words (i.e., for which an impulse was set up) will allow the transition to occur.

As far as the position of elements within WEDNESDAY 2 is concerned, one can specify in a natural and nonredundant way all the gradations from obligatory positions to obligatory priorities to simple likelihoods of relative positions.

The Parser

The parser builds on the idea of chart parsing (Kaplan, 1973; Kay, 1980). Previous nondeterministic parsers usually incorporated a backtracking mechanism so that when the analysis following the current alternative failed an earlier context was restored and the process continued following one of the possible alternatives in that context. Using backtracking in this way means that a fragment might have to be reanalyzed many times along different alternative paths. Chart parsing avoids all this; a chart parser is willing to adopt any strategy of analysis, but whatever the adopted strategy, work is never duplicated. Basically, a chart can be seen as a working memory structure in which representations are kept for complete constituents, for incomplete constituents (together with the indication of what is needed to complete them), and for working hypotheses. The chart is built "around" the sentence and therefore both the relations of dominance and precedence are represented within it. The basic entities of the chart are called "edges" (in fact, they indicate the portion of a string that they refer to). "Inactive edges" denote completely recognized constituents whereas "active edges" refer to constituents that have been recognized only partially. The process of parsing is basically a process of introducing new edges into the chart in order to extend the existing edges so as to include larger portions of the sentence. In WEDNESDAY 2 active edges are used as search spaces in the sense just outlined. Actually, they are complex data structures with rich information including a semantic interpretation of the fragment, syntactic data, pending impulses, an overall measure of likelihood, and so forth. Data on an edge are unified (merged together) dynamically as indicated later.

The mechanism is capable of processing different subproblems in parallel. In fact, working on a serial machine, a multiprocessing scheme is realized with an agenda that at every moment of the computation includes the list of tasks to be carried out. A scheduling function decides the priorities to give the various tasks. An interesting aspect is that heuristics easily can be included to guide the parser (Stock, 1989), thus implementing strategies that may take the context into account: For instance, the semantic relevance of a certain partial interpretation can be evaluated and can cause the selection of that particular task to be carried on first by the processor; or more structural criteria can be adopted such as, "Carry on the task that will extend most a partial analysis chosen amongst the largest active edges present so far in the chart."

The parser works asymmetrically with respect to the "arrival" of the main element. Before the main element arrives the extension of an edge has almost no effect. Upon the arrival of the main element, all the candidate fillers must find a compatible impulse and all impulses concerning the main element must find satisfaction. If all this does not happen then the new edge expected to be added to the chart is not added: The situation is recognized as a failure—an impossible tentative analysis. After the arrival of the main, each new head must find an impulse to merge with and each incoming impulse must find satisfaction. Again, if all this does not happen the new edge will not be added to the chart.

Mechanisms for handling certain forms of ellipsis and for treating long-distance dependencies such as those found in relative clauses also are included in the system. These mechanisms again rely on lexical data and impulses on the one hand, and on constraints defined in the networks on the other.

The relevance of the chart-based approach can be appreciated best through an example. Let us consider the parsing of the sentence, "The king gave the girl with the long black hair to the sheikh." The fragment "the girl with the long black hair" is analyzed only once, resulting in a noun phrase (NP), to which a certain semantic interpretation can be associated; this analysis is always available, regardless of how it originated. For example, the lexical entry for the word *gave* may have specified the alternatives that an NP following the verb can be either the direct object (semantically, the transferred object) or the indirect object (semantically, the recipient). In the lexicon, the likelihoods of these situations are specified; but in addition, the compatible situations for the other grammatical functions involved with the word *gave* are specified. So if the first NP processed after *gave* is to be considered the direct object, then a prepositional phrase (PP) marked *to* must appear subsequently in the sentence and semantically specify the recipient. Alternatively, if the first NP is to be considered the recipient, the transferred object will follow, specified as an NP.

At the sentence level, the material "the girl with the long black hair" can occupy two completely different roles. When the material is processed in combination with the previous partial analysis of the sentence, the parser establishes two possible tasks that are inserted into the agenda. In principle they could be considered in parallel; if we have a single processor, one of the tasks is chosen first (say the one with the NP having the recipient interpretation, because of its semantics). When it is noticed that the following PP ("to the sheikh") is not compatible with this partial interpretation, the other task is executed, finding as already completed and available the analysis of the fragment "the girl with the long black hair." The final PP is compatible with the second interpretation and the sentence is interpreted completely.

Specification of Idioms in the Lexicon

The power of WEDNESDAY 2 idiom processing is bound to flexible idioms. Nonflexible idiom forms that are to be treated as big words constitute no problem for any parser. Idioms as big words can be represented in the lexicon indexed by the initial words of the string.

Flexible idioms are represented in WEDNESDAY 2's lexicon as further specifications of words just as in a dictionary. In this first realization, idioms are bound to the particular word that represents the crucial part of that idiom. In WEDNESDAY 2 terms, the word that represents the crucial part of the idiom is the one that bears the main of the immediate constituent including the idiom. For instance in *build castles in the air* it would be the verb *to build*. The choice of the present realization can be extended to other elements of the idiomatic expression and possibly to multiple entries of the same expression.

Each idiom is described in two sections: The first describes the elements characterizing that idiom, expressed coherently with the normal characterization of the word. The second section describes the interpretation, that is, which substitutions should be performed when the idiom is recognized.

Constituents of an idiom are described as particular fillers of linguistic functions or particular modifiers. Again using the example of *build castles in the air,* when *build* is in an active form it has *castles* as a further description of the filler of the object (OBJ) function and the string *in the air* as a further specification of a particular modifier that may be attached to the main element. In addition, there is an indication of the weight that the particular idiom element carries for the overall recognition. At the same time it always remains possible to specify a new alternative for a filler for an existing function including the description of the component and its weight. For instance, a new alternative might be a partial NP instead of a complete NP as in "take care" or an NP marked differently from usual. Finally, the entry can include the information that a certain impulse specified for the word is to be considered to have been removed for this idiom description (e.g., "go tell some one else" where the direct object of *tell* is absent whereas in literal expressions it must be there).

Elements of an idiom can be specified in the lexicon as string patterns, semantic patterns, value restrictions (and so forth), and morphological variations. Coreferences among parts of an idiom (such as "John made up his mind," where the mind is John's mind) also can be specified there. Substitutions to be performed when the idiom is recognized include the semantics of the idiom that are supposed to take the place of the literal semantics, plus a specification of the new main and of the bindings for the new functions in relation to the "literal" ones. For analyzable idioms, substitutions are only possible for referent mappings that map the main-functions (i.e., predicate-argument) structure of the idiomatic phrase into the new idiomatic representations. In the case of non-analyzable idioms, the semantics of the idiom must be substituted as a whole unit because the lexical entries for the idiom's constituent lexemes do not contain idiomatic readings that preserve the main-function information relaxing to the internal structure of the phrase.

Idiom Processing in WEDNESDAY 2

Idiom processing in WEDNESDAY 2 is integrated into the nondeterministic multiprocessing-based behavior of the parser. As the literal analysis proceeds and partial representations are built, the background impulses are monitored, checking for possible idiomatic fragments. Monitoring is carried out only for fragments of idioms not in conflict with the present configuration. A dynamic activation table is introduced with the occurrence of a word that has some idiom specification associated. The weight associated with each constituent of an idiom expresses the relevance of the constituent in the recognition of that idiom; so the occurrence of an expected fragment of an idiom gives strength to that hypothesis in proportion to the relative weight of the fragment.

If the configuration of the sentence conflicts with one element then the idiom that includes that element is discarded from the table. For example, with the sentence "John built a house for his parents," after *a house* is interpreted as the direct object of *built,* the idiomatic entry associated with *build castles in the air* is discarded from the activation table. The normal processing goes on, including the possible nondeterministic choices, the establishment of new processes, and so on. The activation tables are included in the edges of the chart.

The weights associated with the different constituents of (many of) the idioms represented in WEDNESDAY 2 were taken from the results of an empirical study of idiom comprehension conducted by Cacciari (1988). Cacciari created six lists of (Italian) idioms, each comprised of 13 idioms and 40 literal sentences as fillers. Each list contained a fragment of each idiom and of a filler in a random, prespecified order. The length of the fragments varied in the six lists, so that in the first list the fragments were the shortest (e.g., "He was . . .") and in the list sixth list, the longest (e.g., "He was sitting on pins and . . ."). Each list was submitted to a different group of 15 subjects in such a way as to ensure that no subject saw the same idiom twice. Subjects were presented with incomplete sentences written in a booklet and were asked to complete them in a meaningful way. The percentage of subjects correctly completing an idiom with the different amount of information given in the six lists was used as the basis for determining the weight of the constituents of the 80 idioms constituting the corpus.

When the activation level of a particular idiom crosses its associated threshold (corresponding to the recognition point mentioned previously), another process is introduced dedicated solely to that particular idiom. The function of this process is to build the idiomatic interpretation. The process begins by introducing an edge in which substitutions are carried out that are compatible with all the information derived by the analysis up to that point. The process continues as long as the incoming information is consistent with the idiomatic representation it is building. The original process goes on as well (unless the fragment giving rise to the new process is not syntactic, being peculiar to that idiom alone); the only change being that the idiom is removed from the active idiom table. At this point there are two working processes and it is a matter for the (external) scheduling function to decide on the priorities. That is, according to different processing models one can decide at that point to assign priority to the literal interpretation or to the idiomatic interpretation.

But still the processing is open and the idiomatic process may result in failure: Further analysis may not confirm what has been hypothesized as an idiom. Furthermore, a different idiomatic process may be separated from the literal process at a later stage when its own activation level crosses the threshold.

As an example, we consider the idiom *to build castles in the air* in the context of the (defective) sentence, "The tycoon built castles in the Highlands." At some point, an attempt at an idiomatic analysis of the sentence will be undertaken and fail at which point it will be replaced by the literal analysis:

1. When *built* is analyzed, its idiom activation table is instantiated.

2. When *castles* is interpreted as the direct object of *built,* the activation of the idiom referred to previously crosses the threshold as specified in the lexicon. An additional (idiomatic) process starts at this point with the new interpretation unified with the previous interpretation of the subject: The process just departs from the literal process; no backtracking is performed. At this point we have two

processes going on: an idiomatic process in which the interpretation is already "the tycoon created unrealistic plans," and the literal process that, of course, incorporates the background monitoring for other potential idioms that might feasibly be consistent up to that point of the analysis.

3. The modifier "in the Highlands" is recognized; the idiomatic process fails because the spatial modifier is different from the one expected.

4. The literal process yields its analysis.

The flexibility inherent in the WEDNESDAY 2 analysis of idioms is required to accommodate the phenomenon of word-order flexibility that is present in a language such as Italian, even if it is of minimal importance in English. For instance, in the Italian version of the same idiom, namely *costruire castelli in aria*, it is acceptable to have a form like "Mario costruí nella sua vita diversi castelli in aria" (word by word: "Mario built in his life several castles in the air") and even, with sarcasm in the topicalization: "In aria Mario costruí diversi castelli" ("In the air Mario built several castles"). Although in English this idiom might be processed as a big word, it is clear from the examples that this cannot be the case in Italian.

EXTENSIONS AND PROBLEMS

In principle, this view can be extended quite easily by linking an idiom description not just to one entry (e.g., the verb for sentence(s) or verb-phrase-(VP) level idioms) that "monitors" the recognition, but to more entries that refer to the same description (such as the NPs or PPs involved). With this refinement, the most meaningful component of an idiom will instantiate the table. The same process would be established and the same representation could be used. The important aspect here is that idioms are recognized by means of the literal analysis and therefore the process makes uses of the syntactic productivity and of the syntactic constraints available. Van der Linden (1991) proposed a hierarchical organization of the lexicon for specifying idioms. We think this is very much in the spirit of our proposal and may lead to a better kind of factoring of common parts of larger idioms.

So, this is a framework in which one could insert data relative to the access of idioms and a theory about how idioms might be processed. This framework is compatible with relevant experimental results. For example, it allows for the simultaneous accessibility of the literal meanings of the component words of an idiom during comprehension. Cacciari and Tabossi (1988) provided direct evidence for such activation during idiom comprehension. Using a cross-modal priming paradigm they showed that the literal meanings of the component words of an idiomatic expression are activated immediately, but that the idiomatic meaning is not activated until 300 ms later, when both the literal and idiomatic senses are active. Even in studies using contexts that are appropriate to the idiomatic meanings of the phrases, both the idiomatic and literal meanings are directly accessible. Such data are consistent with the organization of a parser that accesses both the idiomatic and literal lexical entries for the input words and is able to construct both literal and figurative interpretations of the input in parallel. The actual distribution of processing resources over the two interpretations is determined by various higher level factors such as immediate semantic and discourse constraints.

Dead metaphors could fit well into this picture. Through semantic interpretation of the autonomous parts (going on in the literal interpretation), in particular as far as modifiers are introduced, one could import something into the new idiomatic/metaphoric meaning. For instance, in the current setting of WEDNESDAY 2 a modifier of the head of the idiom (like "John kicked the bucket 2 months after the accident") is correctly interpreted as modifying the idiomatic meaning ("John died 2 months after the accident"); the same holds for morphological modifiers (like "Jack rehit the road"); and there is also the possibility of using material that modifies a nonverbal component in the idiomatic interpretation. For instance, one could specify that material that modifies a noun can be used to modify the "verb predicate" of one of its arguments in the idiomatic interpretation. A case of this kind could be "Mary built professional castles in the air," meaning that she had unrealistic professional fantasies. Novel metaphors, however, require a different mechanism because they involve specifications at the knowledge level.

The framework we are proposing incorporates the recognition of idiomatic reference as an integral component of natural language processing, but at the same time accommodates the syntactic flexibility exhibited by idioms in most languages. However, no attempt is made to capture other forms of productivity, as we believe them to be the product of processes independent of the recognition process.

REFERENCES

Cacciari, C. (1988). *La comprensione delle espressioni idiomatiche: Il rapporto fra significato letterale e significato figurato* [The comprehension of idiomatic expressions: The relationship between literal and figurative meanings]. Unpublished doctoral dissertation, University of Bologna, Italy.

Cacciari, C., & Glucksberg, S. (1990). Understanding idiomatic expressions: The contribution of word meanings. In G. B. Simpson (Ed.), *Understanding word and sentence* (pp. 217–240). Amsterdam, Netherlands: Elsevier.

Cacciari, C., & Tabossi, P. (1988). The comprehension of idioms. *Journal of Memory and Language, 27,* 668–683.

Clark, H. H., & Lucy, P. (1975). Understanding what is meant from what is said: A study in conversationally conveyed requests. *Journal of Verbal Learning and Verbal Behavior, 14,* 56–72.

Cottrell, G. W. (1988). A model of lexical access of ambiguous words. In S. L. Small, G. K. Cottrell, & M. Tanenhaus (Eds.), *Lexical ambiguity resolution*. San Mateo, CA: Kaufmann.

Dyer, M., & Zernik, U. (1986). Encoding and acquiring meaning for figurative phrases. In *Proceedings of the 24th Meeting of the Association for Computational Linguistics* (pp. 106–111). New York.

Gibbs, R. W. (1983). Do people always process the literal meanings of indirect requests? *Journal of Experimental Psychology: Learning, Memory and Cognition, 9*, 524–533.

Gibbs, R. W., & Nayak, N. (1989). Psycholinguistic studies on the syntactic behavior of idioms. *Cognitive Psychology, 21*, 100–138.

Gibbs, R. W., Nayak, N., Bolton, J. L., & Keppel, M. (1989). Speakers' assumption about the lexical flexibility of idioms. *Memory and Cognition, 17*, 58–68.

Gibbs, R. W., Nayak, N., & Cutting, C. (1989). How to kick the bucket and not decompose. Analyzability and idiom processing. *Journal of Memory and Language, 28*, 576–593.

Gibbs, R. W., & O'Brien, J. (1990). Idioms and mental imager: The metaphorical motivation for idiomatic meaning. *Cognition, 36*, 35–68.

Glucksberg, S. (1990). *Beyond literal meanings: The psychology of allusion*. Paper presented at the annual meeting of the American Psychological Association, Boston.

Hendrix, G. G. (1977). LIFER: A natural language interface facility. *SIGART Newsletter*, No. 61.

Jacobs, P. (1985). PHRED: A generator for natural language interfaces. *Computational Linguistics, 11*(4), 219–242.

Kaplan, R. (1973). A general syntactic processor. In R. Rustin (Ed.), *Natural language processing*. Englewood Cliffs, NJ: Prentice-Hall.

Katz, J. (1973). Compositionality, idiomaticity, and lexical substitution. In S. R. Anderson & P. Kiparsky (Eds.), *A festschrift for Morris Halle*. New York: Holt, Rinehart & Winston.

Kay, M. (1980). *Algorithm schemata and data structures in syntactic processing*. Xerox Palo Alto Research Center, Palo Alto, CA.

Lakoff, G. (in press). Metaphor: The contemporary view. In A. Ortony (Ed.), *Metaphor and thought* (2nd ed.). New York: Cambridge University Press.

Nayak, N., and Gibbs, R. W. (1990). Conceptual knowledge in the interpretation of idioms. *Journal of Experimental Psychology: General, 119*, 315–330.

Ortony, A. (Ed.). (in press). *Metaphor and thought* (2nd ed.). New York: Cambridge University Press.

Ortony, A., Schallert, D. L., Reynolds, R. E., & Antos, S. J. (1978). Interpreting metaphors and idioms: Some effects of context on comprehension. *Journal of Verbal Learning and Verbal Behavior, 17*, 465–477.

Stock, O. (1989). Parsing with flexibility, dynamic strategies, and idioms in mind. *Computational Linguistics, 15*, 1.

Swinney, D. A., & Cutler, A. (1979). The access and processing of idiomatic expressions. *Journal of Verbal Learning and Verbal Behavior, 18*, 523–534.

Van der Linden, E. (1991). Idioms, non-literal language and knowledge representation. *Proceedings of the IJCAI workshop on computational approaches to non-literal language: Metaphor, metonymy, idiom, speech acts, implicature* (pp. 141–150). Sydney, Australia: Conference Organization.

Van der Linden, E., & Kraaij, W. (1990). Ambiguity resolution and the retrieval of idioms: Two approaches. *Proceedings of COLING-90* (Vol. 2, pp. 1–6). Helsinki, Finland: Conference Organization.

Waltz, D. (1978). An English language question answering system for a large relational database. *Communications of the Association for Computing Machinery, 21*(7), 526–539.

Wasow, T., Sag, I. A., & Nunberg, G. (1982). Idioms: An interim report. *Proceedings of the XIII International Congress of Linguistics* (pp. 102–105). Tokyo: CIPL.

Wilensky, R., & Arens, Y. (1980). *PHRAN—A knowledge-based approach to natural language analysis* (ERL Memorandum No. UCB/ERL M80/34). Berkeley: University of California, Electronic Research Laboratory.

Wood, M. W. (1986). *A definition of idiom*. Bloomington: Indiana University Linguistics Club.

11 The Recognition and Interpretation of Idioms

Stephen G. Pulman
University of Cambridge Computer Laboratory and
SRI International Cambridge Computer Science Research Centre

Here are some examples of phrases that have been described as idiomatic in both the traditional and the generative linguistic literature:

1. John *turned on* the light.
2. Joe *put up with* the noise.
3. Bill *took advantage of* her generosity.
4. He did it *for* his mother's *sake*.
5. The old curmudgeon finally *kicked the bucket*.
6. We got him to *spill the beans*.
7. That really *put the cat among the pigeons*.
8. He was chasing *a red herring*.
9. We feel they are *skating on thin ice* with that project.
10. He shouldn't have *counted his chickens before they were hatched*.

Intuitively speaking, these examples are ranged on a scale from the more grammaticalized, like *turn on,* to phrases that legitimately might be regarded as proverbs rather than idioms, like the *count your chickens* example. In between are examples like *spill the beans,* or *skate on thin ice.* What they all have in common is that their meanings are not deducible from the ordinary meanings of their components by the usual rules of compositional semantics. We do not get the meaning of *turn on* in this context from a combination of the meanings of *turn* and *on,* and although the meanings of *skate, thin,* and *ice* surely play some kind of part in our interpretation of Sentence 9, the example nevertheless conveys something over and above a picture of people moving rapidly across ice on skates.

To say that idioms are not interpreted compositionally is not intended to be claiming that noncompositionality is a sufficient condition for an idiom. Nor is it to deny that there is no trace of compositionality in these examples. Not everything that is noncompositional normally would be counted as an idiom. For example, a phrase like *on top of,* which corresponds to no productive compositional semantic pattern (*on bottom of), is probably best thought of as a "compound preposition." And *for X's sake* is recognizably the same idiom as *for the sake of X* and, with the exception of the contribution of *sake,* is as compositional as possessives in general are. Nevertheless, idioms are not wholly compositional.

This lack of total compositionality may be for one of several reasons: Perhaps the components do not in isolation have a meaning distinct from their occurrence in the idiom, as with *sake* in *for X's sake,* or *tabs* in the idiom *keep tabs on;* or it may be that they have several meanings (or one radically underdetermined one), the correct one of which can be determined only in the context of the idiom, as with *up* and *with* and *on* and so forth in the first two examples. More characteristically, perhaps, it may be that the components of the idiom have literal meanings, but that these are not what is involved in their interpretation as an idiom. This latter type of idiom often is characterized (metaphorically) as a frozen or dead metaphor. However, its meaning is not completely lexicalized: It is certainly the case that someone unfamiliar with the idiom nevertheless can arrive at an appropriate meaning for it by processing it as a metaphor (Examples 7, 9, and 10). As one might expect if one is treating it as a metaphor, one sometimes arrives at rational interpretations that are nevertheless not that of the idiom; for example, detecting connotations of cruelty in the *cat among the pigeons* example: There is no such connotation in its ordinary usage.

Idioms are pervasive in all styles of language use. The problem they present to the theoretical and computational linguist is not the fact that their meaning cannot be worked out by the usual syntactic and semantic rules, for if it were not for other factors this could be overcome by treating them as multiword lexical items to be looked up in a list in a fairly straightforward way. (A treatment like this is all that is necessary for things like *on top of*). The problem is rather that unlike (most) lexical items, (most) idioms have considerable internal structure that seems to interact with the usual productive syntactic and semantic mechanisms of a language in ways that render a "look-up" approach impossible in the general case. It is as if idioms have some of the properties of lexical items, in that some aspect of their meaning simply has to be looked up in a dictionary, or some repository of idiosyncratic information, but also have some properties of regular syntactic and semantic structures, in particular a fair amount of variability in the actual forms in which the idiom can be encountered: a problem for look-up-based approaches. Thus a grammatical theory that does not allow for this interaction between conflicting sets of properties is likely to be found wanting in crucial respects: The ability of a theory to accommodate the behavior of idioms has been seen therefore as a major argument in its favor, whether in Standard Theory transformational grammar (Fraser, 1970; Katz, 1973), Generative Semantics (Newmeyer, 1972), more recent transformational theories (Chomsky, 1980), Lexical-Functional Grammar (Bresnan, 1982), Generalized Phrase Structure Grammar (Gazdar, Klein, Pullum, & Sag, 1985), or Tree Adjoining Grammar (Abeille, 1990).

The main point of the present article is to establish that there are some properties of idioms that are not captured satisfactorily by any of the current grammatical frameworks, and that these properties suggest that idioms are in fact not properly to be considered as part of the domain of a grammatical theory at all. Instead, the recognition and interpretation of idioms belongs in the relatively unexplored areas between compositional syntax and semantics on the one hand, and contextually interpreted, fully resolved, interpretations of utterances on the other. Getting from compositionally derived meaning syntactic and semantic representations to fully resolved contextual interpretations involves what can be called *contextual reasoning*. This is the process of taking the information that can be derived linguistically from a sentence and fleshing it out with information supplied by the local context or general background knowledge, leading to a fully specific interpretation of that utterance of the sentence in that particular context. Contextual reasoning includes the various processes that establish the referents of pronouns and other anaphoric devices, the resolution of ellipsis, and the filling in of contextually dependent "vague relations" such as that associated with possessives, compound nominals, and verbs like *have* or *do:* In order to interpret them correctly, one needs to know that the *have* of "John has measles" is not quite the same as the *have* in "John has a sister."

PROPERTIES OF IDIOMS

First let us review some of the properties of idioms that have figured in recent discussions of them (Bresnan, 1982; Chomsky, 1980; Gazdar et al., 1985; Wasow, Sag, and Nunberg, 1982). The first observation is an old one: that in pragmatically appropriate contexts some idioms can appear in syntactically variant forms:

11. John turned the light on.
12. Her generosity was taken advantage of.
13. Advantage was taken of her generosity.
14. He did it for the sake of his mother.
15. The beans were spilled.

16. It was thin ice that they were skating on.
17. Chickens that are counted before they are hatched aren't a good basis for a bank loan.

But some idioms seem fairly resistant to this kind of paraphrase:

18. ?*The bucket was finally kicked by the old curmudgeon.
19. *It was among the pigeons that he put the cat.
20. *He was chasing a herring that was red.

The only interpretation these sentences easily receive is a literal one. It has been claimed (Chomsky, 1980) that there is a difference between syntactic constructions in this respect: that, in particular, most idioms do not appear in *tough-movement* variants of basic forms even though other transformational paraphrases of them are permitted:

21. She is easy to take advantage of.
22. *Advantage is easy to take of her.

(Tough-movement is the term used informally to describe the relation between the approximate paraphrases "it is easy to please John" and "John is easy to please," associated with a group of adjectives that include *easy, tough,* and *difficult.*) However, it seems likely (see following examples) that this is not a syntactic matter so much as one of finding the appropriate context in which the "focusing" effect of tough-movement can seem natural:

23. She's playing hard to get.
24. That's a course which is proving hard to steer.
25. That lie is difficult to nail.

A second important observation about the properties of idioms is that they are in the main capable of "internal modification":

26. I have a theoretical axe to grind.
27. He cut through a lot of red tape.
28. They were skating on very thin ice.

Here it is the components of the idioms that are being modified: Example 26 means "I have a theoretical point to make," not "Theoretically, I have a point to make" (on the most natural reading of the latter, at least). Likewise, it is the amount of red tape that is being quantified, not the action of cutting through red tape. Furthermore, these modifications feel entirely natural and straightforward:

There is no sense of "playing with words," humorous intent, or metalinguistic comment. Contrast these in both respects with the following examples:

29. He kicked the proverbial bucket.
30. I'll keep a close eye on his progress.
31. That turned out to be a very red herring.

Kick the proverbial bucket is clearly metalinguistic; in the next example, although *close* syntactically modifies *eye,* it is felt semantically to modify the whole phrase: It means "I'll watch his progress closely." In *a very red herring* most people feel that there is an element of play or humor involved in arriving at the interpretation, although in order to do this some modification of a component of the idiom is involved: We could paraphrase the result as something like "That was an unusually irrelevant diversion." Now, most people would agree that to deal adequately with examples like these three examples, we have to go outside grammar to some theory dealing with the stylistic properties of language. But for the previous set of examples, where there is no feeling that anything other than the normal processes of syntactic and semantic modification are at work, the implication is that we must assign independent meanings to the components of the idioms in order that there is something there for the modifiers to modify.

This conclusion is further reinforced by the observation that, contrary to the traditional generative wisdom (e.g., Bresnan, 1982, quoting Grimshaw), parts of idioms can serve as antecedents to pronouns and ellipsis:

32. He turned the tables on me and then I turned them on him.
33. They said the tide would turn, and eventually it did.

This possibility seems to correlate with that of internal modification: An idiom that cannot be modified internally cannot provide anaphoric antecedents:

34. *I'll keep an eye on him and one on her too.

The inference from these observations is that the components that serve as antecedents must be individually meaningful, as usually is assumed in the cases not involving idioms.

A further observation that we can add in support of this general conclusion is that some idioms can be recognized, albeit in something of a stylistically marked way, even when incomplete:

35. That's a case of counting your chickens *(before they are hatched).*
36. This is just smoke without fire *(there's no smoke without fire).*

37. That suggestion came from the bottom of the barrel *(cf. scraping the bottom of the barrel)*.

For examples like at least the 36 and 37, to assemble the correct interpretation requires the components to be individually meaningful.

CANONICAL FORM THEORIES

Until recently, most linguistic theories, to the extent that they have tried to capture the properties of idioms at all, have adopted one version or another of what I call a *canonical form* approach. Starting from the point of view that the idiosyncratic nature of idioms is a lexical property in some sense, and that this idiosyncrasy should be stated only once, rather than having to be repeated for all the variant forms in which the idiom may appear, these theories adopt some level of linguistic representation provided by the theory as the *canonical level* for this statement. That is to say, this level provides a *normal form* to which all different occurrences of the idiom can be reduced: The properties of the idiom then can be stated at this level once and for all, and the normal mechanisms provided by the theory for syntactic variation will ensure that alternative variant forms of the idiom are related in some systematic way to the canonical form, allowing the properties of all the different forms to be deduced.

For example, Chomsky (1980) proposed that idioms should be catered for by using a special class of lexical rules operating at the level of "D-structure," a level of underlying grammatical representation at which semantically important properties are exhibited via a canonical syntactic form. Chomsky's lexical idiom rules are sensitive to the presence of particular groups of lexical items and operate so as to reanalyze, or provide an alternative analysis for, independently generated structures. Thus structures like:

38. John [VP [V kicked][NP the bucket]], and
39. John [VP [V took][NP advantage][P of][NP Bill]],

will be reanalyzed lexically as:

40. John [VP [V kicked the bucket]], and
41. John [VP [V took advantage of][NP Bill]],

with the idiomatic meanings being assigned as those of the newly created complex V: *kick the bucket* = "die," *take advantage of* = "exploit," roughly. The original syntactic structures are retained, though, allowing for the observed syntactic variation. The inability of some idioms to undergo certain rules can be described via a mechanism for marking the output of the idiom rules with a list of transformational processes that are allowed or disallowed. Chomsky did not go into any formal detail on the properties of these idiom rules but it seems fair to conclude on the basis of his examples that they have at least the following properties: (a) They operate on constituents, not arbitrary sections of tree; and (b) there is only one rule per idiom. The first property is required if the proposed mechanism for handling the semantics is to be viable: Idioms are "like lexical items"—that is, they are single semantic units. The second is not required logically but seems to be the intent of all canonical form approaches: The point of stating facts about the idiom at a canonical level of representation is that it allows only 1 statement of the facts about the idiom.

Bresnan (1982) proposed a mechanism with some similar features, but here the canonical form is a level of lexical representation. Idiomatic meanings, she posited, are to be stated in the lexicon, associated with the main functor of the idiom: Thus one sense of *keep*, that which appears in the idiom *keep tabs on* will be as follows:

keep: V, keep-tabs-on ((subj),(on obj)); (obj form)=tabs

The verb will have a special meaning, and will be marked syntactically as requiring the other components of the idiom: *on* followed by an NP consisting of the head N *tabs*. Alternative forms, such as the passive version, will be derived via the normal mechanism of lexical redundancy rules, just as for other transitive verbs:

...
$\Leftarrow$ *passive* $\Rightarrow$
keep: V, passive, keep-tabs-on ((by obj/null), (on subj); (subj form)=tabs

These redundancy rules allow variant lexical entries to be deduced from a single basic one, where the variant forms are predictable. They fulfill many of the functions served by lexically governed transformational rules in earlier theories. The interaction of such rules suffices to derive all the valid alternative forms: Exceptions presumably can be marked as such. Bresnan's (1982) approach, given the properties of lexical redundancy rules, seems to share, *mutatis mutandis* both of the properties (a) and (b) of Chomsky's (1980) approach. It is a firm prediction of both theories that all the alternative variant forms in which a particular idiom can appear will be relatable to each other through the syntactic or lexical mechanisms of the grammatical theory: that all the variants can be "derived" from the single canonical form at which the properties of the idiom are stated.

Both of these theories have their problems. Firstly, as Gazdar et al. (1985) pointed out, it is not clear how a theory that regards idioms as essentially synonymous with atomic lexical items can assign to them enough internal structure to allow for internal modification and the apparent appearance of some of their components as antecedents. Likewise, our ability to recognize partial or incomplete idioms remains unexplained on such a view.

Second, it seems that the predictions of these theories about the variety of idioms are false. Sets of sentences like these are (correctly) not related by regular syntactic or lexical processes in any current theory of grammar known to me:

42a. He turned the tables on me.

42b. The tables have turned.

43a. Now he's let the cat out of the bag.

43b. Now the cat's out of the bag.

44a. I've got some loose ends to be tied up.

44b. I'm tying up a few loose ends.

44c. A few loose ends need tying up.

45a. He really put the cat among the pigeons.

45b. Now the cat's well and truly among the pigeons.

Nevertheless, in these groups of examples, it is intuitively obvious that it is the same idiom appearing in each sentence, rather than several separate, accidentally related idioms. However, this fact is not something that can even be described in the canonical form theories, for there is no canonical form at which the properties of the idiom can be represented. At best, there will have to be several different statements for the various syntactic forms in which the idiom appears. Although workable, this is a clumsy and unattractive position to be forced into taking.

As well as there being no syntactic canonical form shared by examples like these, it is also true that the components of the idiom, in some cases, are not grouped together under the same constituent. There are other examples of the same thing, where the idiomatic component of a sentence consists, roughly speaking, of the subject and verb, but where the complement can vary:

46. The ceiling fell in on Pedro.

47. The earth finally moved for Ernestina.

48. Fortune smiled on Bonzo.

In Tree Adjoining Grammar (TAG), as described in Abeille (1990), a lexical head simply is associated with the different syntactic constructs ("elementary trees") it can appear in. In the case of idioms, these are regarded as having "multicomponent" heads, like *kick, the,* and *bucket,* and they are associated directly with a set of elementary trees representing the variant syntactic forms the idioms can appear in. In contrast to the preceding theories, there is no requirement that such families of elementary trees be "natural" or predictable in the sense that, say, the tough-movement predicates or the passivisable verbs would be assigned to a natural set of elementary trees. Other than the fact that they have distributed heads, there is apparently no important distinction made between idiomatic constructions and nonidiomatic constructions. Although not strictly speaking a canonical form theory, TAG does make the claim that the mechanisms of syntactic variation for idioms are the same for nonidioms.

TAG fares somewhat better than the other two theories in accounting for many properties of idioms, but suffers the same problems with respect to those cases where not all of the idiom is present. In those cases no elementary tree will match the entry for the idiom and it will not be recognized.

All these theories fare badly on examples of idioms where there is lexical variation in one component, such as:

49. Put/lay/spread your cards on the table.

TAG has the same problems as the other theories in capturing the fact that these are versions of the same idiom, intuitively, not three separate idioms with identical meanings.

THE PARTIAL FUNCTION APPROACH

A second type of approach to the properties of idioms is taken by both Wasow et al. (1983) and Gazdar et al. (1985). Their proposals are couched within a monostratal theory of syntax: There is only level of syntactic analysis, and thus syntactic or lexical canonical forms are not an option. This approach to syntactic description (which of course has been enormously influential) is wedded to a semantic theory that is basically that of Montague (1974). Semantic interpretation consists of translation into a (theoretically dispensable) logical form—an expression of a formally defined artificial language called *Intensional Logic*— which has a recursively defined model-theoretic interpretation. In general the meaning of a constituent is either a function or an argument (which itself may be a function). Meanings of complex constituents are built up by applying the meaning of some of the components to the meanings of the others, as function to argument. The denotations (logicians' proxies for meanings) of these functions are built up from a basic ontology of individuals, possible worlds, and set theoretic constructions based on these.

Normally speaking, the interpretations of these various functions, and the predicates and constants of Intensional Logic, are total functions: that is, they are defined for every object in the domain of the interpretation. Thus (to simplify) the interpretation of something like *table* might be a (function from possible worlds to a) function from objects to truth values: a function that tells you, for every object, whether or not it is a table. Mathematically speaking, we also can have "partial functions"; functions that are defined for some arguments, but not others. A simple example of such a function might be division: division of X by Y is defined for all values of X and Y except where Y = zero. In these cases the value of *divide (X,Y)* = *undefined*. Thus, division is a function that is defined for some numbers, but not all (all except zero, in fact).

The partial function approach to idioms advocated by Gazdar et al. (1985) is as follows: We assign to each of the words appearing in the idioms, as well as its usual literal meaning, if it has one, an idiomatic meaning. This is a partial function that is defined for some arguments and not others. It is defined, in fact, only for the arguments corresponding to the other components of the idiom. Thus in the case where all the components of the idiom appear in an appropriate configuration, we will end up with a meaning that results from the combination of all the components with each other. If some of the components are missing, we will have something that is not fully defined, that is, not meaningful.

This can be illustrated informally as follows: We assign to *turn* its usual meaning, which we represent as **turn** and also an idiomatic meaning, roughly corresponding to **seize.** We treat the other components of an idiom in a similar way. To suggest (to us) that the idiomatic components all belong together, we assign them all a numerical subscript. This also serves to distinguish the idiomatic meanings from their literal counterparts: *Turning the tables* is not literally (i.e., physically) to **seize** anything, but it is to seize_{21} something. Now, the basic idea is that the grammar will assign to a sentence containing the words in question analyses corresponding to all possible combinations of the entries for the words. However, of these combinations, only those that have all the literal or all the idiomatic senses (in our informal illustration, those with the same subscript), combined in the appropriate function-argument pattern, will have a properly defined meaning:

turn: **turn, seize_{21}** . . .
the: **the, a_{21}** . . .
tables: **tables, position-of-strength_{21}** . . .
turn the tables =
(i) **turn (the (tables))**
(ii) **seize_{21} (a_{21} (position-of-strength_{21}))**
(iii) *__turn (a_{21} (position-of-strength_{21}))__
(iv) *__seize_{21} (the (tables))__
etc.

Combinations of literal with idiomatic senses are not defined: They do not combine into a sensible meaning.

Because according to this view the components of idioms are independently meaningful, it is not surprising that they can be modified, can serve as antecedents, and so on. (Those idioms that do not have these properties are treated essentially as complex lexical items by the Generalized Phrase Structure Grammar (GPSG) account: They thus distinguish two subtypes of idioms).

There are, unfortunately, one or two problems with the partial function account. One question concerns the basis on which meanings are categorized into literal and nonliteral. An intuition behind the GPSG treatment (I am grateful to Gerald Gazdar for making me aware of this) was that the mechanism could be regarded as an extension of the notion of a "sorted logic." In a sorted logic, the objects in the domain are separated into sorts, and the various expressions of the logic are categorized as to what sort of thing they can be predicated of meaningfully. To give an informal example, one might say that the predicate *drink* in English was (ignoring metaphorical uses) required to have something of sort "living thing" as its subject and sort "liquid" as its object. It is not meaningful to combine *drink* with arguments of differing sorts: "The book drank the flower" sounds odd.

In the case of idioms, the effect of this mechanism is to make a combination like "*seize$_{21}$ (the (tables))" as anomalous as "the book drank the flowers," and for essentially the same reason. But if the motivation behind the assignment of things to sorts is semantic, it is not obvious that the restrictions on combination that are required actually could be obtained in a way that ensures overall consistency of the sortal system. For example, if we assume that the idiomatic meaning of *axe to grind* is essentially that of *point to make,* then we might assign the sort of *point* to the idiomatic sense of *axe,* and that of *make* to *grind.* However, there then would be no obvious reason why I cannot say "I want to consider this axe" with the meaning "I want to consider this point." If *consider* can combine nonidiomatically with *point,* it is not obvious why it cannot combine with the relevant meaning of *axe* without sortal violation.

If we carry out the assignment of partial meanings on some other basis, there are still problems in ensuring that only the right combinations are permitted. The initial assumption is that literal verbs will have to be defined in such a way that they do not combine with idiomatic arguments, for otherwise we would be able to say things like "seize the tables," meaning "seize a position of strength." This suggests that the sortal structures erected for idiomatic expressions should be insulated from those that apply to nonidiomatic expressions, although parallel to that one in various respects. However, things are not quite so simple, for at least some literal verbs do seem to combine with idiomatic components, provided the rest of the idiom is there too:

50. He tried to break **the ice** which *inhibited our conversation.*

In order to account for the interpretation of the relative clause, in which *the ice* is the subject of *inhibit* (via its connection to *which*), we would need to assume, it seems, a special sense of *inhibit* that is capable of combining with idiomatic senses.

Gazdar et al. (1985) apparently were willing to acknowledge this multiplication of word senses. They pointed out that partial functions will "permeate the entire lexicon" (p. 239), even though this proliferation apparently leads to the prediction that combinations like:

51. The ice inhibited our conversation.

Should be easily interpretable, without contextual priming, and with the idiomatic components receiving the interpretations they would have in the full idiom. My intuition is that this is not the case. However, even if it is, there surely will be a considerable combinatorial explosion problem if this program is carried through systematically: Just consider a phrase like *see the light*. This will have many different analyses: a literal one, an idiomatic one involving the special sense of *see* required to combine with *the light* of *the light at the end of the tunnel;* a second idiomatic one in which a complete idiom is present (meaning something like "suddenly have the truth revealed"); all possible combinations of these, resulting in structures with no fully defined meaning; combinations of each of these with analyses in which the *the* is the *the* of *kick the bucket* (nb. **kick a bucket*), or of *cat among the pigeons* (nb. **cat among no pigeons*), likewise yielding no fully defined meaning, and so on and so forth.

Nor is this multiplication of meanings restricted to the nonlogical vocabulary of the meaning representation. It is also the case that all the logical constants of Intensional Logic will have to be made systematically ambiguous between total and partial function uses. For example, if the partialness of idiom denotations is to be made to do the work it is required to do, it must be inherited by functions applying to those partial functions. This will happen straightforwardly in most instances, by the normal compositional rules of the grammar. But in some cases, the components of an idiom are in structures where they are not operating on each other as function to argument, being combined in some other structure. Consider the case of:

52. That has put a cat among the pigeons.
53. Now there's a cat among the pigeons.

Assuming that the relevant parts of the idiom are *a cat* and *among the pigeons,* then the rules assumed for these constructions by Gazdar et al. (1985) will deliver structures like these (ignoring intensional operators for simplicity) for the two sentences:

54. Put (among (the pigeons))) (a cat)).
55. Be (a [λx. cat(x) ∧ [among (the (pigeons))](x)]).

In the first of this pair, *put* combines with *among the pigeons* to form a predicate that can apply to *a cat*. *Put* will pass on the partialness of its argument. But in the second, there is no verb that applies to *among the pigeons* and *a cat* in a similar way. Thus in order to rule out combinations of literal cats with idiomatic pigeons, and suchlike oddities, it seems that it must be arranged that *and* is defined in such a way that it only accepts two idiomatic arguments or two literal arguments, and not combinations. This is technically possible, of course (though the resulting adjustments to the model theory of Intensional Logic are not trivial), but is beginning to seem a somewhat less than elegant solution. It is, of course, also an approach that will present some serious practical problems if one is interested in being able to produce a computationally feasible analysis of idioms: It in effect makes the problem of automatic word-sense selection many times more complex than it was before. For now, many sentences that do not obviously contain ambiguous words will do so under this analysis simply because of the fact that they contain some words that are a component of some idiom, the other components of which are not actually present in the current sentence.

IDIOMS AND QUASI-INFERENCE

It seems to me that the way out of the inadequacies and problems of the preceding theories is to acknowledge and make use of the observation that in order for certain types of idiom to be regarded as having a canonical form, either of the syntactic-lexical type envisaged by Chomsky (1980) and Bresnan (1982), or "purely semantic," which is what the Gazdar et al. (1985) proposal amounts to, then we must give up the assumption that this level of canonical form corresponds to anything made available in current theories of grammar as an independently motivated level of representation. More specifically, the relationship between pairs like the two examples just discussed, or the following is not anything that could or should be captured by syntactic or lexical rules, or directly by compositional semantics:

56. John let the cat out of the bag.
57. The cat is out of the bag.
58. He turned the tables on me.
59. The tables have turned.
60. He laid his cards on the table.
61. His cards are on the table.

If anything, what we have here is a relationship of entailment. In each case the first member of the pair entails the second. In the case where we are dealing with the more usual examples of idioms appearing in related constructions, the same thing is true: Characteristically, what makes us decide that two syntactic constructions are related is that sentences in one form entail sentences in the other form, and sometimes vice versa.

If this observation is correct, then several consequences follow: First, if we want to state the facts about an idiom just once—if we regard pairs of sentence like Examples 56–61 as involving the "same" idiom—then that statement will have to be at some postgrammatical level of representation. Second, it follows from the nature of some of these entailments that the properties of the idiom will have to be stated on the entailed member of the pairs in the aforementioned examples, not the entailing member. That is to say, the idiom must be *the cat . . . out of the bag, a cat . . . among the pigeons,* and not *let the cat out of the bag,* or *put a cat among the pigeons.*

Let us see how such a proposal might work out in detail. We first of all outline a purely mechanical solution, which is capable of being implemented in a practical natural language understanding system, and then go on to discuss the theoretical status of the constructs involved.

We assume some grammatical theory providing translations of sentence meanings into logical forms directly. Thus if we envisage such a grammar as used by a parser, the parser will deliver, for a given input string, one or more logical forms, if the input string was covered by the grammar. These logical forms will feed into an inference mechanism of some kind. This inference mechanism also will have access to various meaning postulates governing the behavior of all the nonlogical constants of the logic that we are translating sentences into (at least as many constants as content words in the language, let us assume). Among these will be postulates giving information about the inferences arising from causal verbs like *let, put, lay,* and so on, as follows:

62. $\forall x, P.\text{let}(x,P) \rightarrow \text{cause}(x,P)$.
63. $\forall x,y,z.\ \text{put}(x,y,z) \rightarrow \text{location}(y,z)$.

We now add to these a set of "idiom rules" somewhat similar in form but describing the relation between literal and idiomatic interpretations:

64. $\forall x,y.\ \text{cat}(x) \wedge \text{bag}(y) \wedge \text{out-of}(x,y) \approx \exists a,z.\ \text{secret}(z) \wedge \text{revealed}(a, z)$.
65. $\forall x,p.\ \text{cat}(c) \wedge \text{pigeons}(p) \wedge \text{location}(c,p) \approx \exists y.\text{disturbance}(y)$.

The application of these rules is triggered by the appearance of a logical form that "matches" the left-hand side of an idiom rule. When this is the case, the idiomatic meaning is a possible one for the sentence as well as, or perhaps instead of, the literal meaning, depending on the context.

From:
John let the cat out of the bag
let(John,$\exists c,b.\ \text{cat}(c) \wedge \text{bag}(b) \wedge \text{out-of}(c,b)$)
via:
$\exists c,b.\ \text{cat}(c) \wedge \text{bag}(b) \wedge \text{out-of}(c,b)$
and:

$\forall$x,y. cat(x) $\wedge$ bag(y) $\wedge$ out-of(x,y) $\approx$ $\exists$a,z. secret(z) $\wedge$ revealed(a, z)
to:
$\exists$a,z. secret(z) $\wedge$ revealed(a, z)

From:
John put a cat among the pigeons
$\exists$c,p. cat(c) $\wedge$ pigeons(p) $\wedge$ put(john,c.p)
via:
$\exists$c,p. cat(c) $\wedge$ pigeons(p) $\wedge$ location(c,p)
and:
$\forall$x,y. cat(x) $\wedge$ pigeons(y) $\wedge$ location(x,y) $\approx$ $\exists$z.disturbance(z)
to:
$\exists$z.disturbance(z)

We can treat, purely mechanically, the process of matching idiom rules and drawing out the idiomatic meaning as ordinary proof theoretic inference operating on the logical forms produced by a natural language system for some given input sentence. We just treat the connective $\approx$ as if it were $\rightarrow$, take the logical form representing the literal sentence meaning (perhaps transformed into some kind of normal form), and by a process of forward chaining inference on it use the idiom rules to produce all the derivable "conclusions." Among these will be the idiomatic interpretation of the sentence "deduced" by the idiom rules.

Using something that has the properties of inference has several advantages. So, for example, the ordering of conjuncts in the literal logical form does not matter; nor does the presence of extra conjuncts reflecting the appearance of internal modifiers of components of the idiom. Treating the process as akin to inference provides the necessary flexibility to deal with these types of variation, whereas a simple "pattern-matching" approach would have problems characterizing the range of permissible variant forms from the target pattern. A simple pattern-matching approach would require, for example, that all of the inputs that should trigger a particular idiom rule had the same overall pattern: But of course this cannot be guaranteed to be the case easily if there are many variant syntactic forms of an idiom. Partial idioms and modifying phrases also would produce structures not necessarily matching the patterns provided. Inference, on the other hand, simply requires that variant forms logically entail the "antecedent" of the rule: They do not have to be syntactically similar, much less identical.

Under this quasi-inference scheme, then, the sequence of events in analyzing the purely compositional meanings of a sentence, in a naive "classical" natural language processing system will be: (a) Parse it, (b) apply compositional semantic rules to give the set of literal logical forms for the sentence, and (c) use the relevant set of meaning postulates and idiom rules to expand the set of interpretations.

This set of literal and idiomatic interpretations then can be checked against the context to discover what the most plausible meaning of the sentence is on this particular occasion.

However, it is very important to notice that our idiom rules are neither ordinary meaning postulates nor inference rules. They are not meaning postulates, because they do not restrict the meanings of the literal interpretations on their left-hand side. The literal meaning is what it is and is not changed by the fact that an idiomatic reading is also possible. Nor are they inference rules, because these require it to be the case that their antecedent is true before their consequent can be regarded as true: Inference is the process of going from true premises to true conclusions. But in the case of the rules giving idiomatic interpretations, in almost all but a few unusual circumstances it is precisely the fact that the antecedent is not literally true that makes the idiomatic interpretation plausible.

This makes it rather important to discover exactly what these idiom rules are. One possible interpretation, suggested to me by Robin Cooper (personal communication), of the status of idiom rules is as follows. Think of the rules cited earlier, of the general form *literal* ≈ *idiom,* as being a quantification over situations, meaning roughly, "in any situation in which idiom would be literally true, it is permissible to use literal to describe it." This is a plausible view, although it seems to me to give idioms more of a metalinguistic status than one might have thought they deserved.

A more simple rationalization for the idiom rules might be along somewhat similar lines, but without the metalinguistic flavor or the vocabulary of situation theory of the previous suggestion. The ordinary definition of truth for a logical language like that we have been assuming might supply a statement of the truth conditions for a logical form like:

66. $\exists c,b.$ cat(c) $\wedge$ bag(b) $\wedge$ out-of(c,b).

This would be in terms of something like the following: ". . . is true if and only if there is some a cat c and a bag b and the pair $\langle c,b \rangle$ is a member of the denotation of the predicate *out-of.* Such descriptions of truth conditions for logical forms are deduced in a recursive way from statements of truth conditions for the basic predicates, constants, and logical devices of the language. What we do now is to think of idioms as simply adding extra clauses to this set of basic definitions, to the effect that a logical form like the aforementioned also will have the truth conditions: ". . . is true if and only if there is some secret $s,$ and there is some agent, $a,$ and the pair $\langle a,s \rangle$ is a member of the denotation of *reveal.*

Of course, the mechanism for recursively assigning truth conditions will have to operate in a way analogous to our quasi-inference described earlier, if it is to be able to recognize when these extra clauses can apply. But this picture of the process of interpreting sentences is not completely unfamiliar. Many aspects of the interpretation of compositionally derived logical forms involve a process syntactically indistinguishable from inference but without requiring the semantic warrant usually demanded of "real" inference. For example, one needs to make "deductions" about possible resolutions of ellipsis, pronoun reference, and so forth, in order to arrive at a fully fledged logical form that can be assessed for truth and falsity. A sentence as such does not contain all the information necessary to build a proposition: Some must be supplied by the context. The process by which this is done, in many computational approaches at least, involves something that looks like reasoning, but with hypotheses rather than established facts (Alshawi, 1992). (Some of the inferences do involve facts, too, of course). The general term for the types of reasoning involved in this aspect of computational linguistics is *contextual reasoning*. The application of idiom rules should be thought of as simply another instance of this kind of reasoning, in which questions about the truth of the propositions involved is suspended. (There might be a connection here with the "methodological solipsism" of Fodor, 1981). The reasoning simply is cranked out on a purely syntactic basis and it is not until those wheels have finished turning that the results are evaluated for truth.

On the assumption that this picture is unproblematic, then the status of our idiom rules also becomes unproblematic: They just operate to give an extra set of truth conditions to sentences interpretable as idioms. For some idiomatic sentences, the usual mechanism for assigning truth conditions in fact will fail: For example, "John has a large sake" should receive no truth conditions, because *sake* is meaningless outside of the idiom it usually occurs in.

FALSE POSITIVES

This mechanism for the interpretation and recognition of idioms enables us to do without special senses for the words involved in an idiom. The idiom rules can be defined in terms of the constants representing the literal meanings of the words present. This avoids the technical problems raised earlier, as well as the potential combinatorial explosion of literal-idiom hybrids caused by the partial function approach. All the words, or rather, their translations into logical constants, must be present, and they must combine in an appropriate way to produce a particular logical form for the idiom to be recognized. (Notice that this presupposes a fairly fine-grained view of the relation between lexical items and logical constants: that the word sense is pretty much the primitive element of meaning, no further decomposition into "semantic atoms" or suchlike being required. This view is argued for in some detail in Pulman, 1983).

However, using literal senses of words to trigger the recognition of idioms brings some potential problems. We might find some idioms accidentally, through the use of other lexical items connected to those triggering the idiom rules via meaning postulates. Take the following example:

67. We watched the chandelier being switched on.

This might be taken to entail:

68. We saw the light.

This particular example has an idiomatic reading. But the former does not have the idiomatic meaning associated with the latter.

In some cases, though, we can find "inferred idioms," as in the following example:

69. John put the tabby among the pigeons.

Then, assume the following is given:

70. $\forall$x. tabby (x) $\rightarrow$ cat (x).

This in turn will entail:

71. John put the cat among the pigeons.

Then, the idiomatic quasi-inference will go through.

One in fact does hear circumlocutionary versions of common idioms for humorous effect ("then the manure really entered the ventilation system"), and it is possible, given an appropriate setting, to interpret "put the tabby among the pigeons" along similar lines. Nevertheless, there is often a conscious piece of reasoning to do in order to arrive at these interpretations, with associated implicatures generated. I take it that the normal process of interpreting idioms does not involve such conscious reasoning, and, accordingly, that we have to solve the problem of "false positives."

It may be that in deriving idiomatic interpretations from a level of meaning representation at which the original lexical items are no longer present, we have gone too far. Nevertheless, we do not want to make too much depend on actual lexical items, because of the fact that we discussed earlier: Some idioms can allow any of a range of semantically similar words to occur in a particular position.

We could retain some connection between the actual lexical items used and the idiom rules by developing some kind of indexing scheme for idiom rules based on the occurrence of particular lexical items in the input sentence. Thus, any sentence mentioning, say, *cats* and *bags* might cause the relevant inference rule to be triggered. On sentences like the following, the rule would be invoked, but would not succeed:

72. The cat meowed as her owner emptied the fish out of her shopping bag.

On sentences like this one, however, the idiom rule would not be invoked, even though the sentence might entail a cat being out of a bag:

73. The tabby emerged from the sack with a mouthful of salmon.

When a sentence is processed, only those idiom rules suggested by the indexing mechanism are used in trying to find extra idiomatic readings. The fact that some idioms display some lexical variation then can be accommodated, because presumably the varying item is not crucial for the presence of the idiom.

With a scheme like this, the circumlocutionary idioms mentioned earlier should be recognized only when this mechanism has been overridden: Their self-conscious nature suggests that a fair degree of problem solving may be involved in recognizing them. One other benefit of a mechanism for lexical indexing is that it would enable us to account for the possibility of recognizing incomplete idioms. If a particular sentence makes no literal sense, but the lexical items present narrow down the range of possible idioms to a manageable number, then the retrieval of the appropriate idiomatic meaning still will be possible. If recognition was only by the idiom rules, then nothing less than the complete idiom would suffice for its successful recognition.

Here then is a simple scheme for lexical indexing. We associate an identifier with each distinct idiom rule, and for each such identifier we decide on some set of lexical items (in their morphological base form) that we take as a cue for the presence of that idiom:

$$\{skate,on,thin,ice\} = idiom\_31$$
$$\{break,the,ice\} = idiom\_256$$
$$\{cat,out,of,bag\} = idiom\_45$$
$$\{cat,among,pigeons\} = idiom\_42$$
$$etc.$$

Now, when in the process of working out the interpretations for a sentence, we take the set of lexical items in it, **L,** and for each of the aforementioned sets of words, **S,** if **S** is a subset of **L** then the idiom may be present. Notice that this does not tell us whether the idiom is present: For that, we have to go though all the mechanisms outlined earlier. All that this indexing does is to tell us which idiom rules in principle can apply to this sentence: Whether they actually do or not will depend on the logical form that the sentence has. For example:

74. John was skating on thin ice. *(idiom possible and rule fires)*
75. They wanted to skate but the ice was too thin. *(idiom possible but rule fails)*
76. The ice was thin. *(idiom not possible)*

In the case where we have an idiom fragment, then, in the absence of any satisfactory literal meaning we can perform the aforementioned indexing test using "intersection" rather than "subset" to generate candidate idiom rules. This will tell us that if there is no other interpretation for Example 76, the idiomatic one is a possibility, although some more powerful mechanism than the ones we have developed will be necessary to produce it.

SYNTACTIC VARIATION

A further consequence of the quasi-inferential treatment of idioms is that there can be no stated connection between an idiom and the various syntactic configurations that it can or cannot appear in, at least on the assumption that syntactic properties are not encoded into logical form and thus available for inference. Thus any syntactic variant that produces the same logical form should be capable of giving rise to an idiomatic inference. This is apparently not so, at least for some examples. However, I think it is possible to explain away this apparent problem for our account for this along lines suggested partly by Newmeyer (1972) and partly by Gazdar et al. (1985).

Consider what the pragmatic function of syntactic variation is. Presumably a passive, or a clefted, or a topicalized form of a sentence is chosen, not because a proposition expressed in this way cannot be expressed any other way, but because the demands of the discourse context are such that the information contained in the proposition must be presented in a certain way. At a simple level, this much can be demonstrated by the relative oddity of discourses like the following:

77. Speaker 1: Who hit Bill?
78. Speaker 2: It was Bill who was hit by John.

Although Speaker 2 expresses a proposition that gives an answer to Speaker 1's question, he does it in an odd way. The emphasis is on Bill, whereas the emphasis of the question was on whoever it was that hit Bill. On the assumption, then, that syntactic forms are going to sound odd if there is no context in which the way they present their information is plausible, we can explain the oddity of many syntactic forms of idioms as follows: For a syntactic form to be appropriate, there must be a context in which it makes sense to focus or contrast the discourse entity that the construction does focus or contrast. In the case where there is no such discourse entity, oddity will result. Thus, roughly speaking, the following sounds odd because it focuses on *the bucket:*

79. *The bucket was kicked by John.

But *the bucket* does not correspond to any discourse entity, and thus there is no context in which this will be appropriate. In other words, as suggested in a different framework by Newmeyer (1972), the sentence sounds odd for much the same reason that the following sounds odd:

80. *John was died.

However, in an idiom like *spill the beans,* it is possible to associate (idiomatic) discourse entities with the components of the idiom:

81. $\forall x, y.$ beans (y) $\wedge$ spill(x,y) $\rightarrow$ $\exists i, a.$ information(i) & reveal (a, i).

Thus it is possible to find a context in which it makes sense to focus one or the other:

82. The beans were spilled.

This sounds fine, roughly because the following sounds fine:

83. The information was revealed.

Even cases where in isolation a syntactic variant sounds peculiar, the idiomatic meaning can be rescued by providing a context in which it makes sense to emphasize the discourse entity that is being focused. Consider the idiom *drop a brick,* meaning "make a stupid or embarrassing mistake." It is very difficult to recover the idiomatic interpretation from a single sentence like:

84. What John dropped was a brick.

This is because the pseudocleft construction is emphasizing the discourse entity referred to by *brick* and in a null context no such entity is available. But in contexts where the pragmatic function of the pseudocleft makes sense, the idiomatic interpretation is perfectly accessible.

We need a context in which it makes sense to give extra emphasis to an idiomatic brick that has been dropped. Fortunately there is an idiom that gives us the right contrast: *To drop a bombshell* means to reveal some surprising or shocking information. So we can now contrive a context in which two idiomatic things are dropped:

> When he revealed the company finances,
> John thought he'd dropped a bombshell,
> but what he'd really dropped was a brick.

I find this occurrence of the pseudocleft perfectly natural with the idiomatic meaning, in contrast to the earlier uncontextualized one.

It thus seems legitimate to regard all idioms as being able in principle to occur in any syntactic configuration, and therefore we can put the responsibility for explaining why some variations sound better than others on to some future theory of information structuring in relation to syntax.

ACKNOWLEDGMENTS

This chapter arose from a talk given to a conference on figurative uses of language organized by Bar-Ilan University, Israel, in 1986. I am grateful to the British Council for funding my trip there, to Ellen Spolsky for making it possible, and to the participants at the conference itself for their good-humored guidance around a culturally (in several senses) unknown landscape. Subsequent versions of the article were given to the Linguistics Association of Great Britain, in Edinburgh, and in talks to the Moral Sciences Club of the University of Cambridge, and to linguistics departments in Essex, Manchester (UMIST), and Sussex. I am grateful to participants on all these occasions for their comments, and in particular to Hiyan Alshawi, Robin Cooper, Gerald Gazdar, Malka Rappoport, Susan Rothstein, and Graham Russell.

REFERENCES

Abeille, A. (1990). Lexical and syntactic rules in a tree adjoining grammar. In *Proceedings of 28th annual meeting, Association for Computational Linguistics* (pp. 292–298). Pittsburgh: ACL.

Alshawi, H. (1992). *The core language engine*. Cambridge, MA: MIT Press.

Bresnan, J. (1982). The passive in lexical theory. In J. Bresnan (Ed.), *The mental representation of grammatical relations* (pp. 40–65). Cambridge, MA: MIT Press.

Chomsky, N. (1980). *Rules and representations*. Oxford, England: Basil Blackwell.

Fodor, J. A. (1981). *Representations: Philosophical essays on the foundations of cognitive science*. Sussex, England: Harvester.

Fraser, B. (1970). Idioms within a transformational grammar *Foundations of Language, 6*, 22–42.

Gazdar, G., Klein, E., Pullum, G. K., & Sag, I. (1985). *Generalised phrase structure grammar*. Oxford, England: Basil Blackwell.

Montague, R. (1974). *Formal philosophy*. New Haven, CT: Yale University Press.

Newmeyer, F. (1972). *The insertion of idioms*. In P. M. Pergateau, J. N. Levi, & C. Phares (Eds.), (pp. 282–295). Papers from the 8th regional meeting. Chicago Linguistics Society, Chicago, IL.

Pulman, S. G. (1983). *Word meaning and belief*. London: Croom Helm, and Norwood, NJ: Ablex.

Wasow, T., Sag, I., & Nunberg, G. (1982). Idioms: An interim report. In *Preprints of the plenary session papers, XIIIth International Congress of Linguists* (pp. 87–96). Tokyo: CIPL.

12 The Determiner in English Idioms

Christiane Fellbaum
Princeton University

Idioms have been the subject of investigation by linguists and psychologists for a number of years. Both groups have been concerned largely with the representation and status of idioms in the lexicon, that is, with the question as to whether idioms are stored, accessed, and subject to grammatical rules in the same way as single lexical items. Whereas the experiments of psychologists by and large have investigated how speakers process nonliteral language, linguists generally have tried to determine the status of idioms in the lexicon by comparing their syntactic behavior with that of single-word lexical items. The central question is whether or not idioms can be shown to have a meaningful internal structure, that is, whether or not they are decomposable into individual chunks or constituents that are semantically nonvacuous (Nunberg, 1978; Pulman, 1986; Wasow, Sag, & Nunberg, 1983; and many others).

Contrary to earlier findings, the general consensus among researchers in the field now is that many idioms are compositional. These idioms are distinguished from noncompositional ones where the meanings of the individual lexical components are opaque, that is, where such components cannot be assigned either literal or figurative interpretations that contribute to the meaning of the entire idiom. Examples of noncompositional idioms are *trip the light fantastic* and *kick the bucket,* which are unanalyzable except as wholes, and thus function semantically as a single word. (Like compositional idioms, these strings are subject to certain low-level syntactic operations such as subject-verb agreement.)

By contrast, speakers treat compositional idioms as analyzable strings. Evidence for this comes largely from the syntactic operations that idioms tolerate compared with nonfigurative strings; for example, passivization commonly has been taken as a test for the semantic transparency of nouns in idioms. Idioms vary with respect to the degree of syntactic and lexical frozenness, and their flexibility appears to be straightforwardly correlated with their compositionality (Gibbs & Nayak, 1989; Gibbs, Nayak, Bolton, & Keppel, 1989; Newmeyer, 1974; Wasow et al., 1983); Nunberg's (1978) important distinction between normally and abnormally decomposable idioms accounts for some of the syntactic and semantic behavior of many idioms.

Our work follows this line of investigation by showing how the nature of the determiner points to the semantic status of noun phrases (NPs) in many idioms, which in turn predicts the range of possible determiner variations.

The syntactic operations (Fraser, 1970; Ruwet, 1973; and others) and lexical substitutions (Gibbs & Nayak, 1989; Gibbs et al., 1989; and others) that have served to test the robustness of the idiom's figurative meaning always have involved content words, usually nouns and verbs. No attention has been paid to the status of the determiner apart from the noun that it precedes in assessing the syntactic or lexical frozenness of idioms. Although it is undoubtedly the content words that make an idiom a special kind of lexical unit, we argue that, in many cases, the determiner carries a considerable semantic load; its shape in a given idiom contributes to the interpretation of the noun and hence to the particular quality of figurative language. Like nouns and verbs, determiners are polysemous in that a given determiner can precede nouns with different kinds of semantic status.

Determiners behave like nouns and verbs in that some idioms tolerate their alterations or substitutions whereas others do not. Although a strong correlation can be shown to exist, the flexibility of the determiner in an idiom is not necessarily a predictor of the idiom's overall syntactic or semantic flexibility; for example, an idiom whose indefinite determiner can be exchanged for a quantifier does not necessarily passivize.

Flexibility of the determiner is found only in compositional idioms, where it is largely an indicator of the noun's referential status. In the large class of noncompositional, unanalyzable idioms like *trip the light fantastic* and *buy the farm,* the determiner is invariable. Moreover, the forms of the determiners here cannot be explained in terms of the rules for literal language that appear to operate in many of the compositional idioms. However, we suggest that the definite article that is found in most of these strings has a particular function relating to the figurative nature of these strings.

PROPERTIES OF THE DETERMINER
IN IDIOMS

Sentences 1–3 show that, like in literal language, different kinds of determiners and nondescriptive adjectives occur with the NPs in verb phrase (VP) idioms (this study will be limited to VP idioms of the form [V][NP][PP], where V = verb and PP = prepositional phrase):

1. Torture can make you *spill the beans*. (definite)
2. Mary will *take a shot* at the bar exam. (indefinite)
3. The minister resigned in order to *save face*. (zero)

I refer to the expressions in Sentences 1–3 as idioms in their *dictionary forms,* and I assume that these citation forms correspond to the context-neutral representations in which idioms are stored in the mental lexicon of speakers. The determiners that occur in the dictionary forms of idioms constitute only a subset of the determiners available in literal language. For example, it is hard to find idioms whose VP-internal nouns in their dictionary forms are preceded by general quantifiers such as *every* and *many,* or by a negative determiner. Similarly, no demonstrative or specificity-inducing adjectives seem to occur in idioms listed in dictionaries. However, as Sentences 4–7 show, idioms can be used with such determiners and adjectives without a resultant loss in the figurative reading:

4. Mary had several shots at the exam, but always failed.
5. Mike has no bone to pick with Joe.
6. I knew all the chairmen of the committees, but I thought it too risky to pull those strings.
7. John had a specific axe to grind with Bob.

The fact that idioms can preserve their figurative meaning when the determiner is changed contradicts the assumption that they are represented as single lexical items in the mental lexicon of native speakers (Bobrow & Bell, 1973; Swinney & Cutler, 1979; and others). The determiner changes in Sentences 4–7 occur inside the idiom, showing that its individual constituents are subject to syntactic and and semantic operations. This supports the now common contention that idioms do not differ in many ways from "literal" strings. The data in Sentences 4–7 confirm the observations made by a number of researchers that many other syntactic and semantic alterations do not result necessarily in the loss of the figurative reading of idioms. More important, because the determiner, as well the adjectives in Sentences 6 and 7, reflect the referential status of the nouns, the possible changes give important clues to the nouns' semantics.

The substitution of a quantifier in Sentence 4 and a negative in Sentence 5 constitute semantic alterations, in that they change the meanings or truth values of the sentences. These changes are analogous to Gibbs et al.'s (1989) substitution of semantically related nouns and verbs in VP idioms and Nunberg's (1978) insertion of descriptive adjectives. The specificity-inducing adjective in Sentence

7 distinguishes this noun from, for example, *shot* in the idiom *have a shot at,* which does not tolerate the presence of *specific*. This indicates that the role of *axe* and *shot* within the VPs somehow must differ, despite their identical dictionary forms.

The use of a demonstrative adjective, as in Sentence 6, shows that the idiom can be altered in accordance with *pragmatic* discourse requirements, that is, that the lexical material inside the VP is discourse sensitive: The use of the demonstrative is licensed by the reference to the preceding material.[1]

However, although there is considerable flexibility in the determiners of idioms, this flexibility is not unconstrained. Like other lexical items or strings, idioms can be manipulated syntactically and semantically only in accordance with speakers' grammatical competence and the pragmatic conditions in a given discourse. These rules of language use constrain the possible grammatical configurations of both literal and figurative language. But in addition to the constraints that apply to idioms as grammatical strings there are constraints whose violations, although not affecting a sentence's grammaticality, will result in the loss of the phrase's figurative meaning. Thus, Wasow et al. (1983) pointed out that speakers know whether a given VP idiom can or cannot be passivized, without ever having been exposed to the relevant data. Furthermore, asyntactic idioms like *kiss ass* should not be available for the rules governing literal language because they do not match the input strings for those rules; yet, their NPs can be modified. This knowledge, too, is part of a speaker's linguistic knowledge.

If idioms were represented in speaker's lexicons as individual items, both syntactic idioms and such asyntactic strings like *kiss ass* and *kiss a lot of ass* would have to be acquired and stored separately. However, it seems more plausible that the NP has its own semantic representation, which determines, according to the same rules as in literal language, which changes are tolerated by the NP and which ones result in a loss of the figurative meaning. We show that the semantics of many idiom NPs decide the range of permissible determiners.

Although most NPs in literal language are compatible with several different determiners (subject to the semantics of the noun and discourse-pragmatic factors), the determiner in many idiom NPs can be varied to a lesser extent; speakers know that whereas the VPs in Sentences 4–7 preserve the idiomatic reading, the sentences that follow are to be interpreted either literally or as idiosyncratic variations by a humorous speaker:

8. Mary had shots at the exam but always failed.
9. I thought it too risky to pull the strings.

---

[1]We are not concerned here with NP-internal syntactic rules like the one requiring agreement of the possessive adjective with the subject applying in the many body-part idioms like *put one's foot down: John finally put his foot down.*

10. John spilled no beans.
11. Max had the axe to grind with Bob.

In other idioms, the determiner tolerates no alternation; thus, Sentence 13 does not receive the figurative interpretation of Sentence 12:

12. You will have to bite the bullet.
13. You will have to bite {a/no/every} bullet.

The nonarbitrariness of the determiner indicates that it is an important part of the idiom. Its behavior with respect to insertion, deletion, and substitutability resembles that of the content word constituents of most idioms. We examine the systematic constraints on the semantic, syntactic, and pragmatic uses of determiners in idioms. We see that, in many idioms, the nature of the determiner follows from the semantics of the NP, and that its behavior can be accounted for along the same principles that hold for NPs in the literal language.

THE LEXICAL REPRESENTATION
AND VARIABILITY OF IDIOMS

The lexicon of a language can be thought of as a mapping of meanings, or concepts, and words, which are the lexicalized realizations of these concepts (Saussure's signifiés and significants, respectively). We refer to words that are linked with a meaning in this way as "denoting." NPs in idioms, when they are denoting, are just like words receiving a literal interpretation in that they are linked to certain specific meanings. These meanings may or may not be expressible by other, nonfigurative nouns. For example, the sense of *ice* in the idiom *break the ice* cannot be referred to easily by a single English noun; only the word *ice* lexicalizes the relevant concept including *tension, shyness, stiffness, uneasiness in a group.*

Denoting nouns in idioms resemble conventional metaphors, which are nouns used figuratively independent of a certain circumscribed idiomatic context. Both metaphors and denoting nouns occurring in idioms are represented multiply in the mental lexicon; that is, they are polysemous. Thus, the noun *bean(s)* in the context of the VP idiom *spill the beans* is associated with roughly the same meaning as the words *secret* and *(confidential) information; bacon* in *bring home the bacon* is interpreted in the same way as *financial support, earnings, income.* The difference between the sense of *beans* that is linked to the meaning *legume* or *vegetable* and the sense of *beans* that is linked to the meaning *secret* is that the latter interpretation is generally available only in the context of the VP idiom *spill the beans,* whereas the former can occur in many more contexts that are less constrained. Standard dictionaries, such as *Collins,* reflect this by including in the entries for *spill* and *bean,* besides their nonfigurative meanings, the idiomatic phrase as a whole.

Another way to look at the lexicon is to think of the word form *bean* as associated with (at least) two different concepts or meanings, one being "legume," the other, roughly, "secret."

Many meanings are associated with more than one word, giving rise to the familiar phenomenon of synonymity. Although in one of its senses, the word *beans* is a close synonym of *legume,* in its other sense it is a synonym of *secret.* In the literal language, synonyms may be substituted more or less freely for each other without a resulting change in the meaning or truth value of the phrase or sentence. In idioms, however, substituting synonyms of either the literal or the figurative meaning often results in the phrase or sentence receiving a literal interpretation only. Thus, Sentence 14 is very likely to be interpreted literally, and Sentence 15 is interpretable only as a speech error or a pun:

14. He spilled the legumes.
15. He spilled the secret.

Some idioms have slightly varying dictionary forms. Thus, Boatner, Gates, and Makkai (1975) list both *button one's lips* and *zip one's lips;* here, two closely related, though non synonymous verbs, can appear in the same idiom. But we do not find substitutions of other, similarly related verbs such as *tie/clip/knot/velcro one's lips.*

Gibbs et al. (1989) replaced verbs and nouns in idioms with semantically similar words and asked subjects to rate the meaning similarity between the altered phrases and the original idioms. They found that subjects judged many idioms with lexical substitutions such as *burst the question* to be semantically close to their canonical forms; in this case, *pop the question.* In general, Gibbs et al. found that subjects rated lexical alterations in semantically normally decomposable idioms less disruptive to the idioms' meaning than in abnormally decomposable and nondecomposable idioms. Thus, subjects stated that they found the similarity between phrases like *punt the bucket* and *kick the bucket* to be weaker than between the two phrases mentioned previously. Gibbs et al. concludes that the relative lack of meaning disruption is due to the fact that some synonyms preserve the metaphorical relation between an idiom's individual component and its real-world referent. But their experiments did not involve speaker's comprehension of variant idioms, and thus they cannot be regarded as evidence that strings like *burst the question, pop the request,* and *burst the request* are indeed all interpreted as *propose marriage.* Therefore, the results do not show that the particular sense of the (polysemous) word *pop,* which is related to *ask,* also is represented in the lexicon by the word *burst.*

Glucksberg, McClone, and Cacciari (1991) cite a few real-life utterances such as *Convicted minimalist spills bean* and *eat the golden goose*. They tested speaker's comprehension of altered idioms, noting that although the canonical forms of idioms are processed fastest, the comprehension of altered idioms takes no more time than the comprehension of literal strings. Glucksberg et al. conclude that variant idioms in fact are processed in the same way as nonfigurative speech, because the constituents of idioms, through frequent use, often have come to be associated with their appropriate meanings, for which ordinary synonyms then can be substituted via standard linguistic processing.

Although this hypothesis seems quite plausible and accounts for the processing times that Glucksberg et al. (1991) measured, it does not address the question as to why a literal word often can be substituted for an idiom constituent whereas the idiom constituent is not necessarily free to be used outside the idiomatic phrase. Thus, although speakers may understand the phrase *He spilled the secret(s)*, it is not clear that they will understand a phrase like *He told me some beans about her*. In other words, the close association of the idiomatic and the literal word with one given concept does not necessarily permit a two-way exchange of these two words expressing that concept. This indicates that there is a difference between denoting nouns in idioms and conventional, free metaphors. A free metaphor such as *angel*, meaning roughly *kind person*, can occur outside of specific idiomatic phrases; it has the same distribution as the corresponding literal NP *kind person*. But nouns like *beans* and *ice* cannot be substituted in all contexts for *secret(s)* and *tension/shyness*. The same can be said for idiomatic uses of verbs, which often receive the intended meaning only in the presence of a specific NP. Thus, the sense of *drop* corresponding to *write* is available only in the context of *a line* but not in sentences like *She dropped her grandparents/her term paper/beautiful French/legibly/all afternoon*.

Nevertheless, the results of Gibbs et al. (1989) and Glucksberg et al. (1991) show that the canonical forms of idioms are subject to considerable morphological and lexical variation, and the question arises as to how such variations are both generated and constrained.

Our knowledge of words and idioms, that is, our lexical knowledge, is part of our language *competence*. But much of our linguistic behavior must be explained in terms of *performance*, that is, the way language is used in actual communication (this distinction is due to Chomsky, 1956, and was also drawn by Saussure, who contrasted *langue* and *parole*). Competence guides our intuitions and judgments about distinguishing between grammatical, well-formed utterances, and ungrammatical or ill-formed ones. By contrast, our language performance accounts for both the production and the successful processing of grammatical errors, unfinished sentences, pronunciation mistakes, and puns.

Idioms are subject to word plays and puns that result in alterations of their canonical forms just as much as other strings. Idiosyncratic variations are created by speakers to fit certain discourse-specific contexts. A priori there is no limit to the changes one could make to an idiom and still expect one's interlocutors to process it. Given the appropriate context, it does not seem unreasonable to assume that even an utterance like *Under great pressure, he finally disgorged the legumes* can be understood by a listener who is aware of the speaker's humorous intent.

An analysis of the lexical, morphological, and syntactic flexibility of idioms, and the possible systematic constraints on this flexibility would represent a very considerable undertaking. In the absence of such a study, this chapter limits itself to a discussion of the canonical forms of idioms and the alterations that are possible in the absence of specific contexts. In the literature on idioms, authors commonly make judgments about which changes preserve the figurative meaning of idioms and which ones do not, and readers generally accept these judgments. For example, people do seem to agree that *have a certain axe to grind* is a permissible alteration of the idiom *have an axe to grind,* and they also agree that *have the axe to grind* does not preserve the intended idiomatic sense. It is important to note that such judgments are made in the absence of any context on the basis of our language competence only. These judgments, and speakers' agreements about them, clearly set off the competence-ruled data that are the subject of this study from the potentially open class of possible variations, including those studied by Gibbs et al. (1989) and Glucksberg et al. (1991). We take the fact that speakers uniformly agree about the canonical forms of idioms and the limits on their context-free variations as a license to limit our study and to disregard the idioms' many possible discourse-conditioned alternations.

The variations in VP idioms that are examined here are limited to the determiner. These determiner changes are often acceptable in context-free uses of the idiom, much like subject-verb agreement or changes in the tense of the verb. Other variants of the determiner, although not created for humorous purposes, are discourse-conditioned and show the speaker's analysis of the NPs as denoting entities. We see that the determiners of NPs in many idioms can be analyzed along the rules of literal language, and that the nature of the determiner frequently reveals the metaphoric status of the nouns.

THE REFERENTIAL STATUS OF NPs
IN IDIOMS

Unlike denoting nouns like *beans* in the expression *spill the beans,* nouns like *dust* and *bucket* in *bite the dust* and *kick the bucket* are not mapped onto a meaning in the lexicon and are therefore semantically empty. Their literal interpretations (i.e., *pail* and *fine dirt particles,* respectively) are not available here, nor can the nouns as separate parts of the idioms receive a metaphoric interpretation (such as *death*) that is related to the meaning of the idiom as a semantic unit. Each of these noncompositional VP idioms as a whole is linked to the meaning of the intransitive verb *die*. We call NPs like *bucket* and *dust* in these idioms "nondenoting."

The distinction between denoting and nondenoting NPs in figurative speech is frequently made on a purely intuitive basis. Although it does seem intuitively obvious that *dust* in *bite the dust* receives no independent figurative meaning outside the VP, and although it seems similarly intuitively obvious that *hatchet* in *bury the hatchet* has some independent figurative meaning, these intuitions are hard to back up, because the use of the noun with the particular figurative sense is usually limited to a single specific occurrence.[2]

Another kind of evidence for the denoting or vacuous nature of an idiom NP often has come from the syntactic shape of the idiom: When the idiom consists of a verb plus a direct object, and its literal equivalent is an intransitive verb, then the fact that the idioms NP cannot be matched onto a literal NP is thought to indicate the nonreferring status of the former: There is simply no way to "translate" the noun. However, the nondenoting status of a NP is not linked necessarily to the lack of a NP in the literal equivalent of the idiom. Although *die* is undoubtedly the most felicitous, and most frequent, word for expressing the sense of *kick the bucket* or *bite the dust*, the same meaning also could be expressed by *cease all biological activity* (*Collins* dictionary). This VP structurally matches the idiomatic VPs, yet we do not interpret *bucket* or *dust* to stand for *biological activity* here. (This raises the thorny issue of how to determine the literal equivalent of an idiom, especially in less clear-cut cases than these.)[3] Consider also the expression *eat humble pie*, which is glossed in Boatner et al. (1975) as *accept insult or shame* or *admit your error*. Here, too, the idiom and its literal counterpart are structurally (syntactically) equivalent. Yet, *humble pie* seems to have no metaphorical relation to *insult*, *shame*, or *error*. Conversely, the noun in *hit the road* appears to be semantically interpretable (literally, in fact), but it does not seem to fit into the literal equivalent of this idiom (*leave*, *depart*).

The strongest support for the semantic status of idiom NPs has come from the syntactic behavior of idioms. Idioms whose nouns are presumed to be semantically empty, such as *kick the bucket* and *bite the dust*, turn out to be highly frozen syntactically; this is commonly taken as the reflex of the fact that the NPs

---

[2]There are very few cases of idiom constituents that preserve (part of) their figurative meaning in more than one context. An example might be *beans*, meaning *information*, in both *spill the beans* and *I don't know beans*. By contrast, *sack* has a completely different meaning in each of the idioms *hit the sack*, *get the sack*, and *leave someone holding the sack*. (But cf. Ruhl, 1989, who argues for monosemy across literal and figurative language.) Wasow et al. (1983) claimed that *strings* in *pull strings* is semantically sufficiently transparent to be used independently of *pull*; however, they were unclear on the constraints of such uses.

[3]Nunberg (1978) notes that *give up the ghost* can passivize, which he interpret as evidence that speakers assign an interpretation to *ghost*.

here have no referent. By contrast, idioms with denoting nouns tend to be available for syntactic movement operations such as passive, and tolerate the insertion of lexical material like adjectives. The flexibility of an NP in an idiom appears indeed to be tied to the referential status of the NP (Newmeyer, 1974; Nunberg, 1978; Wasow *et al.*, 1983; and others), although this correlation is not always straightforward.[4] We show that, similarly, the nature of the determiner in the dictionary form of the idiom and the determiner's alterability yield important clues to the referential status of the NP, as well as to its specificity, and its known, presupposed or inferred status.

IDIOMS WITH A DEFINITE DETERMINER

In literal language, the definite determiner is polysemous; that is, it can precede nouns with several different kinds of semantic status. With a denoting NP, the principal uses of the definite determiner in the literal language can be summed up as follows: (a) unique: *The sun rises in the east;* (b) institutional: *I am going to the post office/The radio broadcast the news of the demonstration;* (c) inferable from general knowledge, or pragmatically presupposed: *Ring the bell twice when you come for dinner/Attach this antenna to the television;* (d) inferable from the preceding discourse: *John told a joke. The punchline wasn't really funny;* (e) known from previous mention in the preceding discourse: *We went to see a play. . . . The play was terribly boring;* (f) definite, specific: *The biology textbook we used last year is bad.* The NPs in their definite, unique, inferable, and known uses all denote specific referents; "institutional" NPs have nonspecific referents. Most of these uses of the definite determiner also can be distinguished in VP idioms.[5]

The nouns referring to unique entities in the idioms that follow are not metaphors, but receive the same literal interpretation that they would be assigned outside the idioms. Just like in nonfigurative contexts, they are preceded by a definite determiner.

16. He promised her **the moon.**
17. The bank robber told the teller to reach for **the sky.**

[4]Wasow et al. (1983) observe that whether or not idiom NPs can pronominalize indicates their metaphorical status: "We thought tabs were being kept on us, but they weren't." But note that some apparently denoting NPs do not pronominalize so easily: "John and Sam finally buried the hatchet, and then Bob and Jane buried it." This indicates that pronominalization is not a sufficiently reliable indicator of a noun's status as a metaphor.

[5]Other nonspecific referents preceded by a definite article are generic NPs as in *The astrolabe is one of mankind's great inventions* and specific indefinites like *The person who guesses the right number will be an instant millionaire.* There is no evidence for such generic or specific indefinite referents in VP idioms.

The definite article here cannot be exchanged for an indefinite one, a negative, or a quantifier; this confirms the literal interpretation of these nouns:

18. He promised her {a/no/every} moon.
19. The bank robber told the teller to reach for {a/no/each} sky.

These nouns are like proper names and refer to specific individual entities. The reason that unique entities are referred to literally in idioms may be the following: The literal equivalent of a noun in most idioms is somewhat vague and admits of several semantically similar interpretations. Thus, *axe* in *have an axe to grind* may refer to *a grievance* or *an ulterior motive;* the exact meaning is not important, because the meaning of the idiom as a whole is not dependent on such a fairly subtle difference. However, the meaning of an idiom like that in Sentence 16 depends crucially on the uniqueness of the noun's referents, and with unique referents, such vagueness of interpretation is not possible. A nonliteral noun with a unique referent would be difficult to interpret, because the word-meaning relation in an idiom tends to be valid only for the one particular context. But note that conventional metaphors, whose exact meaning is less vague than that of idiom NPs, can occur in idioms as well: *Heaven(s)* commonly stands for *sky* in many contexts, and also occurs in the idiom *go to heaven; the (great) maker,* a conventional metaphor for *God,* also has this meaning in the idiom *meet one's maker.*

Note the use of the indefinite article in accordance with the rules of literal language in *He only goes fishing once in a blue moon:* Blue moons, a natural phenomenon, are rare, but not unique.

The use of the definite article in such nonspecific NPs as *the post office, the supermarket,* and *the TV* could be called *institutional* (somewhat differently from the use of that term in Quirk, Greenbaum, and Svartvik, 1985). It also can be found with NPs in some VP idioms, which receive this institutional interpretation:

20. This court ruling will {turn/set/put} **the clock** back.
21. In this house, the wife wears **the** {**pants/trousers**}.
22. John's wife is the one who brings home **the bacon.**
23. After dinner, he decided to hit **the road.**

The clock in Sentence 20 refers to *progress; the pants/trousers* in Sentence 21 stands for *(traditionally male) authority* or *power,* and *the bacon* in Sentence 22 means *financial support.* These senses are institutional in that their referents are understood and known without having been mentioned previously, similar to *the post office* in a (nonidiomatic) sentence like *I went to the post office this morning.*

The road in Sentence 23 is not a metaphor, but is interpreted literally in a way similar to *post office*.

When the definite article is exchanged for another kind of determiner, the referent of the NP no longer receives the institutional interpretation. This is the case for both literal and figurative NPs:

24. I went to {a/each} post office this morning.
25. This ruling will set (all) clocks back.
26. In this house, the wife wears {trousers/pants}.
27. John's wife brings home some bacon.
28. After dinner he decided to hit that road behind our yard.

A somewhat similar case is presented by the *pragmatically presupposed* referents in the following idioms:

29. When John heard the news, he hit **the {roof/ceiling}**.
30. Mary went through **the {roof/ceiling}** when her rent was raised.
31. He pulled **the plug** on her activities.

The definite determiners here are justified because of the pragmatically presupposed, and thus "given," referents of the NPs, which resemble those in the (nonfigurative) strings listed next:

32. When you get home, put this in **the freezer.**
33. This antenna must be attached to **the TV.**

People commonly assume the existence of *a freezer, a roof, a ceiling, plugs,* and *a TV* in everybody's life. These quasi-generic, nonspecific referents therefore are presupposed and constitute a kind of world knowledge. They are referred to without having occurred prior in the given discourse. The substitution of another kind of determiner in both literal and figurative speech removes this reading.[6] Compare the following sentences:

34. When you get home, put this in {a/each/some} freezer.
35. When John heard the news, he hit a {roof/ceiling}.

Whereas such referents as *roof, ceiling,* and *freezer* can be interpreted independently of a given discourse situation or context, the definite determiner in some

---

[6]The common use of the "generic" possessive *your* illustrates the assumption or presupposition on the part of the speaker that his interlocutor possesses certain things: *Put this in your freezer./This antenna must be attached to your TV.*

idioms precedes a NP whose referent is inferable from the context or discourse in which it occurs:

36. At every party John manages to break the ice with his jokes.

The existence of *ice,* that is, tension and uneasiness between people in a social situation, is inferable from *party.*[7] The use of the definite article parallels that in a similar sentence like Sentence 37 that follows next, which receives a literal interpretation; just as *party* licenses the interpretation of *the ice, lecture* makes *the notes* inferable:

37. When John gives a lecture, he always forgets the notes.

An indefinite article in both kinds of sentences would result in an interpretation of the NP that is disjoint semantically from the preceding discourse. The interpretation of such indefinite NPs accounts for the oddness of Sentences 38 and, especially, 39:

38. At every party, John manages to break ice with his jokes.
39. When John gives a lecture, he always forgets notes.

The string *break the ice* receives an idiomatic reading naturally in a context where such tension is inferable; Sentence 40 that follows is odd, even though social uneasiness is not inconceivable even in a grocery store:

40. At every grocery store, John manages to break the ice.

Contrast this with the distribution of a noncompositional idiom like *kick the bucket,* which is not context-dependent and which can occur in virtually any context, because *the bucket* does not refer to an inferable entity:

41. John kicked the bucket at the {grocery store/birthday party}.

The inferences we make, such as interpreting *ice* on the context of *party,* are a consequence of the structure of our mental lexicon. There is strong evidence that semantically related words and concepts are stored together (Gross, Fischer, & Miller, 1989; Miller, 1969; and others). And in natural, coherent communication, related words tended to co-occur, (Charles & Miller, 1989; Fellbaum, 1992; Justeson & Katz, 1991) because we usually communicate about a given topic or a

---

[7]Evidence that *ice* stands for *tension, uneasiness* also comes from the fact that it is a mass noun, just like its literal counterpart, and cannot pluralize: *John breaks the ices at every party* is no longer distinctly odd.

range of related topics. Whereas the nonidiomatic word form *ice* with its associated meaning, *frozen water,* is semantically connected to, and occurs naturally in context with, such words as *cold, winter,* and so on, the same word *ice* that is associated with the meaning *tension, uneasiness,* is connected to words denoting such concepts as *party, strangers, shyness, social interaction,* and so forth.[8]

It follows that the entities that can be inferred from the context of a figurative noun are more likely to be semantically linked to that figurative meaning, rather than to the literal one. Thus, sequences like Sentences 42 and 43 receive either a literal reading or can be interpreted as humorous variants of the underlying idioms. In fact, the continuing discourses must be controlled carefully to permit such humorous readings; not every discourse that is compatible with the literal interpretation is possible with the humorous idiom variant: It is not clear what *the pieces* in Sentences 42 and *the fat* in Sentence 43 would refer to if *the ice* were interpreted figuratively as components of *tension, shyness* and *earnings,* respectively:

42. He broke the ice at the party. There were many small pieces left.
43. John's wife brings home the bacon. She always removes the fat.

Note also Pulman's (1986) discussion of the impossibility of substituting a specific hyponym for the noun in an idiom, as in the sentence **John put the tabby among the pigeons.*

NPs that are definite because they were previously mentioned are common in literal language (Clark & Haviland, 1977; Prince, 1981; and others), but not in idiomatic language. This is necessarily so because the figurative NP receives its interpretation only by virtue of its setting within the idiomatic VP; the NP, not being a conventional metaphor, cannot be repeated with its intended meaning in another context. Thus, whereas Sentence 44 is a plausible discourse, Sentence 45 is not:

44. We saw a play the other night. . . . **The play** was boring.
45. John has a bone to pick with Bob. . . . **The bone** is small.

We can distinguish yet another kind of idiom NP with a definite determiner that corresponds to a semantic class of NPs in literal language. These are NPs with a specific referent known to the discourse participants. The fact that the NP is interpreted figuratively makes no difference; this use of the article is the same as it would be with an NP that receives a literal reading, that is, with any

---

[8]In Glucksberg et al.'s (1991) model of idiom representation, both literal and idiomatic senses are available and permit speakers to create and interpret variants based on literal properties of the components. But the figurative and the literal NPs that denote a given concept are not equal in that they are not interchangeable in all contexts.

synonym of the known referent. For example, *the beans* in the VP *spill the beans* must refer to a secret whose existence and contents are known to the discourse participants. Thus, Sentence 46 is an acceptable sequence, whereas Sentence 47, where the contents of the secret is made known to the previously ignorant listeners, is odd:

46. John spilled the beans (about his girlfriend).
47. John spilled the beans that his girlfriend once worked for the CIA.

The noun *secret* can be both definite or indefinite; if it is definite, it obeys the same constraint as *the beans:*

48. John told {a/the} secret (about his girlfriend).
49. John told the secret that his girlfriend once worked for the CIA.

Thus, *the beans* in the idiom refers to a particular, known secret or confidential information. Note that because this noun refers to a specific secret it can be modified only by a quantifier that is semantically compatible:

50. ?John spilled {some/many/hundreds of} beans about Mary.
51. John spilled all the beans about Mary.

Note also that due to the specificity of *the beans,* only the VP-external negation is possible; the VP-internal negation in Sentence 53 is decidedly odd:

52. John didn't spill the beans about his girlfriend.
53. John spilled no beans about his girlfriend.

The idiom *bury the hatchet* can be analyzed in the same way: Sentence 54 can be uttered felicitously only when the discourse participants are aware of the existence and nature of the hostile relationship between John and Bob:

54. Yesterday, John and Bob buried the hatchet.

By contrast, Sentence 55 sounds odd, because the idiom is used without the referent of the NP having been established in the listeners' minds:

55. Yesterday, John and Bob buried the hatchet about property lines.

In the cases of idioms like *spill the beans* and *bury the hatchet,* we saw that the definite article is justified by the semantic nature of the noun's referent, and that the determiner choice follows the same rules as in literal language. In every case, the definite article is fixed and cannot be exchanged for an indefinite or a negative determiner, which would remove the presupposition of there existing a secret or a relation of enmity:

56. Bob and John buried {a/no} hatchet.
57. John spilled (no) beans about his girlfriend.

The NPs in these idioms often can be modified by a demonstrative adjective so long as the referents have been activated in the given discourse. Because the use of the demonstrative adjective is discourse-dependent, demonstratives do not occur in the dictionary forms of idioms. Note the following examples:

58. Bob and John finally buried that old hatchet.
59. We'll cross that bridge when we get to it.
60. I'll take THAT bull by the horn.
61. Those windmills not even he would tilt at. (Wasow et al.'s Sentence 13)

The demonstrative here always modifies a "given" NP; it seems that its deictic meaning is not available for NPs in idioms. The reason may be that the referents of NPs in idioms generally denote abstract referents lacking a physical extension, rather than concrete entities that can be pointed to.

The particular word used to denote the referent may be new in the discourse if the idiom is used for the first time, but the associated concepts *enmity, obstacle/difficulty,* and *imaginary opponent* must have been activated in the discourse; the nouns in the idioms function just like synonyms for other words expressing the same concepts. The use of the demonstrative here, then, is no different from that in literal language.

The remaining cases of definite determiners in VP idioms do not fall into any of the uses that have been distinguished for literal language. The nouns here do not have generic, unique, specific, known, or inferable referents and seem to violate the normal rules of determiner selection. Examples are *kick the bucket, bite the dust, chew the fat, shoot the breeze, give the slip to,* and many others. The nouns in these idioms cannot be interpreted either literally or metaphorically, and appear to be nondenoting. This fairly large class of idioms has been noted for both its semantic opacity and its syntactic frozenness with respect to passivization, insertion of lexical material, and so on. (Nunberg, 1978; and others). Gibbs et al. (1989) also show that these idioms do not tolerate lexical substitution without losing their figurative meaning. The emptiness of the noun that has been demonstrated by the syntactic inflexibility of the idiom is confirmed by the fact that the definite determiner is not accountable for by the usual principles. We call the use of the definite determiner here the *idiomatic use,* as it seems to be the one use of the definite article that has no correspondence in literal language.

The syntactic and lexical rigidity of these idioms that has been noted (Cutler, 1982; Fraser, 1970; Gibbs et al., 1989; Newmeyer, 1974; and others) also is found within the NP, where the definite determiner cannot be altered without a resultant loss of the figurative meaning:

62. Mary finally gave the slip to her boyfriend.
63. Mary finally gave that particular slip to her boyfriend.
64. Mary finally gave a certain slip to her boyfriend.
65. Mary finally gave {no/some/every} slip to her boyfriend.

We suggest that the idiomatic use of the definite determiner has a specific function, namely, to alert the hearer to the nonliteral nature of the expression. The hearer cannot assign any of the standard meanings of the definite article to the NPs in such idioms, and, by default, interprets it as idiomatic. Note that if the article preceding such nondenoting nouns were indefinite, the listener would interpret them according to the rules of literal language, that is, as entities newly introduced into the discourse for which a referent must be established, as in *John kicked a bucket.* We see that, in fact, there exist very few VP idioms where a nondenoting noun is preceded by an indefinite article.[9]

VP IDIOMS WITH INDEFINITE NPs

Dictionaries commonly classify VPs such as *take a nap* and *have a drink* as idioms. These constructions are characterized by the presence of a semantically empty "light" verb such as *do, have, make,* or *take,* and a singular indefinite NP; they denote actions that also can be referred to by verbs that are homophonous with the nouns in the VPs (*to nap* and *to drink,* in the examples just mentioned). Because these VP constructions are productive in English (but see Wierzbicka, 1982, for a principled account of the constraints on their productivity), and because of their semantic transparency, we do not consider them as true idioms. These VPs also exhibit a high degree of semantic and syntactic flexibility, similar to nonidiomatic strings. They could be classified as the kinds of pseudoidiomatic

[9]This hypothesis could be checked in an experiment monitoring the on-line processing of idioms like *bite the bullet* and *chew the fat* to determine whether hearers assign a nonliteral reading to the expression soon after they hear the definite article. Cacciari and Tabossi (1988) and Tabossi and Cacciari (1988) raise the question of determining the *key* in an idiom, that is, the particular constituent that alerts the hearer to the nonliteral meaning of an expression; in these idioms, the key may be not a content word, but the definite determiner. Another test might consist in presenting made-up idioms (or idioms literally translated from another language) with definite NPs to speakers and let them judge whether or not the string is to be interpreted literally, figuratively, or whether it is a nonsensical string. We would predict that even though the meaning of the made-up idiom is opaque to the hearers, they should be able to distinguish it as an idiom, rather than as a nonsensical string.

constructions (like *the X-er the Y-er*) studied by Fillmore, Kay, and O'Connor (1988).

Apart from these constructions, there are relatively few VP idioms whose dictionary form shows an indefinite NP. This makes sense given that the listener is likely to interpret an indefinite noun literally, assigning it a "new," nonspecific referent, rather than interpreting it idiomatically. There is no a priori reason why the listener would not follow the normal rules for interpreting an indefinite article, which precedes a noun that cannot be linked to an entity that is old in the discourse or otherwise presupposed. The listener is likely to assign a referent to the noun on the basis of its literal interpretation, unless both the larger context and the verb in the idiomatic VP are semantically sufficiently incongruous to indicate that a literal interpretation is not appropriate here.[10]

Even when the idiom is interpreted figuratively, the indefinite article maintains its function, and the referent of the NP is is assigned a new reading. This is the case, for example, in the sentence that follows:

66. Mike smelled a rat.

Consider also the following idioms:

67. Mike danced up a storm.
68. You are building castles in the air.
69. When she heard the news, she made a scene.

Here, too, the indefinite article is used in accordance with the rules of literary language, signaling that the noun is to be interpreted as new. The verbs *dance up, build* and *make* denote the "creation" of something new. Similarly, the indefinite article in idioms like *turn over a new leaf* and *sing a different tune* is used just like in literal language, with the adjectives *new* and *different* reenforcing the semantics of the NP.

The entities denoted by the objects of creation verbs do not exist prior to the action denoted by the verb. Therefore, they cannot be referred to by specific NPs, and do not tolerate the insertion of adjectives like *specific* or *certain:*

70. She was singing a specific new tune.
71. Mike danced up a certain storm.
72. She turned over a specific new leaf.

Sentence 74 shows that the same holds true for literal language. In Sentence 73, the verb is not one of creation, so the object noun may be specific. By contrast,

[10]The generic use of the indefinite article, as in *A lion won't attack when it has just fed,* does not occur in idioms.

in Sentence 75 the passive topicalizes the noun, which results in its referent having an (indefinite) specific reading:

73. Mary bought a certain rug.
74. Mary wove a (*certain) rug.
75. A certain rug was {woven/bought} by Mary.

Similarly, negation in these idioms must have scope over the entire VP. In literal language, negation of only the argument often implies a contrast, but suggests that an argument is presupposed; negation over the entire VP lacks such a presupposition, as Sentences 76–79 show (see Babby, 1980, for a discussion of contrastive negation). Although Sentence 80 may mean that Mary is weaving something other than a rug, Sentence 81 does not seem to imply that Mike danced up something other than a storm. There does not seem to be any presupposition in Sentences 81–83—that Mike danced up something, Sue made something, and Larry will turn over something—that is responsible for the non-idiomatic reading. The reason that these sentences are not meaningful is that the verbs do not receive an interpretation independent of their noun arguments:

76. Mary isn't weaving a rug.
77. Mike didn't dance up a storm after all.
78. Fortunately Sue did not make a scene.
79. Larry won't turn over a new leaf.
80. Mary is weaving no rug.
81. Mike danced up no storm after all.
82. Fortunately Sue made no scene.
83. Larry will turn over no new leaf.

It might be argued that the nouns in these idioms are semantically empty, which would account for their inflexibility. However, note that some of these these idioms can undergo passivization or topicalization, which has been taken to indicate that people assign an interpretation to the noun (Nunberg, 1978; and others):

84. A new leaf was turned over when the management changed.
85. What a scene she made when she heard the news!

The fact that the use of the indefinite article here conforms to that of literal language indicates that the NPs in these idioms function as metaphors and have a referent, but only in composition with the particular verbs. The relation between the figurative NP and its referent here is maintained by the use of the indefinite article.

Consider next the idiom in the following sentence:

86. John has a {bone/crow} to pick with Bob.

The NPs here have a referent whose meaning is rather close to *the hatchet in bury the hatchet;* namely, *a point of contention* or *quarrel.* But unlike in that idiom, the referents of *bone* and *crow* are new to the listener, as the indefinite article indicates. Indeed, the sequence in Sentence 87 is fine, and should be compared with the less felicitous Sentence 88:

87. John has a {bone/crow} to pick with Bob about property lines.
88. John and Bob buried the hatchet about property lines. .

The same analysis applies to the idiom *have an axe to grind.*

Although the referents of the NPs in these idioms are indefinite, that is, not known to the listener, they are specific. This can be seen by the fact that the idioms tolerate the insertion of adjectives that induce a specificity reading:

89. John has a {specific/certain/particular} bone to pick with Bob.
90. Mary had a {specific/certain/particular} axe to grind with her boss.

The NPs in these idioms can be negated and quantified:

91. John has {several/no} bones to pick with Bob.
92. Mary had {more than one/no} axe to grind with her boss.

In contrast to the idioms in Sentences 76–79, the negation and specificity data indicate that the interpretation of the nouns' referents here do not seem to depend closely on the verbs.

A small number of idioms have indefinite NPs without a referent:

93. It seems John has a chip on his shoulder.
94. We had a ball watching the comedians.

The NPs here cannot be negated or modified either by quantifiers or by adjectives that denote specificity:

95. We had no ball last night.
96. It seems John has several chips on his shoulder.
97. John seems to have a specific chip on his shoulder.

The question arises why these idioms do not have a definite determiner that prevents the hearer from assigning a new referent to the NP, such as in the idioms *kick the bucket* and *bite the dust*. To begin with, a survey of an idiom dictionary such as Boatner et al. (1975) shows up far more opaque idioms with definite NPs than with indefinite NPs, which make up a very small class. Second, although they are completely inflexible, such nouns as *ball* and *chip* seem semantically slightly more transparent than do *bucket* and *dust*. *Ball* could be glossed with *good time* (which, in the same construction, can be focused in passivization and thus apparently has a referent); *chip* seems to refer to *grudge*. Although there is no evidence that people analyze the nouns in this way, such an analysis is least plausible here, unlike in idioms of the *kick the bucket* type.

Some VP idioms have bare plurals, for example, *cut corners* and *keep tabs on*. These are plural indefinites, and like singular indefinites, they tend to be flexible if the noun has a referent. Thus, the *corners* in *cut corners* refer to *shortcuts*, and they can be negated or quantified:

98. He cuts {lots of/no} corners.

A much-discussed idiom VP is *pull strings/wires;* the relation between the surface NP and its meaning, *connections,* is particularly salient here. As has been observed (Wasow et al., 1983; and others), this idiom shows great syntactic flexibility, and the NP can be modified in any way compatible with its semantics:

99. Her mother pulled {many/no/these/certain} strings.

By contrast, *tabs* refers to *watch, guard,* and is not quantifiable:

100. *The FB kept many tabs on him.

Thus we see that the behavior of the indefinite determiners in idioms NPs parallels that in literal language.

BARE NOUNS

Many VP idioms contain a singular count noun with zero determiner, and, by the criteria of literal language, thus could be called "asyntactic" (Cruse, 1986, and others):

101. In this war, the generals {saved/lost} face.
102. They could not make head or tail of his story.
103. John {took/lost} heart when he heard the news.

One could argue that the nouns have become incorporated into the verbs (Baker, 1988), that is, that they form a syntactic unit with the verbs. The idioms are syntactically frozen and cannot undergo such movement operations as passivization. However, the NPs here seem to be metaphors that refer to a mass noun: *Face* is synonymous with *(personal) honor; head or tail* stands for *sense;* and *heart* has the sense of *courage.* Given these alternate, metaphoric senses of the nouns, idioms such as in Sentences 101–103 are no longer asyntactic; a singular mass noun standardly occurs with zero determiner. Thus, the asyntacticity arises only under the literal interpretation of the noun, when it is a count noun.

The nouns in such idioms can be preceded by determiners that are compatible with their semantics. For example, a quantifier can be inserted when the referent of the NP is quantifiable:

104. They couldn't make much head or tail of his story.
105. The teacher took ({little/no}) stock in the student's report.
106. The movement lost ({much/no}) ground in the '90's.
107. He had to kiss ({quite a bit of/his colleagues'}) ass to get the promotion.[11]

---

[11]The idiom *kiss ass* does not follow the usual pattern of idioms with body-part nouns: Expressions like *stab someone in the back, pat someone on the back,* and *hit someone in the face* display what is known as *possessor ascension* syntax, where the "possessor" NP is the direct argument of the verb and the "possessed" body part appears in a prepositional phrase (Fox, 1981; and others). In the literal language, but not in the idioms, an alternative syntax is possible:

1a. John kissed his daughter on the forehead.
1b. John kissed his daughter's forehead.
2a. John stabbed his best friend in the back.
2b. John stabbed his best friend's back.
3a. The news hit her in the face.
3b. The news hit her face.

It has been noted (Fox, 1981) that the possessor ascension syntax seems to express a greater degree of affectedness of the possessor. In body-part idioms, the possessor always is affected by the action, whereas the body-part noun usually does not receive a literal (and affected) interpretation: In sentence 2a, under the idiomatic reading, John's *best friend* is being acted upon, but *his back* is not. This may explain the obligatory possessor ascension syntax in the idioms; it would be evidence for Nunberg's (1978) claim that their syntax may be sensitive to fairly subtle semantic properties of the idioms. But *kiss ass,* when it occurs with a possessor, behaves differently; only the configuration with *ass* as the direct argument is idiomatic, whereas the possessor ascension version must be interpreted literally:

4a. John kissed his colleagues' ass.
4b. John kissed his colleagues on the ass.

Note also that the possessor does not have to have a surface form in this idiom, as sentence 107 shows. Unlike the body-part NPs in such idioms as *stab someone in the back* and *hit someone in the face, ass* in *kiss ass* is interpreted as a mass noun and therefore does not follow the canonical syntax of body-part language.

The nouns with zero determiner in the following idioms have no referent:

108. His opponent had to eat {humble pie/crow}.
109. The salesman started to talk turkey.

These highly frozen idioms resemble the class of idioms with definite determiners that includes *bite the dust* and *shoot the breeze,* and those with indefinite determiners like *have a ball.* Predictably, they tolerate no NP-internal modification whatsoever:

110. His opponent had to eat {some/no/a piece of} humble pie.
111. The salesman started to talk {a lot of/no} turkey.

CONCLUSION

An examination of the nouns in many VP idioms shows that their semantics are reflected in the determiners they are compatible with. The range of determiners is constrained by the same semantic and pragmatic principles as in literal language.

The definite determiner occurring in the dictionary forms of many idioms is inflexible when it modifies nouns that can be shown to have unique, institutional, or discourse-determined referents. When these referents have been activated in the discourse, demonstratives may be substituted—a pragmatic principle operative in literal language.

The indefinite article in the VP idioms we investigated also can be shown to follow from the nouns' semantics; it is used with new or specific indefinite referents. As predictable from the corresponding case in literal language, quantifiers or negative adjectives can be substituted.

The zero determiner occurs in apparently asyntactic idioms with count nouns; however, these nouns have figurative meanings corresponding to mass nouns, which are compatible with zero determiner. The interpretation of these nouns as mass nouns is further supported by their compatibility with certain quantifiers.

In sum, the analysis of the determiners in the kinds of VP idioms we examined supports a compositional of idioms, and, in particular, serves to test and strengthen intuitions about the referential status and the meaning of metaphoric nouns.

The class of idioms where these principles fail shows inflexibility not only with respect to the determiner but also with respect to lexical changes and syntactic operations such as passivization, indicating that the noun has no semantic content. We suggested a special, pragmatically based function for the definite determiner that is found in most of these noncompositional idioms.

ACKNOWLEDGMENTS

Preparation of this chapter was supported in part by contract N00014-86-K-0492 with the Office of Naval Research (ONR) and in part by a grant from the James S. McDonnell Foundation. The views and conclusions contained herein are those of the author and should not be represented as official policies of ONR, the McDonnell Foundation, or Princeton University. We thank Cristina Cacciari and Patrizia Tabossi for valuable comments, and members of the Cognitive Science Laboratory for help with some of the data.

REFERENCES

Babby, L. (1980). *Existential sentences and negation in Russia.* Ann Arbor: Karoma.

Baker, M. C. (1988). *Incorporation: A theory of grammatical function changing.* Chicago: University of Chicago Press.

Boatner, M., Gates, J., & Makkai, A. (1975). *A dictionary of American idioms.* New York: Barron's Educational Series.

Bobrow, S. A., & Bell, S. M. (1973). On catching on to idiomatic expressoins. *Memory & Cognition, 1,* 343–346.

Cacciari, C., & Tabossi, P. (1988). The comprehension of idioms. *Journal of Memory and Language, 27,* 668–683.

Chomsky, N. (1956). *Syntactic structure.* The Hague, Netherlands: Mouton.

Clark, H., & Haviland, S. (1977). Comprehension and the given-new contrast. In R. Freedle (Ed.), *Discourse production and comprehension* (pp. 1–40). Norwood, NJ: Ablex.

Cruse, D. A. (1986). *Lexical semantics.* Cambridge, England: Cambridge University Press.

Cutler, A. (1982). Idioms: The colder the older. *Linguistic Inquiry, 13,* 317–320.

Fillmore, C. J., Kay, P., & O'Connor, M. C. (1988). Regularity and idiomaticity in grammatical constructions. *Language, 64,* 501–538.

Fellbaum, C. (1992). *Co-occurrence and antonymy* (Technical Report No. 52). Princeton, NJ: Princeton University, Cognitive Science Laboratory.

Fox, B. (1981). Body part syntax: Towards a universal characterization. *Studies in Language, 5,* 323–340.

Fraser, B. (1970). Idioms within a transformational grammar. *Foundations of Language, 6,* 22–42.

Gibbs, R. W., & Nayak, N. P. (1989). Psycholinguistic studies on the syntactic behavior of idioms. *Cognitive Psychology, 21,* 100–138.

Gibbs, R. W., Nayak, N. P., Bolton, J. L., & Keppel, M. E. (1989). Speakers' assumptions about the lexical flexibility of idioms. *Memory & Cognition, 17,* 58–68.

Glucksberg, S., McGlone, M., & Cacciari, C. (1991). Semantic productivity and idiom comprehension. Manuscript submitted for publication.

Gross, D., Fischer, U., & Miller, G. A. (1989). The organization of adjectival meanings. *Journal of Language and Memory, 28,* 92–106.

Justeson, J. S., & Katz, S. M. (1989). Co-occurrences of antonymous adjectives and their contexts. *Computational Linguistics, 17,* 1–19.

Miller, G. A. (1969). The organization of lexical memory: Are word associations sufficient? In G. A. Talland & N. C. Waugh (Eds.), *The pathology of memory* (pp. 223–236). New York: Academic.

Charles, W. G., & Miller, G. A. (1989). Contexts of antonymous adjectives. *Applied Psycholinguistics, 10,* 357–375.

Newmeyer, F. L. (1974). The regularity of idiom behavior. *Lingua, 34,* 327–342.

Nunberg, G. D. (1978). *The pragmatics of reference.* Bloomington: Indiana University Linguistics Club.

Prince, E. (1981). Towards a taxonomy of given/new information. In P. Cole (Ed.), *Radical pragmatics* (pp. 223–255). New York: Academic.

Pulman, S. G. (1986). *The recognition and interpretation of idioms.* Unpublished manuscript, University of Cambridge, Computer Laboratory, Cambridge, England.

Quirk, R., Greenbaum, S., & Svartvik, J. (1985). *A Comprehensive grammar of the English language.* London: Longman.

Ruhl, C. E. (1989). *On monosemy: A study in linguistic semantics.* Albany: SUNY Press.

Ruwet, N. (1983). Du bon usage des expressions idiomatiques [Concerning the correct use of idioms]. *Recherches Linguistiques, 11,* 5–84.

Swinney, D. A., & Cutler, A. (1979). The access and processing of idiomatic expressions. *Journal of Verbal Learning and Verbal Behavior, 18,* 523–534.

Tabossi, P., & Cacciari, C. (1988, July). *Context effects in the comprehension of idioms.* Paper presented at the tenth annual conference of the Cognitive Science Society, Montreal.

Wasow, T., Sag, I., & Nunberg, G. (1983). Idioms: An interim report. In S. Hattori & K. Inoue (Eds.), *Proceedings of the XIIIth International Congress of Linguistics* (pp. 102–115). Tokyo: CIPL.

Wierzbicka, A. (1982). Why can you have a drink when you can't have an eat? *Language, 58,* 753–799.

13 Idiomaticity as a Reaction to *L'Arbitraire du Signe* in the Universal Process of Semeio-Genesis

Adam Makkai
University of Illinois at Chicago, University of Hong Kong, and LACUS, Inc.

It generally is assumed by both linguists and lexicographers all over the world that DeSaussure's famous dictum identifying the relationship between *le signifié* (content) and *le signifiant* (expression) as basically "arbitrary" is correct.

The principle of arbitrariness may be illustrated as follows: The concept of *dog* and the word "dog" are in an arbitrary relationship to one another, because dog, spelled backwards yields "god" and the concepts of *dog* and *god* are not the reverse of one another. Furthermore, the concept dog can be expressed as the French word *chien,* the German word *Hund,* the Russian word *sobaka,* and the Hungarian word *kutya,* to mention just a few. Outsiders to any of these languages can easily be fooled by teaching them the wrong word. Thus, if you do not know Indonesian and are confronted with the choice between *anjing* and *kuching* (the one being cat and the other one being dog), you may have a hard time choosing the right word. As it happens, *anjing* means dog and *kuching* means cat in Indonesian, but in introductory linguistics courses students can be easily fooled by asking them to choose between the word *minum* and *susu* for dog and cat, respectively. Some will vote for *minum* some for *susu,* although the former means drink and the latter means milk. *Kuching minum susu* means the cat drinks milk.

The principle of arbitrariness was first formally worked out by DeSaussure who, in his *Cours de Linguistique Générale* (1915), defined the linguistics sign as consisting of a concept (the signified) and a string of sounds (the signifier) whose relationship was essentially arbitrary. Human societies get used to these arbitrary designations of concepts by sound strings and hand this down to their children. Insiders to human societies take these concept–sound relationships for granted, whereas foreigners and children tend to question them.

In this chapter I argue that the concept of *l'arbitraire du signe* is a historical product in the evolution of mankind's universal sign-producing activities and that as such it had a beginning, a peak period, and a period of decadence. The evidence for this thinking comes from publications such as Koestler's influential book *The Ghost in the Machine* (1967), in which brain evolution is traced, and M. A. K. Halliday's (1975a) classic on children's language acquisition, *Learning How to Mean,* in which it is convincingly demonstrated that children, as they acquire speech, seem to move through the main phases of human speech development in general. This, in turn, seems to be a logical extension of Haeckel's theory which, ever since its first formulation in the 19th century, maintained that ontogeny recapitulates philogeny.

But let us see in detail how such a concept relates to the problem of *l'arbitraire du signe* in general and idiomaticity in particular.

ON THE NATURE OF LINGUISTIC SIGNS

From "Martian" and "Venusian" to "Tellurian"

Primitive humanity (Neanderthals and their predecessors) are thought to have had no more than 250 to 300 distinct noises to communicate with; these are believed to have corresponded to roughly 250 to 300 concepts in their daily routines such as signs of warning of danger, cries of pain and joy, indications of thirst, hunger, and the mating urge, signs and sounds of territorial defense and aggression, and so forth. It is believed—and there may be room for doubt or disagreement—that this state of affairs is roughly comparable, *mutatis mutandis,* to the *holophrastic phase* in the language development of contemporary children. Neanderthal speech is correlated by anthropologists and brain researchers as traced in Koestler (1967:129) with a stage of human brain development before the "mushrooming out of the human neo-cortex" (p. 129), which is much closer to us in time—35,000 to 40,000 years—and is correctable with the skull measurements of Cro-Magnon man. Depending on the anthropological and archaeological sources one reads, Neanderthal man and Neanderthal speech can be thought of as 1 million years old. I am anxious to point out that I wish to take no sides in any debate related to "evolutionism" versus "creationism" as they are irrelevant to this discussion.

If the human voice, in terms of pitch, rhythm, intonation, and tempo, was capable of being a manifestation of sensations such as hunger, pain, joy, danger, playfulness, grooming, and so on, and if the imaginable or reconstructable social structures associatable with Neanderthals were steady over long stretches of time, this type of communication, although lacking "logic" in the modern mathematical sense, must have been rather "logical"; after all there was not much room for misunderstanding. If a fairly limited set of concepts (250 to 300) is

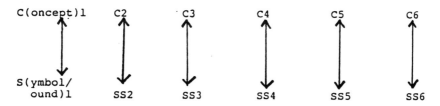

FIG. 13.1. Neanderthal communication, computer communication, Martian communication.

related reasonably steadfastly to 250 to 300 distinct signs manifesting in simple noises, the communication system so reconstructed is not really basically different from modern computer languages, as shown in Fig. 13.1.

In modern parlance one might say that Fig. 13.1 shows a system characterized by *direct realization*. There is no *synonymy* and no *homonymy* in this system as there is also no *composite realization, diversification,* or *neutralization.* For those phenomena to arise we must look at another group of humans, much closer to us in time. Before we do that in order to characterize the languages of modern humanity, let us ask the question: What would be the logical opposite of this "Neanderthal-Martian-Computer Language" system, in which one concept always leads to one and the very same sound (or symbol)? It would have to be a system in which any concept can be related to any sound symbol available to the speakers. It would look as in Fig. 13.2.

As can be seen by comparing Figs. 13.1 and 13.2, Fig. 13.2 is the logical opposite of Fig. 13.1. In Fig. 13.1 each concept is expressed exclusively by its corresponding sound-symbol; in Fig. 13.2 all of the concepts can lead to all of the sound symbols. How realistic is this in modern terms?, we might ask. The answer is that Fig. 13.1 is commonplace: The payroll of a large firm done on a computer uses language very much like that depicted in Fig. 13.1. Computers are inanimate machines that lack human consciousness; they take nothing for granted. This kind of language is used in science classes, during the instruction of mathematics, in usage instruction manuals, and so forth. Merchandise in modern supermarkets is bar coded for the convenience of electronic pricing and

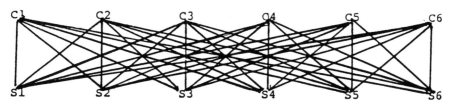

FIG. 13.2. Telepathic communication, poetic communication, Venusian communication.

checking out; the bar codes always and unambiguously differentiate a can of bean soup from a can of mushroom soup and indicate the correct price.

But just as man does not live by bread alone, neither do we manage to use the "language of logic" all the time. Ever since the first lover called his lady a "flower," Venusian communication has been with us and it just will not go away. We, as a species, no sooner invented the convenience of direct realization in logical communication as we found it constitutionally necessary to rebel against it and to turn to the device of *phoricity*. Derived from the known term *metaphor*, phoricity refers to the feature of human languages whereby signs point not only at their references but at other signs as well and through these at a series of networks of interrelated references. Modern human languages are so engineered that they always bring something "down," "over," "across," "forward," or "backward"; hence we have the phenomena of the *metaphor, anaphora,* and *cataphora*—to mention for now only the commonly recognized types.

Now modern Earth languages, or "Tellurian," to borrow John Algeo's term (1970), exhibit a combination of the communication systems diagramed in Figs. 13.1 and 13.2, shown in Fig. 13.3.

In the type of modern communication system outlined in Fig. 13.3, we have a fair amount of direct realization as in the words "the square root of 16 is 4" and "may I have a pound of granulated sugar, please," but we also have a great deal of neutralization, as in the case of the English syllable *well,* which is a noun in the sentence "the farmer dug a well," a verb in "tears welled up in my eyes," an adjective in "yesterday I was sick but I am well today," an adverb in "John speaks Mandarin well," and an interjection in "well, I think so."

When we notice that a concept such as ᶜ[male parent] can be expressed in English as *father,* which is neutral, as *Dad,* which is affectionate, as *Daddy* which is affectionate and diminutive, as *old man* which is slang, we have encountered the phenomenon of diversification.

Our human languages today, then, are characterized by the fact that besides a large amount of direct realization they show *neutralization* and *diversification* to be universally widespread features.

One of the most important realizational relationships for our purposes is composite realization. The notion is familiar enough: Major sentence types answering the S (sentence) $\Rightarrow$ NP (noun phrase) + VP (verb phrase) formula manifest in the composite realization mode; sentences such as "dogs bark,"

FIG. 13.3.   Modern human communication: Earth language or Tellurian.

"cats meow," and "children play loudly" are all "compositely realized" in surface syntax due to the linear display of subject, verb, adverb, and so forth. In terms of signs composite realization works as follows: The sign *elephant* is a simple sign in direct realization to the concept ᶜ[large African or Indian pachyderm mammal with a trunk], and so is the sign *white* to the concept ᶜ[light frequency reflecting all of the sun's rays']. If one encounters an elephant that is an albino, one therefore may call it a *white elephant*. The manifestation mode of the expression will be composite in surface syntax, but the expression will not be an instance of composite realization but of direct realization, because the creature that is an elephant is of the white color; hence the words *white* and *elephant* do realize an "elephant" and the "white color," respectively. However, as time goes on, societies become more complex and certain historic events take place that leave an imprint of *internal borrowing* on natural languages. (cf. Halliday 1975b, Lamb, 1966).

The King of Siam is said to have disliked a courtier once, and so, in order to punish him, gave him a white elephant as a gift. One must realize, of course, that in ancient Thailand the white elephant was considered a holy animal somewhat as cows still are considered in India today. To kill or to neglect a white elephant was considered a capital crime. Yet to care for a white elephant properly meant financial ruin. Because the white elephant was a gift from the King, it could not be refused.

So what does *white elephant* mean today in spoken North American English? It stands for "unwanted property, such as a large house, difficult to manage or to sell." It helps to know the story of the King of Siam and the courtier who was punished with the expensive gift, but it is strictly speaking not necessary; there are many fluent speakers of American English who use the expression *white elephant* in the aforementioned sense as used by real estate people who never heard of the story from ancient Thailand. One must, as semanticist-lexicographer, treat *white elephant* as a separate entry in the lexicon of English from both *white* and *elephant* with a definition all its own, that of "unmanageable property." This, to be sure, is a complex bundle of ideas—indeed entire networks are needed to express what is involved in the notions of "manage," "un," "-able," and "property"; yet the whole designation of "unmanageable property" can be seen as a unitary conglomerate, or Gestalt of meaning, hence a *macrosememe* or a definable unit of meaning, rendered familiar by social use and acceptance.

An Introductory Example

What kind of a sign, then, is *white elephant* in terms of our sign types depicted in Figs. 13.1, 13.2, and 13.3? It can be diagramed in simplified form as in Fig. 13.4.

As can be seen from Fig. 13.4, the complex new expression *white elephant* meaning "property difficult to manage or sell" has not lost its connections to the

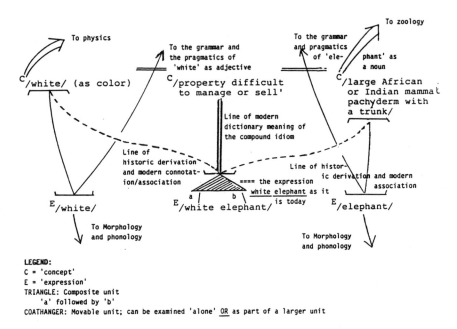

FIG. 13.4. *White elephant* as an idiom and its place in a line-up of concepts and expressions.

concepts "white" and "elephant." That this is so is easily proven: Children and foreign learners of English, who are not familiar with a given idiom, try to work out its meaning by the traditional route of Fig. 13.1; they tacitly assume that each concept has only one way of being expressed, and conversely, that each expression leads to one and only one concept that is always the same. And this is how children and foreigners are misled.

Permit me to illustrate from children's usage on some examples collected in the United States:

When a child is naughty and the father wants to administer a spanking, he may say, "I will fix your little red wagon," where the *little red wagon* refers to the child's bottom and *fix* refers to the spanking. I heard children naively and innocently reply to this, "but I don't have a little red wagon, Daddy!"—meaning quite literally that they had no toy wagon that was little and red. The fathers involved laughed and gave up the idea of the spanking; one picked the child up, spanked him while laughing, and said in an amused tone, "this is your 'little red wagon' [the bottom] and this is how I fix it." I imagine that this child will never forget the meaning of the phrase "fix your little red wagon" (cf. Makkai, 1976).

The expression *a monkey on my back* in the United States or the corresponding British expression *an albatross around my neck* (with the latter being borrowed from Coleridge's "Rime of the Ancient Mariner" and being therefore literary) both mean "an unpleasant, nagging problem, such as a complex of guilt, or debt, that will not go away." A mother once said in front of her child, "those Wednesday afternoons at the hospital sure are a monkey on my back." What she meant to say was that her volunteer work at the hospital is an unwelcome obligation she cannot get rid of. Her 4-year-old daughter replied, "But Mommy, there is nothing on your back, not a monkey, not a birdie—nothing!" The mother, who was greatly relieved by spontaneous laughter, explained to her child what a *monkey on one's back* meant, and then went on to her hospital visit in a much improved mood.

I was a recently arrived refugee immigrant in the United States when, shortly before the end of my 6th month in Boston, someone said, "You can't be serious, you're pulling my leg." I was startled and in broken phrases apologized, "pardon me, Sir, I did not mean to touch your foot." Amidst general hilarity I thus got my first practical lesson in English idiomaticity; I learned that *to pull one's leg* means to "tease someone." Only years later did I find possible historical explanations as to why and how the phrase probably arose—as it happens through the mercy killing of hanged prisoners who were suffocating: Pulling their legs broke their spinal cords and ended their misery faster.

Composite Realization

White elephant, then, is an instance of composite realization, where the individual constituents of the composite form have some secondary connections to the meanings of the constituents now suppressed in the composite form, but freely in the foreground when the lexemes *white* and *elephant* are used outside the given construction referring to "unwanted or unmanageable property."

If one bears in mind the story from ancient Thailand, the designating of "unwanted or unmanageable property" as *white elephant* begins to seem less arbitrary. To illustrate what arbitrary might be like in this connection, imagine that "unwanted or unmanageable property" is called *woopy-woop* or *toopy-toop.* These are pronounced easily in English and presently unused and carry no meaning whatsoever.

The language has opted for two familiar words in conjunction in a new context; one might argue, not because of the story from ancient Thailand, but because elephants are big as are houses, and a white elephant is rare; hence the image of a white elephant is not a bad tag for a large house that is odd or unusual. This sounds realistic enough, yet fails to be convincing, because "unwanted or unmanageable" property also could have been compared to any number of large objects of an unusual nature such as a possible *golden whale,* but no such form actually is on record whereas *white elephant* is.

THE CONCEPT OF IDIOMATICITY—A MORE FORMAL APPROACH

It is now time to discuss the concept of idiomaticity more formally. The curvy arrows leading out of the concepts of "white" and "pachyderm" in Fig. 13.4 lead us to physics and zoology, respectively; this is in the realm of general semantics or pragmatics, as some might prefer to call it. The dictionary meanings "white," "property difficult to manage or sell," and "elephant" are *sememes* or units of meaning, which are, of course, like all units of meaning in every human language, semantically complex. The reason why they are units, nevertheless, is because in human memory they correlate with a unitary dictionary entry on the one hand and, on the other, contrast with their known meanings in isolation. *White,* on the lower level qua dictionary entry, is an adjective that can modify a noun; its meaning is its sememe, which can be expressed in a variety of styles colloquially or scientifically or may be illustrated by a dash of white paint on a dark surface. The entry *elephant* is a noun and as such can partake of the grammatical behavior of English nouns referring to animate objects; its meaning is the SEMEME "African or Indian pachyderm with a trunk," which, again, can be rendered colloquially, scientifically, on a drawing, or on a photograph. What interests us particularly here is the complex expression *white elephant*. It must be seen as a single unit. It is a complex lexeme whose constituents *white* and *elephant* have preserved their historic connections to the sememes "white" and "elephant." Yet *white elephant,* which is a unitary noun, now has its own primary connecting line to the sememe "unwanted or unmanageable property," and for modern speakers this is the really important line. The fact that *white* elephant (n) = "unwanted or unmanageable property" obviously must be spelled as two familiar words alphabetical under *w* and *e* in the dictionary, can be a source of confusion, psychologically speaking. Two words simply seem to be two words and nevertheless to have to think of them (in layman's terms) as one word presents an uncomfortable contradiction, as if we were told that 1 = 2, the prime example of a falsehood we are taught to reject from early childhood onward. One certainly does not equal two arithmetically and so there can be no denying that the expression *white elephant* (whatever it means) somehow contains two words. What we must come to tolerate here is that we are dealing not with prima facie physical sight and identification but with a much subtler state of affairs, in order to do justice to this built-in mendacity in modern human languages that forces us to see two as one and in order to introduce the main theme of this chapter, that of the gradual evolution of linguistic sign creation or *semeio-genesis.*

Pound's Poetic Typology Describes Word Formations

We need some terms in order to designate word creation in its various phases. The temptation arises to borrow three terms from poetic aesthetics, namely from

304

Ezra Pound (Eliot, 1963) who was, as is commonly known in literary circles, heavily influenced by the orientalist Ernest Fenollosa (Chisolm, 1963; Fenollosa, 1920; Yip, 1969). I quote from Pound verbatim as given in Pound's essays edited by T. S. Eliot (1963):

> That is to say, there are three "kinds of poetry":
> *Melopoeia,* wherein the words are charged, over and above their plain meaning, with some musical property, which directs the bearing or trend of that meaning.
> *Phanopoeia,* which is a casting of images upon the visual imagination.
> *Logopoeia,* "the dance of the intellect among words," that is to say, it employs words not only for their direct meaning, but it takes count in a special way of habits of usage, of the context we *expect* to find with the word, its usual concomitants, of its known acceptances, and of ironical play. It holds the aesthetic content which is peculiarly the domain of verbal manifestation, and cannot possibly be contained in plastic or in music. It is the latest come, and perhaps the most tricky and undependable mode.
> The melopoeia can be appreciated by a foreigner with a sensitive ear, even though he be ignorant of the language in which the poem is written. It is practically impossible to transfer or translate it from one language to another, save perhaps by divine accident, and for half a line at a time.
> Phanopoeia can, on the other hand, be translated almost, or wholly intact. When it is good enough, it is practically impossible for the translator to destroy it save by very crass bungling, and the neglect of perfectly well-known and formulative rules.
> Logopoeia does not translate; though the attitude of mind it expresses may pass through a paraphrase (pp. 19–20).

In order to properly distinguish my present use of the terms from Pound's and Fenollosa's aesthetics, I use the term *logopoeia* in its etymological sense as "word creation" from the Greek *logos* ("word") and *poein* ("to make"). Instead of the Poundian *melopoeia* for "sound poetry," I use the term *onomatopoeia,* more familiar in linguistics for "sound imitating words," and for the idiomatic habit of putting new signs together via an image, I use the hybrid Latino-Greek term *imagopoeia.* There is one additional term that we need, referring to "language via gesturing," and this I call *kinetopoeia.* My indebtedness to Pound and Fenallosa is very great indeed and my tampering with their designations for types of poetry is in no way contradicted or detracted from by my borrowing from their word-coining habits in order to introduce my concept of idiomaticity via image-based word formation; that is, *imagopoetic logopoeia,* for that is what idiomaticity is really all about.

Generally humanity, in creating signs, is always engaged in some form or other of semeio-genesis via logopoeia, and the kind of logopoeia we discover at various levels is characteristic of the stage of development of the language group in question. But how does this all take place?

I suggest in this article that roughly at a time when the human neo-cortex begins to "balloon out" as suggested in Koestler's brilliant book on brain development (1967) and Neanderthal language yields its place to the much richer and more complex languages of Cro-Magnon man, we abandon the elementary phonetopoetic-onomatopoetic way to verbal creation and embark on the more modern course of imagopoetic internal borrowing.

The question arises: What are the probable reasons for abandoning meaning designation by the allocation of sounds for the device of borrowing an image? The answer probably lies in the discrepancy between the available and distinguishable sounds and the number of new concepts humans need for survival. The *Oxford English Dictionary (OED)* has almost 500,000 entries in it (lexemes); these in turn, require minimally 10 to 20 words (lexemes) to define these entries. The *OED,* therefore, contains minimally 5,000,000 but more likely 10,000,000 individual sememes, certain well-chosen configurations of which constitute *definitional macrosememes.* To illustrate: If the entry *dog* (n) is defined as "domesticated canine mammal of the canidae species," the words between the quotation marks are the definitional macrosememe and the constituents therein are sememes inside of it such that each one correlates to a lexeme and, therefore, can be looked up in turn. (It happens not infrequently that one has to look up the meanings of words one finds in a definition before one can make sense of the definition in itself.) All definitions are intrinsically highly complex and lead to *encyclopaedic knowledge* of various disciplines. The notions of "domesticated," "canine," and "mammal" all can be studied *in extenso* so that one has to have an entire library at one's disposal. It is therefore very difficult to estimate the number of *pragmo-semantic linkages* that one can reach from 5 million to 10 million sememes, but a conservative multiplication by a factor of 10 seems not unreasonable. We can imagine informally, therefore, that the *OED* shows an upper line-up as follows:

1. Number of entries: half a million.
2. Number of definitions (macrosememes): half a million.
3. Number of sememes: 5 million to 10 million.
4. Number of pragmo-semantic linkages: 50 million to 100 million

Yet all of this information is encapsulated in far fewer morphemes and only a few dozen phonemes. This would be the *OED*'s lower line-up:

1. Number of morphemes: A few thousand.
2. Number of phonemes: A few dozen.

Let us think of a class of 30 students, their individual biographies, and let us imagine that they have to share one single typewriter to write down their condensed biographies on one page each. The phrase "I was born in X" probably would appear in all 32 biographies; some students will be born in the same city

(X), others elsewhere; the year may be the same or not; the months and days will differ, but there might be an occasional pair of "birthday twins." Each biography will constitute an individual text; after all, these are separate individuals. Yet each text will have a great recurrence of similar or identical phrases, the words will be even closer and, given the fact that they had to use the same typewriter, they will have used the same limited set of letters to express their individual life histories. If one of the students wants to be "original" and wants to say how hard he intends to work after graduation, he will be unlikely to invent a new word and write "I shall be working *brummmmmmmmmmmmmmmmmmmm*"; on the other hand, he might try to say something like "I shall be working more diligently than seven Vietnamese shopkeepers, seven Polish farmers, and seven Chinese restaurant owners put together."

The student who wrote *brummmmmmmmmmmm,* to express the notion of "very hard work" engaged in *phonopoetic logopoeia.* The student, however, who promised to work harder than seven Vietnamese, seven Poles, and seven Chinamen put together is availing himself of the possibility of *imagopoetic logopoeia.* Everybody knows that the Vietnamese, the Poles, and the Chinese are some of the most diligent immigrants in the United States and one easily can visualize the restaurateur, the farmer, and the shopkeeper at work. Multiplying their effects by seven is, of course, a difficult calculation to perform exactly, but resorting to such numerical hyperbole is, nevertheless, a possible way to express the notion of "to a high degree."

The instance just cited is imaginary, and even if it did happen would not amount to anything we could lexicalize in a dictionary; it would amount to what Hockett (1958) called a "nonce form" without social significance.

The Birth of a Famous American Idiom

Next, I would like to illustrate the imagopoetic creation of the idiomatic lexeme *red herring.*

In the 19th century, fugitives from justice on the run, when pursued by bloodhounds with a sharp sense of smell, would try to escape by rubbing pieces of herring on low-lying branches of the trail in order to confuse the sense of smell of the hounds. Herring tends to be reddish in color and, when old, has a foul smell. As American civilization developed during the course of the 19th century and legal issues arose, people found it necessary to make quick and handy reference to false or phony issues. They just could have said, of course, "this is a false/phony issue" and no doubt many did. But people, whether in law enforcement or private life, who were familiar with the habit of escapees who had gone to the West Coast (particularly Oregon where this phrase is said to have originated) knew about the habit of rubbing "red herring" on branches along escape trails and began to use the phrase *red herring* in the sense of "confusing/phony/false issue."

One who does not know the meaning of the idiom *red herring* is forced by the expression to think of the color "red" and of the fish called "herring"; the reason, of course, is that the hearer already knows those terms but cannot make sense of them in combination. As time went on, the phrase became so popular that nowadays all dictionaries carry it. As shown in Fig. 13.5, its structure is the same as that of *white elephant,* adjective + noun, with the resultant combination functioning as a new noun with a nondeduceable, hence unitary meaning (a macrosememe), which, of course, is polysemantic in cognition and the pragmatics of the "real world." There is a subtle but real difference in the *degree of transparency* of the two expressions: *White elephant,* according to many speakers, is easier to identify with an unsellable building than *red herring* with a phony issue. Characteristically, *white elephant* refers to an object—hence the relative simplicity in visualization—whereas *red herring* refers to people's verbal behav-

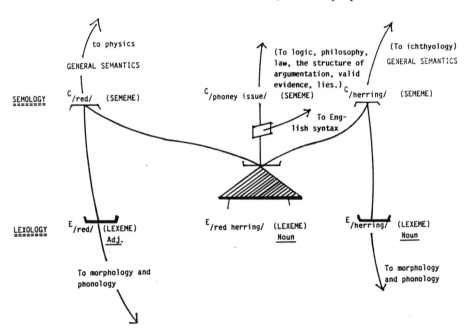

LEGEND: The shaded triangle in the middle is the contemporary nominal lexeme red herring with the contemporary meaning 'phoney issue'. Its two constituents red and herring, respectively, can be looked up in a dictionary separately and arrive at physics on account of the color 'red' and ichthyology on account of the fish 'herring'. The idiomatic meaning 'phoney issue' can lead the investigator to logic, philosophy, law, the syllogism, the structure of argumentation, lies and the subterfuge. All of this is SIMULTANEOUSLY AVAILABLE or IGNORABLE with concentration on what is necessary at the moment. If red herring were a Chinese idiom written with the characters for 'red' and 'herring', the etymology of this expression would be outwardly visible as it is in the case of 'quickly-fast-immediately' which is written by the characters for 'horse' and 'back'.

FIG. 13.5. *Red herring* as bimorphemic lexeme.

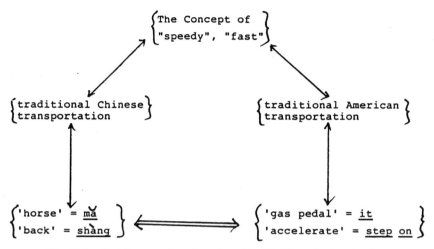

FIG. 13.6.   A Chinese and an American English idiom, both using images from a common mode of nonpedestrian transportation.

step on it in American English are *lexical facts* the linguist-lexicographer must account for.

The Chinese expression for "danger" is *xiǎo xìn;* it is written by the characters 小心; the literal meaning of compound is "small heart," an interesting example for our consideration. The human heart is invisible to the eye, but fear and anxiety can cause a sensation of narrowing in the chest. In English one speaks of a "sunken heart" when one is shocked or frightened.

In modern times, as Western technological inventions reached China, the choice arose whether to create new native expressions for these commonly used goods or to name them in some other way. Consider the telephone. We in the West take this as a single concept and seldom analyze it; one has to go to etymological studies and Greek to see *telephone* as a complex sign made up of *telos* ("goal, distance") and *phōnē* ("sound"). If understood etymologically, *telephone* means "distance sounder," a fact well echoed in its German name *Fernsprecher* ("distance talker"). Yet when in the 1960s in Kuala Lumpur, Malaysia, the National Language Institute (Dewan Bahasa Dan Pustaka) were given the suggestion to call the telephone *bunyi jauh* (from Malay "distance" and "sound"), the suggestion was rejected and they decided to use *talipun* instead with the customary substitution of /p/ for /f/. Not so the Chinese. They call the telephone *tiàn huà,* written 電話; the characters stand for "electric" and "talk/speed." The idea of sound is not expressed, but electricity, a primary notion in Chinese, is favored in a number of similar expressions.

When computers were introduced in China, a similarly ingenious idiom arose: To "electric" as in *tiàn hùa* ("telephone"), they now added the character for "brains": The result is *tiàn năo,* written 電腦 ("computer"), literally "electric brains." The third member of this triad is *tiàn yĭng,* written電影("electric shadow/image"), which stands for "motion picture, movies."

ARE IDIOMS CASES
OF PRAGMATIC METONYMY?

In Western linguistic speculation (Ruhl, 1989) there has been a recent trend trying to question the existence of idioms and explaining as many idioms as possible as cases of *pragmatic metonymy.* Ruhl (1974, 1975, 1976, 1978, 1979, 1980, 1982, 1989) reiterated on numerous occasions that idioms exist only in the heads of foreigners and that mature native speakers always know the literal meaning that is the base of a given idiom. This notion, attractive to many, is challenging to the semanticist-lexicographer working with idioms and so I feel obligated to devote attention to Ruhl's arguments against idiomaticity.

The well-known expression *kick the bucket* ("to die") is not an idiom in Ruhl's scheme of affairs, because of the following considerations: *Kick* ("rapid motion with the foot resulting in hard contact") is a sign of incipient life and death both, in general. Thus the first sign of an embryo's continued healthy growth inside the womb is when it first starts to kick, usually in the 5th month of pregnancy. When a cold engine in a car first refuses to start and requires repeated effort either by start-key and battery or by hand cranking and then finally starts, it is said to *kick in,* to "start coming alive." The phrase *to kick in* is now so extended as to cover the meaning "take effect" in general; one hears statements such as "My salary kicks in after the 28th of each month." To signal the end of life, *kick over* is used, as in "Mrs. O'Leary's old cow kicked over this morning."

Ruhl (1982) had no explanation for the *bucket* in *kick the bucket* and so he admitted that "there is something idiomatic" (p. 304) about the expression. The truth is that nobody really knows where *bucket* comes from in this phrase. Some people think that it is in memory of Western-style hangings in which the criminal is stood up on a bucket with the noose in his neck and the rope looped around the branch of a tree; then the sheriff comes and kicks the bucket out from under the criminal whereby he is hanged. According to Flavell (1972), *bucket* comes from the French *bucqet,* which meant "beam." According to Flavell, the phrase originated in 16th- and 17th-century English farmhouses where pigs were slaughtered with their feet being tied to the beam, or "bucket." The pigs as their last sign of reflex were "kicking the beams" to which their feet were tied. Whereas it makes sense for such a widely spread idiom to have originated in England, the question remains as to why and how French *bucqet,* now dead in English, predominates over the common word *beam?*

Ruhl's (1982) assertion that *kick the bucket* is not an idiom has the partial merit of calling attention to kicking as a sign of last reflex and incipient life, but the acceptance of these side associations heavily depends on diachronic information (as in the case of the story in England of old-fashioned pig slaughter) and on all sorts of other cultural information beyond the scope of work for the descriptive lexicographer. As Bolinger (1976) convincingly argued, idioms have outside relations, and the associative links that parts of idioms have with other lexemes in the language rest on diachronic awareness.

Ruhl (1978, 1980) devoted a separate article to to each of the following expressions *hit the sack* ("go to sleep") and *break the ice* ("start talking"); his intention was to explain that these are not idioms but metonymic extensions of the underlying common senses of *hit, break,* and *ice.*

The *hit* of *hit the sack* also occurs, Ruhl (1978) convincingly demonstrated, in *hit the deck* ("lie down suddenly") and *call me the moment you hit town* meaning "when you arrive in town." From these and other examples collected from modern American fiction, Ruhl concluded that *hit* has the meaning "make sudden contact with." Because *sack* is used in slang to mean "bed" as in "John is a sack-rat" ("he sleeps a lot"), Ruhl suggested that *hit the sack* is, in fact, understandable as the combination of "to make sudden contact with" and "informal place to sleep."

Break the ice is similarly dismissed as an idiom. Ruhl (1980) demonstrated that *break* means "suddenly to disjoin, to dissociate" and also "suddenly to release" as in "Finally my fever broke" and "The news broke around 8 o'clock." The word *ice* can be shown to enjoy widespread use referring to isolation, frozenness, sadness, and so forth, as one talks about the *icy look* one someone's face, and so on. To *break the ice,* then, Ruhl concluded, is not an idiom but a metonymic sense extension, which understandably says "make the frozen silence/sadness go away."

If the concepts "go to bed quickly" and "start talking" were expressed as /hummmmmmmmmm/ and /wheeeeeee/, respectively, the question whether they are idioms or not never would arise; speakers would accept them as phonopoetically created, arbitrary signs of ancient origin. Because, however, in the late 20th century we have these two compound expressions with a familiar syntactic pattern (to verb [V] the noun [N]), speculation naturally is aroused regarding their origins and the question of just how arbitrary they are. Any descriptive lexicographer, whether working on a bilingual dictionary of English or on an *OED*-style, monolingual defining English dictionary would be well advised to include both *hit the sack* and *break the ice* under the lemmas for *hit* and *break,* if the task at hand is a description of contemporary English usage. Ruhl's point, however, that literal senses can be found in such expressions by educated native speakers who also have a broad range of literary and cultural associations is a valid one. We thus come to a crucial question in the analysis of idioms: for whom is a given expression an idiom?

THE RELATIVITY OF IDIOM PERCEPTION

"For whom" is a dangerous and loaded question because it arouses the specter of relativism in linguistics, a discipline, which is experiencing a hard time acting as an objective science (Yngve, 1974, 1986). The question "for whom?" would have been difficult to raise during the 1950s when the neo-Bloomfieldian structuralists were generally somewhat discouraging of meaning, and in transformational generative grammar (based on Chomsky, 1965) "for whom?" was, once again, a nonquestion as the grammar worth describing was the "competence of the ideal hearer-speaker in a homogenous society," a situation that does not exist in reality and that had to be artificially created by Chomsky in order to to make language fit the Procrustean bed of symbolic logic. Yet with the 1960s there came urban sociolinguistics (Labov, 1964, 1976) with a resultant more or less standard acceptance of *variationism*. In grammar (mainly syntax), we are no longer shocked when we hear "this is 'grammatical' in my speech, but it may be 'ungrammatical' in yours." An utterance such as "I ain't got nuttin' to do with you no more," once held up as the prime example of "illogical speech" where negations of negatives allegedly created unwanted assertions, is viewed calmly nowadays as an instance of "emphatic denial" in Appalachian speech and in Black English. The question of "for whom?" should be, I think, no longer taboo in modern linguistics. Yet in lexical semantics, an important and sensitive area where tolerance must be practiced, the issue of "relative understanding" never was raised, with two notable exceptions, Welch (1974) and Lamb (1990). The former deals with the layman's and the Latin scholar's awareness of English polysyllables of Latin origin; the latter warns against the hazards of either-or thinking.

The thrust of Lamb's (1990) argument is that whether *hit the sack* and *break the ice* are perceived as idioms or as metonymic extensions of literal phrases depends on the cognitive capacity of the user/analyst and the intended target-audience. The situation is paradoxical in the true Greek sense of *paradox* ("an apparent contradiction that displays a hidden truth"): The only realistic way to account for these phrases is to state that they are both literal and idiomatic. This chapter then, is offered as an argument for the inclusiveness of both-and thinking in contrast to the exclusiveness of either-or thinking.

"Regularity" can be found in *break the ice* and *hit the sack* where the grammatical behavior of these forms under inflection is concerned: The past tense is *he broke the ice* and never **he break-the-ice-ed;* the past tense of *hit the sack* is *he hit the sack* and never **he hit-the-sacked*. The same is true about *kick the bucket;* the past form is *he kicked the bucket* and never **he kick-the-bucketed,* which shows that the morpohemes *break, hit,* and *kick* remain in these expressions with their customary morphological behavior whether or not they also refer to the acts of "breaking," "hitting," or "kicking." Consider as further examples of the same principle English *understand-understood* and *withstand-*

316

withstood, which are never inflected as weak-verb forms **understanded* and **withstanded,* although physical "standing" is not necessarily involved in the mental act of "comprehension" and the social act of "resistance." One makes the best descriptive sense, therefore, by suggesting that the morpheme *stand* is present in these expressions but the lexeme *stand* ("be positioned erect on one's feet") is not.

What is required is that modern linguists give up, at long last, their unconscious adherance to the Bloomfieldian notion of the morpheme (Bloomfield, 1933) as a "meaningful unit" (p. 160) where Bloomfield used the term sememe for the "meaning of a morpheme" (p. 160), and come to accept the existence of the *intervening lexical stratum.*

The recognition of lexemes is of potentially great benefit for linguistics because the *lexemic stratum* can handle syntax in its tactical dimensions. Meaning and "deep structure" can be handled on the next stratum higher up, in semology, the place where the definitions of the lexemes, the actual entries in the dictionary, must be handled in any event.

But let us return to Ruhl's examples *kick the bucket* and *hit the sack* in order to see how they could be used literally. Imagine a scene of target shooting: Among the targets to be hit there are some beer cans, some wooden dolls, and behind them, covering the wall, an old sack. Max, a novice, keeps missing both the wooden dolls and the beer cans. The instructor says: "Max, stop hitting the sack! Aim at the bottles!"

On a narrow corridor in a boarding house, where the running water is shut off for repairs, there are some buckets with water in them for people to wash in the morning. Max, who is unaware of the water shutdown and the water storage buckets, moves around in the dark. Accidentally his foot comes into collision with a pail that makes a loud rattling noise. One of the boarders gets up to see what caused the noise and tells his roommate: "Max, the newcomer, kicked the bucket." The point is that no native speaker can say this without knowing that he is punning. In Stanley Kramer's motion picture, *It's a Mad, Mad, Mad, Mad World,* actor Jimmy Durante, who fell out of a car in a hairpin curve, tells the onlookers where some hidden money can be found, and then his foot comes into violent collision with a pail that rolls down the hill before he dies. The audience rewards this visual literalization of the idiom with uproarious laughter. No one ever denied, accordingly, that idioms do behave partially as if they were literal constructions, but we must observe the native population in their daily interactions of how they actually use idioms.

Lamb (1990) has convincingly shown in terms of the formalism of relational network diagramming what I am saying here in plain prose: The question whether or not a form is an idiom or not is relative to the consciousness of the user. Because some users are both native speakers and linguists—or even literary scholars—the range of possible associations is rather wide.

Speakers of dialects other than American English when coming to the United

States tend to acquire idioms such as "He has two strikes against him" and "He'll never get to first base" entirely outside of the baseball-based sport context with which they are not familiar. The first one means "to have wasted two chances out of three after which one must stop trying" and the second means "to establish oneself in a position of strategic importance from where further moves become possible." Only after prolonged stay in the United States do such naive users of baseball idioms discover where the phrases come from.

A SECOND LOOK AT CHINESE IDIOMS

But let us return to some of our Chinese examples used in this chapter earlier. Chances are that native speakers of Mandarin hardly ever speculate on what a given character originally stood for; for Chinese people the character 馬 simply indicates the segmental phonemes /m/ and /a/, which must be pronounced with different contrasting tones, depending on the meaning. With the rising tone *mǎ* means "horse," and in the written form no additional character is required to express the idea of horse. If the same segmentals are pronounced on a high-level tone as *mā*, the word means "mother," and the character for "woman" must be added before the character for "horse." The question arises: Is the meaning "horse" at all present in Mandarin "mother" then? Of course not. Yet the character for "horse" is there! What does that make the combined character 媽 ("mother") in Chinese? My suggestion is that it is an independent lexeme on the spoken level; after all it has its own tone, which is in contrast with that of both "horse" and "scold." Graphically, however, it is an idiom that in the "horse" character calls attention to part of the pronunciation (the segmentals) and in the "woman" character reminds users of a "human female." The fact that the combined character does not mean "mare" (female horse) or "woman rider" or a "woman as big or strong as a horse," or any such possible combination, shows that the combined character is a *grapho-lexemic idiom*. The Chinese language is probably unique in having developed this kind of idiomaticity. A native speaker of Chinese has no need to rationalize to himself or herself the composition of the character for "mother" in this way, but it is said here in Hong Kong that it is a powerful mnemonic device for foreigners and for children. We thus can understand why the question "for whom?" is far from being irrelevant.

CONCLUSIONS

What theoretical conclusions can we possibly draw from all of this? There appears to be a universal constraint on all idiom formation and it is this: Whereas nonidioms probably arose through phonopoetic arbitrariness, idioms tend to arise via imagopoetic arbitrariness, thereby amounting to a new phase in the evolution of human logopoetic, that is word-building, activity. Imagopoetic arbitrariness seems to be closer to the real world from the point of view of our contemporary inclinations toward logic. Societies that already have developed a fair number of signs via the usual *l'arbitraire du signe,* where arbitrariness means the linkage of a sound sequence to a macrosememe, when forming newer sets of concepts do not resort to the ancient phonopoetic arbitrariness, but start to engage in an activity of a nonacoustic but visual order: They now select already existing signs and start recombining them in terms of a suggestive image. Hence the name of this kind of idiomatic logopoeia as imagopoeia, that via image-creating word formation.

The Chinese idioms *mǎ shàng* ("quickly"), *tiàn huà* ("telephone"), and *tiàn nǎo* ("computer") are all such imagopoetically created idioms whose structure would indicate that they are younger formations in the history of the language than the primary signs that were created phonopoetically.

At the beginning of their lingual evolution ancient humans were, it would seem, more orientated toward sound than toward visual images. The fact that writing is so much younger than speech would seem to support such a line of speculation. Phonopoetic activity was, in all likelihood, onomatopoetic, the notion of onomatopoeia, sound-imitating designations, is, in fact, the motivation for the coining of terms *phonopoetic-phonopoeia* (sound), *logopoetic-logopoeia* (words), and *imagopoetic-imagopoeia* (images) as used in this chapter.

Also consider the fact that in ancient Greece, Homeric epics were memorized and performed, with performance sometimes lasting a day or two without any written records. The invention of the hexameter by the Greeks certainly must have been a help in the memorization process as syllable length, stress, and the openness or closedness of the syllables involved correlated with the lexemes in question whose linear syntax, in turn, "told the story" of the *Iliad* and the *Odyssey.* As children grow up, they, too, show tendencies of having their memories first rooted in touch, second in sound, and only around the age of 6 years when elementary school starts to bring drawing and literacy, in visual images.

It is not difficult to see how the sound-based systems had to start breaking down as the brains of social humans expanded cortically and developed further and further needs to build connections between concepts and expressions. The once more or less natural connection between pleasure and danger as notions and the cries that expressed them, although remaining in the archaic residue of the onomatopoetic word stock of modern languages, gradually gave way to sapient modes of logopoeia whose chief characteristic, by necessity, became De Saussure's *l'arbitraire du signe.* But as more and more such arbitrary connections were built and allowed to proliferate, speech communities reached a certain saturation point. The resultant *homonymic overload* started to threaten social usefulness, and speech communities began semiconsciously to rebel against the exclusive and total arbitrariness of the sign system. When speech communities reached their respective stages of homonymic overload, they also reached the phase of phonopoetic saturation. What this means is easy to see and to validate: Hardly ever do we manage to create a neologism in one of today's languages built on the archaic residue of phonopoetically anchored nonproductive patterns. The number of strong verbs of the *sing-sang-sung* type are limited and fixed in English; newly made-up verbs are all weak and have their past tenses in *-ed.* Onomatopoetic words such as *hiss, thud, bang,* and *meow* are much more reluctant to sprout new buds in the lexicon of English, whereas the sciences and technology have no difficulty coming up with abstract new terms by cleverly remobilizing a few Greek and Latin stems, prefixes, and suffixes.

With neocortical expansion comes the phase of sapient logopoeia which, historically well before the invention of writing, starts using visual imagery. The Homeric "standing epithets" of *ox-eyed Hera* and the *rose-fingered dawn,* embedded in the rhythmic repetition of the Homeric hexameters, were, in fact, visually based images.

What are some of the favorite sources of imagery in modern idiom formation? They seem to include parts of the body—nouns such as hands, arms, feet, legs, the head, the eyes, the ears, and so on, with "primary verbs," which after first being used for some bodily function such as *break, kick,* and *take,* may become the subjects of Ruhl's metonymic extension principle.

Another heavily favored area is that of animals and familiar elements of nature. The notion of slipperiness/dishonesty tends to be characterized by words referring to fish, which are slippery and elusive; slyness/evasiveness tends to be compared to the nature of the fox—a sly and elusive predator. Wolves, tigers, lions, cats, and dogs all have contributed to modern idiom formation across languages and cultures. So general is this tendency to build from already existing materials that entire proverb-length statements also can be found in different languages and cultures. Consider English "don't count your chickens before they're hatched," which means something such as "refrain from celebrating the success of an undertaking prematurely lest it misfire involving you in embarrassment." In the unrelated Hungarian, one says *"Ne igyál előre a medve bőrére,"* which translates as "do not drink [a toast] to the bear's hide in advance." The same idea is expressed in French as *"Ne vendez pas la peau del'ours avant de l'avoir tué,"* echoed by the Italian *"Non vendere la pelle d'oso prima di averlo preso"* ("do not sell the hide of the bear before having taken [captured] it"). Russian has *"Medved' esčë v lov'e, a ty uže medved'a porodaëš"* ("the bear is still in the hunt [being hunted], but you are already selling it [the bear]"). It is fairly transparent, I think, that these five different versions in five different languages, by using different words and making different propositions still are saying, at a deeper level, the same thing. Certainly, any translator of a literary or colloquial text who found this saying in any of the language would be well advised to try to find the corresponding idiom in the target language and to use it in its totality instead of laboriously translating the idiom word for word.

This fact of the popularity of animals is interesting because the English version of "Don't count your chickens . . ." can be traced back to the fables of Aesop, whereas the continental versions involve a hunting scene with a resulting celebration or the anticipated sale of the hide of a bear. The common underlying moral, that the premature celebration of success can end in failure and embarrassment, must have been a common experience to the societies that have this proverb. The versions using the "bear" as the object of capture may have been influenced by one another—certainly the French and the Italian are much too close to ignore the similarity—the Hungarian mentions "drinking"; the Russian, as well as the French and the Italian, are concerned with the "sale" of the hide. It seems that comparative literature and ethnographic history have much unfinished business in common in digging up the exact route such proverbs have traveled over the centuries.

The tendency toward internal borrowing of materials created via phonopoetic arbitrariness into the higher level of imagopoeia is at the heart of idiom formation on a global basis. In my article "Idiomaticity as a Language Universal" (Makkai, 1978), I gave a long list of heavily reinvested words such as French *coup* ("strike" or "blow"), which has produced hundreds of idioms. In this chapter I have suggested that idiom formation is a reaction to the arbitrariness of earlier modes of sign formation, chiefly by the less conscious phonopoetic approach to logopoeia. Figure 13.7 (overleaf) presents this hypothesis of logopoetic evolution from phonopoeia to imagopoeia. I regret that I cannot at this stage of my work on idioms offer irrefutable proof that languages always evolve in this fashion. It is, of course, possible that a limited number of complex expressions are image based from the very start just as it is possible, though a rather rare event, for modern languages to introduce onomatopoetic or other phonopoetically coined lexical items that then are accepted socially.

It was the Italian jurist, historian, and philosopher, Gianbattista Vico (1770/1961) who in his recently rediscovered and increasingly influential book on science first suggested in Western speculation on language that the most ancient form of communication was probably a gestural one. I have devoted a longer article to Vico's relevance in modern linguistic speculation (Makkai, in press b), which will be included in my collection of essays (Makkai, in press a).

In closing then, we should observe that idioms are the price we pay for the vast proliferation of concepts vis-à-vis the relatively arrested development of our phonological abilities. Here, again, linguistic ontogeny may be seen to recapitulate linguistic philogeny: Children have a much more flexible phonetic-articulatory apparatus than even young adults after the age of 21 years. Children can learn a foreign language without a "foreign accent" without any effort—after the age of 21 years most people speak a foreign language with an appreciable foreign accent. This foreign accent, which shows their phonetic limitation, however, does not preclude people older than 21 years to acquire new concepts, indeed to acquire a college or graduate education in many a technically exacting field. Conceptual development thus easily continues when phonetic (hence pho-

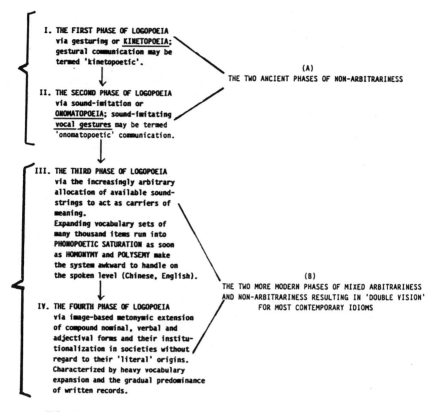

I. THE FIRST PHASE OF LOGOPOEIA via gesturing or **KINETOPOEIA**; gestural communication may be termed 'kinetopoetic'.

II. THE SECOND PHASE OF LOGOPOEIA via sound-imitation or **ONOMATOPOEIA**; sound-imitating **vocal gestures** may be termed 'onomatopoetic' communication.

(A)
THE TWO ANCIENT PHASES OF NON-ARBITRARINESS

III. THE THIRD PHASE OF LOGOPOEIA via the increasingly arbitrary allocation of available sound-strings to act as carriers of meaning. Expanding vocabulary sets of many thousand items run into PHONOPOETIC SATURATION as soon as HOMONYMY and POLYSEMY make the system awkward to handle on the spoken level (Chinese, English).

IV. THE FOURTH PHASE OF LOGOPOEIA via image-based metonymic extension of compound nominal, verbal and adjectival forms and their institutionalization in societies without regard to their 'literal' origins. Characterized by heavy vocabulary expansion and the gradual predominance of written records.

(B)
THE TWO MORE MODERN PHASES OF MIXED ARBITRARINESS AND NON-ARBITRARINESS RESULTING IN 'DOUBLE VISION' FOR MOST CONTEMPORARY IDIOMS

FIG. 13.7. A schematic outline of human semeio-genesis in natural languages.

nopoetic) flexibility is no longer there. Idioms almost always can be literalized, but such literalizations are perceived either as comical, exaggerated, or based on historical hindsight, which is not immediately relevant to a synchronic description of the use of the form at hand.

REFERENCES

Algeo, J. (1970). *English: An introduction to language.* New York: Harcourt, Brace & World.
Bloomfield, L. (1933). *Language.* New York: Holt.
Bolinger, D. L. (1976). Memory and meaning. *Forum Linguisticum, 1,* 1–14.
Bolinger, D. L. (1977). Idioms have relations. *Forum Linguisticum, 2,* 157–169.
Chisolm, L. W. (1963). *Fenollosa: The Far East and American culture.* New Haven, CT: Yale University Press.
Chomsky, N. (1965). *Aspects of the theory of syntax.* Cambridge, MA: MIT Press.

De Saussure, F. (1959). *A course in general linguistics* (W. Baskin, Trans.). New York: Philosophical Library. (Original work published 1915)

Eliot, T. S. (1963). *Literary essays of Ezra Pound*. London: Faber & Faber.

Fabricius-Kovács, F. (1961). A propos d'une loi sémantique [Regarding a semantic law]. *Acta Linguistica Hungarica, 11,* 405–411.

Fenollosa, E. F. (1920). The Chinese written character as a medium for poetry. In E. Pound, *Instigations of Ezra Pound together with an eassay on the Chinese written character by Ernest Fenollosa.* New York: Boni & Liveright.

Flavell, R. H. (1972). *Dictionnaire des locutions idiomatiques anglaises employant certains mots de couleur* [Dictionary of English idiomatic expressions using certain color words]. Unpublished doctoral dissertation, Université de Paris.

Halliday, M. A. K. (1975a). *Language as social semiotic.* London: Edward Arnold.

Halliday, M. A. K. (1975b). *Learning how to mean.* London: Edward Arnold.

Hockett, C. F. (1958). *A course in modern linguistics.* New York: MacMillan.

Koestler, A. (1967). *The ghost in the machine: The urge to self-destruction: A psychological and evolutionary study of modern man's predicament.* New York: Macmillan.

Kronasser, H. (1952). *Handbuch der semasiologie* [Handbook of semology]. Heidelberg: Karl Winter Universitätsverlag.

Labov, W. (1964). *The social stratification of English in New York City.* Washington, DC: Center for Applied Linguistics.

Labov, W. (1976). On the use of the present to explain the past. In A. Makkai, V. B. Makkai, & L. Heilmann (Eds.), *Linguistics at the crossroads* (pp. 226–261). Padova and Lake Bluff, IL: Liviana Editrice and Jupiter Press.

Lamb, S. M. (1966). *Outline of stratificational grammar.* Washington, DC: Georgetown University Press.

Lamb, S. M. (1990). Linguistic model and linguistic thought: The case of "either-or" thinking. In *The 17th LACUS forum* (pp. 109–120).Lake Bluff, IL: LACUS, Inc.

Makkai, A. (1972). *Idiom structure in English.* The Hague, Netherlands: Mouton.

Makkai, A. (1976). Idioms, psychology, and lexemic principle. In *The 3rd LACUS forum* (pp. 467–478). Columbia, SC: Hornbeam.

Makkai, A. (1978). Idiomaticity as a language universal. In *Universals of human language: Vol. 3. Word structure* (pp. 401–448). Stanford, CA: Stanford University Press.

Makkai, A. (in press a). *Ecolinguistics: Toward a new paradigm for the science of language.* Budapest and London: Akadémiai kiadó and Frances Pinter.

Makkai, A. (in press b). On positive and negative logic in modern linguistic theorizing: A Vichian perspective on the development of the philosophy of language and semiotics. In M. Danesi (Ed.), *Proceedings of the 1990 University of Toronto symposium on semiotics.* Berlin: Mouton-De-Gruyter.

Makkai, A., Makkai, V. B., & Heilmann, L. (Eds.) (1976). *Linguistics at the crossroads.* Padova and Lake Bluff: Liviana Editrice & Jupiter Press.

Pound, E. (1920). *Instigations of Ezra Pound together with an essay on the Chinese written character by Ernest Fenellosa.* New York: Boni & Liveright.

Pound, E. (1963). *Literary essays of Ezra Pound.* London: Faber & Faber.

Rohsenow, J. S. (1984). Idiomaticity in Mandarin Chinese. In *The 11th LACUS forum* (pp. 323–340). Columbia, SC: Hornbeam.

Ruhl, C. E. (1974). Primary verbs. In *The 1st LACUS formu* (pp. 436–446). Columbia, SC: Hornbeam.

Ruhl, C. E. (1975). Pragmatic metonymy. in *The 2nd LACUS forum* (pp. 370–380). Columbia, SC: Hornbeam.

Ruhl, C. E. (1976). Idioms and data. In *The 3rd LACUS forum* (pp. 456–566). Columbia, SC: Hornbeam.

Ruhl, C. E. (1978). Alleged idioms with "*hit.*" In *The 5th LACUS form* (pp. 93–107). Columbia, SC: Hornbeam.

Ruhl, C. E. (1979). The semantic field of "*break,*" "*cut,*" and "*tear.*" In *the 6th LACUS forum* (pp. 200–214). Columbia, SC: Hornbeam.

Ruhl, C. E. (1980). The noun "*ice.*" In *The 7th LACUS forum* (pp. 257–269). Columbia, SC: Hornbeam.

Ruhl, C. E. (1982). Figurative "*kick.*" In *The 9th LACUS forum* (pp. 301–310). Columbia, SC: Hornbeam.

Ruhl, C. E. (1989). *On metonymy.* Buffalo: SUNY at Buffalo Press.

Vico, G. (1770/1961). *La szienza nuova* [The new science] (M. Fisch & E. Bär, Trans.). Ithaca, NY: Cornell University Press.

Welch, D. H. (1974). Latinate and English verbs and nouns: A synchronic, diachronic and panchronic description. In *The 1st LACUS forum* (pp. 458–471). Columbia, SC: Hornbeam.

Yip, Wai-lim (1969). *Ezra Pound's CATHAY.* Princeton, NJ: Princeton University Press.

Yngve, V. (1974). The dilemma of contemporary linguistics. In *The 1st LACUS forum* (pp. 1–16). Columbia, SC: Hornbeam.

Yngve, V. (1986). To be a scientist. In *The 13th LACUS forum* (pp. 5–25). Lake Bluff, IL: LACUS, Inc.

Author Index

Subject Index

lexical, 10
logical, 257, 262–265, 267–268
semantic, 238
syntactic, 10, 35, 129, 139, 184, 238, 254, 256, 263, 268
Formedness, 277
ill-, 65–66, 129–132, 134–137, 139–140
well-, 65–66, 79, 135–137, 139–140

G

Grammar,
Generalized Phrase Structure (GPSG), 251, 259
Lexical-Functional, 251
Montague, 257
Standard Theory transformational, 251
transformational generative, 316
Tree Adjoining (TAG), 251, 256–257
Grammatical
theory, *see* Theory

H

Hemispheric,
lateralization, 203, 216

I

Identification, 85
word, 155, 172
Idiom (or Idiomatic), 3, 4, 5, 6, 7, 9, 10, 24, 27, 29–34, 40, 42, 49, 57–59, 61–62, 65, 164, 272, 276
acquisition, *see* Acquisition
analizibility, 27, 32, 35, 39, 62–64, 231, 234–236, 242
compositional, 5, 6, 13, 15, 17, 19–20, 22–23, 35, 74, 271–272, 278, 283, 293
constituent, 8, 10, 14, 19–20, 35, 37, 231, 234–235, 237, 242–243, 256, 271, 273, 277
decomposition, 17, 35, 37, 62, 65, 79, 173, 271
development, *see also* Acquisition
familiar, 5, 8, 9, 10, 11, 39, 41
flexibility, *see* Flexibility
formation, 57, 63, 80–81, 84, 105, 135–

137, 139, 145–146, 164–165, 184, 309, 318, 320–321
frozenness, 16, 30, 57, 63, 80–81, 84, 105, 135–137, 139, 145–146, 164–165, 184, 208, 212–213, 219, 272, 278, 286, 292, 293
key, 147–149, 151–156, 287
list, 4, 5, 47, 83, 164
mental, 4
motivation, 35
noncompositional, 6, 15–17, 19–20, 23, 34, 61, 271–272, 278, 283, 293
opaqueness, 15, 17, 20–21, 35, 37–39, 43–44, 46–47, 65, 80–81, 83, 87, 91–95, 145, 185, 231, 235, 271, 286–287, 291
phrasal, 4, 7, 15, 24, 35, 79, 82, 89
quasi-metaphorical, 22, 24, 45
structure, *see* Structure
transparency, 15, 17, 20–21, 37, 39, 43–44, 46, 49, 80, 88, 91–92, 95, 145, 181, 185, 231, 234, 271, 287, 291, 308–309
transformability, 135–137, 139–140
variant, 8, 9, 10, 11, 12, 14–15, 277
variability, 14, 19, 250, 275
Idiomaticity, 27–28, 31–33, 57, 59, 62, 69, 71, 74–75, 93, 129–130, 134, 136, 145, 290, 303–305, 309, 314, 318
Image, 41, 320
mental, 36, 67–69
Imagery, *see* Image
Inference, 37, 42, 72, 102, 104–105, 111, 122, 165, 217, 262–266, 268, 283
quasi-, 261, 263–264
Intent,
communicative, 8, 14–15, 20–23
Intention,
communicative, 101, 104, 121–122, 125
Interpretation, 17, 22–25, 29, 32, 36–37, 39–41, 45, 49, 64, 70, 74, 79, 81, 84–85, 87–88, 91, 93–97, 105, 115, 121, 123, 145, 165, 172–174, 178, 181–185, 201–202, 204–205, 215, 219–220, 222, 237–241, 243–244, 250–251, 254, 257, 260, 263–266, 272, 281–282, 284, 288–290, 292–293
figurative, 62–66, 71, 73, 108, 115, 146, 148, 166, 170, 174–175, 177, 179, 181–183, 187, 202, 204–206, 208, 214, 217, 219–222, 245, 271, 275